W9-DGP-302

THE WORD WAS MADE FLESH

Unlike religions whose founders were *mediators* of their faiths, Christianity exists in the *person*, God and man, of its Originator. Thus the Church is a continuing testament to the divinity of Jesus Christ.

In this inspiring dissertation, Father Adam compares the Christology of the Catholic Church with non-Catholic theology. He examines the Christ of the Scriptures, particularly the writings of Paul and John; and he traces the deepening historical awareness by the Church of the mystery of Jesus as God-man, as Redeemer, Priest and king. He notes the rational approach to the gospels which has too often led to the denial of Christ's divinity and to an image of Christ as a bloodless myth and liberal ideal.

In the first part of his book the author considers the person of Christ, His humanity as well as His consciousness of His divine nature. The second part is devoted to the works of Christ and the Catholic dogma that upholds them—the doctrine of redemption, Christ as the Saviour of mankind, the mystery of the Mass, and that Apostolic communion which unites the faithful under one living Church.

"Only the professional theologian can detect the enormous amount of learning hidden behind the fluid and readable presentation and the tremendous power of synthesis that produced this classic, to be read, we hope, by thousands of thoughtful and intellectually mature Christians."

—*Commonweal*

Other MENTOR OMEGA Books

The Dead Sea Scrolls and Primitive Christianity *by Jean Danielou.* A Jesuit Professor at the Catholic Institute of Paris demonstrates the relationship between the facts revealed in the ancient scrolls and the traditional view of Christian faith.
(#MP405—60¢)

American Catholic Dilemma *by Thomas F. O'Dea.* A well-known sociologist scrutinizes the contributions of his fellow Catholics to American intellectual life. (#MP404—60¢)

The Dynamics of World History *by Christopher Dawson.* A renowned historian examines the relation between religion and civilization, and shows Christianity as the central, dynamic force in man's historical progression.
(#MQ378—95¢)

A Preface to Metaphysics *by Jacques Maritain.* Seven lectures on metaphysics by the distinguished French Neo-Thomist. (#MP403—60¢)

TO OUR READERS: We welcome your request for our free catalog of SIGNET and MENTOR books. If your dealer does not have the books you want, you may order them by mail, enclosing the list price plus 5¢ a copy to cover mailing. The New American Library of World Literature, Inc., P.O. Box 2310, Grand Central Station, New York 17, N. Y.

THE
CHRIST
OF
FAITH

The Christology of the Church

by KARL ADAM

A MENTOR OMEGA BOOK
Published by the New American Library

From twenty centuries of literature and scholarship, Mentor Omega Books present a treasury of Catholic thought for the modern reader.

© Copyright 1957 by Pantheon Books Inc.

All rights reserved. No part of this book may be reproduced in any form without written permission from the publisher, except for brief passages included in a review appearing in a newspaper or magazine. For information address Pantheon Books Inc., 333 Sixth Avenue, New York 14, New York.

Published as a MENTOR OMEGA BOOK By Arrangement with Pantheon Books Inc.

First Printing, June, 1962

NIHIL OBSTAT: HVBERTVS RICHARDS, S.T.L., L.S.S.
CENSOR DEPVTATVS
IMPRIMATVR: ✠ GEORGIVS L. CRAVEN
EPISCOPVS SEBASTOPOLIS
VIC. CAP. WESTMON.
WESTMONASTERII: DIE VIII OCTOBRIS MCMLVI

This translation from the original German, Der Christus des Glaubens (Patmos-Verlag, Düsseldorf), was made by JOYCE CRICK

MENTOR TRADEMARK REG. U.S. PAT. OFF. AND FOREIGN COUNTRIES REGISTERED TRADEMARK—MARCA REGISTRADA HECHO EN CHICAGO, U.S.A.

MENTOR OMEGA BOOKS are published by The New American Library of World Literature, Inc. 501 Madison Avenue, New York 22, New York

PRINTED IN THE UNITED STATES OF AMERICA

FOREWORD

This work is in essence a summary of lectures I gave over a number of decades at the University of Tübingen. Their historical perspective has been deepened by the valuable and penetrating study of a former student of mine, Professor J. R. Geiselmann, *Jesus der Christus* (1951). My particular thanks are also due to Professor F. Hofmann, who is also numbered among my students. In his contribution to the collection *Das Konzil von Chalkedon* (ed. A. Grillmeyer and H. Bacht) he was able to throw light on the confused disputes of the schools of Alexandria and Antioch, and in particular upon the much-contested Christology of St. Cyril of Alexandria. As for liturgical history, the *Missarum Solemnia* of J. Jungmann, S.J., came as a most welcome addition to my own exposition. For the rest, I was not so much concerned with extending academic theology as with bringing into relief the values of life that can be apprehended in the actual development of the Church's Christology. In the evening of my life, it is an especial joy and an undeserved happiness to be able to present to my numerous students by means of the printed word the noble image of God become man, and in unison with them to receive his blessing and his Grace.

I wish to thank my niece Frau Roma Haag for her help in preparing the manuscript. For the lively interest and wise criticism with which she has followed all my works, I dedicate this book to her.

KARL ADAM

Tübingen
August, 1954

DEDICATED
TO MY DEAR NIECE
FRAU ROMA HAAG

CONTENTS

CONTENTS

CONTENTS

CONTENTS

CONTENTS

CONTENTS

x

THE
CHRIST
OF
FAITH

BOOK I

THE PERSON OF CHRIST

I

INTRODUCTION: THE SOURCE OF THE BELIEF IN CHRIST

The place of Christology within Church dogma

CHRISTIANITY is the good tidings of Christ. *Christianity is Christ.* This is the message that gives foundation and content not only to the moral imperatives and ethical standards, but also to the dogmas, the truths of our faith. For ultimately it is the annunciation of Christ that is our confirmation of the dogmas of the *Deus revelans* and the *Deus trinus:* that there is a living God, revealing himself to man, and that this God is triune. Only through him has the world attained the unfailing certainty that a Father reigns in heaven, and that this Father begat in eternity a Son of his essence, to whom he is bound in eternal love by the Holy Spirit, and through whom he binds himself to us. Thus far the idea of the triune God is of the heart of Christ's message. We pray to the Father through the Son in the Holy Spirit. In the history of our salvation, it was not as if the Son were reached through the Father, nor as if the belief in the Trinity came first and the belief in Christ second. "No one knows the Father except the Son, and him to whom the Son chooses to reveal him." Only in the Son do we attain certainty of the Father and the Holy Spirit. For the Son is the living revelation of God's paternal goodness in the Holy Spirit. And only the conviction that the Son is of the same nature as God, and that he is the Son of God, led Christian thought to ascertain processes and sources of life within the Godhead, and to develop the dogma of the Trinity on all sides. Only the belief in Christ produced the belief in the Trinity. Although in our creed the dogma of the Trinity has logical priority, in the history of the revelation it came second. Christology, the doctrine of the person and the work of Christ, comes prior in the

17

history of revelation to the dogma of God the one and three-in-one.

Similarly with the dogmas of the creation, of the first state of man, of original sin, and salvation. It is the belief in the Son of God made man that gives to all these articles of faith their particular place in the Christian gospel as a whole, their particular form and foundation. The attempt to understand the mystery of Jesus and his significance for the salvation of man nurtured the searching faith which was to illuminate the relationship ordained by God between creation and the Creator, and to uncover the deeper causes why redemption should be necessary. These were the questions directed towards the first state of things, towards the fall of man, towards the meaning of the Lord's incarnation and of his death on the cross. Only Christology brought permanence and light to these questions.

The same holds for the Church's doctrines of Grace, the sacrament, eschatology, and, last but not least, the idea of the Church itself. All these dogmas grow from the seed of the Christological dogma. What they do is to describe the intensive and the extensive influence of the mystery of Christ, both in the individual soul and in the bosom of the believing Church. The articles of faith of Grace, the sacrament, and the Church are fundamentally the universal contemplation and confirmation of the salvation wrought by Christ and his spirit in the individual and in the community. Without Christ there can be no Grace, no sacrament, no Church, no hope for the future.

This leads us to maintain that Christology lies at the heart of all Catholic dogma. Catholic dogma is centred on Christ. The mystery of God become man is the holy tabernacle of the Church. From it the light of our faith shines out on all sides, interpreting and explaining, but also wakening, kindling the spirit, bringing new birth. Thus do we say in truth: Christianity is Christ. In the name of "Jesus Christ" this is exactly what our faith avows: Jesus is the Christ.

Thus our entire religious position stands and falls with the belief in Christ.

The living Church as the source of our belief in Christ

But where do we draw this belief from? That is the first question of significance we must answer. *We have received this belief from our mother, the Church.* But let us first make clear to ourselves this connexion between the belief in Christ and the Church. At the beginning of our belief in Christ stands the Credo of the Church. It was from this *"credo in Jesum Christum"* that the Church arose. Only this, her avowal of Christ, enabled her to become the congregation of the faithful and the Christian Church. In manifold suffering, in the martyrdom of body and spirit, and under countless attacks from doctrines opposed to Christianity, the Church has preserved this faith through the centuries. Ever since Paul said that Christ was a stumbling block to the Jews and a foolishness to the Gentiles, Christ has made his way through mankind as the one sublime stumbling block and the one great foolishness, the incomprehensible paradox of the *Deus crucifixus*. As Simeon the old man said (Luke 2.34), he was destined for the fall of many, and for a sign that was to be contradicted. But, as the same Simeon rejoiced, he was also destined for the rise of many. This summoning, wakening power of Jesus is developed in the living Church. In the Church's consciousness of faith, in her ordinances and sacraments, in her life of Grace and her miracles, she is the living revelation of the spirit of Jesus, and of the powers of resurrection he issues forth. She is his body.

Thus it is that we receive the belief in Jesus from the Church, and not from philosophical and textual criticism. As the congregation of faith, she is in her essence the annunciation of Christ; grown aware of her mission, she is his herald, imposing that task on herself; she is, in herself, the living tradition of his holy word and works. Thus she knows out of her own being, out of her living communion with Christ, out of the fullness of Christ that is her essence, that Christ is more than Solomon, more than one of the prophets, that he is "the Lord." She knows it *through herself,* out of her living self-awareness which through the centuries is its own ever-renewed testimony. Whoever seeks Christ without the Church, putting his trust in his own insight and what goes by the name of criticism, deprives himself of all possibility of finding the living Christ. Only the living comprehends and affirms the living. If there were no living Church in which Christ's influence perpetuated itself, the Gospels and Epistles would be for us but a dead letter, breathing no life. The hammer of criticism would always be able to quash their testimony to fragments, and make a joyful, victorious faith impossible. The history of Gospel criticism is enough proof of this. Even Schleiermacher, father of the Lutheran church, confesses: "Reverence for the Holy Scripture cannot be the foundation of faith in Christ. This faith must rather be the presupposition, that the Scriptures may be guaranteed the reverence due to them." And so Schleiermacher is able to ascribe authority to the Scriptures only in so far as they are "a genuine testimony of the common spirit of the Christian Church." Without the living Church, the Gospels and, indeed, the entire New Testament would be simply a more or less stirring literary composition, raised, it is true, high above all other religious literature, even the Old Testament, but all the same just a body of writing robbed of the breath of life, the fresh inspiration of flesh-and-blood reality. The Gospel image of Christ touches us directly; it breaks out of its literary frame, as it were, into the present, into the Here and Now; we see him and experience him in living shape; he addresses us in person. All this is certainly not to be explained from literary testimony alone, but from the confession of the living Church that puts this testimony into our hands, or, more precisely, from the testimony of the Apostles, sealed by their martyrdom, which is handed down to us by the *successio apostolica,* the succession in time and the coincidence in space of the Apostolic bishoprics. By the Apostolic succession, time is undone. In the teaching of the Apostles, there is no yesterday and no morrow, but only today. The Church has them to call upon, and thus can say in a real sense: "I myself have seen Jesus, who is the Christ, I myself have heard him preach, I myself stood beneath his cross, and at the tomb of his resurrection. What is written in the Gospels is of my own awareness. From the beginning it lives and moves and has its being in me. The Gospels are the expression of my understanding of myself." To the outer testimony of the Gospels, the inner testimony of the Holy Spirit is united. As our hearts receive the Gospels in faith, they experience an inner transformation, a new purity, a new profundity, rebirth in the Holy Spirit. And thus it is that they also experience the resurrection, the peace and joy of Easter. To this extent the Christian community is nothing more than Christ's power of resurrection, working on in history, Christ eternal unfolding himself in history, the "fullness of Christ." "Flesh and blood has not revealed this to thee, but my Father in heaven," Christ said to Peter, when his disciple first recognized him as the Christ. Peter was enabled to gaze upon the mystery of the Christ in Jesus, to believe in Christ by divine power, by entering upon a new, supernatural course of life. This faith leapt like a divine spark from Peter to the other disciples until on that Whitsuntide it blazed into flame. It was a new insight, a new power that issued forth from Jesus. And this power bound the Apostles and their followers into a new unity, into the body of Christ, into an inner receptiveness to the spirit of Jesus. This was the beginning of the Church.

So we have to go to the living Church if we wish to know the living Christ. In all the history of religion, there is *no* analogy to be found to this relationship between the Church and Christ. Why? Because it is only in Christianity that the personality of the founder constitutes the entire content of the religion. The Christian is the man who has made Christ his own, who is animated by the spirit of Christ. All other religions that have demonstrably been founded by an historical personality do not regard their founder as the content, the object of their faith, but simply as its mediator. The faith itself does not coincide with the figure of the founder, but can be presented independently of this figure and separated entirely from him. This is so in the case of the religion of Israel, and its founder Moses. It is so in Buddhism, and in Islam. In all these religions, the founder is not at the centre but on the periphery of the religious interest. At the centre is his doctrine. And that is why it is not important for these religions to take over the image of their founder in its original lines, as drawn by the first congregation. For it is not the image of the founder that is ever present in the consciousness of the faithful, but his proclamation and teaching. The image of the founder can grow indistinct, new ideas can be superimposed upon it even to the point where it is no longer recognizable. But Christianity is totally different. At its very first entry into history, Christianity proclaims itself as the tidings of Christ the Lord. "What do you know of Christ?" is what Jesus asks his disciples. These tidings constitute the true content of the religion. Then as now, there was no need to know anything else but Christ. In knowing him, they knew everything. Peter and Paul, John and James live and move and have their being in this One, in the mystery of the Lord. Subsequent centuries have attempted to fathom this mystery in all its depth and all its breadth, and bring it to consciousness. In doing so, they took over certain ideas and concepts from elsewhere—from Judaism, from Greek and Hellenistic philosophy. Afterwards they applied regular Scholastic concepts borrowed from Plato and Plotinus, and later from Aristotle too. All these borrowings were only using the resources of the age to make still clearer what was inscribed direct and living in all hearts, the image of the Lord. Fundamentally, it was always one and the same thing—what the early Church of Jerusalem meant by the designations "Son of David" and "Messias," what the community of Antioch meant by the word "Kyrios," what John expressed by the term "Logos," and what later theology called the second "Hypostasis of God," and "Homoousios." It was always one and the same Christ, proclaimed with ever-new tongues, and with ever-growing penetration and clarity.

This overwhelming fact, that Christianity never was anything but the tidings of Christ, that Christ was and is the object of contemplation and thought across many hundreds of years, assures us that the image of Jesus cherished by the congregation of the faithful can never be distorted, that it is the true, original image of Christ, and that therefore we must go to the living Church, and not to the critics outside the faith, if we are searching for the true Christ.

Certainly we *cannot do without* the Gospels and the other Scriptures of the New Testament for details of the life of Jesus. "Without the Scriptures, we would be deprived of the characteristic form of Jesus' utterances. We would not know how the Son of God spoke, and I think I would have no more wish to live if I could no longer hear him speak" (A. Möhler, *Einheit,* p. 60). "However," that same Möhler goes on to say, "without a tradition we would not know who it was that spoke so, nor what he proclaimed, and all joy in his words would also be lost." The bond unifying the conflicting or at least divergent trains of thought in the Scriptures is the Church's self-perpetuating, living consciousness of faith. Only in the light of this faith can the New Testament be properly understood. This faith is its presupposition throughout. We may say that through all the gaps and cracks in the Biblical proclamation, the living stream of the Church's faith shines out to meet us. It alone can present us with a unified and complete version of the Biblical image of Christ. Without the testimony of the Church, what the Bible alone has to tell us of Jesus would be insufficient. It becomes alive for us only in the hands of the Church. Thus Church and Holy Scripture belong inextricably together. We may not tear them apart. The Holy Scripture is the literary expression and precipitate of the Church's original awareness of Christ, of her experience of Christ.

Errors in the criticism of liberal theology

It is necessary to stress this most emphatically at the outset of the lectures. The young theologian is especially exposed to the danger that his perception of the great simple line leading from the living community of faith that is the Church to Christ might be clouded by the overwhelming number of questions of New Testament exegesis. Concern with problems of what goes by the name of criticism involuntarily leads him astray to the assumption that his faith will depend on the results of criticism, that he is at every moment delivered into the hands of the historian and the textual critic. That would be a miserable kind of Christianity, living in constant anxiety as to whether today or the next day criticism would pronounce its death penalty.

This over-estimation of Biblical criticism is based upon *two false assumptions*. The first is that Christianity is nothing but Bible Christianity, that it has its origin solely in the Bible, and that as a result it can be explained and understood from the Bible alone. This is the false assumption that Luther and Calvin made. In the face of modern Biblical criticism, the theology of the reformers is in a far more difficult position than Catholic theology. Every advance against the Bible is for them at the same time an advance against the very understanding of Christ. In the creed of Catholic theology, it is not the Bible but the living proclamation of the Church that is the true basis of Christianity, in face of which all Biblical questions are secondary. Christ's sermon, the sermons of the first Apostles, their *living word* first planted the seeds of faith, even long before a Christian literature existed. So this literature did not produce faith, but was itself the product of faith. It is the more or less complete precipitate of the early Christian consciousness of faith. It is missionary literature. And thus the most superior source of Christianity is not the word of the Bible, but the living word of the Church's proclamation of faith. Even if the Bible did not exist, a Christian religious movement would be conceivable. Without the firm support of the letter, it would constantly be in danger of obscuring the abundance of concrete detail in the unique and mighty experience of Christ. But nevertheless, the Church would have been able to communicate the image of Christ to us, even without the Bible, because the content of her faith is, to such a vast degree, this very image. And that is why the Bible is and always will be an exceedingly valuable source of material, but not the primary source of the Christian faith. All critical exegesis of the Bible, all questions of the higher and the lower textual criticism, do not touch the substance of our faith. We turn from the Bible to the consciousness of faith in the Church, which first produced the Bible and supports its import with her dogma.

This brings us to the second false assumption made by those young theologians who constantly keep their ears pricked for every echo of every blow from the hammer of the higher criticism. The textual critic assumes that Christianity and Christology are something finished and inflexible, lying before us complete down to the last impulse and the last article, complete in the Bible and in Christian literature, in every Christian movement and institution from the early Fathers down to the present. They assume that Christianity poured all its vitality into its literature and other foundations, and became as it were fossilized in them. They go on to assume that only the historian acquainted with Christian literature and its monuments is capable of passing judgement on the nature of Christianity. According to this theory, the sole source of our faith, and its exclusive standard, would simply be the historical evidence for it. And therefore, they claim, it is up to the historian, the expert, to decide on the nature of Christianity, not to the living Church. What is wrong in these assumptions? They are wrong in regarding Christianity, not as a living movement, but as something frozen and extinct, something whose fossilization in the strata of history can and must be entirely uncovered. They misjudge the living, inward, invisible quality of Christianity, which can be comprehended only by inner experience, and not by external verification. This way of regarding Christianity turns it into a mummy, or rather into a corpse, which the anatomist can dissect down to the last fibre. It is false when the anatomist declares, "What I have under the knife is the whole man," and it is equally false when the critic would have us understand the nature of Christ and of Christianity solely from his historical analyses. Our modern critics of the Bible, from Bruno Bauer to Reitzenstein and Bultmann, set to work upon Christianity as if it were a corpse. They treat the Biblical texts and other traditional Christian documents like an anatomist dealing with a human limb; they take their sections and they dissect; they cut a piece away here, join it on there, and reassemble the disparate parts according to some hypothesis or personal intention, and then declare: *ecce Christus,* lo, this is what Christ was really like, this is what Christianity really was in its earliest beginnings. This radical Biblical criticism misjudges the *living quality of the Christian mystery.* Hence it can assess neither the Christianity of Christ nor the Christianity of the present day. All they can see is a series and succession of ideas and concepts. They have no inkling of the unifying bond that animates these parts and makes a unity of them. "Dissection" is their only true task. They dissect Christ and dissect Christianity. Thus, Christ, for example, originally regarded himself only as the child of God, like the pious figures of the Old Testament. Later, they maintain, this awareness of being the child of God developed into an awareness that he was the Messias, and finally it was transfigured into the inner consciousness of his Godhead. These successive stages in the Lord's consciousness of his mission persist in the successive stages of the Christian proclamation. They make their distinctions: Jewish Christianity, Hellenistic Christianity, Old Catholic Christianity, Alexandrine Christianity, Augustinian Christianity, and so on. After they have set to work, they leave only fragments behind. And when some critic or other feels urged to put these fragments together again, the strangest formations arise. Because the critic will not use the support offered by the objective spirit of living Christianity, self-perpetuating in the community of faith and love, he has to give free play to his own critical intellect and personal intuition. Instead of the objective spirit of the living Church, transcending every individual and every culture, he falls back upon *his own subjective intellect.* And since no human intellect is utterly independent, but is open to manifold outside influences, particularly to social and philosophical trends, systems of thought arise in whose aspect one can tell at a glance whether they have been fathered by Hegel or Marx, Schleiermacher or Nietzsche, Heidegger or Sartre. At one moment Christ parades in the Rationalist's toga, as Goodman Enlightenment. The next, he sobs and sighs like Goethe's Werther. Now he is the stern moralist, firmly upholding the categorical imperative; and now he wears the Jacobin's stocking cap. Or perhaps he is the lonely dreamer, going through the world misunderstood, and dying misunderstood. One thing is certain: "It was not only each epoch," remarks A. Schweitzer, "that found its reflection in Jesus; each individual created him in accordance with his own character" (*The Quest of the Historical Jesus,*

Eng. tr., New York, 1948, p. 4). The spectacle that Gnosticism presented as early as the second century, the struggle
between all possible tendencies for the possession of Christ, is
forever repeated anew. Certainly, this kind of subjectivism is
fruitless. "We are divided. So many heads, so many opinions"
(A. Harnack).

This subjective spirit has its counterpart in a subjective
method that also requires some brief discussion. "Every ordinary method of historical investigation proves inadequate to
the complexity of the conditions. The standards of ordinary
historical science are here inadequate, its methods not immediately applicable. The historical study of the life of Jesus
had to create its own methods for itself. . . . There is, however, no direct method of solving the problem in its complexity; all that can be done is to experiment continuously,
starting from definite assumptions; and in this experimenta-
tion the guiding principle must ultimately rest upon historical
intuition" (Schweitzer, *loc. cit.*)

With these words, Schweitzer has all unwillingly pronounced
the death sentence upon modern criticism of the Life-of-Jesus
kind. For an approach that does not use a clear method based
on assured principles, but consists in continuous experimenta-
tion according to shifting assumptions, simply cannot call itself a scholarly method. It can never guarantee that it is
aiming at a scientific result. It is always able to raise new
problems, and bring new possibilities to light, but it can never
offer a scholarly solution to any of the problems it poses. A
method that can only ask questions is no method. The only
true method of approaching Christianity is one that receives
its final standards not from the subjective spirit of the individual scholar, but from the objective spirit of the living
Church, the source of all Christian trends and documents.

Troeltsch attempted to make good the lack of a strict
method by formulating three principles necessary for any con-
sistent historical scholarship: historical criticism (i.e., con-
scientious probing and assessment of sources); the analogy
with contemporary occurrences (i.e., events in the life of
Jesus are to be judged according to criteria that are also valid
for life today); and correlation (i.e., the interactions of all
manifestations of life in history must be regarded in terms of
their most fundamental connexions with one another).

Troeltsch's first condition receives our assent without further
ado, for the basis of all historical knowledge is a thorough
assessment of sources. But what does he mean by his second

and third principles, analogy and correlation? At their root, these formulations go back to an *a priori* philosophical assumption that a break in the chain of cause and effect, the interruption of something absolutely new, is impossible. For if the law of analogy and correlation is to be the guiding star of historical investigation, all it will recognize are things analogous, things similar, things causally related to previous events. So miracles cannot exist in this scheme of things. But the great characteristic of Christianity is that it is a history of miracles. Thus Troeltsch's two principles betray an unproved and unprovable presupposition that cuts off from the start all understanding of Christianity, and which Renan expressed in the confident words: *"Il n'y a pas de surnaturel."*

The very abundance of Lives of Jesus, from Venturini to Santayana, that have been presented with pretension to scholarly discipline, is proof enough that the historical appearance of Christ and Christianity is not to be understood in all its aspects merely with the means of historiography. There will always be something left over that cannot be understood. If the historian would rather examine dead texts than listen to the living testimony of the Church, if he hesitates to grasp Christianity and the living image of Christ through the living Church, they will forever remain an unsolved problem for him.

We must be clear about this before we continue with these lectures in Christology: critical scholarship cannot help us here. The liberating solution can be achieved only by entering into the living faith of the Church. When I listen to a dying man pray: "Jesus, in thee I live; Jesus, in thee I die," and when I perceive what courage and joy this prayer brings him, then I know what Jesus is. Then I have no need of the critics and historians of religion. *The same* feeling throbs in the dying prayer of the Christian today as compelled St. Peter to the acknowledgement "Thou art the Christ," and which St. Stephen expressed in these words: "I see the heavens opened and the Son of Man standing at the right hand of God." All the differences of the aeons and the generations are dissolved in the living faith of the Church. All is present in it. For in it, Christ is as near to us today as he was to Peter.

Belief in Christ and the Apostolic succession

But the objection could be raised: Does not this make a *subjective* experience the *basis* of our belief in Christ? If I should ask a dying Christian uttering his last prayer, "Why do you believe in Christ?" it may well be that his eyes will come to rest upon the priest, who is the witness of Christ most near to him. And the priest will refer to his bishop, and the bishop to the *successio apostolica*, the long series of episcopal witnesses of faith leading back to Peter and John. At the end of the succession stands Peter, with the disciples. In their midst stands Jesus himself. Thus, across space and time the *successio apostolica* has brought me into the midst of the community of disciples and face to face with the Lord. My situation, in my heart and towards Christ, is now the same as the Apostles'. By means of the succession of bishops, I have reached the same plane as the Apostles. This is not a question of any subjective experience or personal whim, but the concrete, visible reality of Christ's witnesses, from Peter down to the priest standing at the Christian's death-bed. The objective reality of the whole Church embraces me. For the sick man offers his dying prayer as a member of Christ's body, not in lonely isolation. The entire strength—vast, objective, holy—of all the members of Christ all over the earth is praying with him, through him. The entire *Ecclesia orans*, embracing earth and heaven, here and beyond, comes to meet me in the dying man's prayer. His act of faith is no more difficult than St. Peter's at Cæsarea Philippi. For through the all-embracing Catholic Church he has attained the same historical and religious feeling for Christ as Peter had for his divine master. The distances of time and space do not exist for him. Like Peter, he stands before Christ and hears his question: "But who do you say I am?" The *reply* is not denied him; no one can take it from him. Thus far the Christian's act of faith is something completely personal. But that he should be in the position to make this act of faith, that he should be objectively and subjectively directed towards the mystery, this he has from the testimony of the Church alone.

We have established that only the living Church is the true means of attaining a living faith in Christ. How can we define this belief in Christ more closely?

Belief in Christ and the motiva credibilitatis

My belief in Christ is not a purely natural act of cognition, not a merely rational conclusion drawn from precisely verifiable premises with all the support of philosophical and historical method. My belief includes, rather, an irrational element; or, better, one beyond all conceptualizing, a power that does not come from this earth and its scholarship, but is purely supernatural. And this supernatural element is the decisive one. Why I believe in Christ, under the aegis of the Church, takes us back to the act of love of the *Deus revelans*. It is Grace, the "gift of God," as Paul calls it in his Epistle to the Ephesians. St. Thomas Aquinas emphasizes that there is a *duplex causa* in the assent of faith. The one is external, i.e., the objective revelation and the doctrine of the Church. It reaches its zenith in the signs and wonders of the *Deus revelans*. It is the preparation for faith. It makes us attentive to the potentialities of God, and prepares us for them. But this external testimony is not enough. According to St. Thomas, the *principalis et propria causa fidei* is much rather the inward cause, Grace, wrought by God alone. The external word of revelation and the sermon must be united with the *inner* word of the Holy Spirit. My faith is always a Pentecostal miracle, the intervention of divine spiritual powers into my little world, "instructed" by God, as John puts it, "sealed" by the Spirit, as Paul expresses it. And that is why the ultimate source of my belief in Christ does not lie in any written document, not even in the word of the Gospels, and certainly not in the human commentators on the Gospels, with their textual criticism, Biblical criticism, and apologetics; it does not even lie in the external authority of the Church. All these, according to St. Thomas, are a *causa exterius inducens*. They make my spirit attentive to God, but do not convince it. Only God himself can make me receptive to God. My eyes are opened to the divine in Christ only when the Pentecostal Spirit breathes upon me. Thus the source of my faith is primarily to be found where the Pentecostal Spirit breathes—in the community of the Holy Spirit, in the company of the saints, in the Church as the Pentecostal congregation. Here alone there burns that holy fire that the disciples felt at Emmaus, as, all unwittingly, they walked with the resurrected Christ. This is holy ground.

Take off thy shoes. He who in faith and love loses himself in this holy spirit of the living Church is assured that he stands in the realm of the divine, the holy and supernatural, and the realm of primal truth and reality, that he drinks directly of the water of life, and hears the beat of the wings of the holy dove.

And that is why we repeat: The first, the purest, the most direct sources of Christology are not the Gospels, not books and writings, not even the Church in her external form, but only the Church as the *Pentecostal congregation,* the Church of living faith and unwearied love. We are chosen to be born into this Church by God's incomprehensible Grace. The breath of its supernatural being surrounded us like a holy ether. All unknowing, we absorbed it. The "potential" faith planted within us at our baptism unfolded in this atmosphere into an "actual," effective faith. And so today we are members of the Church of the faithful, and theologians.

According to what I have just expounded, we may well ask whether our belief in Christ is not a sheer experience of Grace. But the reply is "No." As in all religious belief, natural and supernatural powers work *together* in our faith in Christ: on the one hand the Grace of God, for that is what gives the belief its peculiar form (*ratio formalis*), and on the other hand man with his rational, ethical powers. This belief is thus primarily a gift to receive, but it is also a task to fulfil. Grace wakens and illumines our meditation on the rational basis of Christianity, so that in its light we gain an insight into the reasons for its credibility (*motiva credibilitatis*). And it inflames our will, so that we grasp and affirm the divine, this absolute and highest good, shining forth in these reasons for our believing, even when it is surrounded by darkness. For whenever the divine breaks through into this earthly, limited, imperfect world of ours, our soul does not apprehend it in perfect clarity. For here we see "through a mirror in an obscure manner," but then, face to face. We make our way through this world only *per umbras et imagines.* All the reasons that our intellect, illumined by Grace, can discover, everything that renders our Christianity credible, can serve only as an indication to point the way, like the pointing finger of St. John in Grünewald's famous picture. Our full and convinced affirmation of Christ in spite of these obscurities is wrought by Grace, or, more precisely, by our will which has been penetrated by Grace. By its nature, this will is directed towards the good. Good, above all the highest good (*summum bonum*), is its specific object. Good, in theological terms, is its *objectum formale,* or *propter quod.* Since it is naturally directed towards good, in particular the highest good, the moment good is borne to it by the intellect, the will affirms it. The more distinct the good, the more certain the affirmation. The intellect, illumined by the light of Grace, eager for what is divine and holy, discovers all those traces, indications, and testimonies in the historical appearance of Christ that make his heavenly nature and divine calling credible. At the same time as the soul is approached by the highest divine good, which is able to bind the will the faster, the more God's constant love diverts the will from mere earthly values and opens it to the world of supernatural values, the purer man in his striving becomes. In spite of all the obscurities that continue to oppress its intellectual thinking, the will makes its affirmation of Christ, because in the image of Christ it encounters that *summum bonum* to which its nature is directed, and which completes, fulfils, and commits it. So in formal terms, the belief in Christ is an *actus intellectus imperatus a voluntate* in so far as it is the will alone, inspired by the *summum bonum* and animated by Grace, that compels the human understanding despite all the darkness, through all the darkness, to make its affirmation of Christ. From the psychological point of view, then, the belief in Christ is *an experience of good,* wrought by God, and not an *experience of certainty.* In its depths it is irrational, incomprehensible, or rather, beyond all conceiving; but nevertheless it is also rational to the extent that the intellect can at least make the good it has experienced credible.

If the intellect were capable of making this experience absolutely certain, it would show us the divine mystery of Christ in utter clarity, without obscurity or covering, and our belief in Christ would be transformed into knowledge. Then the belief would be the object of rational cognition alone, and only the clever and the knowledgeable would be summoned to the faith. Faith would no longer be a moral act, a leap of the heart and the shaken conscience up to the living God; there would be no moral reservation plunging through the shadows and mists to sainthood. And it would no longer be a mystical, supernatural event, no "planting of the Father" within us, no descent of the Holy Spirit into our soul, no Pentecostal experience, but a simple act of intellectual understanding like any other, like examining the structure of an insect's wings. It would be something purely human. But faith is more than that; it is a moral act, and a straining towards the highest, a struggle with God, and it is all this because of the darkness that surrounds the highest like the clouds around Mount Sinai. It is the darkness that makes of faith a moral achievement, a truly creative, supernatural process, an act of God.

Once more: we do not learn the ultimate truth about Christ at the scholar's desk or in the sobriety of his study. We will learn it only in the sacred spaces, flooded with supernatural life and the powers of moral man, in what we call the "body of Christ," in his living Church.

The significance of miracles for the belief in Christ

To gain some further insight into this fundamental state of affairs, let us come to a close by recalling the importance that is accorded to the miracles of Christ in the process of faith. The Gospels as well as the lives of the saints tell us of marvellous and supernatural events which we could not countenance as historical fact or proof of a religion if we denied *a priori* the possibility of miracles. Confronted with these occurrences, sober common sense will be quiet and watchful, and honestly admit that the natural chain of cause and effect has been broken through here, and that a gap, a vacuum, yawns in the natural succession of events, something left over that cannot be accounted for by the means of natural, exact thinking. In face of this vacuum, our questioning intellect is compelled to reckon with the possibility, even the probability, that a supernatural causality is at work here. But this is still by no means faith. We will say these things are incomprehensible, marvellous. We may perhaps repeat Du Bois-Reymond's *"ignoramus et ignorabimus,"* but we will still not be able to utter our "credo" straightway as long as we put our trust exclusively in our intellect and refuse to judge *out of the entirety of our existential situation,* out of the entirety of our questionable human existence and our inextricable tie to God. It is a long, long way from external apprehension, and inner wonder at the strange and incomprehensible, to a personal recognition of the divinity that reveals himself in it, and from this in turn to man's faithful yielding to the *Deus mirabilis.* We can travel it only if we embrace ethical and religious powers as well as the intellectual, the will directed towards the *summum bonum* as well as the critical understanding, and, as the decisive power, the loving approach of divine Grace. Only when we are prepared for the divine to this extent may it happen that the divine itself will overcome us like a new light and bring us to the shattering confession of the Apostle Thomas when he saw the wounds of the resurrected Christ: "My Lord and my God." God must come to us first, before we can come to him. We cannot even utter the "Abba, Father," unless it be in the Holy Spirit. Thus I can believe in Christ only if he has already cleaved to me, if I lay myself open to the personal impression which is urged upon me by his divine and holy being. *The miracles lead me up to Christ, but they do not lead me into Christ.* Certainly they enable me to look up to Christ, they waken the desire for salvation within me. "Lord, help thou mine unbelief." But they are only *causa exterius inducens.* He alone can creatively arouse the affirmation of Christ within my breast. By means of the miracles, an ether must issue forth from him, an utterly personal impression that takes possession of me in face of the miracles, and makes me his own. This is not effected by the miracle alone. Thus Corozain and Bethsaida remained in their unbelief, although they were witnesses of many mighty deeds of the Lord. All they had heeded was the external event and the pragmatic results, not the man of miracles himself, only the *factum,* not the *faciens.* That is why they were not taken up into his personal sphere, into the circle of redemption. And that is why Jesus "was unable" to work any miracles in Nazareth, because the inner moral and religious assumptions were lacking, without which God the all-holy cannot achieve a miracle (see Mark 6.5). Indeed, he never works a miracle just for the sake of the marvel. It is never an end in itself. He works a miracle in order to draw us to him by its means and fill us with his saving power.

This, too, teaches us that to attain the living belief in Christ, mere intellectual processes, *sola scientiae principa,* as the oath against modernism rightly emphasizes (H. Denzinger, *Enchiridion symbolorum,* 20th ed., Freiburg, 1932, 2146), are not enough. Rather, in the process of faith, intellectual and ethical powers work together, and even these two purely human powers have their ultimate basis in the supernatural workings of God. "No one can come to me unless the Father who sent me draw him" (John 6.44). And thus it is usually not in the university lecture hall that we encounter Christ, but in the holy place of the living Church, in which the Holy Spirit dwells, and which draws all members together in an inner unity, so that they become spirit of his spirit, and flesh of his flesh.

Let us affirm once again: It is the Church's image of Christ, the *dogmatic image of Christ,* that supports our faith, and not the image of Christ that any journalist, Renan, Rosegger, or D. F. Strauss, may have sketched according to his own intuition. This dogmatic image of Christ alone has made its way victorious through the centuries. All the Christian dogmas have grown out of it. It has given meaning and form to the Christian ethics and Christian cult. The human spirit has struggled and split up into sects over this dogmatic image of Christ. It has remained the source and native ground of all the Christian denominations, and a different image of Christ has never, in the course of history, been able to assert itself.

This glance at the dogmatic image of Christ now brings us into the field of Christology. According to the nature of the subject, our discussion is divided into two main parts. In the first (Book I) we will describe the *person* of Christ, the mystery of his human and divine nature, within a theological frame of reference. This is Christology in the narrower sense. In the second (Book II) we will describe the *work* of God made man, his act of redemption. This is what we mean by soteriology. First we will expound the development of the Church's doctrine in order to assess these problems in their historical interaction, and to appreciate their growing clarification in the course of history.

II

THE DEVELOPMENT OF CHURCH DOCTRINE IN THE LIGHT OF THE CHRISTOLOGICAL DISPUTES

Monarchianism

THE Christological heresies of the first centuries after Christ arose partly from a rigid adherence to the Jewish concept of God and partly from the adoption of pagan, Hellenistic ideas about God. The Jewish influence can be seen in the continuing efforts to preserve within the Christological mystery the oneness of God (*monarchia*) in the sense of one divine person. These arose from the first postulate: There is only one divine person; "Jahve hath not wife or child." This led directly to the heresy we call Monarchianism. According to this doctrine, the main Christological question was not whether there is more than one divine person, but simply whether Christ is identical with the Father—a different manifestation of God, perhaps; or whether he can be regarded only as a creation wrought by the Father's power. According to which solution they adopted, two kinds of Monarchianism arose: Modalist, or Patripassian, and Dynamistic. The first held that what we call "person" in God is only an external manifestation (*modus*) of the one God. One and the same *Monas* reveals itself—in the creation as the Father, and in the salvation as the Son. One and the same *Monas* both created the world and became flesh and suffered on the cross. To this extent it could be said· God the Father has suffered and has died. Hence the name "Patripassian." This kind of Monarchianism was propagated by Noëtus of Smyrna, and by his pupils Praxeas and in particular Sabellius. It was opposed by Tertullian, Hippolytus, and Dionysius of Alexandria. Indeed, in his attack on Modalist

Monarchianism, the last-named emphasized the distinction between Father and Son so strongly that he was in danger of founding a fresh heresy. He maintained that the identity of Father and Son was so slight that the Son could be regarded as the creation (ποίημα) of the Father. Pope Callistus had already declared himself against Modalism, and Pope Dionysius of Rome (d. 268) later published a bull rejecting Patripassianism in 260, at the same time correcting the ambiguous utterance of Dionysius of Alexandria. These debates resulted in the establishment of the doctrine that on the one hand the Son is a divine person distinct from the Father, and that on the other this distinction itself did not arise from the Son's being created by the Father. Thus the Pope's letter tried to suppress not only the Patripassian heresy but also the first traces of nascent Subordinationism, according to which the Son was but a creation of the Father.

But there was a second heresy more dangerous for Christology than this Modalist Monarchianism. It too was propagated by the Judaeo-Christian Ebionites, who maintained that since there can be only one divine person, Christ himself cannot be that divine person but simply the vessel of an impersonal divine power (δύναμις). This would make Christ merely human (ψιλὸς ἄνθρωπος) and deny the whole basis of Christianity, the idea of God become man. At bottom, these heretics were still haunted not only by the orthodox Jewish concept of God but also by the old Jewish view of the Messias as one specially sent from God, the chosen human organ of God's decree, but not as the historical revelation and a manifestation of God himself. Modern liberal assessments of Jesus as the great, unique, but purely human means of divine revelation are remarkably close to this heretical dynamism nourished on Jewish ideas. Its chief representatives were Theodotus, a shoemaker from Byzantium, and his pupil Theodotus the Banker, but in particular Paul of Samosata, Bishop of Antioch. The former was excluded from the Church by Pope Victor (189–198). Paul of Samosata was deposed at an Antioch synod in 268. Rome's judgement was confirmed in 272 by the pagan Emperor Aurelian. This was the first example of the influence of a political power upon purely ecclesiastical affairs, but on the other hand a clear proof that towards the end of the third century Rome's dominance was admitted and recognized even among the pagan authorities. Paul of Samosata tried as clearly as possible to express the living dynamic, though not the divine, person in Christ by using the Gnostic terms ὁμοούσιος to express the power, and ὁμοούσιος τῷ Πατρί to express the Son. But he did not use the term ὁμοούσιος in the sense of consubstantiality with the divine nature, but referred it solely to the spiritual power of the Father endowed upon the Son. The divine quality alive in Christ was the spiritual power (δύναμις λογική) of the Father himself. Because Paul of Samosata's interpretation of the term "homoousios" had been heretical, the Synod of Antioch rejected the expression outright, although the Council of Nicaea was later to make use of it to express unequivocally the consubstantiality of Father and Son.

In rejecting Dynamistic Monarchianism, the Church removed once and for all from Christology the narrow Judaistic idea of the Messias, and also broke with the Judaistic concept of God, according to which the Godhead was only one person. Thus it ensured the basis of the belief in Christ, the mysterious fact that the one divine being is so eternally fruitful that it shines both in the Father and in the Son. Thus the end of the third century saw the Church's clarification of these Christological points: Christ is not mere man; rather, his place is on the side of God. But he is not identical with the Father, but distinct from him. However, it is not enough to speak here of a spiritual power similar to God's. And it certainly does not do to follow Dionysius of Alexandria in calling Christ the creation of God.

Christology of Christ's inferiority, and Arianism

Passionate debates were still kindled by this last proposition, in spite of Pope Dionysius' quite unequivocal letter on the subject in 260. The dispute with the Monarchians had settled once and for all the Jewish version of the Christian concept of God, which regarded God as a single divine person of which Christ was but a new manifestation, or held Christ to be simply the vessel of a divine power. The question that now arose was how to define more closely the second divine person. On the one hand Christ's essence is divine rather than human, but on the other he is not identical with the Father. How, then, is he distinguished from him? This was the problem of the relationship of the second divine person to the first.

Now the pagan, Hellenistic turn of mind was close and familiar to the Christian who believed in the incarnation of

God's Son (the idea of the divinity's descent into the world
of men was, after all, not strange to Hellenism); but it became
very dangerous when the Christian sought an answer to his
question: What relationship of essence persists between this
Son of God come down to earth, and the Father, Lord of
heaven and earth? Even St. Paul had given the name of "God"
(ὁ Θεός) only to God the Father, and had distinguished him
most carefully from God become man, "the Lord" (Κύριος).
And John had recorded Jesus' words: "The Father is greater
than I." In the Synoptic Gospels, Jesus' prayers to the Father
always put himself in the position of the subject rather than
the object of worship. And did he not give the sick young man
the strange reply: "Why dost thou ask me about what is good?
One there is who is good, and he is God" (Matt. 19.17)?

Subordinationism

These New Testament texts would seem at first glance to
indicate an inferiority of the Son to the Father. A mind trained
in the Hellenistic school would read even more into them. A
Christian in the tradition of Plato, or even Philo, could hardly
understand this inferiority of the Son except in the sense of the
Platonic view of God and the world. According to this, God
is the transcendent pure and simple (τὸ ἕν), whose essence is
totally unrelated to the world and who thus requires a mediator, lesser in nature than himself but higher than the world, to
bring about a connexion between himself and the world. In
Philo's terminology this mediator was called the "Logos,"
which increased the temptation to regard the Logos of St. John
and thus the Christ of the New Testament as identical with
this concept, seeing Christ as a being mediating between God
and the world, a creature higher than the angels but less than
God himself. Thus arose the Christology of Christ's inferiority,
or Subordinationism, as it is called. This Christology of
Christ's inferiority had in common with Monarchianism a reluctance to regard Christ as a true divine person, of the same
substance as the Father. They knew that in essence he was on
the side of God but did not have the courage to draw the conclusion that he could be God in the same sense as the Father.
This shows very clearly how closely the development of the
problems of Christology is related to questions as to the nature
of the Trinity. As long as the Trinity was regarded in terms

of the history of our Lord, and Christ recognized only in his historical works and deeds, not only were these works but the Lord's essence itself made dependent upon the Father. For he became the Logos only because the Father freely willed his issuance from the Father's seed, that Christ might create the world, or take on human form. On the day of the creation of the world, or at the hour of his incarnation, he came to birth in his full personality as Logos. The conclusion was not far to seek that the Logos which had reached its full being only in *time* must necessarily be less than the eternal Father.

This interpretation of Christology in terms of the history of our Lord was not wholly replaced until Origen's doctrine of the begetting of the Son in eternity, which gave Christology a point of departure within the Godhead. Only then was the way free to confirm the necessity within the Godhead for the existence of the Logos, and thus to establish that Logos and Father were of the same substance. Origen died in A.D. 254. But it was a long time before the sound parts of his speculation were able to find their way into theology as a whole; for Origen himself did not draw the final conclusions from his doctrine. He too clung to the idea that the Son was inferior to the Father, even though he had suggested the eternal begetting of the Son. There were a number of factors supporting this Christology of Christ's inferiority. We have already mentioned them: first, those passages in the New Testament that appear to range the Son below the Father; secondly, the whole current view of God and the world deriving from Plato which was unable to imagine any impression of God upon the world without a subordinate mediator; and thirdly, the Christology of the early Christian Apologists which was dominated by this Platonic concept of God and sought to base the mystery of the Lord not in his eternal divine essence, but in historical events of the period and of his life, i.e., in Christ's appearance in time. In emphasizing that the Logos became fully itself only through the creation of the world, or through the incarnation, and that the Holy Spirit became divine spirit only in the Pentecostal miracle, they introduced the idea of time into the concepts of Logos and Holy Spirit, and hence made both appear inferior, at least temporally, to the Father.

Of course, this is not to say that the Christology of Christ's inferiority to the Father was for any length of time exclusively supported by the Church. This is sufficiently proved by the letter from Pope Dionysius to his namesake the Bishop of Alexandria in which he confirms as official doctrine the consubstantiality of Father, and Son, and μία τριάς. There was also the tradition of the Alexandrian school, who followed their master Origen in maintaining that the Son was begotten in eternity, thus rejecting the Apologists' doctrine of the Trinity which was based on the history of our Lord. And thirdly, there was the Church's energetic protest which Subordinationism encountered all along the line when Arius, Presbyter of Alexandria, came forward in his chief work *Thalia* as its interpreter and promulgator.

It is not necessary to go into Arius' doctrine in detail here. It is characterized by the utter isolation of God the highest (ὁ Θεός), and his complete separation from the cosmos. The Platonic note is easy to discern. God is so transcendent that of himself he can have absolutely no relationship to the world. This offers the conclusion that the Son was a mediator, a God of secondary order not begotten in eternity and out of the inner necessity of the Godhead, but created by God's free will. He has not issued forth from the substance of the Father *ex sinu Patris,* but was created of God's free will. Above all, *created.* He is thus the Son of God not by nature but by Grace. In a brief time, Arianism spread to an amazing extent. It found the support of the worldly power, the imperial ἐπίσκοπος, who led the non-Christian cults in the office of Pontifex Maximus. It was in tune with the philosophy of the age, and likewise went more than halfway to meet the doctrine of the Apologists which was based upon the history of our Lord. "The world was astonished to find it had become Arian" (St. Jerome).

However, this very astonishment was proof that Arianism was not originally a Christian growth, and did not express the Christian confession of faith in Christ, untouched by Neo-Platonism. It is clear that Arianism presents us with a pagan, Neo-Platonic system. It was the attempt at a synthesis between Hellenism and Christianity.

The history of Arianism, seen from the outside, presents a picture of un-Christian strife and wrangling, but from the inside it is a proof of the spirit and power in Christianity, the ever-renewed confession, drawn from all its depths: "Thou art the Christ, Son of the living God."

The most important opponents of Arianism were Alexander, Bishop of Alexandria, and in particular his deacon Athanasius. Athanasius had recognized at once the questionable conclusions that could be drawn from Arius' doctrine. For if Arius were right, neither was the Trinity a single divine nature nor was it eternal. It was formed only *in time,* and there would always be the possibility that in later aeons new developments could take place within the Godhead. The three-in-one of the Trinity could become the four-in-one, or the many-in-one. The divinity of the Father itself was most dangerously threatened. For one could conclude from Arius' teaching that the first divine person had not always been the Father, and had not from eternity borne the Word and the wisdom within him. A further criticism levelled against it was that the three divine persons were not of equal value, if the Son were not of the same nature as the Father. As well as the creator there would be a created god, a demigod. This would be pagan polytheism, and would make the worship of the Lord impossible. Anyway, why should God not be able directly to intrude into the fate and affairs of mankind? If some such mediator had been necessary, God would have required yet another mediator, in order to create the Logos, and the series of go-betweens would stretch on into infinity. But for Athanasius, the decisive criticism of Arius was in the question of the redemption of mankind. He took his starting point, like many of his predecessors, in mankind's need of salvation. His entire Christology is dominated by the question: How is redemption possible? If Christ is not God, then all our hope of redemption is built upon sand, for only God can redeem mankind. It is due to Athanasius that in 325 the Council of Nicaea included in the second article of the Apostolic Creed the item that Son and Father were of the same substance (ὁμοούσιος τῷ Πατρί). It is true, this idea of Athanasius was not yet fully developed, the less so since the Council had given express definition neither to the begetting of the Son in eternity nor to whether the Holy Spirit was of the same substance as Son and Father. So Subordinationism could always go on flourishing underground, to distort the Church's image of Christ. It was not until the Christology of the Cappadocians, and really not until Augustine, that the Nicene doctrine gained dominance to the exhaustion of all others; and the Emperor Theodosius I made its way to general recognition easier by a decretal in the year 380.

The dogmatic result of the Arian disputes could be summed up thus: Christ is not a god of secondary order, a god by Grace. He is rather God's Son, the historical revelation of God himself. He is consubstantial with God, begotten in eternity of inner divine necessity, and not created by a Grace-bestowing will.

At last the mystery of the incarnation was ensured against

all misinterpretation. Pagan deification was kept remote from the image of Christ. Christ does not stand in the line of the ancient gods and sons of gods, subordinate to the highest god. He is God himself, the personal revelation of the Father. This was the basis of the formulation "God-man," as Athanasius had already used it. In this God-man, the absolute Self assumed historical appearance. What Christ does, thinks, utters, works, has absolute validity. All Christianity is thereby exalted above the mere human and historically conditioned. This is the occurrence of something utterly new, without any causal connexion to what has gone before, without any "correlation." It is in essence supernatural.

From now on, the dogma of God incarnate plays a far more important rôle than it had in the earlier Christian cult. Whereas the original liturgical prayers were addressed to the Father, the canonical prayer of St. Athanasius preserved in the Georgian-Jacobite liturgy was addressed to the Son. From here, it made its way into all the Oriental liturgies, and in Egypt created the Gregorian liturgy which is addressed solely to the Son. Prayers to Christ do not make their way into the Latin Mass until later. The Kyrie Eleison, a prayer to Christ from the start, was not taken over by the Roman liturgy from the Greek until the fifth century. The Gloria, "an inheritance from the early Church's treasury of hymns" (Jungmann), was originally a hymn of praise to God the Father uttered by Christ, the High Priest. Only after later development was the thought of mediation transferred by this act of praise to the Son. The canon of the Roman Mass, the main part of which goes back to the fifth century, has to this day preserved in its essentials the old decree to address prayers to the Father through the mediation of Christ. The Agnus Dei was apparently taken over about 700 by Pope Sergius I from the Syrian liturgy. The three prayers in the name of Christ before the communion originated as late as the ninth and tenth centuries. In general we may say that the defence of Christianity against Arianism had no small influence upon the order of prayer in the liturgy.

Earlier, the liturgy had always been offered "through thy servant Jesus" (διὰ Ἰησοῦ τοῦ παιδός σου), "per Christum Dominum," or "in the name of Jesus," and prayers had been offered through Jesus directly to the Father—indeed, as late as 393 a Synod of Hippo praesente Augustino required that the collect should always be said to the Father. However, there was now a great fear, particularly in those Greek and Oriental churches that had been haunted by Arianism, that the preposition "through" was an encouragement to Arian Subordinationism. The Arians did in fact call upon this liturgical formulation to support their doctrine of the Son's inferiority to the Father. To counter this Arian objection, not a few Oriental liturgies altered the old formula "through Christ our Lord," and substituted "with him" (as Athanasius and Chrysostom had already done). Instead of the old doxology, "Glory be to the Father through the Son in the Holy Spirit," from now on they prayed: "Glory be to the Father and to the Son and to the Holy Spirit." In fact, the old formulation was perfectly correct if, in regarding Christ *in forma Dei,* i.e., according to his divine nature, the Son issues from the Father; and also if, in regarding him *in forma servi,* i.e., according to his human nature, the word "through" is intended to signify that mediation and priestly office which the New Man exercises as *primus inter pares* for all mankind. In contrast to the Oriental liturgies, the Roman Church has in general faithfully preserved the *"per Christum Dominum nostrum."* Most of its liturgical prayers call upon the Father *"per Christum Dominum nostrum."* But an anti-Arian tendency still shows itself in the addition of the word *"Deus,"* to ensure the divine issuance of the Son from the Father. This in any case was the reason why, even in the early Church, prayers were addressed directly to Christ himself, if not in solemn liturgy, then at least in private prayer. Even in the Apocalypse of St. John (5. 9–13) there is reference to worship of the Lamb. When St. Stephen was stoned, he cried to the Son: "Lord Jesus, receive my spirit" (Acts 8.59). The *Acta Petri,* dating from the time of Origen, a work that mirrors the popular religious temper of the third century, offers all the prayers directly to Christ so exclusively that the word "Pan-Christianism" has been coined. Similarly, in the true early Christian martyrdoms (*Martyrium Polycarpi, Martyrium Carpi*) Christ is constantly called upon. After the Arian disputes had died down, such prayers to Christ came to be included even in solemn liturgy.

In its dogma that the Son was of the same substance as the Father, the Council of Nicaea created the basis for subsequent Christological thinking. Such theology could not depart from this dogma without ceasing to be Christian. Liberal Protestant theology is unfaithful to this common ground nourishing all Christian confessions; it refuses it, as it were, "civic rights"; and when its particular aim is to take from the simple image of Christ in the Gospels his "mantle of gold brocade," his divine nature, then it is reverting to this old Dynamistic Monarchianism. The entire course of historical Christianity even in the most confused of its heretical offspring gives the lie to this procedure. It is folly to continue to speak of Christianity and pretend to the name of Christian while denying it the very element that was the dynamic of its historical development: the belief in the supernatural essence of Jesus.

The Christological question in the narrower sense

In the disputes against Arianism, the Christological question was one with the problem of the Trinity—how to define the relationship to one another within the Godhead of the three divine persons. But subsequently theology withdrew the Christological question completely from its connexion with life within the Trinity, and it became the Christological question in the narrower sense, i.e., What is the relationship of the consubstantial divine nature in Christ to his human nature? The dogma of consubstantiality has solved one side of the problem, i.e., that Christ's divine nature was not granted him by Grace, that his divinity was not of a secondary order, but that it was, quite simply, identical with the Godhead. The second question demanded a solution so much the more urgently: What is the relationship between the divinity in Jesus and his humanity, the humanity in Jesus and the divine Logos? This was not only an ontological but also a psychological question: What is the relationship between Jesus' consciousness of his divinity and his purely human consciousness, his awareness of hunger, anxiety, thought, will, suffering, and death?

Docetism

The simplest, crudest solution was to deny absolutely this purely human consciousness. According to the view of the Docetae, Jesus' entire human nature is mere outward appearance: his body is appearance, his suffering is appearance. All that is real in him is his divinity. It is exceedingly instructive to follow the philosophical roots of this Docetism, in so far as we can speak of such. Once again we realize that the real root of every heresy is to be found not in the sphere of revelation, but in the pagan philosophies. Tertullian had already understood this and called the philosopher the father of all heresies. The heresy of Docetism went back to Greek thought, in particular to Neo-Platonism. But the system was made still cruder by clumsy thinking. To Plato, true spiritual being, the Logos, is to be found in the ideal image of things, in which all spiritual essences have their reality. Ultimately, true being is the divine itself, whose image and expression is the Logos. Everything existent is constructed according to this pattern. Thus Plato regarded the empirical existence perceived by the senses as a secondary order of being, which, in so far as it can be perceived only by the senses, is transient and mutable. Only what is spiritual does not pass away, and is thus the true reality and source of reality. This sharp distinction between divine spiritual being and empirical sensuous being was intensified by Oriental influence into an antithesis between spirit and matter. Oriental thought is essentially dualistic. It is based upon a system of antagonistic opposites: heaven and earth, spirit and matter, soul and body. Apart from Brahmanism and its offspring, this dualistic thinking was established and propagated in particular by the religion of the Parsees. When Alexander the Great conquered Persia, Greek thought too was penetrated by this Persian dualism, giving rise to Hellenistic thought, which was characterized by this very tension between spirit and matter. It held that the sensuous world has no real existence. To the crude-thinking it was just one further step to regarding what has no existence as something that *should* have no existence (the οὐκ ὄν as the μὴ ὄν). So now God and the world, soul and body were not merely distinct, they were opposites, indeed contradictory. Neo-Platonism, which was more a religion than a philosophy, added the further interpretation that the aim of all spiritual education and effort was absolute release from the world of the senses, especially in ecstatic mysticism, in order to emphasize the purely spiritual in man. A strong anti-sensuous tendency, which we know as Encratism, spread, particularly in those circles that were repelled by the advance of uncontrolled sensuality. As Christianity made its way into these circles, its ethics were understood primarily in Encratic terms, and its metaphysics primarily in Docetic terms. We may say that the first misinterpretation of the Christian teaching took place on Hellenistic ground in the sense that it contested the Lord's corporeality and sensuous existence. Even the writings of St. John (1 John 1.1; 4.1; 2

John 7) already had to do with Docetism. That is why the
Evangelist is eager to emphasize that the Word became flesh.
This Docetic Gnosticism regarded the body as something unworthy of man. With this as its starting point the Gospel
according to the Egyptians did not hesitate to call woman, the
symbol of closeness to nature, "a garment of shame." These
Gnostics emphasized the Docetic view of Christ all the more
in the hope of countering the pagan objection that the idea of
God crucified was folly.

The Docetic Gnosis was decisively rejected, even in the
very beginnings of Christianity, not least in the *"verbum caro
factum est"* of St. John. All the symbols of our faith emphasize that Jesus was truly born of Mary, and that his suffering and death were real. The soteriology of the early Church,
as first formulated by St. Paul, is based upon the assumption of
the reality of Christ's incarnation, and the reality of his death
on the cross. Among the Apostolic Fathers, Ignatius of Antioch
in particular countered the Gnostics of Judaic tendency by
stressing the corporeality of the Lord. Docetism was furthest
advanced by Marcion, who had come from Sinope to Rome
about A.D. 140 and was soon excommunicated there. On the
one hand his dualism made him reject the entire Old Testament as the work of the evil Demiurge; on the other hand he
tried to support his Docetism by exegesis from a Gospel according to St. Luke and ten Epistles of St. Paul which he had
himself cut and arranged to fit his views. For him, Christ is
the manifestation of the good God. His body is mere outward
appearance, and he first came forward before the world in the
fifteenth year of Tiberius' reign. Only this illusory body was
crucified. These fantastic ideas were passionately rejected
primarily by Irenaeus and Tertullian. When Docetism emerged
again in the Middle Ages among the Albigensians and Bogo-
milians it was refuted afresh at the Council of Lyons (1245)
and the Council of Vienne (1311-12).

The first attempt to reconcile Jesus' divinity with his low
human estate by regarding the latter as mere outward appearance was rejected at the very beginning of Christianity. The
Church's consciousness of faith clung just as firmly to the
Lord's true humanity as it did to his true divinity. This alone
withdraws the image of Christ from the oppressive realm of the
pagan mythologies and theogonies. The pagan gods that had
come down to earth had absorbed all their human quality into
their divinity. They were not God become flesh, but gods upon
earth whose human form was mere outward appearance. In

contrast to this, the Christian faith firmly maintained that Christ was not a god upon earth, but God become flesh.

The Logos-Sarx Christology of Arius and Apollinaris

The second attempt to approach a solution to our question derived from Arius and Apollinaris. Arius, of the school of Lucian of Antioch, regarded the Logos as the creation of the Father. Thus it belonged in the category of created powers, even if foremost among them. As a created power it is fit and capable of becoming an essential part of created nature, and of entering human nature as its highest, noblest power, and thus of becoming part of human nature. Arius' concept of the Logos furnished him with a basis upon which to explain the mystery of the incarnation in such a way that in the true humanity of Christ the Logos should take the place of the human soul, the soul being conceived as the principle of both vital animal life and spiritual life. Thus in the incarnation the Logos would not take up human nature as a whole, but only the flesh, the somatic part, and not the soul (σάρξ, ἄψυχον σῶμα). The Logos itself would take over the functions of the soul. The incarnation itself was thus understood as the animation of the body by the Logos. God incarnate is made up of human body (Sarx) and divine Logos. Thus the Logos did not become man, but only flesh. Arius' interpretation of the interpenetration of God and man in Christ is every bit as crude and naïve as his theory of the Logos. Christ is half man and half god, the monstrous product of a synthesis. Arius gives no explanation of how the Gospels' clear statement of the full humanity of Christ, and St. Paul's teaching of the meaning of Christ's death for our salvation, are to be understood in terms of his theory. Above all, he is not aware of the contradiction in his scheme: How can our soul be redeemed if the Logos is not united to a purely human soul?

Apollinaris, Bishop of Laodicea (d. about A.D. 390), formulated a far more profound theory of the unity of humanity and divinity in Christ, taking the same Logos-Sarx scheme as his point of departure. The object of his speculations was to make as close as possible the union of true divinity and true humanity in Christ, which, he recognized, were both truly essential parts of Christ's nature. This union seemed closest to him if the divinity and humanity in Christ complemented each other so as to constitute one nature and being, if together they composed a single divine-and-human nature. However, he concluded, drawing upon Aristotle, two complete perfected natures are not able to compound themselves into any such unity of nature (δύο τέλεια ἕν γενέσθαι οὐ δύναται). They cannot interpenetrate each other, but only exist side by side. If all the same a true unity of nature should be established, it could be only by diminishing, as it were, the human nature of Jesus at its highest point. He tried to clarify this with the aid of Trichotomistic psychology, which distinguishes in man's soul a lower, sensuous soul (ψυχή, *anima sensitiva*) and a higher, spiritual principle (πνεῦμα, νοῦς, *anima intellectiva*). In the incarnation, the Logos takes the place of this spiritual soul. The incarnation is brought about by the joining of the divine Pneuma and the Sarx, living but deprived of its higher spirit, into a union. In agreement with the Alexandrian tradition, which arose under the influence of Stoicism, Apollinaris regarded the Logos as the really effective principle in Jesus' higher spiritual life, and thus as the dominating, animating, fundamental power in Jesus' humanity too. Thus Christ was bound to transience and the earth only in his organic, sensuous being. His spiritual thinking and willing were divine, the wisdom and omnipotence of the Logos. He had but a single consciousness: the divine. Thus Christ is a "heavenly human" in so far as he derives his body from the Virgin but his soul from the Logos. These two parts are related to each other as parts of a whole, and are therefore together μία φύσις μία οὐσία, ἕν πρόσωπον, expressions which for Apollinaris are almost identical. But it is the Logos that controls all life in Christ. In this sense, Apollinaris speaks of the "one nature of God-Logos become flesh," an expression later taken up by Cyril and used in a somewhat different sense. This was the only way Apollinaris believed he could save the unity of the image of Christ and avoid a split of Christ's self-consciousness into human and divine. On the other hand, this seemed to him the only certain and dependable way of explaining the redemption of mankind. For if Christ thought and willed purely as a man, he could not be denied freedom of decision, and must also have had the freedom to sin. But this would mean the end of all the certainty of redemption, which, according to Paul and John, had from eternity been part of the divine ordinance for salvation. For in the last resort it would depend upon the free decision of Jesus' human thought and will, something accidental. The great divine dispensation in its entirety, above all the mystery of the incarnation, would be dependent upon the good will of Jesus' humanity. And this would be unworthy of God and his wisdom.

Apollinaris' theory is distinguished—to its advantage—from that of Arius by the fact that it recognizes in Christ not merely the human body but also a human soul. But by depriving this soul of its dominant spiritual principle, the nous, it can hardly claim to speak of a fully human nature in Christ. In order to establish in Christ a true unity of nature, Apollinaris denatures the humanity of Jesus. It remained something incomplete, a fragment, at bottom near to what the animals have, an animal soul. This was a great threat to the whole divinity and sublimity of Christ's humanity. What would Christ's example have to say to man if it were based not on the anguished struggling of the human will, but on the all-holy Logos? How could man's innermost will have been redeemed by Christ if Christ's own will had been not human but divine? This was and is an axiom of soteriology: *quad non est assumptum, non est sanatum.* If the entire human thought and volition were not assumed into the divine person, it could not be led by the latter to experience any objective purification and salvation. We may well say: "The two heretical forms of the Logos-Sarx Christology, Arianism and Apollinarianism, were probably the most dangerous invasion of Hellenistic ideas into the traditional conception of Christ" (*Das Konzil von Chalkedon,* I, p. 115). Apollinarianism bears the first seeds of the later heresy of Monophysitism, which laid the gilding of divinity onto the picture of Christ so thickly that the Lord's human traits disappeared completely and Christ reverted to the ranks of pagan mythologies.

Apollinarianism could not be combated from the position of Alexandrine theology. Even the great Athanasius puts so little stress on the human soul in Jesus that it never becomes the express object of theological avowal in his scheme. He recognizes and worships the pattern of the human soul so exclusively in the Logos that the image of the Logos, Christ's human soul, retreats completely. The Logos itself is represented as the animating and energizing principle of Christ's body, the physical source of all his actions as living man. In a more moderate form than Apollinaris, Athanasius too is bound to the Logos-Sarx pattern of thought. Indeed, we may say that even later, the Eastern Church never completely threw off her bondage to this pattern.

The great achievement of the theology of Antioch was that

it overcame Apollinarianism; indeed, it was in dispute with the heresy that the school first developed. It countered the Logos-Sarx scheme with a Logos-Anthropos scheme. In this respect we owe a particular debt to Eustathius of Antioch and Theodore of Mopsuestia, although their strong emphasis upon this contrast itself ran the danger of preparing the way for a dualistic Christology which was carried to its logical conclusion in Nestorianism. The place of Christ's human soul in their theological scheme was this: Without it, redemption from sin, which cleaves in particular to the human soul, is impossible. With this doctrine they were able to point out the inadequacy of the Arian and Apollinarian Christology.

At the Synods of Alexandria and Rome, Apollinarianism was condemned. The first Council at Constantinople (381) pronounced its solemn sentence (Denzinger, 86). Since then, Church theology has expressly emphasized that God became flesh *mediante anima,* through the mediation of the human soul, and not in place of the human soul. The rejection of Apollinarianism anticipated the later rejection of fully developed Monophysitism, Monotheletism, and Monenergism.

It is true that terminologically the expressions "became flesh" and "incarnation" remained in use. Didymus the Blind in particular used them so frequently and recklessly in his early period that theologians were tempted to range him close to Apollinarianism. St. Augustine, too, was fond of the phrase *caro Christi,* but he always used it in the sense of the entire humanity of Jesus. The early Scholastics remained faithful to this usage of Augustine's. The high age of Scholasticism, however, preferred the unambiguous phrase "made man." Since then, theology has no longer spoken of an *assumptio carnis* alone, but of the *assumptio carnis et animae,* i.e., *hominis.*

The disputes with Apollinaris had made the following dogma clear: Both divinity and perfect humanity are in Christ. This humanity is fully conscious of itself and its peculiar spirituality. It is in no sense replaced by the Logos. The unity of divinity and humanity in Christ may not be brought about by any diminishing or denaturing of humanity in Christ. This prepared the way for the realization that the union of divinity and humanity in Christ can take place only *secundum personam,* not *secundum naturam.* It cannot be that divine powers poured themselves, as it were, with natural necessity, into the humanity of Christ and transformed it into divinity. Rather, Christ's human nature remained completely unabsorbed after the union. What the Logos imparts to Christ's human nature

can be only the identity of the second person, the consciousness of being this person, the independence, the autonomy. It
is true, this conclusion did not come fully to light until the
disputes with Monophysitism. The question that this heresy
raised was this: If Christ is truly God, and in body and soul
wholly man, and if both parts of his being, divine and human,
remain undiminished, how can the *unus Christus,* the unified
self, arise, and how can this unified self be more precisely
defined?

The Christology of the schools of Antioch and Alexandria

The preceding discussion has indicated that the Christological controversies of the early Church were settled by two
schools of theology, the school of Alexandria and the school
of Antioch. The former favoured a metaphysical and contemplative view of God and the world; the second tended to
stress empirical data, i.e., what is historically given. Where the
school of Antioch aspired to God from the world of experience, the Alexandrians laboured to understand the world of
historical data from the divine. Where the school of Antioch
worked from the depths to the heights, Alexandrian speculation moved from the heights to the depths.

This characteristic distinction between the two schools became the more apparent as the question became more important of *how* divinity and humanity were united in Christ.
The school of Antioch started from the historical appearance
of Jesus: Christ came into the world wholly man, with a consciousness of human identity. The disputes with Apollinaris
had clearly established that Christ possessed a consciousness
not only of divine but also of human identity. This led them
to the conclusion that Christ also had a human self. Hence
their question: If Christ's human self is historically given,
indeed has priority, how can the divine self be united with this
human self? From the start this question involved the danger
of deducing the existence of an autonomous human self from
the peculiarity of the human consciousness of self, and thus of
destroying the unity of Christ's person. The school of Antioch
was strongly tempted to regard the union of divinity and humanity in Christ not as an inner union of essence, but as
merely external, accidental. It would regard the human self
as coexistent with the divine self. Their unity would be not

physical, but moral; not of being, but of will; a mere reciprocal relationship (ἕνωσις σχετική) which arises out of the loving inclination of divine and human selves towards each other, and thus must be renewed. Thus a continual exchange of love, a constant movement of love, would take place in Christ between the divine self of the Logos and the human self. The continual obligation of love (συνάφεια) elevates even the human self to the Son of God. So there are two Sons of God in Christ, the natural and the adopted. Mary bore only this adopted son. Hence she cannot strictly be called the mother of God, but only the mother of Christ.

Nestorianism

These conclusions, it is true, were first seen clearly and drawn expressly only in the course of the disputes. At first glance it would seem that the Antioch doctrine of the *unio caritatis* was supported by the Church's condemnation of Arianism and Apollinarianism, which had tried to demonstrate a natural union between divinity and humanity in Christ. And so Nestorius, Patriarch of Constantinople, confidently believed he was thinking along strictly orthodox lines when he allowed Anastasius the priest to spread Antiochian ideas among the people. This popularization necessarily made the ideas both cruder and stronger than originally. This was particularly clear in the practical conclusions which the preacher imagined he was drawing from the doctrine of the two Sons of God. He held that the characteristics and activities of the divine and the human self in Christ were to be rigidly separated. It would not do simply to call Christ God and worship him as God without any further distinction. Only the Logos in Christ was the true God. Thus there was no *communicatio idiomatum*. Thus it would also not do to address Mary as the mother of God. She was the Christotokos, but not the Theotokos. This last conclusion in particular threw sharp light upon the doctrine of the two Sons of God. It appeared in crass contradiction to the Christian creed, which had always honoured Mary as blessed among women, whose offspring was the whole Christ, and not merely his human self alone. Ever since Origen, theology had designated Mary as the mother of God. This new doctrine was dangerously near to ascribing a dualism to Christ, a dichotomy to his being. Christ appeared as a duality, as holiness walking the earth, in whom the human high priest honoured his God. This was no longer the Christ of John and Paul, and it was no longer the mighty miracle-working self of the Gospels, who died on the cross and rose again on the third day. In the history of dogma Nestorianism was closely related to Dynamistic Monarchianism, particularly to such ideas as Paul of Samosata's reduction of Christ's historical appearance to mere man.

It was understandable that Nestorius should have roused the protest of the Alexandrian school, which, ever since Clement of Alexandria, had characteristically viewed the Logos as the unifying principle directly animating Christ's human actions. So this school did not judge Christ primarily according to his external human appearance, but according to his inner dignity, accessible only to faith, according to the relation between his essence and God. So the question they posed was this: If Christ is the true God, how can his divinity assume human nature without endangering the inviolability of this human nature? This question certainly ensured the unity of Christ's person, but there was also the fateful danger that it would not do justice to the human nature in its effective sphere. Where the Alexandrians from their point of departure were disposed to overstrain the unity of person in Christ into a unity of nature, the school of Antioch was inclined to extend the duality of natures to a duality of persons. It is only natural that even Cyril should, at the beginning of his speculation, base it on the traditional Logos-Sarx scheme and even go on undisturbed to use Apollinarian formulations. Only in the course of the disputes with Nestorius did he come to recognize that for its part Alexandrian theory did not do justice to the peculiar importance of Christ's human soul and its deeds. It was the particular achievement of his speculation to unite the insights of both schools, and thereby to furnish a sufficiently clear basis for further correct development of the truths of Christology.

The characteristics of his speculation can be summed up briefly: The process of incarnation had its starting point not in the human but in the divine self. Christ the man did not become the Logos—that would be an apotheosis after the fashion of pagan mythologies—but rather the Logos became man. The subject of the union is solely the Logos-self. Thus we can speak only of a single self in Christ, the divine self of the Logos. Even after the incarnation, there is only one self in Christ. "One and the same is Christ." This Logos has assumed human nature to such an extent that it possesses human nature physically (ἕνωσις φυσική) in its being, and not through some moral act of faith and love on the part of human nature. The union of God and man in Christ is accomplished once and for all in the incarnation. It does not depend upon free will or a moral act. This formula of Cyril's, ἕνωσις φυσική, is not to be understood in the sense that the later Monophysitism ascribed to it, that the union of both natures took place *secundum naturam divinam* so that all the characteristics of the divine nature of themselves poured into the humanity and completely absorbed it. The formula rather means: The union is not accidental and dependent upon will, brought into being through a voluntary act of human nature, but is permanent, unique, brought into being by the fact of the incarnation. The self of the Logos is thus not the result but the permanent principle of the union, which already existed before any moral act that Christ was capable of, and is so close that the divine and the human in Christ can be separate only theoretically in idea. In reality it is one and the same divine self that performs not only the divine but also the human deeds, so that both divine and human actions are equally expressions of Christ. This is the *communicatio idiomatum*. From the self in Christ named after his divine nature, one can adduce human actions, and from the self in Christ called after his human nature, one can adduce divine actions. I can avow: The Logos became man and suffered, just as I can affirm: The crucified one is the prince of life. I may say this because the subject of my avowal is always one and the same: the self of the eternal Word. This is why our worship is due not simply to the Logos in Christ but to the whole Christ, including his humanity, because this humanity belongs to the Logos and is not to be separated from it. This is why Mary is truly the mother of God, because the living being that she bore is the Son of God become man.

This powerful emphasis on ἕνωσις φυσική, which Cyril derived from the Alexandrian tradition, preserves the image of Christ from all antinomies and stresses the divine basis of Christ's life, the mighty fact that God himself, the second divine person, is the true bearer of all human and superhuman characteristics and powers of the Lord. At last the *verbum caro factum est* of St. John, and the believing conviction that the selfsame historical Jesus is also the Son of the living God, was once again given lucid expression and clear spiritual perception.

It is true, the liberating word had not yet been uttered, that the union was not a *unio secundum naturam* but only *secundum personam*. Cyril had not yet attempted to draw a clear distinction between nature and person, or to establish that existence as person is not an essential part of nature, but that existence as person can rather be distinguished from existence as nature, and that it is hence conceivable, and indeed really the case, that in Christ a human nature can certainly exist, but not a human person. Since Cyril had not gone as far as this, the suspicion could still arise that at root the Alexandrians taught the assumption of human nature into divine nature in such a way that the divine nature could absorb and assume even human qualities and powers. This possibility was first grasped at a later date by Monophysitism.

After the Synod of Alexandria, Cyril followed the Pope's injunction to anathematize the errors of Nestorius in twelve articles. In the same year (429) Pope Celestine rejected Nestorianism at a Synod in Rome. Since Nestorius would not humble himself and accused Cyril of Apollinarianism in twelve counter-anathemata, in 431 the Emperor Theodosius II summoned a general council to Ephesus. With Cyril presiding, Nestorianism was again rejected and the Church doctrine formulated in Cyril's version. Nestorius and his followers were angered at the harsh and hasty way Cyril urged a decision even before the Nestorians had reached the Council. There is no doubt that Cyril was not entirely motivated by unselfish reasons. He introduced his personal interest and private antagonism to Nestorius into the dogmatic dispute. So the opposition persisted. Not until 433 did the Eastern Church reach agreement on the Symbol of Antioch (known as the *symbolum Ephesinum* and as the "symbol of Union") which designated Mary as the mother of God, Theotokos, but nevertheless continued to teach an uncommingled union of divinity and humanity in Christ. By assumption into the Logos, the humanity of Christ does not receive the qualities and powers of divine nature, but remains unconsumed humanity. The equivocal slogan of μία φύσις τοῦ Θεοῦ λόγου σεσαρχωμένη, "one nature incarnate of God the Word," deriving from Apollinaris and taken over by Cyril, was not included in the symbol of Union. But in spite of this, Cyril gave his assent to the symbol composed by the school of Antioch, as it presented a meaningful reconciliation between the two schools of thought.

The essential result of the anti-Nestorian dispute was this: that there is not a double identity in Christ, but only the one self, that of the Logos, the second divine person. The humanity of the Lord is so closely and permanently united in its essence to this Logos-self that all the human actions of Christ are at the same time actions of the Logos. Christ cannot do or think anything that does not belong to his Logos-self.

Monophysitism

After Cyril's death, the old Alexandrian Logos-Sarx scheme was revived in its most rigid form; its followers regarded the decisions of the Antioch symbol of Union as needing revision. The dispute blazed up anew, and its leader was at first Eutyches, Archimandrite of a monastery near Constantinople. He took over Cyril's formulations, and interpreted them to mean that in the power of the incarnation the divinity and the humanity of Christ fused together into one *physis,* into one divine nature. The old Apollinarian Logos-Sarx Christology which the formulation of 433 on Christ's unity, composed by the school of Antioch and approved by Cyril, was to have overcome, led Eutyches to the view that the incarnation brought about a "fusion" (κρᾶσις, σύγκρασις) in which the human nature was entirely subsumed into the divine. He was supported primarily by such Alexandrians as the mighty Patriarch Dioscurus, who defended Eutyches' formulations at the so-called "Robber-Council of Ephesus" against the orthodox Patriarch Flavian of Constantinople and against the *Epistola dogmatica* of Pope Leo I to Flavian. The general council of 451 that was called at Chalcedon took up Pope Leo's *Epistola dogmatica* and rejected all Monophysitist interpretations of the Antioch symbol. As the Council of Nicaea had proclaimed Christ to be ὁμοούσιος τῷ Πατρί, the Council of Chalcedon was equally emphatic in proclaiming the ὁμοούσιος ἡμῖν, too. Christ is of the same essence as we are. He is our brother. Of course the two natures in Christ must not be torn asunder, as the Nestorians had done. The Logos is now and ever shall be the unifying principle in Christ. God become man is one and the same Lord, without division (ἀδιαιρέτως) or separation (ἀχωρίστως). Nestorianism remained condemned. But on the other hand it is not as if the two natures in Christ might be fused with each other. Rather, they stay side by side without any transformation (ἀτρέπτως) or fusion (ἀσυγχύτως). The peculiarity of each nature is preserved even after the incarnation, but they are united in one person.

Christ is not a divinized man, but God become man, God made flesh (Denzinger, 148).

As we see, the Council of Chalcedon is significant for its renewed emphasis upon the faith of the early Church in the complete, full humanity of Jesus, in face of the emergent Monophysitism unleashed by the anti-Nestorian disputes. It averted the dangerous conclusions that were being drawn from the *symbolum Ephesinum,* and in some cases from certain of Cyril's formulations. As God become man, Christ is the mediator between heaven and earth, between God and man, not only on account of his deeds and his mission, but also in his entire incarnate manifestation. His place is not only on the side of God, but also on the side of man.

However important the Council of Chalcedon was in keeping the stream of Church doctrine in the right channels, it still did not offer a positive and exhaustive solution to the question raised by Monophysitism: In what manner are the two natures in Christ united? Its achievement was defensive rather than constructive. Speculative thinking came up against the uncompromising truth: Christ is unique. He is no less than the Logos itself. His human nature is taken up into this Logos, but it is not entirely subsumed by it. Even after the incarnation, Christ remains fully and wholly man. By stressing this last truth in particular, the Council of Chalcedon made the old problem still more urgent: How can Christ be fully and wholly human, if this humanity does not exist of itself, but only in the Logos? How can a unique Christ arise from the union of unabsorbed human nature and unabsorbed divine nature? What is the meeting point between the divine self in Christ and his human nature? It is true the Council's formulation now distinguishes between φύσις and ὑπόστασις (πρόσωπον), ideas that formerly were constantly being confused, especially by the Alexandrians; but the Council refrained from explaining more precisely in conceptual terms where lay the distinction between the two. To grasp this clearly was obviously beyond the powers of the Fathers of the Council of Chalcedon. The issue was clarified by the theologian Leontius of Constantinople and the philosopher Boethius. In a more precise conceptual analysis they distinguished between person and nature and demonstrated that existence as person could be detached from nature, and that hence it was conceivable that the Logos as creative principle was at the same time the mainstay of the human nature. Now they expressly distinguish the terms "nature" and "essence" (οὐσία, φύσις) from the concept "person" (ὑπόστασις, πρόσωπον). Person they define as that which gives nature its independence, its autonomy. Resting upon this terminology, the Council of 553 defined the ἕνωσις καθ' ὑπόστασιν (*unio hypostatica*). The Symbol of Union and the Council of Chalcedon had indeed already made use of the ὑπόστασις, but without distinguishing it sharply from the concept φύσις Pope Leo's dogmatic epistle went back to Tertullian to maintain expressly: *una persona in utraque natura.* From now on the term ὑπόστασις referred exclusively to the person, the self in Christ. So, according to this, Church doctrine ran as follows: Not the divine nature, but the divine (second) person, is the principle uniting the two natures. Their union is strictly hypostatic—i.e., it does not signify a communication of divine nature and its attributes to the humanity of the Lord, but only the communication of the autonomy, the existence as person. As full, complete human nature usually belongs to itself, so Christ's human nature belongs to the eternal Word. It loses its independence in face of the higher, divine principle. Or rather, even as it loses its human autonomy, it is taken up and supported by a far higher, divine autonomy (ἐνυπόστατος).

Monotheletism and Monenergism

But this clear terminology was not created until the sixth century, so it is not surprising that until that time new misunderstandings and heresies were constantly spreading. Monophysitism certainly was not dead, but found increasingly passionate expression, and branched out into countless sects—even in orthodox circles it still had its secret adherents who sought a formula that would reconcile the creed of the Church with their own convictions. In many cases there were more distinctions in the formulation than in the issue that divided the adherents of Chalcedon and Monophysitism. Political interests had played a certain part in encouraging these attempts at a compromise with Monophysitism ever since the Emperor Heraclius had conquered Syria and Armenia, two countries in which the heresy was widespread. What Monophysitism found particularly repellent was the duality of will in Jesus implied by the Council of Chalcedon. Like Apollinaris formerly, its adherents believed that the whole dogma of redemption was endangered if Christ possessed free human will and free human action. This presented the unanswerable conclusion that with his free human will he would have been able to oppose the divine will, and sin, and thus bring our redemption to naught. The Monophysitist Patriarch Sergius of Constantinople attempted to put aside this objection by recognizing only one effective power, only one will and operation in Christ (ἕν θέλημα καὶ μία ἐνέργεια). It was not far to the conclusion that the human will in Jesus, and hence his human nature, was only potential, by disposition, something autonomous and independent. In reality, *in actu,* it coincided with the divine will. To this extent, one could speak only of a will of the Lord (ἕν θέλημα). For what in fact was active in Christ was the divine Logos and his energy alone. This did not work through the freedom and properties of the human nature, but through its own divine power. And it worked to such mighty effect that the potential human volition was *in actu* completely assumed and absorbed into the divine volition.

This is not the place to describe the passionate disputes released by this attempt at a compromise, which for political reasons also had the recommendation of the state. Pope Honorius did not go to the heart of the question. He believed wrongly that it was just a question of whether Christ could ever misuse his free human will and oppose the divine will— as if Sergius had only tried to maintain the commonplace that the human and divine will would never come into conflict. Honorius had only the *de facto* moral union of both wills in mind, not the oneness of their natures, as Sergius had meant. This is why he writes in his Epistle to Sergius only of "one will of our Lord Jesus Christ." For a time it seemed as if the old Monophysitism was to make its way into the Church again by way of Monenergism. The situation was saved by the two monks Sophronius (later Patriarch of Jerusalem) and the learned Abbot Maximus the Confessor. As early as the Vatican Synod of 649 Pope Martin I sternly repudiated Monotheletism in the name of the Roman Church. And the General Council at Constantinople (680–81), with the confirmation of Pope Agatho, declared it a heresy, and excommunicated not only the originators of error, in particular Sergius, but also those who had "favoured" it—above all, Pope Honorius. In connexion with Pope Agatho's dogmatic epistle, the solemn confession was made: "Thus according to the doctrine of the Fathers we proclaim in Christ *two natural wills* and two natural activities of will (δύο φυσικὰ θελήματα καὶ δύο φυσικὰς ἐνεργείας, *duas naturales voluntates et duas naturales opera-*

tiones), undivided, unchanged, unseparated, uncommingled. And the two natural wills are not opposed to each other. The human will does not contradict the divine and almighty will, but rather is subordinate to it." With this decision, both duality of will in Christ and his moral unity were preserved.

The decision of the Council of Chalcedon that both natures preserve their characteristics even after the incarnation (*salva proprietate utriusque naturae*) was further strengthened, and its conclusions further ensured, by this doctrine of the Council of Constantinople that in Christ there were not only two wills but also two natural *functions* of will (*operationes*). Not only did the two natures in Christ remain uncommingled, but also their manner of functioning. This is not to say that under the overwhelming power of the divine nature the human nature just managed, more as a potential disposition, to survive. The human will is rather an autonomous instrument of the Logos, obeying its own laws, wielding its own power. The human will retains its full freedom. It is violated by the divine will as little as our will is by Grace.

The achievement of the dispute with Monotheletism lay above all in its confirmation that the union of human nature with the divine self in no way diminishes human nature, but countenances and preserves it in its peculiarity, its *proprietas*, down to its last act of will; that the laws of physiology and psychology that guide human development have their place and their permanence in the image of Christ of our belief. Not only would the one doctrine be heretical—to identify the spiritual life and thought of our Lord with the fount of divine reason. It would also be heretical to claim that his will, his free decision, was the divine almighty will. Our Lord's decisions are characterized by his humanity, in so far as they are inspired by purely human thought and carried out with human freedom. Christ is not a miracle walking on earth, performing acts only apparently human, but in reality accomplishing only divine achievements. Of course he is not mere man. Because he is God made man, the union of his human activity and will with the divine in him is incomparably closer than it is in us. It is permanent and of his person. It is one of the most difficult, but also one of the most fascinating, problems of an understanding psychology to trace the mysterious connexions between the human and divine will in Christ and describe how they interpenetrate each other, and subsist side by side.

Adoptionism

The Council's decision in 681 really brought an end to the Christological disputes. In the West, only Nestorianism flickered up again here and there, once in Spain in the eighth century in the form of what we call Adoptionism. It held that according to Jesus' human nature, he could be regarded only as God's adopted Son, not his true Son, but his Son by God's Grace. In 794 a Synod at Frankfort repudiated this error in the presence of a legate of Pope Hadrian I. Its argument ran that even the human nature of our Lord had as its mainstay a divine self, the second divine person. A similar kind of Nestorianism showed itself under modern guise in the nineteenth century in the theory of Anton Günther (d. 1863). He held that a dual self-consciousness, human and divine, was to be distinguished in Christ. Justified though this conception certainly was, its assumption that this self-consciousness embraced the entire essence of the person was just as certainly false. The quality that makes the person is not the autonomy but the consciousness of autonomy, the self-consciousness. From the proposition that the consciousness creates the person, but that on the other hand in Christ two consciousnesses must be maintained, Günther came to the conclusion that in Christ two persons could be assumed, one potentially human and one divine. With the awakening of reason, the former consciously and freely unites itself with the divine, to form a moral or dynamic unity. And only in the sense of this moral dynamic unity might one speak of a unity of person in Christ.

The affinity of this theory to Nestorianism was too apparent for the Ecclesiastical Office to be silent. If it were true that the self-consciousness creates the person, then a dual person, in the Nestorian sense, would also exist in Christ. So Pope Pius IX condemned Günther's kind of Nestorianism (Denzinger, 1655).

Since Günther, there have not been any more serious Christological disputes within ecclesiastical theology. Of course, this is not to say that there have not been any more Christological problems. As we have seen, the Ecclesiastical Office has played a purely defensive part in all Christological questions that have arisen. The charisma of the Ecclesiastical Office is in fact to preserve the tradition in its purest form. That is why it has rejected every misinterpretation and distortion of the true image of Christ. But it also has avoided a positive solution to urgent questions, particularly to the problem of what was really meant by the existence of person in Christ, what was the function of the Logos in assuming or becoming person. Even today theologians are not agreed on this point. It is something we shall have to take up later. This exposition of the Christological disputes was simply intended to map out the firm ground on which we must tread in order to sketch out and preserve an image of Christ within the Church's belief, that "dogmatic" image of Christ which alone has permanence in history and alone has made history.

III

THE IMAGE OF CHRIST IN
NON-CATHOLIC THEOLOGY

IN its attempts to grasp Christ's essence more deeply, Catholic theology had looked for guidance to the faith and doctrine of the Church. At first Protestant theology took over this image of the Christ of faith, but ever since the Enlightenment of the eighteenth century, it has fallen victim to the far-reaching and destructive analytical tendency of rationalistic thinking. These rationalistic circles sought many ways to tear the belief in the divinity of Jesus out of the Christian creed. Some would have Christ be the ideal man; for others, his figure vanished completely into myth. The question whether Christ was in truth God's Son was no longer asked; the only important thing was to explain how this (impossible) faith could have arisen in the Christian communities. In particular they attempted to find a solution to the eschatological problem raised by certain statements of Jesus. But they no longer looked for it in the tension of the relationship between the human and divine nature in Jesus, and in his peculiar consciousness that he was the Messias. They sought their solution in contemporary errors, to which he too was bound, or in the arguments of modern Existentialism, which in reality make of Christ's message an empty thing.

The questions posed by modern non-Catholic theology are based on the rationalistic assumption that the divinity of the Lord, the figure of God made man, is *a priori* impossible and therefore unhistorical, because it contradicts every comparison with experience and destroys the sequence of cause and effect —new, disrupting, miraculous. So the question as to whether Christ was God could from the start never be an object of historical investigation. It belongs, they would maintain, rather to the realm of subjective belief. The only genuine object of scholarly probing was to *explain* historically how the belief in Christ's divinity came to be held among men. What are the historical roots of the belief in Christ?

It was D. F. Strauss who, influenced by Hegel and following Reimarus, the author of the Wolfenbüttel fragments, contested the tenet that the Christ of faith was the Jesus of history. In his *Leben Jesu* (1835) he took great pains to prove the Christ of faith to be a product of myth fashioned by the credulous. This axe was laid at the root. From now on the true Christological problem was: How is the belief in Christ to be historically explained? Is it possible to accept unquestioningly the testimonies of Paul and John and the Synoptic Gospels as sober historical documents? Or are these testimonies themselves already secondary, produced by the faith of the community, and not original historical truth? In the crude light of this most radical of questions, the questions of the Monarchians, Arians, Apollinarians, Nestorians, Monophysites, Monotheletists, and the rest seem tame and harmless.

The image of Christ of the mythological school

Three judgements on Jesus derive from Strauss. The first is represented by the mythological school. It is inspired by certain fundamental ideas of Hegel's according to which the seminal creative force in history is not historical personalities but ideas. So Christianity too arose not from the act of a single personality but under the impetus of ideas, be they religious or literary, economic, political, or social. These ideas embodied themselves in myth. Thus the Christian faith can be explained without reference to Christ. Christianity is an anonymous movement. Even then Bruno Bauer, at that time a lecturer at Bonn University, called this kind of Gospel criticism of Strauss' reactionary and apologetic He himself described the oldest portrayal of Christ as a free literary creation from the pen of the first Evangelist Mark. So in the last analysis, Christianity was a literary production. Its existence had been brought about by ideas that had been spread abroad solely by means of literature. Certain ideals, such as love of mankind, equality and fraternity, which at that time had been put forward by individual Platonic, Neo-Platonic, and in particular

Stoic writers, had gradually merged to form a movement among the people, and found their expression in Christianity. Kalthoff, of Bremen, regarded the entire content of the Gospels merely as the personification of such collective social ideals. It was the social distress of the dying ancient world that found liberating expression in the figure of him who was killed on the cross and yet rose again the third day. This was also related to Nietzsche's conception that Christianity was in essentials a movement of resentment on the part of the repressed plebeian instinct of the mass to assert itself against the high heroic instincts of the superman. The mathematician W. B. Smith went so far as to explain the name of Jesus as the name of a pre-Christian cult god, and to interpret the mystery of his suffering and resurrection as a reproduction of an old mystery drama. Jensen even found in the Gospels the main lines of the Babylonian epic of Gilgamesh, and maintained that in our cathedrals we serve a Babylonian god. The philosopher Drews considered the Gospel tradition to be a conglomeration of mythical elements, and was convinced that one Jesus of Nazareth had never really existed. We find further similar attitudes in D. Schulz, J. M. Robertson, S. Lublinski, M. Maurenbrecher, K. Kautzky, *et al.*

The image of Christ of the liberal school

The second trend proceeding from Strauss is the so-called liberal study of Jesus. In contrast to Hegel, it emphasizes that history is made not by ideas but by personalities. So for them the major factor in explaining Christianity is the personality of Jesus. But they are disposed to think that the personality of Jesus must submit to being grasped with the means of historical method—i.e., the tools of secular history, a thorough analysis of sources, and the laws of correlation and analogy. They hold that those things in Jesus that go beyond similar historical situations and parallels, and transcend historical correlation—i.e., demonstrably go beyond the historical chain of cause and effect—are unhistorical and must be removed from the picture. The liberal school aims on principle at proving everything that is mysterious and supernatural in the life of our Lord to be unhistorical, and merely the product of the faith of the community—what they call the dogma of the community. But they conscientiously restrain themselves from regarding the entire Gospel tradition outright as creating nothing but myth. They find many a solid stone surviving from the original structure that cannot be destroyed by any critical chisel. It is true, all that their criticism has left is mere disparate fragments. But all they have to do is put these fragments together again the right way. When the model for their reconstruction is the ideal current in their culture, they succeed in setting up a Jesus according to the taste of the moderns. In essentials, this Jesus reveals ethical and religious traits. He is the master of the inner life, who leads us to the Father, the first of the religious geniuses. Their refusal to see in this "historical" Jesus the supernatural being of Christ has provoked the coinage "Jesuanism." For they maintain that the object of historical investigation is not the Christ of faith, but only the Jesus of history. Indeed, if we do question the history of faith there is no place where this "historical" Jesus can be found. Even the Dynamist Monarchians, who believed that the effective principle in Christ was only a spiritual power "of the same essence" as the Father, did not recognize an historical Jesus in the liberal sense. In fact, such a one never has had any effect in history, and has remained merely the fabrication of journalists.

The image of Christ of the eschatological school

The third trend proceeding from Strauss, which we know as the eschatological school, rejects both the mythological and the liberal trends in the study of Christ. It rightly perceives in them a dogmatic *a priori,* a compulsion based upon unproven assumptions, which has made their criticism the slave of an ideology. So, independent of these schools, it sets out once again to cull the image of our Lord quite factually from the sources. The eschatological school regards itself as the sole critical historical school. Among its adherents are numbered, *inter alia,* W. Bousset, Albert Schweitzer, J. Wellhausen, R. Bultmann, and M. Werner. With the help of a thorny textual criticism, they attempt to lay the original stones bare, and free them from all the secondary and tertiary strata. But indeed, pathetically little turns up by way of original stones. In his work *Was wissen wir von Jesus?* Bousset explains that all we possess directly from Jesus is on the whole brief pronouncements only. These sayings are like pebbles, over which the stream of tradition has rolled, polishing them, shifting them here and there, merging them in this or that conglomerate. There remains to us perhaps the parable of the prodigal son, the saying about God's fatherly love, or Jesus' dispute with the Pharisees. Christ's fundamental eschatological attitude in particular survives, i.e., his conviction that the kingdom of God was at hand and that the present generation would live to experience the return of the Son of Man from heaven. The eschatological school arrives at the so-called eschatological Christ by calling upon those texts that foretell the coming of Christ in this generation, and by violently forcing all other texts into this eschatological pattern. They hold that the historical Jesus was in fact guided by the fantastic delusion that the kingdom of God would come down to earth in this generation. This would make his mission no different from John the Baptist's. By preaching repentance he would prepare the way for the coming Parousia of the Lord. It is possible, they maintain, that towards the end of his life he became certain that he himself would be the one who would come again, bringing the kingdom of God; in this case, his self-consciousness would already have degenerated into morbid over-excitement. In any case, these theologians make of the historical Jesus something very different from the Jesus of faith—an eschatological fanatic.

The image of Christ of the dialectical school

Even this image of Christ could not be upheld in historical criticism as soon as it became clear that these eschatological texts were not at the centre, but rather on the periphery, of Jesus' teaching, and that Jesus had striven to realize the kingdom of God in the present rather than intended that it should come about in the future.

All these images of Christ were withdrawn from circulation almost overnight, and replaced by the so-called "dialectic" theology of Karl Barth, Emil Brunner, Gogarten, and others. They follow the reformers, especially Calvin, in confirming anew the divine in Christianity, the absoluteness of its manifestation, in face of all the humanized versions of the liberals, tailored to meet the taste of the time. With incomparable passion, Barth in particular has condemned the modern ideological Jesus. His school seems to have reconquered the theological field. However, the school itself can hardly be regarded as a unity. On the one hand Karl Barth and Emil Brunner have drawn ever nearer to the traditional image of Christ. But on the other hand Rudolf Bultmann has combined his attempt to rehabilitate Christian teaching with a radical rejection of all those events in the life of Jesus that imply the break-through of transcendence into this world; he denies the incarnation, Christ's miracles, his expiatory death, his resurrection and second coming at the Last Judgement, and so on and so forth. He is of the opinion that only by stripping the Christian message bare of all traces of myth can it be salvaged to have any significance for modern man; for Bultmann the essence of the Christian faith lies in man's realization, as he apprehends the teaching of Christ, of his complete surrender to the world of the senses; by accepting the message of Christ's death and resurrection, man succeeds in conquering the world and redeeming himself. In spite of Bultmann's protestations to the contrary, his doctrine has abandoned Christ's teaching, which is centred precisely on the supernatural events of his life. Revelation becomes a mere philosophy of religion, which has its roots in Kierkegaard and in Heidegger's Existentialism. On the one hand Bultmann agrees with Barth in seeing in the faith in the cross the miracle of forgiveness wrought by divine Grace. But on the other hand it is equally clear that his systematic contestation of the possibility of a scholarly foundation for Christianity carries the line of liberal critical theology to its very end.

The teaching of the Church and contemporary Christological errors

Now the Catholic Church derives her image of Christ not from dead texts wilfully rearranged, but out of her own living self-consciousness; she knows that in the unity of the Church's testimony to the faith, animated by the Holy Spirit, and above all in the *successio apostolica* she perpetuates the consciousness of faith of the first Apostles. So she has on principle not concerned herself with the extravagant problems raised by non-Catholic Christology. Her interest in them is only secondary. Only in so far as the non-Catholic questions have threatened to disrupt her own theology has the Church found it necessary to draw certain guiding lines for the Catholic theologian to observe in his discussion of modern Christological problems. These guiding lines are there to preserve the Church's Christology from infiltration by the basic ideas of Strauss and his successors. They are not intended to hinder the apologist in any way from proceeding in his defence against "liberal" criticism in a strictly scientific manner, paying exact attention to the sources, and their thorough exegesis. But the Church does want to prevent taking over these radical theories into her own theology, so that the Church's Christology becomes the home not of the thoughts of the Apostles and saints but of Strauss, Bousset, and Bultmann. In the Encyclical *Pascendi* of 1907, the Church repudiated above all the distinction between a Christ of faith and a Jesus of history, who was solely man, and was transformed into the divine by transfiguration and defiguration. This was a repudiation of the view that the Jesus of history was someone other than the Christ of faith. Furthermore, it rejected the related idea that only the Jesus of history could be demonstrated with the tools of historiography while the Christ of faith on the other hand could simply be put down to the religious experience. On the contrary, it affirmed that the belief in Christ, too, rested upon assured, historically verifiable facts, above all upon the historically demonstrable claim of our Lord to be the Messias sent by God. The decree *Lamentabili* (propositions 27–35) further rejected a series of propositions tending in this direction, in particular the statement that Christ's divinity cannot be proved from the Gospels. Against this the Church firmly held that the content of the divine mystery of Jesus (the mystery of his eternal begetting by the Father, his incarnation and redemption) certainly cannot be learned by historical means, but only by way of faith; but on the other hand the fact that Jesus knew himself to be the true Son of God and testified to this can nevertheless be proved scientifically with historical methods. If this is granted, the further statements of radical criticism no longer hold water—for example, that the expression "Son of God" in the Gospels always means the Messias in the Judaic sense, and never the Son of God in the Christian sense, or that during his public life Jesus never claimed to be the Messias, or that the Jesus of the Gospels never did have absolute knowledge, but rather was under the error that the Parousia would come very soon; or their contention that the historical Jesus, like all things human, was to be placed and judged within the framework of his age; or that the figure of Jesus had been rendered absolute only by the work of faith;

that the Christ of Paul and John, and certainly the Christ of
the Council of Nicaea and of all subsequent Councils, was
quite essentially distinct from the plain image of the historical
Jesus.

With this decree, we can see that the Church drew up a
memorandum of all those propositions of modern criticism
that touched her consciousness of faith in Christ. With the
power of her living faith in what has been since the days of
the Apostles the heart and lodestar of her teaching, these statements demonstrate her reaction to that anti-Christian scholarship which, as in the days of St. John, "reduces" Christ anew.
What she opposes to this critical scholarship is her consciousness of faith, and more, her consciousness of the spirit of the
Lord which animates that faith. Had the Church countered
this hypercritical scholarship not with the power of her faith
but solely with the means of scholarship, she would be sacrificing the very thing that characterizes her: the consciousness of
being the self-perpetuation of Christ's teaching, and of having
received her faith in the Lord not from the earth and its scholarship, but through the Apostles from the very heart of Christ.
The Church has no need to prove Christ. She herself in all her
being and becoming is the unfolded faith in Christ the Lord,
the ever-living Christ.

Having traced the development of the Christology of the
Church in the light of the ecclesiastical disputes with both old
and new heresies, and having gained sufficient knowledge of
the dogmatic image of Christ, our next step will be to confirm
the dogmatic image of Christ from the sources of revelation.
Once more, it is not as if our faith were dependent on these
proofs. For the true image of Christ lives in the heart of the
Church and her members, transcending all written testimony.
When we probe the sources of revelation, we are tracing only
the reflection which the living image of Christ in the believing
Church has brought forth in canonical and post-canonical
literature. Only when we constantly relate this reflected image
to the living image of Christ present in the Church's faith will
it take on flesh and blood and clear outline.

We shall proceed according to the *dogmatic* method. Its
chief characteristic is that we do not draw our evidence about
Christ from secular source material, but from the living faith
of the Church, that faith which has found its true precipitate
in the divinely inspired Bible, and in the tradition outside the
Bible. The objective principle of dogmatic Christology is of a
supernatural kind. It is the treasury of those revelations of

Christ which the Holy Spirit wakened in the Church, and which has been preserved in writing and in oral tradition. This is the reason why even the subjective principle of our exposition is not ordinary secular thought alone, but thought seized and illuminated by the Grace of faith (*ratio fide illuminata*). What we desire in our rôle as dogmatists is a new contemplation, borne by the wings of the Holy Spirit, of the image of Christ of our divinely inspired Catholic Church.

This dogmatic method is combined where necessary with the *apologetic* method, which works with purely natural means of perception. Its purpose is to meet our opponents on their own historical ground and answer their criticism by proving our faith in Christ as a faith compatible with reason (*obsequium rationabile*). In adducing its proofs, this apologetic method on principle disregards the supernatural nature of the sources of our faith, its inspiration. It deals with documents and the tradition in exactly the same manner as the secular historian does, simply in their peculiarity as historical sources of the earliest Christian faith. And it interprets these sources only according to the principles of sound critical thinking, and does not allow its judgements to be influenced by any dogmatic considerations. This method deliberately takes its stand on the same ground as negative criticism, because an honest and fruitful dispute is possible only on these terms.

In detail we shall proceed thus. First we shall ask: What do the Canonical Gospels say about Christ? Since to the believer these Gospels are inspired, their image of Christ is fundamental, and furnishes him with his standard. So first of all we shall sketch out the main lines of the image of Christ as it is found in the Gospels. It is the image of the Christ of faith. But since liberal criticism has raised the objection that the Canonical Gospels have already been painted over by the fanatic faith of the earliest believers, we are for apologetic reasons compelled to look for the image of Christ as it was even *before* the Gospels. So our question then will be: What image of Christ did the Church possess before the Gospels were written? Our answer will take us back to the time of the first Apostles, the earliest generation. Their testimony is for us particularly to be respected, for they are the original witnesses of Christ, who saw and heard his teaching. But since negative criticism does not completely trust these witnesses, our apologetics carry us still further back until we come to Jesus himself, his own testimony of himself. This is the one place where we are on sure ground in face of criticism.

THE PERSON OF CHRIST

As we go back in this manner, stratum by stratum, generation by generation, to Jesus himself, our apologetic method at
the same time serves dogmatic interests. For on our way
through the generations, we are able to confirm the confession
of faith in Christ that each congregation and each generation
made. Thus from generation to generation we plunge into the
stream of the Holy Spirit, and the inspired faith which permeated the congregations. We draw sustenance directly from
the Christian experience from century to century. So our
method is both apologetic and dogmatic at the same time.

IV

THE IMAGE OF CHRIST IN THE CANONICAL GOSPELS

Jesus' consciousness of his messianic mission

THE four Canonical Gospels are agreed that from the very beginning of his emergence into public life, Jesus was conscious of his unique mission from the Father. First they testify that the prophets who had been killed by the Jews had been sent from God (cf. Matt. 23.37). But they further testify that in comparison to Jesus, these prophets were only the servants whom the householder sent out to the vine-dressers (21.34 ff.). Jesus applied to John the Baptist, "the greatest of all born of woman," the Biblical prophecy: "Behold, I send my messenger before thy face, who shall make ready thy way before thee" (Matt. 11.10; cf. John 1.6; 3.28). So even John is only the herald. In the most perfect sense, Jesus alone knew himself to be the one called by God. As early as his first appearance in Nazareth, he referred the words of Isaias to himself: "The spirit of the Lord is upon me because he has anointed me; to bring good news to the poor he has sent me, to proclaim to the captives release, and sight to the blind; to set at liberty the oppressed, to proclaim the acceptable year of the Lord, and the day of recompense" (Luke 4.18; cf. Isa. 61.1). The same prophecy of Isaias re-echoes in the voice at Jesus' baptism: "This is my beloved Son." Jesus expresses this awareness of his mission in the ever-recurring succinct and deliberate affirmation: "I have come," "I have not come." This is the one great apocalyptic formulation (cf. Acts 9.21; 16.36; Eph. 6.22) of his proclaimed mission, which introduces the great turning point of our time. With this "coming" of the Lord, the new era is ushered in. He comes from "the right hand of the Ancient of Days." Daniel had already pointed toward this coming, and Jesus refers himself to Daniel's prophecy, calling himself, in Daniel's sense, "the Son of Man," whose coming is so vital for mankind. The Lord insists again and again on this coming. "Do not think that I have come to send peace upon the earth; I have come to bring a sword, not peace" (Matt. 10.34). "I have come to cast fire upon the earth, and what will I but that it be kindled?" (Luke 12.49). "I have come to call sinners, not the just" (Matt. 9.13). "The Son of Man came to seek and to save what was lost" (Luke 19.10). "Do not think that I have come to destroy the Law or the Prophets. I have not come to destroy, but to fulfil" (Matt. 5.17). "The Son of Man has not come to be served, but to serve, and to give his life as a ransom for many" (Matt. 20.28). "The Son of Man will come in his majesty, and all the angels with him, and then he will judge each one according to his works" (Matt. 25.31).

This formulation, "I have come," "I have not come," so certain of its purpose, clearly expresses Jesus' consciousness of having come into this world to fulfil a special task. But it expresses not only the consciousness but also the content of his mission. Jesus knows that he has been sent from God to bring the time of salvation, that he is the fulfiller come to perfect the imperfect, make the weak strong and the crooked straight. In him the great new thing, proclaimed and announced by the prophets, has come to pass. This new thing is summed up in the phrase "kingdom of God" (according to Matthew, "kingdom of heaven"). Hence the first announcement of his good tidings is "The kingdom of God is near at hand." Because he is the fulfiller and bringer of the time of salvation, Jesus stands higher than all the prophets and kings who have preceded him, higher than the noblest figures of Old Testament history. In Jesus one "greater than Jonas" has appeared (Matt. 12.41), and one greater than Solomon (Matt. 12.42). Indeed, "one greater than the temple is here" (Matt. 12.6). The Jews regarded the temple as the holiest thing upon earth. An offence against the temple was punished with death. So really Jesus is assured that he is greater than this most sacred place upon earth. This is how he knows himself to be born Lord of the Temple with the right to get rid of all intrusive abuses, with the whip, if necessary (Matt. 21.12; John 2.14ff.). John the Baptist is certainly greater than all who were born of woman. But he is also less, not just less than Jesus himself, but less than the "least" of those who have followed Jesus into the kingdom of God (Matt. 11.11ff.; cf. John 3.28ff.). Blessed are the eyes of the disciples, that they see what they see. For many prophets and kings have desired to see it, and have not seen it (Luke 10.24). Abraham rejoiced that he was to see the day of Jesus (John 8.56; cf. 12.41). For the miracles that Jesus wrought in its streets, Capharnaum was exalted "to heaven" (Matt. 11.23; cf. John 6.59).

Since he is greater than all the prophets, Jesus stands not only superior to the word and works of the prophets, but even higher than the Law of Moses, in which every Jew was accustomed to acknowledge the inviolable will of God, revealed by God himself. Certainly, Jesus affirms this Law down to the last detail. "I have not come to destroy, but to fulfil" [the Law] (Matt. 5.18). He urges the disciples to accomplish in reality what the Scribes and the Pharisees merely preach from the chair of Moses (Matt. 23.2). The law of the Sabbath is so sacred to him that he commends the disciples to pray that their flight should not be on the Sabbath, for on the Sabbath they might not flee (Matt. 24.20). But Jesus sees in the Law something deeper than the dead letter of the Scribes. To him, the Law is love of God and of one's neighbour applied to life. And it is his mission to "fulfil" it in this deeper sense (Matt. 5.17). This is why his attitude towards the Law is inwardly free and sovereign. "For the Son of Man is Lord even of the Sabbath" (Matt. 12.8). As the Sabbath rests upon Jahve's commandment (Exod. 20.8 ff.; Deut. 5.12 ff.), then it was fitting that Jesus should transgress it, and have his disciples transgress it if the Law's deepest sense, true love, should so require. It was not simply that Jesus called upon the higher meaning of the Law and put aside the accretions of the Scribes' interpretation of the Old Testament—for example, the ceremonial law of the washing of hands before meals (Mark 7.1 ff.; Matt. 15.1 ff.); not simply that he cleared the Old Testament of the rank growth of rabbinical commentary— there was even a law, clearly belonging to the Old Testament, and going back to Moses himself, which had had an enormous effect upon social intercourse—tho law in Leviticus 11 of the clean and the unclean animals, which he dissolved with the simple words: "What goes into the mouth does not defile a man" (Matt. 15.11). Jesus freely disregarded even Leviticus 13–15, which forbade communication with the unclean and the lepers. He heals the lepers and the woman with the haemorrhage without fearing defilement (Mark 5.25). He banishes mere ritual from the field of morality. Jesus disregards with equal sovereignty the Mosaic law of divorce. According to Deuteronomy 24.1, the man may divorce his wife "if she find not favour in his eyes." According to the Scribe Hillel, such a situation arises if the wife should merely burn his dinner. Jesus rejects not only Hillel's loose interpretation of the Mosaic Law but also the Law of Moses itself. "But it was not so from the beginning" (Matt. 19.8). "What God has joined together, let no man put asunder" (Matt. 19.6). And he assured the Pharisees: "Whoever puts away his wife and marries another, commits adultery against her" (Mark 10.11). His royal consciousness of sovereign superiority to the letter of the Mosaic Law is particularly clear in the Sermon on the Mount. With his sharp formulations, Jesus contrasts his new ethos with the old legality of Moses' foundation. "The ancients"—i.e., the lawgivers of yesterday and the day before yesterday, "have said . . ." "But *I* say to you . . ." In Jesus' first two commandments, concerning murder and adultery, there is still a doubt whether the old Law condemning the wicked deed but not the evil intent is only deepened, or whether it is in fact replaced. But in the subsequent contrast between his own prescriptions and the old commandments, there can be no doubt that his commandment against divorce and false oaths goes intentionally beyond the Old Testament, which permits divorce, and forbids only false oaths (Lev. 19.12; Num. 30.3). The fifth prescription, against returning an injury, is the direct opposite of the Jewish *jus talionis* (cf. Lev. 24.19; Exod. 21.23 f.), and is nonetheless meant as the standard for the disciples to follow. "If someone strike thee on the right cheek, turn to him the other also" (Matt. 5.39). But the peak of his new ethos is the sixth contrast with the old order—the commandment of love (Matt. 5.43 ff.). Because the only commandment Moses had given was to love thy neighbour (Lev. 19.18), the Scribes and commentators imagined they were to conclude that one might hate one's enemy. Against this, Jesus commends love of one's enemy, something completely unheard of in Judaism, and, for the most part, in the entire ancient world.

Thus Jesus' attitude to the Law was that of the sovereign Lord who is able to amend the ancient tradition, even the Mosaic Law itself, not, as the prophets did, by calling upon the word of God, but of his own personal authority ("But *I* say to you . . ."). In the consciousness of representing in his person the pure inviolate will of God, the simple assertion of his authority is enough to remove all mere ceremony and ritual from the ethos, cancel out all mere abiding by the external letter of the Law, and complete the line of the prophets in its purest form.

The Gospels tell us that Jesus, as well as being conscious that he had come to fulfil the Law, also knew himself to be the true meaning and content of all prophecy. He knows himself to be so at one with Jahve, that he sees everything the Old Testament expects of the actions of God as realized in his own person. He is himself the Jahve of the Old Testament. Thus he always interprets the prophecies as if he himself were in the place of Jahve. This is particularly clear from a passage in what is known as the oral tradition (Matt. 11.10 ff. = Luke 7.27 ff.). According to Malachias (3.1) Jahve says: "Behold, I send my angel, and he shall prepare the way before my face." Christ makes use of this passage in his speech about John the Baptist: The "before my face" of Malachias, which refers to God himself, is taken over in Jesus' speech to refer to Jesus himself. He sees the coming of God realized in his own coming. Thus in Matthew 11.14 he designates the Baptist as Elias, who, according to Malachias 3.23, was to come before the day of the Lord should break. The same identification with Jahve is present in his claim to forgive sins. There is not a single passage in the Judaic Scriptures that expressly endows the Messias with the authority to forgive sins. In Jesus' time, the question was much disputed by the rabbis. In Isaias 43.25, Ezekiel 36.25, and Jeremias 31.31, the forgiveness of sins is expressly called the attribute of God. But Jesus tells the paralytic, "Son, thy sins are forgiven thee" (Mark 2.5). The Jews immediately react to this with the significant accusation: He blasphemes. "Who can forgive sins, but only God?" So it is clear Jesus interpreted the prophecies of Jahve's messianic forgiveness of sins out of his inner identity with Jahve. He himself knows he is the Lord, who forgives all sins. The same identification with Jahve can be seen in his reply to John the Baptist's disciple (Matt. 11.2–6 = Luke 7.18–23), in which he sees the prophecy of Isaias 35.5 fulfilled in his own works: "The blind see, the lame walk." But in Isaias 35 the prophet is not speaking of the Messias, but of God himself: "God himself will come and will save you." So here too Jesus knows himself to be the Lord who heals the blind and the lame. And again, when the Old Testament prophesies that God will feed his flock like a shepherd (Isa.

40.11; Ezek. 34.11), Jesus knows himself to be this shepherd
who lays down his life for his sheep (John 10.11). "I am the
good shepherd." When the chief priests became indignant
because the children in the temple cried out in rejoicing to
the Lord (Matt. 21.15 f.), he refers back to Psalm 8.3. But
even here the reference is not to the Messias, but to Jahve
himself, who confounds his enemies "out of the mouth of little
children and babes at breast." This identification of Jesus with
Jahve is particularly prominent in the Gospel according to St.
John. Here, Jesus applied the Old Testament designation of
God, "I am he" (Deut. 32.39; Isa. 41.4; 43.10, *et al.*), to
himself: "You are from below, I am from above. You are of
this world, I am not of this world" (John 8.23). "When you
have lifted up the Son of Man, you will know that I am he"
(John 8.28; cf. 13.19). According to Isaias 43.10, the servant
chosen by the Lord shall be the "witness" of God. His testimony shall be precisely this "I am he." This "I am he" is repeated in John.

So, according to the Evangelists, it is for Jesus a hermeneu-
tic rule, as it were, to understand and interpret himself as
Jahve. He knows the prophecies to be fulfilled in his own
person.

This consciousness of being one essence with Jahve which
guides Jesus' reading of the Old Testament also dominates
his own manner of teaching and preaching. In the parables of
the prodigal son, the lost sheep, the lost coin, the talents, and
the labourers in the vineyard, God's behaviour toward men is
always identified with his own behaviour. Where the prophets
of Israel always give their decision in the name of Jahve
("thus spoke the Lord"), Jesus decides of his own authority.
He never once indicates that he gives his decision in the place
of the heavenly Father, or in his name. He passes judgement
on the strength of his own right. He himself, his consciousness
and his conscience, is that right. The same thing is revealed in
his miracles. He does not work his wonders as one empowered
by God, but of his own sovereign power. This is not mere
authorization, but omnipotence. He bids the lame walk.
"Arise, take up thy pallet and go to thy house" (Matt. 9.6).
"Rise, take up thy pallet and walk" (John 5.8). The decision of his will alone is sufficient to heal the leper. "I will; be
thou made clean" (Matt. 8.3). His word is enough to waken
the dead. "Girl, I say to thee, arise" (Mark 5.41).

In this sovereign self-consciousness, directly rooted in his
sense of oneness with Jahve, he knows himself to be the one

and only master, teacher, and guide of mankind. "For one is your master, and all you are brothers" (Matt. 23.8). "For one only is your master, the Christ" (Matt. 23.10). He alone is the Saviour. "Come to me, all you who labour and are burdened, and I will give you rest" (Matt. 11.28). He is the cornerstone of mankind. "The stone which the builders rejected has become the cornerstone; by the Lord this has been done, and it is wonderful in our eyes" (Matt. 21.42). Thus he, in his own person, is the one and only judge of mankind. It is in their attitude to his person that men can be distinguished. He is the crisis, the judgement, the decision. "Everyone who acknowledges me before men, I also will acknowledge him before my Father in heaven. But whoever disowns me before men, I in turn will disown him before my Father in heaven" (Matt. 10.32).

There can be no doubt: the Canonical Gospels see in the person of Jesus Jahve himself. According to them, Jesus thinks, feels, and acts in the clear consciousness that he is not simply one called like the rest of the prophets, but rather the historical manifestation and revelation of God himself.

Jesus' consciousness of being the Son of God

This awareness of his identity with God, which runs like a vein of gold through the Gospels, is also expressed quite unequivocally in what Jesus has to say about himself, and in what others have to say of him—above all, the fact that he refers quite unmistakably to himself as the "Son" of the Father. And this he means in an exclusive and unique sense. In the parable of the vine-dressers he calls himself the "well-beloved son," "the heir," in clear distinction from the prophets, "the servants" (Matt. 21.37 ff.). At first the householder sends his servants to the vineyard. When these are mistreated, he sends his own "well-beloved son." Clearly the relationship between father and son here is the natural one of parent and child, different from the one between master and "servants." As the Son, Jesus stands higher than all men, even higher than the angels (Mark 13.32). No one knows the Day of Judgement, neither the angels in heaven, nor the Son, but the Father only. This gradation is a concrete expression of how the Son is exalted above men and angels. In a famous Logion from the oral tradition he declares in solemnly exalted language, "All things have been delivered to me by my Father; and no one knows the Son except the Father; nor does anyone know the Father except the Son, and him to whom the Son chooses to reveal him" (Matt. 11.27 = Luke 10.22). There can be no doubt that with these words Jesus consciously aligns himself at God's side, not on the side of man, and that his relationship to the Father is not one of Grace, but the natural relation of child to father. It is in the Gospel according to St. John that Jesus refers to himself as the Son most frequently. "He who sees the Son sees also the Father" (14.9 ff.; 12.45). He and the Father are "one" (10.30). Above all, the priestly prayer in Chapter 17 points to the divine essence and dignity of the Son.

His sense of inner unity with the Father also explains Jesus' characteristic way of praying: he approaches the Father very closely, but without including the disciples. He never embraces the disciples in this communion of prayer. God is "his" Father, and "their" Father. This is something we will have to discuss later in greater detail.

Again, this consciousness of the Lord that he is the Son of God is further reflected in the statements made in the Gospels by those who had heard Jesus. Biblical criticism has long outgrown the stage of understanding the expression "Son of God" as the Evangelists use it, in a purely ethical theocratic sense, as if all it meant was the man raised by God's especial Grace to be the Messias. It is true the Jews of that time applied the expression "Son of God" only to created beings, to the angels, the king over Israel, the children of Israel, and indeed, to all the devout. But the Evangelists admit of no doubt that they intend the "Son of God" in the true, strictly metaphysical sense. Thus Matthew and Luke emphasize Mary's virginity before the birth of Jesus to indicate that the child born of Mary had not a man but God himself for its father. The phrase "Son of God" plays a dominant part in the Gospel according to St. Mark. Here, as Bousset points out, it has already taken on the "character of a formula," which points back to the oldest level of faith. The "Son of God" dominates the description of the baptism ("this is my beloved Son"), the temptation ("if you are the Son of God"), and is also at the basis of the scene of Christ's transfiguration. Even if we doubt that the men possessed by devils gave a metaphysical meaning to the phrase, it is certain that the Evangelist telling the story used it in its deepest significance. The same metaphysical significance is at the root of St. Peter's acknowledgement at Cæsarea Philippi: "Thou art the Christ" (Mark 8.29), and in particular is the basis of the high priest's question at the trial: "Art thou the Christ, the son of the blessed one?" (Mark 14.61). If we note that according to Matthew 16.17, Christ responds to Peter's acknowledgement with the solemn declaration: "Flesh and blood has not revealed this to thee, but my Father in heaven," Peter can have seen in Christ only the *filius Dei naturalis*. For the acknowledgement that Christ was merely a human Messias and leader could have been reached by purely natural means of knowing, and Christ's indication of a special divine revelation would be incomprehensible. As for the high priest's question, the high priest himself may well have been convinced personally that the coming Messias would be mere man, son of David. But he surely meant his question whether Christ called himself son of the blessed one in the sense of a *filius Dei naturalis*, otherwise he would not have dared condemn Christ to death, for according to the law of Mishnah, merely to pretend to the name of Messias was not a capital crime, even when the claim was unfounded. The pagan centurion is also thinking of Christ as the natural Son of God when he confesses at the foot of the cross, "Truly this man was the Son of God" (Mark 15.39; Matt. 27.54). He was assuredly a Hellenist, and to the Hellenist pagan there was nothing unusual in the idea of a natural Son of God. As a pagan, he thought of a divinity in the sense of pagan mythology. Bousset is not wrong to point out that most manuscripts of the Gospel according to St. Mark bear the superscription "The Gospel of Jesus Christ, Son of God." Since St. Mark was writing for Hellenistic readers, pagan and Christian, by the phrase "Son of God" he could mean nothing but the idea of the *filius Dei naturalis*. This also applies to St. Luke, the pupil of St. Paul, and in particular to St. John.

To sum up, we may affirm that the Gospels are agreed in their testimony that Jesus felt himself to be the fulfilment and the true content of the Old Testament, the bringer of the highest, most consummate revelation. This consciousness of his calling was rooted in his metaphysical consciousness of being the Son of God, in his clear knowledge and declaration that he and he alone was the Well-beloved Son of the heavenly Father, identical with Jahve. It is in the light of these declarations of his majesty that the Gospels interpret the Judaic references to the "Son of God" as well. Where the Jews gave the term the purely theocratic meaning of the son of David, exalted to be the Messias, the Evangelists, with their Easter faith, gave it a metaphysical interpretation.

Jesus' affirmation of his lowliness

But these declarations of his majesty do not complete the picture of the Lord. At their side we find equally clear declarations of Jesus' lowliness and weakness. Jesus knows himself to be the Son of the Father, but he does not feel himself to be simply a god walking the earth after the manner of the pagan mythologies. As well as a sense of sovereign ascendancy over all earthly powers, all lawful orders and authorities, there is also the awareness of an inward dependence and subordination, of the subjection of his being as mere man to the Father. Jesus prays to the Father. So he is not simply the object of worship, he is also the worshipper. And he does not pray to God only after the manner of the Son—i.e., so that his prayers express his unity of essence with the Father, and are an exchange of life with the Father. Jesus does not always pray to the Father from the same divine level of being, as it were, but sometimes calls upon him from the depths of his human existence. "Holy Father, keep in thy name those whom thou hast given me, that they may be one even as we are one" (John 17.11). He prays for Peter, that his faith may not fail (Luke 22.32), and he promises the disciples that he will pray for the Holy Spirit to be sent down to them (John 14.16). This prayer on the Mount of Olives wells up from the profoundest depths of afflicted humanity: "Father, if it is possible, let this cup pass away from me; yet not as I will, but as thou willest" (Matt. 26.39). In the agony of death, he sees himself borne so far away from his Father that the words of the 22nd Psalm spill over his lips, "My God, my God, why hast thou forsaken me?" (Mark 15.34). The being of his Father is something so sacred and utterly perfect to him, exalted so high above his own holiness, that he will not be called good himself. "Why dost thou call me good? None is good but only God," he replies, when the young man calls him "Good master" (Mark 10.18). So it is not his own perfection, but the Father's, that he impresses upon men: "You therefore are to be perfect, even as your heavenly Father is perfect" (Matt. 5.48). The Evangelists emphasize that he too was tempted to sin. The temptations did not come from within his own nature, but from outside, from the devil. These are evil influences wrought upon his inner life. They rouse thoughts and possibilities within him which he will have to combat. The triumph with which he overcomes these persuasions is proof that within his own soul there is no impulse alive that could bring him into conflict with the divine will. The assured consciousness of the harmony of his being with God is natural to him. And yet, he did experience Satan's persuasions as "temptations," something that touched his soul, without stirring it (Matt. 4.1 ff.; Luke 4.1 ff.). Luke brings his account of the temptation to a close with the remark that the devil departed from Jesus "for a while" (Luke 4.13). So the Evil One drew near him with his temptations later, too. Jesus' human desires were accessible to satanic insinuations. But men too can tempt Jesus. As Peter tries to persuade him to draw back from the way of suffering, the Lord recognizes a temptation of the devil: "Get behind me, Satan, for thou dost not mind the things of God, but those of men" (Mark 8.33). His struggle upon the Mount of Olives is a struggle to accede to the Father's will. Not that Jesus knew himself to be in danger of violating the will of the Father, but that his human feeling recoiled at the terrible form in which the Father's will threatened to manifest itself. It was the plea: "Father, let this cup pass away from me." But he added, "Yet not as I will, but as thou willest"—proof that his soul was still firmly rooted in the will of the Father. The Epistle of St. Paul to the Hebrews represents vividly this life-and-death struggle of our Lord. "For Jesus in the days of his earthly life offered up prayers and supplications to him who was able to save him from death" (5.7). Thus Jesus was also accessible to the temptations of earthly suffering and grief. His animal being (*voluntas ut natura*) resisted the bitter dispensation of God, even though at the same time his moral will (*voluntas ut ratio*) affirmed it as divine Providence.

So the Gospels give us a picture of a struggling Jesus, not simply one of sovereign ascendancy over the world, distant from the earth. But in spite of this, Jesus' human desires are firmly rooted in the will of God, so that all outward temptations lose their force the moment they come up against the will of God in his consciousness. It was this impression of Jesus' moral ascendancy that made his inspired disciples first aware that he was "the saint of God" (Mark 1.20); that made Peter cry out, "Depart from me, for I am a sinful man, O Lord" (Luke 5.8); that made the centurion protest, "Lord,

I am not worthy that thou shouldst come under my roof"
(Matt. 8.8); that even those remote from him like Pilate's
wife (Matt. 27.19) and Pilate himself (27.24) should call
him "this just man," and that John the Baptist should make
his disclaimer, saying, "It is I who ought to be baptized by
thee, and dost thou come to me?" (Matt. 3.14). "One mightier
than I is coming after me, the strap of whose sandals I am
not worthy to unloose" (Mark 1.7).

Something infinitely holy speaks out of Christ's being, the
powerful impression of absolute harmony with the will of
the Father. But this holiness was not anything frozen and
static, the sovereign purity and peace of other worlds than
ours. It was something living, dynamic, an ever-renewed
moral power. This very renewal is the psychological point of
contact that allows his example to rouse and waken and
bring new strength to the weary and heavy-laden. Sin is not
a stranger to him. He has looked it in the eye, yet not as one
afraid of succumbing to it, but as one who knows that it has
no part in him. Thus he can say to his enemies: "Which of
you can convict me of sin?" (John 8.46). It is true, no one
is good, absolutely good, but only God. All earthly good
grows pale in face of this absolute of good, the utter perfection of God. At root, it is more a negative thing, an utter
freedom from sin. Jesus' moral wishes and moral power are
perfect, but perfect only as man's will upon earth can be
perfect. But this is infinite stages away from the perfection
of God. "Why dost thou call me good? No one is good but
only God" (Mark 10.18).

The Evangelists also pass on to us similar indications of
lowliness in the Lord's human knowledge and perception.
There are things that remain inaccessible to his eyes, in so
far as they are the eyes of mere man. "But of that day or
hour no one knows, neither the angels in heaven, nor the Son,
but the Father only" (Mark 13.32). This is not yet the time
to broach the problem of how this ignorance of Jesus (ex
humanitate) is to be reconciled with his necessarily effortless
contemplation of God, which arises from his consciousness of
being the Son of God; the problem of how Jesus can say of
himself that he too does not know when the Day of Judgement will be, although we learn from the same Gospels that
he will be the judge of the world. All we can establish here is
that Jesus' human consciousness does not include the all-
embracing comprehensive omniscience of the Father. He
makes no claim to it, but rather expressly refuses it. To the

extent that his understanding was human understanding, it was limited.

The same limitation we have seen in his will and knowledge also characterizes his powers. It is true he works unheard-of miracles—the lame walk and the dead rise. But the Evangelist does not hide from us that in Nazareth, the town that had been his home, he was unable to work any miracles, beyond curing a few sick people by laying his hands upon them (Mark 6.5). His working of miracles had an inner limit in the impenitence and unbelief of mankind. Here almighty God fails to come to his aid. And where God fails, Jesus' miraculous power fails too. And his powers in heaven are limited, too, as they are on earth. When the mother of James and John requested of him that her two sons might sit, one at his right hand and one at his left in the kingdom, he explains "as for sitting at my right hand and at my left, that is not mine to give, but it belongs to those for whom it has been prepared by my Father" (Matt. 20.23). At the Last Judgement, it is the Father who has the highest power of judging. Jesus' task is only to bear the Father authoritative witness about mankind. "Therefore everyone who acknowledges me before men, I also will acknowledge him before my Father in heaven" (Matt. 10.32).

This limitation of will, knowledge, and power corresponds to the remarkably simple circumstances in which the Gospels tell us Jesus led his human life. It is a life of poverty, lowliness, homelessness. When a Scribe declares he is ready to follow him wherever he goes, Jesus reminds him of his homelessness: "The foxes have dens and the birds of the air have nests; but the Son of Man has nowhere to lay his head" (Matt. 8.20). Jesus lives on what the devout women accompanying him give him. To pay the temple tax, he works a miracle (Matt. 17.26). He tells his disciples: "Take nothing for your journey, neither staff nor wallet nor bread nor money; neither have two tunics" (Luke 9.3), and this he realized in his own way of life. The poorest of the poor in Israel—this is the picture of our Lord the Gospels give us. His path has nothing of the splendour of a divinity walking the earth. And the way he regarded his life, like the way he lived it, radiates this same infinite simplicity. "I have not come to be served, but to serve"—that is the real motto that St. Mark establishes as the foundation of his life. Jesus' life was one of constant service, washing the feet of the poor and sick, of sinners and children. If we put this picture of humbleness and simplicity side by side with the ideas the ancients had of their sons of God in human form, we become aware of the enormous difference that separates the picture of Christ in the Gospels from the ancient ideas of the Saviour: the pagan Hellenists regarded him as a walking miracle, a sort of heavenly phantom, but in contrast to this, Jesus reveals the purest, simplest humanity, the smell of the earth, praying, struggling, suffering out of the depths of his perfect humanity. And if we accompany him as far as the cross, if we hear his plaints and lamentations on the Mount of Olives, if we listen to his cry, "I am thirsty," "My God, my God, why hast thou forsaken me?" we are confronted with a life overflowing with grief and suffering, but overflowing too with a tremendous power of soul, a struggle and a victory such as the earth has never seen before or since. The Gospels throw this into radiant relief: Jesus was the Son of God. Though they do not hide the further factor, but are moved to portray it down to the smallest detail—that Jesus was also the Son of Man.

* * * *

Having presented the picture of Christ as the Gospels, the oldest classical documents about Christ, portrayed it, and having pointed out his divine and human traits, we know how Jesus stood before the Evangelists and the Christians of his time, and what they knew and believed of him. It is a picture of infinite delicacy and tenderness, sublimity and power, but also of vast simplicity and lowliness. And the divine and the human in Jesus do not subsist separately and side by side, but are inextricably interwoven. It is not as if fine sentiments and adages had been woven artificially into this image of Christ in the Gospels, so that they could be picked out with ease. Christ's teaching was his life, or rather, he taught by his life. Every action he performed breathed out the majesty of his being. We are surrounded by living reality. So we must hearken to this historical life. But so far we have reached only the belief of the Evangelists. What was the faith of the earlier Church of the Apostles? From the Christians of the second generation and the Church of the years 60–70, we now turn to the Christians of the first generation.

V

THE IMAGE OF CHRIST IN THE EARLY CHURCH, ACCORDING TO RELIGIOUS HISTORY

SOURCE material for the Christological doctrines of the early Church at the time of the Apostles is available in the first twelve chapters of the Acts of the Apostles, more particularly in the sermons of St. Peter and in St. Stephen's speech, for these were given before any of the Evangelists had begun to write. It is also to be found in those parts of the Epistles of St. Paul that can be regarded not as the Apostle's own particular theorizing but as the common property of the early congregation, that is, as a part of early Christian tradition. And finally we find source material in those passages of the Synoptic Gospels that contain the creed of the Church as a whole—the earliest Christian tradition.

Testimony of the faith in Christ in the Acts of the Apostles

In his very first sermon, St. Peter considers the life, death, and resurrection of Jesus as the fulfilment of Old Testament prophecy, and therefore as the beginning of the great time of redemption. Therein lies his testimony: "The God of Abraham and the God of Isaac and the God of Jacob, the God of our fathers has glorified his Son [or: servant] Jesus, whom you indeed delivered up and disowned before the face of Pilate" (Acts 3.13; cf. 4.10; 5.30; 10.40). Peter uses the phrase "his *servant Jesus*" (Acts 3.13, 26) after the manner of Isaias, to indicate a special service, the service of the

Messias. The expression "servant" or "Son," as the Greek term is sometimes rendered, thus indicates that Chosen One among men who has been called by Jahve into his service. This servant of God has been glorified in the resurrection by the God of Abraham. The formulation "God of Abraham" is typically Jewish, and brings the servant of God into an Old Testament context. It is clear that this sermon of St. Peter's dates from the time when Christianity was still a community within Jewry. Both expressions—"the servant Jesus" and "the God of Abraham"—are archaistic. Later on, both disappear. But they reveal that we are on the threshold of Christianity, at the transition between Judaism and Christianity.

That the servant Jesus was really recognized and glorified by the God of Abraham is proved by his *resurrection*. The fact of Jesus' resurrection is the basis of the early Christian proclamation of the Gospel. It is the Pentecostal faith that colours the old Apostles' view of Jesus. They can all bear witness to Jesus' resurrection (Acts 2.32; 3.15; 5.32). For they, and they alone, "ate and drank with him after he had risen from the dead" (Acts 10.41). The Acts of the Apostles remind us here of the testimony Luke and John gave of the resurrected Christ in their Gospels.

To the first Apostles, the resurrection of Jesus is the conclusive proof that he is the Christ. As they were dealing with devout orthodox Jews for whom the most important issue was whether Jesus really was the Messias, the first Apostles had to put all the stress upon the proof of this fact. To them, the ultimate proof that Jesus was the Messias was his resurrection. This, and his suffering likewise, was not simply a fact of history, but the fulfilment of Old Testament prophecies, and therefore a truth of redemption (cf. 1 Cor. 15.4; Luke 24.27; Acts 13.29).

But while the disciples proclaim Jesus to be the Christ, they are at the same time concerned to establish that this Christ, the Anointed One who has appeared in Jesus, is not only mere man as the Jews expect, son of David and thus "Son of God" in the theocratic sense; they also proclaim that by his resurrection he has revealed himself as the One who sits at the right hand of God. The first Apostles are concerned to throw into sharp relief this distinction between the Jewish expectation of the Messias and the Christian belief. In the same breath as they announce Jesus to be the Christ, they emphasize his divine origin. The stone rejected by the builders has become the cornerstone (Acts 4.11). God has exalted him to his right hand (2.33; 5.31; 7.55), which in the idiom of the time meant: God has invested him with divine power and glory. But withal, the subject of his distinction is still the servant Jesus, the one who gave his all in the service of God. Thus it was a question of the exaltation of Jesus' humanity into the sphere of divine life. Where divine life is must eternal life be also. Thus in the resurrected humanity of Jesus, God the eternal is manifest in the present. But in what way he is manifest in the present, the pre-Synoptic proclamation of the early Christians does not make clear. Paul and John are the first to bear witness that this God manifest in the humanity of the Lord is "God's own Son" (Paul), his "only-begotten Son" (John). But even the pre-Synoptic teaching leaves no room for doubt that the man Jesus, the son of David, was by the resurrection raised to eternal life. The divine Jesus is the starting point of the first Apostles' proclamation of the Gospel. In their mission to the Jews their main concern is to furnish proof that the man who was crucified, whom "all know of," really is the Messias who sits at the right hand of God. That is why they call Jesus "the author of life" (Acts 3.15; τὸν δὲ ἀρχηγὸν τῆς ζωῆς), i.e., him in whom there is the fullness of life, and from whom all life issues forth. This is the monstrous paradox that Peter holds up to the Jews: "The author of life you killed, whom God has raised up from the dead; whereof we are witness" (3.15). His exaltation to the right hand of God meant to them elevation to Divine Being. As author of life, Jesus arisen had received the power of pouring forth his holy spirit upon his own, and thereby had fulfilled the prediction of the prophet Joel (Acts 2.16). "Therefore, exalted by the right hand of God, and receiving from the Father the promise of the Holy Spirit, he has poured forth this spirit, which you see and hear" (2.33). Thus Jesus arisen becomes the true principle of the new life of the disciples' community. His spirit is their spirit. The powers of the Trinity—the God of Abraham, Jesus raised to the right hand of God, and the Holy Spirit—are the three fundamental divine powers that the early Christians are concerned to proclaim. In the name of this Jesus, the man exalted to divine life, their miracles are wrought: "Why do you marvel at this, or why do you stare at us, as though by any power or holiness of our own we had made this man walk?" (3.12). "In the name of Jesus Christ of Nazareth, arise and walk" (3.6).

And thus their leading maxim becomes the early Apostolic

proclamation: "Let all the house of Israel know most assuredly that God has made both Lord and Christ, this Jesus whom you crucified" (. . . ὅτι καὶ Κύριον αὐτὸν καὶ Χριστὸν ἐποίησεν ὁ Θεός, τοῦτον τὸν Ἰησοῦν ὃν ὑμεῖς ἐσταυρώσατε, Acts 2.36). It is "the God" who has wrought this miracle of exalting the humanity of Christ to divine life. Later theology was to put it thus: The act of incarnation, the assumption of humanity by the second divine person, belongs as *opus Dei ad extra* to the *unus Deus,* to the entire Trinity. To this triune God the *gratia unionis,* the miracle of the exaltation of Christ's humanity to divine life, is ascribed. God become man—for that is the subject of St. Peter's proof—has not been "Lord and Christ" from eternity, but has become so only by the miracle of Grace of the incarnation, by the act of the one God. That is why Peter says God has "made" him Lord and Christ. There is an act, a deed here, for it is not a question of the Word that was in the beginning (λόγος ἄσαρκος), but of God become man. This passage too sounds archaistic, in so far as it does not, as present-day theology does, place the divinity of Jesus as such in the centre of contemplation, but rather the exaltation of his humanity. This is significant for the Christology of the early Church, because it confirms the fact that the early Christian proclamation of the Gospel was first and foremost not concerned with the everlasting Son of God, but with God become man. Their starting point was not Christ's divinity but his humanity. But they emphasize: This humanity has been assumed into the divine glory.

The divine dignity of Jesus is expressed even more clearly in the predicate "the Lord" (ὁ Κύριος) than in the predicate "the Christ" (ὁ Χριστός). For in the Jewish as in the Hellenistic idiom, "the Lord" is the true name for God, in so far as he is outwardly revealed. The God become man, then, is "the Lord" of the Old Testament. In a similar phrase, Peter describes Christ as "the Prince and the Saviour" (ἀρχηγὸς καὶ σωτήρ). "Him God exalted with his right hand to be Prince and Saviour, to grant repentance to Israel and forgiveness of sins" (Acts 5.31). The expression could be an indirect refutation of similar Hellenistic formulations which give their rulers and princes the additional honorific title of "Saviour" (σωτήρ). So what Peter really means is that he who has been elevated is alone the true Saviour, not the worldly rulers. "Neither is there salvation in any other. For there is no other name under heaven given to me by which we must be saved" (4.12). To this is related the further avowal: "For heaven indeed must receive him until the times of the restoration of all things" (3.21); "he it is who has been appointed by God to be judge of the living and of the dead" (10.42). This, then, is the early Apostolic Creed: The resurrection was testimony that Jesus, crucified by the Jews, is the servant of God who was raised to the right hand of God; and thus he is the Lord, the Saviour and author of life, who endows us with the Holy Spirit, without which we cannot achieve bliss; and he will be our judge and our fate.

Once again: It is *not* the divinity of Jesus that stands in the foreground of the early Christian proclamation of the Gospel, but his humanity, his *historical appearance*, his confirmation by death and resurrection. Confronted with orthodox Jewry, the burning question was not: Is God himself revealed in Jesus of Nazareth, is he very God of very God?; but solely: Has the Messias really appeared in him, and in what sense has he become our Messias? It was the question of the Messias, not the question of God, that stood in the foreground of the early Apostolic mission. Not until Hellenistic times was raised the problem of the extent to which Christ was the true God. The early Christian question centred on the mission of the historical Jesus. It can further be deduced that the historical humanity of Christ was the true object of the early Christian proclamation from the *standard* that Peter sets up for the selection of an Apostle, necessary after Judas' suicide, in the time before the Gospels were written: "Of these men who have been in our company all the time that the Lord Jesus moved among us, from John's baptism until the day that he was taken up from us, of these one must become a witness with us of his resurrection" (Acts 1.21). This standard would indicate that the early Christian proclamation referred solely to the elevation of the Lord and the related course of his life, from his baptism by John to his resurrection—all of which fell within the field of Old Testament prophecy. The Apostle Peter and his fellows have an eye only for the earthly historical life and works of Jesus, in so far as the Old Testament prophecies are fulfilled in them. In no sense does he refer to the superhistorical, pre-existent, transcendent being of the Lord, not even to the miracle of his supernatural conception and birth. The essential and decisive thing for Peter was not an exposition of the metahistorical, superhistorical, and prehistorical in Jesus, but in the clear testimony of precisely verifiable facts from his public life, above all the testimony of his resurrection. All this in the light of the prophetic witnesses. It is the same pattern of proclamation that in some manner lies at the bottom of all the Canonical Gospels, and was in particular the model for the Gospel according to St. Matthew.

But although this places the humanity of Jesus in the foreground of the early Christian message, it does not mean that they were completely silent about the divinity of Christ. Faith in his divinity is rather the broad undercurrent of their proclamation of Jesus the servant. All the colours with which they paint Jesus exalted blend in with the picture of a heavenly being which, although subordinate in its human form to the Father, nevertheless accomplishes actions that are truly divine, appropriate only to God, but of his own autonomous authority. This is a Messias not in the Jewish but in the Christian sense. However, it is still significant that the early congregation, bringing their message to the Jews, refrain from ever giving Christ the name of God or speaking expressly of the divine functions of the Messias. They were clearly afraid of being misunderstood by the Jews, who believed in one single divine person, and of being accused of blasphemy. Within their message of Jesus "the servant," the Lord's work as redeemer upon earth came to the fore, and not the metaphysical idea of Christ's being the Son of God. A shift of emphasis from the human and earthly in Jesus to the divine and supernatural does not become perceptible until the missionary work among the Hellenists.

Thus the oldest documents of the Christian mission reveal the clear, pure, uncoloured source of their tradition, the fact that the Apostles in no sense glorified or transfigured the picture of Jesus. Otherwise these oldest of testimonies would somehow have made use of the later Christian formulation deriving from Paul and John, that Jesus is pre-existent and God's only-begotten Son. The early Apostolic tradition leaves no doubt that it arose in a time when Christianity was still slowly and painfully emerging from Judaism, in a time of transition from the Jews' rigid belief in one God to the dynamic Christian faith in one triune God.

Radical Biblical criticism would seize upon this circumstance, that the primary interest of the early Christian community was in the history of Jesus the man, as an opportunity to dispute their belief in Jesus' divinity, or at least to advance the theory that this belief, following the law of an inner development, was reached only after going through certain stages. The historian of religion Bousset in particular was of the opinion that by some very daring combinations he could set up a sequence of development that would explain the gradual unfolding of the Christian belief in the divinity of Christ.

What Bousset—and with him most historians of religion—resists is the admission that Christ himself was already conscious of being the Son of God in the true sense, and that the earliest congregation in Jerusalem already addressed him as Lord and Saviour. Bousset maintains that such a belief could strike root only in Hellenistic ground, not in the Jewish-Palestinian tradition, for only the Hellenistic pagans had the psychological possibility of believing in saviours and gods come down from heaven to earth. With this as their starting point, all the critics had to do was to show in detail how these Hellenistic ideas could have arisen in the early Church, which was Jewish. The question whether Jesus already knew himself to be the Messias is at first cut out of this problem entirely. It is simply a question of pointing out the transition that led from the Jewish-Palestinian attitude of mind to the Hellenistic.

Even before Bousset, indeed ever since Reimarus, radical Biblical criticism had regarded its chief task to be the proof in evolutionary terms that the belief in Christ's divinity *developed only gradually*, that it was not something original, but secondary. Wrede wrote a daring book upon the contrast—which he claimed was obvious and irreconcilable—between the picture of Christ in the Synoptic Gospels and the picture of Christ derived from St. Paul and St. John. He maintained that the true creator of the Church's Christology was St. Paul. He alone was able to range Christ with the Godhead because he had never had the opportunity of knowing him personally, so his speculations, nourished upon late Judaic eschatology and mysticism, had not been fettered by the memory of the poor and simple life Jesus had led. This ideal image of Christ soon became the dominant one in the Christian communities, and even overlaid certain features of the Synoptic picture of Jesus.

Wrede's suggestions have found practically no supporters, not even among the Biblical critics. An exact analysis of Paul's writings and of the Synoptic Gospels will show without a flaw that the belief in Christ's supernatural essence had been dominant in those Christian communities which had existed before Paul's time, or had gone untouched by his influence. This made it necessary for the historians of religion to probe the roots not of St. Paul's Christology but of the Christology of the early communities *before St. Paul's time* —i.e., advance the evidence that it was made up of a combination of Jewish and pagan elements, the evolutionary product of certain Jewish and Hellenistic ideas, and not derived from Jesus' own testimony to himself.

The Son of Man

The argument for this mythological, eschatological explanation of the belief in Christ's divinity, which Bousset in particular tends to support in his work *Kyrios Christos* (3rd ed., Göttingen, 1926), runs something like this: Christ's own annunciation itself does not as yet include the basis for the later belief in God the Saviour. Indeed, it is altogether problematical whether Jesus himself wanted to be regarded as the promised Christ. It is rather the Christian community at Jerusalem that should be thought of as the *creator* of early Christian Messianism. This is on account of its peculiar dogma of the Son of Man. Resting on their faith in Jesus resurrected, the Jerusalem community were the first to assume that Jesus was the Son of Man and as such would one day come in the clouds of heaven. This was the only way they could solve the riddle of his death upon the cross: Jesus died, that he might return from heaven as the promised Son of Man and set up the new kingdom of God. By his resurrection, he had testified to his coming as the Son of Man. So, to justify their belief in the resurrection, the community swathed his figure in the myth of the coming of the Son of Man, whose appearance would blaze like lightning from one end of the world to the other. As early Christian literature reveals, Christianity originally was thoroughly eschatological. It was looking exclusively to the coming Parousia. The significance Jesus had for it lay necessarily in the time to come, in his mission to bring the new kingdom down from heaven in the immediate future. To give expression to this belief, they took over from contemporary apocalyptic writings Daniel's image of the Son of Man. They took care that no description of himself was put into his mouth other than this of the Son of Man. So in Jesus' designation of himself as the Son of Man we are confronted with the oldest dogma of the early Christian community, the dogma in which they formulated their faith in the glory of Jesus resurrected, who was to appear upon earth within their generation. Volkmar, Lietzmann, and Wellhausen argue along similar lines. According to them, the name "Son of Man" is hardly comprehensible in the mouth of Jesus. It can be found neither in St. Paul nor in the post-Pauline writings. It is absent in all the Apostolic Fathers, with the one exception of Ignatius of Antioch (*Epistola ad Ephesios*, 20.2). All of which leads the critics to the conclusion that it is a strictly theological construct, and not original.

The Lord

According to this argument, the myth arose originally in the heart of the community of Jerusalem, and underwent a further development in Antioch. Not Judaism, but Hellenism, was dominant there, with its throng of saviour divinities and its cult of the Kyrios. The idea of the divine king had been transplanted to the West from the Orient, largely from Babylon and Egypt, and had been linked with the idea of the Saviour of the mystery cults. The Roman Emperors were called by the honorific title "Saviour of all mankind," "Saviour of the world." The Roman Emperor was as much Kyrios and Soter as the gods. This led to the naturalization of the beliefs in the Lord and Saviour. What they believed of the Emperor they would believe more readily even of the mystery gods Mithras, Osiris, Hermes. These were regarded as Kyrioi and Soteres. Everywhere in the Empire, especially in Syria, Egypt, and Asia Minor, communities large and small gathered together to worship their cult god, the Kyrios. What was more natural than that those Hellenists who believed in Christ—and they came thronging from the most diverse cults to the new faith—should similarly meet in the glorification of their Kyrios, Jesus? But as they raised Jesus to be the god of their cult, and called him Kyrios, they turned the Jewish community's Lord of the future into the Lord of the present or, rather, the Lord of the Second Coming became the Lord of the community. All unnoticed, as it were, the early Christian idea of the Messias, the coming Son of God, merged into the idea of God as the present Lord, who becomes immediately operative within the religious community. St. Paul's later mystical cult of Christ thus arose out of the Kyrios cult of the Hellenistic community at Antioch. Hence, the line of development in early Christian Christology came to be: The annunciation of Jesus; the testimony of the early community at Jerusalem to Jesus resurrected; Jesus the coming Son of Man; Jesus the Lord. From this Paul drew the conclusion: Jesus is God's own Son.

The belief of the early Christian community

This theory is defeated the moment the assured proof is adduced that Jesus had been acknowledged as the Kyrios even by the early community at Jerusalem, made up of original Jews, long before he was by the Hellenistic community at Antioch. For such evidence would break down what the critics would have is the first stage in the evolution of belief in the coming Son of Man, and we would require no further refutation of the monstrous assumption that every description Jesus gives of himself as the Son of Man has been artificially interpolated into the Gospels, and that they must be regarded as dogmatic, not as historical statements. The so-called dogmatics of the Son of Man loses all justification, however, when it is superseded by the belief in the Kyrios within the same community, which, as the historians unanimously agree, includes the belief in Jesus' divinity. It is still less justified, if we can adduce the further proof that the belief in the Son of Man never was at the centre of the early Christian faith, and in fact was not a statement of dogma, but Jesus' own description of himself.

Let us take up the first question: Was it really the community in Antioch that first created the Kyrios belief, or did it already exist in the Jerusalem community?

We have already established the words of St. Peter in Jerusalem as the main point of the early Apostolic proclamation: God has made him (Jesus the man) both Lord and Christ (Acts 2.36). It is true, Bousset makes the most desperate efforts to prove critically that the decisive word Κύριος, Kyrios, in this verse is a later insertion. But the entire context of the speech indicates that the most important thing to Peter was precisely to emphasize Christ's divine dignity as a ruler. Peter starts from the promise made to David "that of the fruit of his loins one should sit upon his throne" (Acts 2.30), and from David's own prophecy, "The Lord said to my Lord: Sit thou at my right hand, until I make thy enemies thy footstool" (Acts 2.34)—i.e., the promise of the Messias as the coming ruler who will sit upon the throne of David. From this, Peter draws the conclusion: "Therefore let all the house of Israel know most assuredly that God has made both Lord and Christ, this Jesus. . . ." (Acts 2.36). In Peter's demonstration, this very position as ruler is the decisive characteristic of the Christ. The Κύριος, the status of Kyrios, is the very thing he wants to prove for his image of Christ. The dignity of Kyrios promised and prophesied for David's offspring had been fulfilled, according to Peter, in the dignity of Kyrios in Jesus resurrected. Otherwise Peter's entire argument would fall to pieces. Moreover, Peter again explains in the house of Cornelius: "He sent his word to the children of Israel, preaching peace through Jesus Christ (who is Lord of all)" (οὗτός ἐστιν πάντων Κύριος, Acts 10.36). This statement, too, cannot be removed from its context. For in converting the Gentile Cornelius, Peter is concerned to prove that God "is not a respecter of persons," but has his worshippers "in every nation" (Acts 10.34, 35), that his rule is all-embracing. And therefore, Peter concludes, Jesus is Lord over all, Jews as well as Gentiles. Thus the Κύριος is an essential part of the argument even of the very first Apostle.

But still further: Peter's words "God has made him Lord" and his quotation from Psalm 109 is itself not original. Its roots lie still deeper, for it goes back to Jesus himself. In Matthew 22.44, 45, Jesus draws the Pharisees' attention to this Psalm with its messianic interpretation to point out the inconsistency of their own purely earthly ideal of the Messias. "If David calls him [the Messias] his 'Lord,' how then is he his son?" Jesus wants to prove by this that the Messias cannot be a merely human descendant of David's, if David himself calls him his Lord. This is how he interprets Psalm 109 —that the Messias is Lord—and in Peter's eyes, this claim of Jesus' is fulfilled in the resurrection and the descent of the Holy Spirit. Of course Bousset is aware of this passage in Matthew 22.44, too. He tries to evade the evidence it offers by regarding it as a theologoumenon, a dogmatic interpolation which the early Christian community did not put into Jesus' mouth until later. But apart from the fact that Bousset merely asserts this, starting from his *a priori* assumptions, without being able to advance the least scrap of evidence for it, even apart from the fact that he is ascribing downright falsifications to the oldest Christian missionaries in maintaining that they put their own formulations into Jesus' mouth, even this dubious path still does not get him out of his blind alley. For he simply cannot deny that Matthew 22.44, arose only on Jewish and not on Hellenistic ground. The problem at issue is strictly a Jewish one—concerning the nature of the promised Messias. Even the way in which the problem is solved is purely Jewish. It is a typical case of a rabbinical, scriptural proof. So Matthew 22.44 could have arisen only against a Jewish background. But this brings Bousset back to the very question he tries to evade: How is it possible for monotheistic Jews to have acknowledged the divine Kyrios in Jesus resurrected?

The well-known early Christian blessing, Maranathâ, "the Lord comes," is further evidence for the early occurrence of the name of Kyrios. It is true, St. Paul is the first to mention it (1 Cor. 16.22). But the Aramaic formulation indicates clearly enough its Palestinian origin. The *Didache* too, the oldest liturgical text, uses this Maranathâ. Since "Hosanna" and "Amen" are also part of this liturgy, there is little doubt that it comes from circles that prayed in the Aramaic language. It is clear that at that time these prayers had already spread to some extent beyond the borders of Palestine. When Paul makes use of the same formula, he assumes that Jews from Palestine were already settled in the community at Corinth, and that these Judaeo-Christians acknowledged Jesus to be "the Lord."

A third piece of evidence for the early occurrence of the name "Kyrios" occurs in the well-known passage in Matthew 7.21 f.: "Not everyone who says to me 'Lord, Lord' shall enter the kingdom of heaven, but he who does the will of my Father in heaven shall enter the kingdom of heaven. Many will say to me in that day, 'Lord, Lord, did we not prophesy in thy name, and cast out devils in thy name, and work many miracles in thy name?' And then I will declare to them, 'I never knew you. Depart from me. . . .'"

Christ himself takes upon him the name of Kyrios here, and indeed understands it in the sense of the cults. He speaks of the time to come, when he will be addressed as Kyrios. For that very reason, the attempt has been made to trace this term to the community's liturgy. But that argument is merely wilful, for the repeated Kyrie was customary in the Jewish prayers too. So Jesus could perfectly well point from past practice to future prayers. But even if this were a case of liturgical formula, its original Judaeo-Palestinian character would still not be called in question, because Matthew, who informs us of this formulation, wrote exclusively for the Judaeo-Christians. So the Judaeo-Christian community in Jerusalem already called upon Jesus as the Lord.

The same divine reverence with which the early community greeted Jesus in this prayer is further apparent, at least indirectly, in the fact that they called upon the name of Jesus. Paul is not the only one to refer to this custom of calling upon the name of Jesus (1 Cor. 1.2; Rom. 10.12, *et al.*). The Acts of the Apostles, too, stress again and again, "Whoever calls upon the name of the Lord shall be saved" (Acts 2.21; cf. 7.59; 9.14, 21). This brought the Christians the name of "callers upon the name of Jesus" (οἱ ἐπικαλούμενοι τὸ ὄνομά σου). The Acts also speak of baptism in the name or on the name of Jesus (22.16; 2.38; 10.48), thereby ascribing divine power to Jesus, and demonstrating him to be the Lord. This power of benediction in the name of Jesus begins even in the time of the Lord's ministry upon earth. There are certain passages in the Gospels in which Jesus speaks of the things that his disciples have done or have still to do "in his name." In the name of Jesus they work miracles and cast out devils (Luke 10.17; Mark 9.38). They will be persecuted and hated for his name's sake (Matt. 5.11; 10.22). After Christ's elevation, the power of his name is manifested still more strongly. In the name of Jesus, Peter healed the lame beggar at the gate of the temple called the Beautiful (Acts 3.6; cf. 4.10). Early Christendom regarded his name as the only one "by which we must be saved" (4.12). Thus even in his lifetime, and especially in the early Church, Jesus was the object of the most fervent of cults. With such worship, the name "Kyrios" comes of itself. All the seeds, at least, are present, for the growth of a Kyrios cult. If the title "Kyrios" were really strange to the early Jewish community, Bousset and his successors would not only be compelled to delete those passages in the Acts of the Apostles where Jesus is expressly referred to as the Lord, but would also have to deny the entire religious temper of the Acts and the Gospels, and the reverence for Christ apparent in them, particularly in the Gospel according to St. Matthew, which was written especially for the Judaeo-Christians in Palestine. Moreover, if Paul had derived the name of Kyrios and with it all his mystical reverence for Christ only from Antioch, if the faith in the divinity of Jesus were first imported from Antioch, how can it be explained that the Apostle's entire belief in Christ was already firmly established when he first came into touch with Antioch? After his conversion, Paul spent many years away from Antioch—three years in the Arabian Desert and in Damascus, fifteen days in Jerusalem, and the rest of the time in his home at Tarsus. At the time Barnabas called him to Antioch he was already a mature Christian, who had nothing more essential to learn, neither in Jerusalem nor in Antioch. He expressly derives his personal belief in Christ exclusively from the miracle of his conversion at Damascus. "Henceforth," he tells us (2 Cor. 5.16), he knew no one "according to the flesh." Ever since that day at Damascus, not before and not after, he knows: "If any man is in Christ, he is a new creature: the former things have passed away; behold, they are made new" (2 Cor. 5.17). The experience that a new life was given to him in Christ, putting aside all laws and causing him to call "Abba, Father," came to him on that day at Damascus. The first word that he uttered then was "Kyrie." "Lord, who art thou?" The historical details to be built into this fundamental experience of the Kyrios he had learned through the Paradosis of Jerusalem, as he himself explains (1 Cor. 15.3). Certainly we cannot overlook the fact that there is a development in Paul's Christology. But this development was not a progression from one new thing to the next, but an increasingly profound comprehension and clarification of the old which was urged upon him by his disputes with the legalistic self-righteousness of the Jews, and with the anthroposophic views of certain mystical Gnostic religions of redemption. He was concerned with attaining out of his experience at Damascus to a comprehensive understanding of the history of revelation and of mankind. As early as his first Epistle to the Corinthians, and the Epistle to the Romans, he was beginning to prepare such an all-embracing system of thought. But the zenith is not reached until his letters from prison. Deissmann is right to emphasize this: "The incident near Damascus . . . must be regarded as the foundational experience in mysticism" (*St. Paul,* Eng. tr., London, 1912, p. 122).

To sum up: The earliest Christians, the first community at Jerusalem, even *Jesus' disciples* during the Master's lifetime, had already made Jesus the object of religious veneration, of a cult. They recognized him to be the Lord, and wrought signs and wonders in his name. The first sermon of St. Peter's already acknowledges Christ as the Lord. Only this can account for the fact that there is absolutely no distinction between the belief in Christ of the first Jewish community and that of the Hellenistic communities. Even Albert Schweitzer, of the eschato-logical school, is compelled to affirm: "But we know nothing of any such controversy. The Hellenistic Christians were on the best of terms with Judaeo-Christian Jerusalem. In fact they allowed themselves to be influenced by the original Apostles in opposition to Paul. In Antioch, Peter counted for more than Paul. Even Barnabas took Peter's side on the question of whether it was right to eat with Gentiles . . . the influence of Jerusalem showed itself stronger than his" (*The Mysticism of Paul the Apostle,* Eng. tr., London, 1931, p. 31). So, if we have to speak of an opposition at all, it is rather an opposition be-tween Paul and Antioch than between Peter and Antioch. Thus it is wrong to say that Paul drew his belief in the Kyrios from Antioch. He had no need to, for the same belief was flourishing in Jerusalem too. And in actual fact he derived it neither from Antioch nor from Jerusalem, but from his experience at Damascus. This is not refuted by the fact that the Apostle, born a Hellenist and calling himself "the Apostle to the Hellenes," should have interpreted his personal experience of Christ to himself in terms and formulations created and made current by the Gnostic Hellenistic mysticism, particularly by the Cilician cult of Mithras, which were part of his environ-ment. Indeed, it made him peculiarly well suited to be the Apostle to the Hellenes.

And now for the second question: Was the original acknowl-edgement of faith, in the first community, simply made to the Son of Man? Was the Son of Man the true content of the early Christian faith? We have shown that in fact the early commu-nity in Jerusalem already recognized Jesus as the Kyrios, as a divine being, and indeed that even in his lifetime Jesus was the object of religious veneration. This already makes the so-called first stage in the evolution of early Christian Christology mean-ingless. For if the first Christian community had already recog-nized Jesus' divinity, then they must also already have under-stood their belief in the coming Son of Man in the light of this fundamental tenet—that is, the source of this belief's ulti-mate sense and content.

Bousset dogmatizes as follows: "Only since the resurrection is Jesus the coming Son of Man, coming on the clouds of heaven, as Daniel foretold . . . the community at Jerusalem swathed his figure in the myth of the Son of Man. . . . Here at the very beginning the creative power of the community's faith and its ability to reshape historical reality are as clear as we could wish . . . the first chord of the hymn is struck, that is to accompany the figure of Jesus throughout history" (*Jesus der Herr*, Göttingen, 1916, p. 11).

This dithyramb of Bousset's on the creative power of community faith is contradicted by hard facts. Bousset bases his hypothesis largely on the eschatological mood of the early community. He maintains that their eyes were fixed not on the present Lord but on the Lord that was to come, so that they regarded Jesus solely as the Son of Man who was to come again. Such an eschatological disposition of mind would make the belief in a Kyrios animating and dominating the community in the present quite impossible. In brief, this is his argument: Because the earliest community expected its salvation only in the future, they could not at the same time venerate Jesus as the present Lord. Their image of Christ could only bear the features of the future judge of the world. But immediately the objection to this comes to mind: Was not Paul, too, of a thoroughly eschatological disposition of mind? Does not the first Epistle to the Thessalonians alone already demonstrate his faith in the immediate coming of the judge of the world? And nevertheless he lives and moves and has his being in the belief in the present power of the Kyrios. Christ in his life and death is his gain. So faith in the present Lord must be quite easily reconcilable with the belief in the future Lord. This alone destroys Bousset's assumption that belief in a present Lord cannot be reconciled with the eschatological vision.

Moreover, Jesus describes himself almost exclusively in the Gospels as the Son of Man. No disciple or member of the community, however, does this. So there is not the slightest trace in the Gospel tradition of any original cult of the Son of Man. Rather, the community in general is painfully careful for its part not to acknowledge Jesus as the Son of Man. The language used is so in accord that we can only conclude that here is a clear historical recollection of the hagiographies—or a conscious falsification. This state of affairs is only obscured by evasion in the theory of community dogma. In the light of Bousset's theory, the Gospels no longer appear as simple, straightforward missionary literature, but virtually as subtle pieces of tendentious special pleading. But even such propaganda would have aimed in the wrong direction if it ascribed the expression "Son of Man" to Jesus alone, and if it did not rather put it particularly in the mouth of the early community too. If the Son of Man had really been the centre of the faith at that time, then the community would inevitably have called upon him as the Son of Man. And anyway, modern Gospel criticism should be the last to think of assuming conscious falsification. At every turn it is borne in upon the critics how naïve and simple the historiography of the Gospels is, how it labours to put down without any omissions the recollections of the Apostles' teachings current in the community, even when it has to take repetitions, inconsistencies, and even contradictions in its stride. An art that was working solely with an eye to literary effect would doubtless have omitted such contradictions. We need only be reminded of the apocryphal books, for example the Infant Gospel of Thomas, in which every action and every word of the child Jesus radiates the omnipotent, omniscient young God. And why should the early Christian community have chosen just this expression "Son of Man"? Neither Jew nor Hellenist of the time could have made much sense of this concept. The average Jew knew only of the Messias, the Son of David, the last prophet that was to come, but nothing of the Son of Man. Only in a small branch of Jewry, in Jewish apocalyptic writings, was his figure known from Daniel. As a constant appellation for the Messias, "Son of Man" occurs only in the apocryphal images of the Book of Henoch. The name "Son of Man" was hardly noticed or emphasized even at the time of Jesus, as a glance at Matthew 16.13 f. will show. The Lord asks: "Who do men say the Son of Man is?" Jesus evidently wants a confession of faith from his disciples but certainly *not* a confession of faith in the Son of Man. He rather takes himself as the starting point. What he wants is a confession of faith in Christ and the Son of God. As soon as Peter makes his avowal, Jesus stresses this with the solemn words "Flesh and blood has not revealed this to thee. . . ." This would indicate that the name "Son of Man" had no dogmatic content. Only the word "Christ" had dogmatic content. This would explain why precisely the oldest parts of the early Apostolic tradition, Peter's sermons in the Acts of the Apostles, nowhere stress or even mention the Son of Man, which they would no doubt have done if the early community had seen the mystery of the Lord mainly in his dignity as Son of Man. Jesus is described as the Son of Man only once in the Acts (7.56), but even here not by a Jewish member of the community but by the Hellenist Stephen, who in his ecstasy beholds the heavens open and the Son of Man seated at the right hand of the Father. The truth is that the idea of the Son of Man, which derives not from the broad stream of prophecy but from the narrow apocalyptic line, was not nearly as familiar to the Jewish people as Bousset's assumption would have us believe, and in no way represented the essential and ultimate experience of the mystery of Jesus within the Judaeo-Christian community.

The concept of the "Son of Man" was even more foreign to the *Hellenistic* circles of the time. There is no need to demonstrate this independently; the formulation comes from Daniel, and is of Jewish origin. Not only was it unknown among the Hellenists but it remained so strange to them that within a few decades it had disappeared completely from Gentile Christian literature. Ignatius of Antioch and Barnabas already contrast the Son of Man with the Son of God. They have lost all understanding of its original mystical sense.

So it was impossible for this suggestion to come from the heart of the community; there were not enough points of contact for it to arise, or assert itself. If it is used throughout each one of the Gospels, as Jesus' own designation of himself, it can rest only upon an exact historical recollection, and thus upon a characteristic of Jesus himself. Only on the assumption that the Lord was pleased to call himself the Son of Man—for reasons that we shall go into later—is it comprehensible that the Evangelists should have taken such pains to stress this fact in their accounts and that now and again they should also interpolate the expression "Son of Man" where Jesus originally spoke in the first person.

Our conclusion is this: The Christian community of Jerusalem had as little to do with originating the avowal of the "Son of Man" as the community at Antioch had with the avowal of the "Lord." The "Lord" was an original part of the Christian creed from the very beginning. "The Son of Man" can be found only in the mouth of Jesus, and not in the cult of the first Christians. This completely disposes of the attempt of the eschatological school to regard what they call the original faith in the coming Son of Man as the preparatory stage for what they call the Hellenistic belief in the Kyrios.

The belief in God the Saviour as a creative power

So the mythological school—which, it is true, cannot be clearly separated from the eschatological school—has tried another way. They too share the assumption that the belief in the divinity of Jesus can go back neither to Jesus himself nor to the first Apostles. On the other hand, they are not satisfied with the view that the early Christian belief in the Son of Man is the natural transition to the Hellenistic belief in the Son of God. They hold that between the Jesus of history and the divine Christ of faith there stands nothing more and nothing less than purposeless poetic legend, the transfiguring power of the communal faith. According to this view, the avowal of the Lord's divinity is to be ascribed to the anonymous myth-making source of the *dogma of the community*. This is the doing either of the early Christian community or, more likely, of the myth-making power of Hellenistic ideas of God as the Saviour which had found their way even into Galilee. The history of religion has furnished a great deal of material for this assumption. The period was of a thoroughly mystical frame of mind; men thirsted after a God and a Saviour. The ground of earthly glory was trembling beneath their feet, with constant civil wars, uprisings, the assassination of emperors. Mankind yearned for a supernatural reality that would assure them of undisturbed happiness. They found this reality only in union with the divine, in the service of the mysteries. And so their hearts were open and their eyes keen to perceive anything that seemed divine or announced the imminence of God's coming. St. Paul, with his experience on the island of Malta, offers a clear example of this frame of mind. Because the Apostle, who had just been saved from shipwreck, did not die of the viper's bite, the people of Malta said that he must be a god (Acts 28.6). This is the milieu, the mythological school argues, which gave rise to the belief in the divinity of Jesus.

We have to consider that Hellenism and its concomitant faith in the mystery cults made up the spiritual atmosphere of Galilee too, and even of Jerusalem in Jesus' time. Since its conquest by the Romans, Palestine had become a country of two languages. Greek was spoken every bit as much as Aramaic, as the Lord's conversations with the pagan centurion and the Phoenician woman make clear. And with the Greek language, Greek ideas and images also entered the country. The mythological school draws its conclusions: The strong impact made by the living Jesus and especially the disciples' visionary experience of his resurrection could within such a milieu lead only to the illusory belief that this Jesus must be of a divine nature, and that the true Lord and Saviour God had appeared in him. This belief in the true Lord and Saviour would thus be a perfectly natural reaction of the mentality of the time to their experience of Jesus.

What can we say to this? When the Christian faith came into the pagan Hellenistic world, of course it found favourable ground for it to develop in the longing for God the Saviour of the Hellenistic mysteries. It is true that it met here a disposition that was dear and familiar—the longing for salvation and the belief in the descent of a divinity to earth, and so on. There is no doubt that Hellenism had no small part in the development of the Christian faith. Christ appeared just at a time that was in the broadest way prepared for the mystery of his divinity made flesh. But on the other hand, the views of God and the world held by the mystery cults and by Christianity are in their main lines so essentially different, indeed so opposed to each other, that to deduce one set of ideas from the other would be a psychological impossibility. The pagan religiosity of the Hellenists could clarify and develop the experiences hovering around the divinity of Jesus, but never create them.

In detail, we can maintain the following. Firstly, the Hellenistic Saviours and sons of God are almost without exception entirely *mythological* fabrications, *without* any historical basis. They are at root nothing but the ancient gods of foreign peoples that had been taken over by Greek and Roman piety because their own national gods were not adequate to the soul's growing need for union with the divinity. These ancient gods for their part were nothing but the old vegetation and fertility gods, originally arising from nature worship and still preserving traces of this nature worship in their ritual. They all bore the stamp of a pantheistic, monistic religion; they were the basic form of the reality of their time, but not the creators of this reality. Gods and men arose rather from *one* mother, from the womb of the one all-powerful mother, nature. Secondly, because these Hellenistic gods were at root only a personification of nature, but not Lord and creator of nature, they were all exceedingly similar, and merged easily into one another. They could exchange names and intermingle rites. The gentle Phrygian shepherd god Attis blended with the Thracian Sabazios-Bakchos, and later took on the form of the Oriental moon-god Men. Finally, he was transformed into Mithras, the Persian sun-god, and with him went through all the transformations that Mithras had gone through. From the Mithras-cult the form of Anahita, wife of Mithras, was assumed by the famous Phrygian mother of the gods and *magna mater* Kybele. Mithras himself was identified with the Phoenician god Adonis, the Thracian Bakchos, the Arcadian Pan, and the Egyptian Osiris.

Isis underwent similar transformations; since the days of the Ptolemies the goddess whose cult centred in Alexandria had held sway over the coastal lands of Syria, Asia Minor, and Greece. Isis was possessed of unutterable powers of transformation. She was the Greek Demeter. She was Aphrodite. She was Tyche. She was Venus, Hera, and Juno: *Una quae est omnia*. Similarly, under Hellenistic guise Osiris became Dionysos, Iakchos, and Bakchos. When in 130 the Emperor Hadrian's favourite Antinoüs was drowned in the Nile, he was at once worshipped as Osiris. Later, he was transformed into Hermes, and an abundance of other gods. A symbolic mythological quality clung inseparably to these divinities of redemption, because at root they were no more and no less than radiations of the one mother, nature. Thus it is that the Hellenistic period is so characteristically marked by the syncretistic nature of its religions.

The entrance into history of the belief in Christ was essentially different. Christ appeared as a flesh-and-blood human being, as a Jew whose birthplace was known, and whose family was precisely named. His lifetime was but recently. His parents were registered by the Roman census in Bethlehem. His trial for treason was called by known representatives of the highest Jewish authorities and the Roman provincial court. This man, whose death had taken place so recently, was called a divinity —and a divinity not in the Hellenistic but in the Jewish sense. He alone is the manifestation of God, the all-powerful and all-holy One. Here was the terrible new and incredible thing in the early Christian proclamation of God: that the one omnipotent God had become man. This historical definitiveness of the image of Christ, and his monotheistic nature, are the source of his exclusiveness. Christ is just as exclusive as the *Deus solus* of the Jews. All the mystery religions are able to blend and melt into one another, and exist side by side. But Christ makes his lonely way through them. "Aloof and great, incomprehensible to the ideas and concepts of the mystery religions, this God of only yesterday suddenly stood in the midst of the others, and high above the others" (Krebs). He would suffer no one by his side, not even the Emperor. The exclusive nature of Christianity becomes clear precisely in its antagonistic attitude towards the Emperor cult. The mystery religions were by nature not at all opposed to the Emperor cult. The nature symbols represented in their divinities had no trouble in assimilating the Emperor's person, too, to express themselves. The characteristic epithets of the mystery gods were easily transferred to the Emperor. The name of "Saviour," "Soter," which Greek mythology had since ancient times ascribed to certain gods, such as Apollo, Asklepios, and Hermes, and which later became an essential attribute of the mystery gods, was conferred upon the Ptolemies in Egypt and the Seleucidae in Syria, in imitation of Babylonian and Egyptian models. In 48 B.C. a decree of the people of Ephesus had declared Julius Caesar to be "God upon earth" and the "general saviour of mankind," and since then, the epithet "Saviour" became an accepted title of the Roman Emperor. The title "Saviour of the entire human race," "Saviour of the world," is always to be found in the list of honorific imperial names, until the Roman Emperor himself bowed before the one true Saviour. Thus the Roman Emperors stood in the same line as the Saviour figures of the mystery religions. Popular devotion made no distinction between them, but identified them as one.

Only the Christian Saviour cannot be placed into this line. He was different, "utterly different," the true Saviour. It was not simply that he claimed to be more exalted than the other Saviours. He did not recognize these others, nor acknowledge their right—not even the Saviour figure of the Emperor. This was the deepest reason for the persecution of the Christians on the part of the Roman state. The Christians were sooner willing to be murdered in thousands than recognize the imperial Soter or range him side by side with Christ.

This leads us to conclude that the Christian belief in the Saviour was felt from the very beginning to be quite different, essentially foreign, indeed essentially opposed to the other ancient Saviour beliefs. It developed not in dependence upon them, but in opposition to them. So they cannot have produced it.

The θεῖοι ἄνθρωποι

The purely mythological Saviour figures of the ancient mysteries are simply irrelevant in the question whether the Christian faith could have developed out of the Hellenistic belief in God the Saviour. But there are in Hellenism certain figures of God the Saviour that are not only of mythological origin but were historical phenomena; divinized men (θεῖοι ἄνθρωποι). Did they perhaps have some effect upon the emergence of the Christian belief in God the Saviour? The facts are these: There are in Hellenism Saviour figures that, like Christ, have not arisen from the symbols of mythology but are historical personalities; in full recognition of their historical origins, they were taken up by the devotion of the faithful into the circle of redeemer divinities. Examples of such divinities are Simon, Menander, Dositheus, and Elchasai, Apollonius of Tyana, and Peregrinus Proteus. Do we really have a case here of a parallel or even of a causal relationship with the Christian belief in the Saviour?

One thing above all we must affirm: these men were exalted to the dignity of gods not by the piety of faith—not even by the strength of the community's faith—but were declared to be gods by some imperial decree or by their own claim. Only then did the faithful gather round them. So their cult cannot be put forward as testimony to the creative power of the community's faith. On the contrary, it is evidence that even in a world yearning after miracles and divinities, the process of divinization can take place only if it is first set afoot by some positive stimulus, from the cult god himself, or by some imperial command. The legend does not create the hero, but the hero the legend. Looking at the impulses and energies that release a mythology, we learn this: Firstly, a fairly long time is necessary for a cult legend to develop. The moment of divinization is usually preceded either by a decree from some high authority, or by the hero's own pretension to divinity. Secondly, it is significant that the divinization of the Hellenistic Saviours was always total. The result of their synthesis of the divine and the human was not a God-man, a God become flesh as in the Christian faith, but a god walking on the earth. A complete transformation of human into divine takes place, so that absolutely nothing is left of the original human but the outward appearance. Hellenistic divinization takes place strictly within the Gnostic and Docetic framework. Simon, Menander, Apollonius are, from the moment they are honoured as Saviours, no longer regarded as men but as gods disguised. And with a grandiose ἐγώ εἰμι, they themselves claim to be the perfect manifestation of the Godhead. Every trace of consciousness that they still belong to mankind has disappeared. As god, they are solely the object of a cult. The faithful see in their Saviour not the means, the way, to the highest divinity, but the divinity itself. This is how these gods come to lose, even for the faithful, every palpable and precise characteristic. They are caught up into the shifting lines of mythology, and the law of mythology fulfils itself in them—i.e., they are soon to be transformed, like all the other gods, melting into each other, until finally they achieve the character of a pure nature symbol.

This very transience of all original human traits, this unchecked, extravagant exaggeration of all attributes, reveals the play of blind popular fantasy, and a quite unrealistic mysticism of feeling. This is sheer irrational emotionalism run wild. For it is founded not upon a certain verifiable historical happening but on uncontrollable excess of feeling.

How differently the early Christians cling to their historical picture of Jesus! From their viewpoint, Christ is now and ever shall be *totus homo,* a man to be comprehended in his historical manifestation, his claims and utterances, his living and suffering, all through an historical approach. And in affirming his divinity, he does not, like the Hellenistic Saviours, lose all measure and moderation. Jesus knows that in his human existence he is dependent upon the Father. The Father is greater than he. Even in John's account, this God become man retains his subordination and obedience to the Father. The whole picture of Christ does not radiate the crude colours of an uncontrolled excess of feeling, but rather the pure light of historical knowledge.

This is why Christianity differs so completely from the Hellenistic mysteries in its way of redemption, and thus in its entire idea of redemption. As far as sorrow and death could come upon the Hellenistic Saviours, their suffering and dying was not filled with a moral content, just as it was not brought about by an act of moral freedom. It was rather a suffering and death that came upon the gods of redemption by fate—accidentally, as it were. This was a suffering without any moral intent—certainly without any intent of redemption. The content of the mysteries is mostly an excessive longing for love, a madness of love, followed by murder of the mystery gods out of jealousy or despair. As far as the Hellenistic Saviours do appear as concrete personalities—for example, Apollonius of Tyana—their suffering and death are certainly not the centre and purpose of their life. Rather they were imposed upon them by fate. When Apollonius was brought before the imperial judges, he made himself invisible, and thus escaped suffering. From the Hellenistic viewpoint the gods were only nature sublimated; they arose from the conditions of nature, and were bound to fate even as nature itself. Thus the redemption the Hellenists expected from these gods was conceived of purely externally. By imitating their suffering in the mystery rites, they thought to experience the gods' revivification also. This is particularly clear in the Isis mysteries, as Minucius Felix presents them in his dialogue *Octavius* (ch. 22): ". . . saw the sacred ceremonies and mysteries. Isis mourns for her lost son, laments him and goes in search of him with her dog-headed companion and shorn priests. And the poor worshippers of Isis beat their breasts and thus imitate the unhappy mother's grief. When her son is found, Isis rejoices, the priests exult, and the dog-headed finder is puffed with pride. And year after year unceasing she goes on losing what she has found and finding what she has "lost." The sad fate that Iris suffers with her child in the mysteries is imitated by the devotee purely in externals. It is essentially *imitative magic,* not a conscious entering into the free sacrifice of the Saviour. And we must not forget: at the centre of all these cult legends was the cult god's extravagant pretension to divinity. The redemption consisted in being completely merged into the god, and becoming one with him. It assumed the annihilation of the self and to this extent was, like the figure of the Saviour, understood pantheistically. Because the idea of redemption was understood not as spiritual and moral, but as physical and ritual, their way of redemption—or rather their technique of redemption—was also purely physical, not to say physiological. By means of harsh asceticism (sometimes, as in the case of the devotees of Attis, by unnatural castration) or by means of the exact opposite in excess of passion, and frenetic exaltation in the intoxication of wine or love, they thought to reach the highest aim of asceticism—complete annihilation of self, and divinization in ecstasy. There is nothing personal or moral to be apprehended in this way of redemption.

This too reveals the enormous gulf between the Christian idea of redemption and the Hellenistic. The same basic concepts are manifest in each: rebirth, life, light, knowledge—and yet the content on either side is utterly different. The Christian Saviour from the beginning is regarded as the Saviour of the soul, as the liberator from sin and redeemer for a new and holy life in God. The Redeemer himself takes the cross upon him, and the burden of man's sin, because he "has not come to be served, but to serve and to give his life as a ransom for many" (Matt. 20.28). Even in its very beginnings, early Christianity was perfectly clear about this, and there was no ambiguity about the Church's proclamation. A careful reading of the New Testament texts—especially the Epistles of St. Paul, the first Epistle of St. Peter, and the Epistle to the Hebrews—shows that even in the time of the first Apostles the avowal of Christ's death for our redemption had come to be a kind of standing formula, a kind of symbol. This is particularly clear in St. Paul's assurance in 1 Corinthians 15.3 ff.: "For I delivered to you first of all, what I also received, that Christ died for our sins according to the Scriptures, and that he was buried, and that he rose again on the third day, according to the Scriptures." This double assurance "according to the Scriptures," as well as the emphasis that he rose again on the third day, is by no means necessary to the context. Obviously Paul is here (and in Acts 13.26 ff.) making use of a formula familiar to the Christians, though we will leave it an open question whether it is a community symbol or a baptismal confession. 1 Timothy 6.1 ff. would suggest that the latter was more likely. Here Paul expressly reminds his disciples of the "good confession" which he made "before many witnesses" (cf. 2 Tim. 2.2). It is a baptismal confession to God and to Christ and to the eternal life (see Feine, *Die Gestalt des apostolischen Glaubensbekenntnisses,* 1925, p. 54). 1 Peter 3.18 ff. points to the same baptismal confession. The Epistle is a kind of baptismal sermon. Peter catalogues the events relevant to our salvation in a sequence strikingly similar to later symbolic formulations, and the suffering, death, resurrection, and transfiguration of Christ in particular are vividly presented to the faithful as the model and authority for their own Christian death. In this respect Hebrews 6.1 ff. is particularly characteristic. The "foundation" (θεμέλιον) of the entire Christian teaching is said to be repentance, faith towards God, baptism, the laying-on of hands, the resurrection of the dead, and the eternal judgement. The basis of later Apostolic symbolism can already be seen here. New Testament studies reveal more and more that the *didactic* formulations of the Christian teachings do not make their first appearance in the pastoral letters, but can be discovered as early as the oldest New Testament epistles. Even in the early Church there was a solid, sharp awareness of doctrine, a clear theology. That is why it had no room for the vagaries of anti-Christian pagan imaginings, and the wild fantasies of the mystery legends. From the beginning the Christian proclamation was presented in clear doctrinal formulations. The Apostles knew what they wanted. From the beginning there was an unmistakable *doctrina christiana.* This was the foundation of the missionary sermons. It was at the heart of the Christian preparations for baptism, and the foremost avowal of the baptismal confession of faith. Within so clear a doctrinal concept there was no room for a gradual unfolding of Christology, and certainly not for a change in the presentation of the figure of Christ.

To sum up: The belief in Christ cannot have been born either of the Hellenistic divine Saviour figures themselves or of the Hellenistic idea of salvation; between the Hellenistic and the Christian Saviours yawns an unbridgeable abyss. The convert from Hellenism to Christianity comes from a world of fantastic excess into a world of clearly delineated bright reality, into daylight—and history. And he comes from a world of naïve superficiality and coarse sensuality into the inner world of the soul and the spirit, where forgiveness of sins, love, and peace are the reigning powers. There is no unison between these, only stark opposition. It is impossible for Christianity to have arisen from something so essentially antithetical to it. It can only have developed not dependent upon the Hellenistic mysteries, but in opposition to them. Acts 12.20-23 offers particularly strong support for this fact. The early Christian community at Cæsarea repudiated the deification of a ruler which appeared there in particularly crude form (see S. Lösch, *Deitas Jesu und antike Apotheose*, 1933, pp. 10 ff.). We need only recall the bloody martyrdoms of the first three centuries. They are overwhelming proof that the first Christians knew how sharply opposed they were to pagan myth and cult, and that they would sooner give up their lives than ally themselves to such imaginings.

Since there is no connexion between the early Christian tidings of Christ and the Hellenistic belief in the Saviour, we may ask where and what are the true sources of the early Christian faith. In subsequent chapters we shall suggest that the immediate source is to be found in the Lord's own statements about himself, in his own consciousness and understanding of his nature and identity, and that the remoter sources come not from Hellenism but from the Jewish prophecies, from the circle of revelation. The longing for the Saviour and even his actual image can in essentials be deduced simply from the Old Testament and its subsidiary writings.

However, before we establish our views about the Lord's self-consciousness, we shall first approach the question whether the Christian faith cannot be confirmed purely psychologically, by merely analyzing the present belief in Christ, above and beyond any historical mediation. This would, of course, by no means detract from the strictly historical foundation of the belief in Christ. Our belief in Christ is not a blind faith, but a rational one, capable of justifying itself in face of criticism. We still have a great deal to say about the intellectual, historically comprehensible foundations of our faith. What we want to answer here is the question: Can the human mind somehow approach the incarnate mystery of the Lord directly, by psychological means, without the intervention of historical insight? Can his truth be experienced in this way above and beyond any labour of the intelligence?

VI

THE APPROACH TO CHRIST OF
RELIGIOUS PSYCHOLOGY

THE HUMAN mind by its very nature has a *disposition* towards the experience of what is holy. It is constructed in a manner that whenever it comes upon a genuine instance of holiness, it is permanently bound to it with absolute certainty. As Rudolf Otto explains in his classic work *The Idea of the Holy* (Eng. tr., rev. ed., London, 1936) this holiness is fundamentally a mystery, something utterly beyond our experience, something "altogether different." The feeling roused in us by holiness is something qualitatively completely different from the feeling evoked by subjective values within us. It is the feeling of being faced by something foreign to us, unknown, strange. The word "mysterious" clearly expresses the content of this emotional experience. We would never call a machine mysterious, even if we had no idea of its construction. Whatever it is, it belongs within our range of experience. But to our sensibilities, what is holy seems on the contrary to belong to a different sphere of existence, occult, transcendent, "numinous," which in its essence seems to be hidden from us. Thus the first mark of holiness is that it has upon us the effect of a mystery, an arcanum. More precisely, it has the effect of a *mysterium tremendum*—i.e., our first impression of it causes us to shrink away from it. A kind of hesitancy, a strange fear rises in us. And this fear too is qualitatively different from the fear we might have of a robber, or of any danger within ourselves. What we fear is this very thing so "altogether different," ineffable, numinous that we discern in holiness. It is not *metus*, but *stupor*. The same kind of shudder is there as in fear of ghosts. Otto maintains that fear of ghosts is nothing but a false offshoot of the true *stupor*, the hesitant fear roused in us at the sight of what is holy. But the same power in holiness that makes us recoil from it as a *mysterium tremendum* draws us to it. It shelters a hidden beauty, loveliness, and nobility which we are unable to utter in words, but which we nevertheless experience. Even as it keeps us at a distance, it draws us to it at the same time. We are compelled, as it were, to look back. A secret longing in us yearns after it. What is holy becomes for us a *mysterium fascinosum*. And this quality of fascination does not entice us after the manner of the beauty and loveliness of this world. It is the ineffable, unutterable, numinous quality that compels us. There is a sense of the awesome in our feeling for its loveliness. And it is this very sense of the awesome that binds us to it, and will not let us go. This tension of opposites, the polarity of these two effects, and the fact that each of these effects is accompanied by the impression of mystery, of the "altogether different"—this is the characteristic of what is holy.

Thus the human soul is organized to experience a value that is qualitatively distinct from all other earthly values. This means there is an organ in our soul sensitive to the supernatural. This supernatural we grasp with our feelings in the experience of the *mysterium tremendum et fascinosum*. It is a peculiar experience, not to be derived from any other, utterly original, but on the other hand directed towards values and realities that cannot be found in the sphere of nature, and in structure utterly different. Everyone can verify this in his own experience. The human spirit is *a priori* possessed of the faculty of discerning the peculiarities of holiness wherever it is genuine and true—not when it occurs in distorted form, as in the appearance of ghosts, but when in fact it works upon us, repelling us and attracting us as the *mysterium tremendum et fascinosum,* thus establishing itself as a genuine manifestation of holiness.

With reference to our problem of whether belief in Christ can be understood on a psychological basis, we can now say that if the figure of Christ were not a genuine manifestation of what is holy, mankind's sense of the numinous would long ago have wearied of him. Christ would not have been able to bind mankind to him for two thousand years, if our numinous sense had not discerned and experienced and gone on experiencing in his incarnate personality a true manifestation of holiness. Simon, Dositheus, Apollonius—all these mystery gods were able to compel the numinous sense of their followers only for a brief while, only for as long as they and their adherents were able to weave the halo of holiness about their heads by magic and suggestion. Once these means ceased—and they could not but cease the moment a critical sense of questioning and doubt arose among the faithful—once the faithful came to look for reasons to support their emotional experience, the devout found nothing more in them to nourish their numinous sense and bind them to their cult. They no longer experienced their Saviours as genuine manifestations of holiness.

Christianity is altogether different. No compulsion, no magic, no suggestion were needed to clothe Christ in the appearance of holiness. He came to his contemporaries as a poor carpenter. As we shall see later on, for a long time he deliberately held back his testimony to his mission. When at last he caused Peter to recognize him as the Christ, he did not work any stupendous miracle and rouse a spurious awe to support this affirmation, but spoke of his suffering soon to come. When he answered Caiaphas' question, "Art thou the Christ?" in the affirmative, he caused himself to be nailed to the cross. The heavenly light had hardly blazed across the darkness before he extinguished it himself. But it was not such lightning, such signs and wonders that led men to him to give him their faith, but, then as now, his mysterious essence, the *mysterium tremendum et fascinosum* of his person. From the moment Peter said, "Master, depart from me, I am a sinful man," for well or ill he was committed to him. From the moment the centurion affirmed, "I am not worthy for you to enter under my roof," he had become one of the faithful, committed to Jesus. This is the same process of flight from Jesus and commitment to him that it has been through the centuries. He will always be the awe-inspiring figure from which we shrink, and always the supremely lovable one towards whom we yearn. There will always be men who cry *"Crucifige,"* and always men to kiss his feet and anoint them. And they will often be the same men. Such is the history of Christianity, the history of the *mysterium tremendum et fascinosum* revealed in the figure of God incarnate. We cannot escape this figure, neither by violence nor by destructive criticism. How rapidly we were able to deal with the mystery gods! The critical sense had only to prick its ears a little, and their shapes became ridiculous. But no critical sense can dissipate the figure of Christ. It will be able to erase or correct this or that historical account in the Gospels. Indeed, if it is bold and frivolous enough, it can condemn the entire Gospel account as a myth. It can accuse the Christian preachers, the Christian Church, the Catholic Church of being a farrago of stupidity and brutality, but it can never prevent men from experiencing the manifestation of holiness in Christ; it cannot prevent their most delicate sensibilities from affirming: He, he alone is the Holy One of God. In him alone truth and light have dawned. "Whither shall we go? Thou alone hast the word of eternal life."

So in the light of the history of the Christian faith, we can affirm this: Just as the belief in God incarnate did not arise merely historically, merely by means of written documents, not by "flesh and blood," but directly from the Father through an experience of Grace, so even today it does not come to us through human arguments, but by way of a direct *encounter in Grace with the Lord,* with the manifestation of holiness. Because this belief was not created by man, it cannot be threatened or destroyed by man either. Neither the sword of the Caesars nor the knife of the critics will ever probe as far as the innermost reaches, the true home of our faith, as far as the *scintilla animae,* as the mystics put it, as far as the point where God and man come into contact, where the delicate sense of the divine dawns upon us, and causes us to testify before the figure of the Son of God: If the divine be anywhere, it is here in Christ Jesus. Certainly, Buddha and Mohammed also live on in the cult of the faithful. But we have already established at the beginning of our lectures that neither religious founder stands as Christ does at the heart of their faith. Not their persons but their messages are central to their religions. So we cannot speak of a numinous commitment to their persons, but only of a religious commitment to their messages. Even from the point of view of Christianity it is certainly possible that genuine numinous elements are to be found in these messages, working upon the faithful. But they lead only to legalized attitudes, confirmed by maxims and standards, and so always bear the stamp of the impersonal and factual. They lack the living, dynamic, inexhaustible, ever-renewed spirit that is to be discerned in Christianity, in which faith is so eminently personal an act, the last surrender to the divine person whose infinite depths are the source of ever new energies and impulses of faith, and ever new possibilities of life and experience.

Having followed the psychological traces of Christ's mystery, we now turn back to the historical way of apprehending it. On this way, we have so far been able to assert the following: Firstly, it is certain and historically demonstrable that the early Christian community in Jerusalem had already set Christ on the side of God and attributed divine properties to him. They called him the "author of life," "the Lord and the Christ," "Judge of the living and of the dead." These articles of faith in the early Church are the more significant when we remember that it was made up of former Jews, who thought in strictly monotheistic terms.

Secondly, it is certain and historically demonstrable that on account of this monotheistic belief in the Jerusalem community there can be no question that the statements of Christ's divinity in the Gospels originated in the community itself.

Thirdly, the essential difference between the pagan-Hellenistic Saviours and the Christian Saviour—who, after all, was confirmed by the early Church's three hundred years of martyrdom—does not admit the possibility that the belief in the divinity of Christ could have arisen on Hellenistic ground. The only conclusion left is that this belief must go back to Christ's own testimony as to himself, to what he said himself about his divine nature. Without some such instigation from Christ himself, it would be incomprehensible how Jews and Hellenists alike could come upon the idea of ranging Jesus, who was crucified, at the side of God.

Now that we have come to know and appreciate the early community's belief in Christ, we may turn our attention to the ultimate historical source of belief, Jesus' own testimony as to himself.

VII

CHRIST'S CONSCIOUSNESS OF BEING THE MESSIAS

WHEN Jesus came into the world, his Jewish contemporaries were full of hope for the immediate coming of a king and a Messias. They called this king and Messias whom they awaited "Mashiah"—that is, the Anointed of God. In John 1.41; 4.25 the Aramaic term "Mashiah" is rendered by the Greek term "Messias."

The Prophetic and late Judaic idea of the Messias

Influenced by the apocalyptic writings, late Jewry had markedly revised the old prophetic idea of the Messias. The prophetic ideal of the Messias had taken up the idea of the offspring of David marvelously born of a virgin's womb, endowed with divine power, wisdom, and holiness, who would renew David's kingdom in a higher spiritual sense, so that the Gentiles would freely bow down to him, and under his leadership create a kingdom of righteousness and peace. The crude nationalistic tendency of the Pharisees coarsened this prophetic image into a political shibboleth. They hoped the Messias would set up a kingdom of earthly glory. But since the decline of the Jewish kingdom had broken down the natural foundation for this ideal, the hopeful gaze of the devout turned completely to the world beyond, and to the last things. The *eschatological* image of the Messias arose. It was in the most devout and quiet circles in the country that a kingdom of the future was awaited, which would come down to earth from the clouds of heaven bringing the new reign of God. The source of this hope was the Book of Daniel. Within the framework of this new belief in the coming kingdom, the Messias was regarded as the *king of the end of the world*. The Psalms of Solomon from the middle of the first century before Christ were the first to put a messianic interpretation on Psalm 2.2: "The kings of the earth rise up and the princes take counsel together against the Lord and against his Anointed," and thus brought the expression Messias (the Anointed) into current terminology. A small circle of the faithful put a purely spiritual interpretation upon this king of the end, but the majority involved it in political ideals. Even Philo says that "a man will come, going out into battle and waging war, who will coerce great and populous nations, and God will send the saints the aid they need" (*De Praemiis et poenis*, 16). Even in the New Testament, the hopes for the coming of a Messias and king glimmer through, though not in a purely eschatological form, but after the manner of the prophets (cf. the Benedictus and the Magnificat). This expectation of the Messias and king can be discovered partly in the doubting question the Jewish authorities addressed to John the Baptist: "Art thou the Christ?" (Luke 3.15; John 1.19); in the Baptist's own question to Jesus: "Art thou he who is to come, or shall we look for another?" (Matt. 11.3); and also in the reception Jesus had among the people. The cry of the demoniac, "I know who thou art, the Holy One of God" (Mark 1.24), shows to what degree these people's minds were living in expectation of the One who was to come. And the enthusiasm with which the people greeted Jesus on his entry into Jerusalem is a major factor too, as is the high priest's question: "I conjure thee by the living God to tell us whether thou art the Christ" (Matt. 26.63). The Acts of the Apostles (5.36) tells of the uprising of Theodas, "claiming to be somebody"—most likely the Messias. The expectation of him who was to come lay in the air. The mental climate in which Jesus lived was messianistic.

Jesus' consciousness of being the Messias

Jesus' entire behaviour demonstrates that he knew himself to be the Messias-King. The entire Gospel tradition assumes this consciousness as a matter of course. For, as all four

Gospels report, Jesus entered Jerusalem as the Messias. In his trial, he is referred to as the "King of the Jews" (John 18.33, 39; 19.3, 14; Mark 15.9, 12). He replies in the affirmative to the high priest's question whether he is the Christ (Matt. 27.11; Mark 15.2; Luke 23.3; John 18.36 f.). Out of mockery he is garbed in purple and crowned with thorns (Matt. 27.27 ff.). The inscription which the Roman Procurator has put at his head on the cross as the reason for his execution was: "Jesus of Nazareth, the King of the Jews" (John 19.19; cf. Matt. 27.37; Mark 15.26; Luke 23.38). It is clear that the public at least was aware that Jesus regarded himself as the Messias and King.

It is true there have been not a few scholars (Wrede, Dalman, Bousset, Norden) who have thrown doubt upon the historical validity of the Gospel account that Jesus was condemned to death because he maintained he was the Messias. The Law of Mishnah did not decree that the claim to be the Messias was a capital offence. It did not regard the offence as *gidduf*, or blasphemy. For the Jews of the time did not regard the awaited Messias as a divine being, but as a man peculiarly endowed with Grace and summoned by God. It was therefore not blasphemy against God if someone falsely pretended to be the Messias. Jewish law could not have condemned Jesus to death because he claimed to be the Messias. Even though his external appearance as a prisoner was in sharp contrast to his claim to be the Messias, it was not a question of this being blasphemy that called forth the judgement upon him. According to the testimony of the Gospels, the situation is rather this: The Roman, Pilate, condemned Jesus to death, even though he was not convinced of his guilt, because Jesus had publicly declared himself to be the king of the Jews ("I am a king, you say")—i.e., for political reasons. The Sanhedrin, however, followed the law and condemned Jesus for a religious offence—blasphemy. But this blasphemy for them did not lie in the Lord's avowal that he was the Christ. According to the idiom of the time this avowal would not have gone beyond the plain claim to be the Messias in the sense of being the Son of God morally and theocratically, but not physically and naturally. Jesus' blasphemy lay rather in his avowal that he was a divine Messias, or more precisely in the additional claim on which he based his messianic divinity: "And you shall see the Son of Man sitting at the right hand of the Power and coming on the clouds of heaven" (Mark 14.62). According to Jewish usage of the period, the image of sitting at the right hand of the Power could mean only taking part in the dominion of God. The Jewish Sanhedrin saw in this a blasphemous self-identification with God. And therefore it condemned Jesus to death.

Jesus' command that the Apostles be silent

But are we still really upon historical ground here? Or has this testimony of Jesus' as to his own identity been put into the Lord's mouth at a later date by the community of the faithful? The negative critics think that they can bring some support to this latter theory, making it probable that Jesus himself acknowledged no awareness of being the divine Messias.

According to the Synoptic Gospels, the men possessed of devils immediately recognized in Jesus the "Holy One of God" —i.e., the Messias (Mark 1.24; 3.11). But Jesus sternly forbids them to speak of it. And Jesus himself keeps to this commandment of silence even after Peter's avowal at Cæsarea Philippi that he was the Christ. "And he strictly charged them to say nothing about him to anyone" (Mark 8.30). And John too reports (John 6.14, 15) that Jesus withdrew to the solitude of the mountains when the crowd began to guess at his messianic secret and cry aloud in their enthusiasm: "This is indeed the prophet who is to come into the world." It would seem that Jesus wanted to avoid proclaiming he was the Messias. Did he himself perhaps have doubts about his calling? The same John testifies that even the Lord's closest relations were uncertain about his messianic mission. "For not even his brethren believed in him" (7.5). So they demanded of him that he work his miracles not only in obscurity but also openly in public in Judaea (6.3, 4; cf. John 10.19 ff.). When John the Baptist sends to ask him if he is he who is to come, Jesus does not give a decisive answer, but refers to the fulfilment of Old Testament prophecies: "the blind see, the lame walk," etc. (Matt. 11.2 ff.). Light is also thrown on Jesus' reluctance to admit in public that he is the Messias when the Scribes and Pharisees challenge him to work a "sign" to prove he is the Messias. "Master, we would see a sign from thee" (Matt. 12.38). He never wrought a miracle of his own accord for the purpose of demonstrating that he was the Messias.

So, according to the Synoptic Gospels, Jesus refrained from publicly claiming to be the Messias. What is the explanation of this? Wrede's answer is that the historical Jesus was never aware of being the Messias. According to this theory, the company of the Apostles did not proclaim him to be such until after his resurrection. And in order to explain why Jesus himself in his lifetime never did so, the Evangelists ascribed to him a policy of subterfuge and silence. They make it appear as if Jesus intentionally avoided speaking in clear terms of being the Messias in order to punish the malice of the Jews, so devoid of any desire for the truth. Jesus' policy of subterfuge and silence, especially as presented in the Gospel according to St. Mark, would ultimately seem to have been a literary device of the Evangelists to disguise the striking fact that Jesus himself never made public proclamation that he was the Messias. In this way they attempted to project the belief in the Messias that first arose out of the belief in the resurrection back into the historical lifetime of Jesus. But in reality, precisely this literary special pleading proves that Jesus never in the true sense declared himself to be the Messias.

Is there any justification for this theory? If we probe the texts, we do in fact seem to be confronted with a strange contradiction. A group of texts does in fact exist in which Jesus forbids any public proclamation that he is the Messias. But this is not the entire historical truth. There is on the other hand a group of passages in which Jesus openly affirms that he is the Messias. With the same distinctness as they testify to the Lord's reserve in his proclamation, the Gospels also testify to the fact that from the beginning he felt himself to be the Messias and the King. They are at one in their account of his baptism, according to which Jesus hears the voice from heaven saying, "This is my beloved Son, in whom I am well pleased." As early as his first appearance in public, Jesus is aware of being the beloved Son of the Father in a quite special sense. The Synoptic Gospels go on to tell how reluctant John is to baptize the Lord, because his prophetic eye discerns one who is free from sin. "It is I who ought to be baptized by thee, and dost thou come to me?" (Matt. 3.14.). The Baptist knows of Jesus' peculiar majesty and peculiar mission. The Evangelists tell how Jesus does not reject the Baptist's avowal, but quietly rejoins, "Let it be so now, for so it becomes us to fulfil all justice" (Matt. 3.15). If Jesus had not known himself to be the Messias, he would have had to reply with a decisive "no," just as in a similar exchange John the Baptist himself had answered the Pharisees' question "Art thou the Christ? Art thou Elias?" His "no" was unmistakable. "I am not the Christ. I am not

Elias. I am the voice of one crying in the desert." From prison, John sent a disciple to ask Jesus if he were really he who was to come, and Jesus' reply referring to the fulfilment of Isaias' prophecies (35.6; 61.1)— "the blind see, the lame walk," etc. —can be understood only as an affirmation of his power as the Saviour, and as a warning not to be mistaken in him. As for the men possessed by devils, who address him as the Holy One of God (Mark 1.24) and the Son of God (Mark 3.11), he does not tell them they are saying what is untrue, but simply forbids them to chatter of his secret. He does not want this secret to be revealed before it is time, because the Jews would misunderstand its import in political terms. On the other hand, he encourages the possessed man in the region of Decapolis to announce everywhere that he has been healed. Among the Gentiles, he has no fear of being misunderstood (cf. Mark 5.19). Similarly, he does not correct the plea of the two blind men, "Have pity on us, Son of David" (Matt. 9.27). To the Samaritan woman, he acknowledges outright that he is the Messias (John 4.26). Among his disciples he himself takes the initiative in rousing them to affirm that he is the Messias. "But who do you say that I am?" (Matt. 16.15; Mark 8.27). Only then, in the name of the disciples, does Peter avow him to be the Christ. In many cases, Jesus' statements are nothing but a disguised proclamation that he was the Messias—for example, his praise of John the Baptist, in which he draws parallels between him and the Son of Man (Matt. 11.7 ff.). "For John came neither eating nor drinking, and they say, 'He has a devil!' The Son of Man came eating and drinking, and they say, 'Behold a glutton and a wine-drinker, a friend of publicans and sinners!' " Here he is comparing himself with the Baptist —whom Christ himself called the greatest among those born of woman—knowing himself to be greater than he. The same supreme consciousness can be seen in his threat to the unbelieving towns Corozain and Bethsaida. "Woe to thee, Corozain! Woe to thee, Bethsaida! For if in Tyre and Sidon had been worked the miracles that have been worked in you, they would have repented long ago in sackcloth and ashes" (Matt. 11.21 ff.). There is no other way of understanding why Jesus called the disciples blessed when they saw what many prophets and just men had longed to see (Matt. 13.17). In this context the famous maxim is significant: "All things have been delivered to me by my Father; and no one knows the Son except the Father; nor does anyone know the Father except the Son, and him to whom the Son chooses to reveal him. Come to me,

all you who labour and are burdened, and I will give you rest"
(Matt. 11.27 f.). This is something we will discuss more
thoroughly later. By way of experimental demonstration, as it
were, Christ is able to show that he is the Messias by driving
out devils. As he expressly declares: "But if I cast out devils
by the Spirit of God, then the kingdom of God has come upon
you" (Matt. 12.28). In defeating Satan, he preserves his messianic power. The challenge of the Scribes mentioned above,
that he should work a sign (Matt. 12.38 f.), would be quite
incomprehensible if he had not already proclaimed rather
clearly to the Jews that he was the Messias.

There is still an abundance of Jesus' statements whose depths
reveal the Lord's claim to be the Messias. We need only recall
his declarations of his majesty. It is not as if this claim to
majesty were to be discerned only intermittently and in disguise in the Gospels. Rather, they make up the underlying
fabric of the narration, without which it could not be wholly
understood. If we tried to repudiate this claim as unhistorical,
it would mean discrediting the Gospels as literary fabrications,
or at least as a collection of fables and legends. And then we
would be landed back with Renan and his senseless hypothesis
that a deception was being practised.

This is the situation before us. Firstly, Jesus consciously
holds back his claim to be the Messias from the public; and
secondly, from the start he knows he is the Messias and proclaims himself to be such. How can this behaviour of the
Lord's be explained?

The content of Jesus' consciousness of being the Messias

There is an answer for those who desire light, and do not
distort the essential meaning of the Gospel accounts with their
preconceived notions. It lies in Jesus' peculiar ideal of the
Messias. There is no doubt that Jesus felt from the beginning
that he was the promised Messias and King, but in an entirely
different sense and with an entirely different purpose from the
intention of the Jewish people. This immediately brings us to
probe the content of his awareness of being the Messias. He
knew that he was the bringer of redemption, and rebirth into
eternal life. He was concerned not with earthly values but
with spiritual. His kingdom is "not of this world." In order
not to endanger the supernatural, heavenly nature of his ideal,

he was compelled to withhold his public claim to be the Messias until a community of disciples had grown up whom he had schooled to appreciate the new and spiritual nature of his calling. If he had confided his secret to the masses from the start, and publicly affirmed that he was the Messias, their crude mass instincts and one-sided insistence upon a political Messias and King would have endangered, if not prevented, the spiritual aim of his messianic mission. John the Evangelist repeatedly draws attention to this danger when he stresses that even his brethren had no understanding for his message (cf. John 7.3), and that the people "would take him by force and make him king" (John 6.15). There is no doubt that Jesus' caution was well founded. We can indeed rightly speak of a policy of silence and subterfuge on the part of the Lord. But it was a policy with an exclusively religious and moral concern, ultimately dominated by his redeeming love. Where holiness and divinity are the issue, the mental climate must be ruled by reserve and reverence. "Do not give to dogs what is holy."

Let us now briefly confirm from the Gospel texts that Jesus was concerned to secure this holiness, and school his company of Apostles to have a care for it; that he did not start from the late Jewish nationalistic interpretation of the coming Messias held by the Pharisees, but resumed the line of prophetic messianism which promised a Messias who would bring the kingdom of God, forgiveness of sins, and Grace.

Christ's idea of the Messias is illuminated in the detailed accounts given by Matthew and Luke of his temptation. In three successive disputes with the tempter, Jesus regards as devilish insinuations the attempts to debase his messianic authority for earthly purposes—above all, the satisfaction of purely earthly needs ("If thou art the Son of God, command that this stone become a loaf of bread"); further, outward achievement and popular recognition ("If thou art the Son of God, throw thyself down from here"); and finally political power ("If thou wilt worship before me, the whole shall be thine"). Jesus' ideal of the Messias, which can be deduced from these temptations, is not concerned with personal influence, success, and power, but with the kingdom of God alone, and religious and spiritual values. His dispute with Peter at Cæsarea Philippi lies along the same line. When Peter tries to dissuade him from taking the way of suffering, Jesus regards it as a temptation of the devil ("Get behind me, Satan!" Mark 8.33). The ideal of power and glory that Peter suggests to him he rejects in order to set up his ideal of simple, pure, unselfish service of the kingdom of God, of the ultimate, absolute commitment to the divine. He knows he has been called to fulfil and develop the "Law," that essence of morality and holiness. "Do not think that I have come to destroy the Law or the Prophets. I have not come to destroy, but to fulfil" (Matt. 5.17). This fulfilment lies in the interpretation and realization down to the last detail of the true meaning of the Law—love of God and one's neighbour, which is the existential pledge for God and his kingdom. With the same breath as he assures his hearers, "All these things have been delivered to me by my Father," he goes on to say, "Come to me, all you who labour and are burdened" (Matt. 11.27 ff.). The power he has from the Father is to him the power of redemption. He is concerned to found the kingdom of God within the newly redeemed soul. That is why the Son of Man is "come" to seek and to save what is lost (Luke 19.10). In the Sermon on the Mount he reveals this as his true plan, and the content of his proclamation. "Blessed are the poor in spirit . . . blessed are the meek . . . blessed are they who mourn . . . blessed are they who hunger and thirst for justice . . . blessed are the merciful" (Matt. 5.3 ff.). What he is saying there means a transvaluation of all values. The Messias is not concerned with outward power and glory, but with redemption from bodily and spiritual suffering. The Messias serves as a Son and a servant for the sake of the kingdom of heaven. "The Son of Man has not come to be served, but to serve, and to give his life as a ransom for many" (Matt. 20.28). At the last supper, this will to messianic sacrifice is concentrated into the moving act of his sacramental sacrifice in the form of the bread and the wine. "Take and eat; this is my body. All of you drink of this; for this is my blood of the new covenant, which is being shed for many unto the forgiveness of sins." This messianic way of sacrifice, poverty, and lowliness was the path along which Jesus wanted to lead mankind to the community of God in which he himself essentially lived.

Such a spiritual ideal of the Messias, with no regard for outward, earthly desires, moving towards the rebirth of the inner man, was something strange and incomprehensible to the majority of Jews of the time. This would explain the incomprehension of the disciples, the dawning doubt of John the Baptist, and the final estrangement of the Jewish masses from him. After all, they had expected an utterly different Messias, one who would bring victory and overwhelming outward achievement. So Jesus the pedagogue did wisely to hide his secret from the masses at first, and disclose it only gradually and cautiously to those who under his teaching had become pure and strong enough to see it.

Only by way of this great restraint was it possible for him to announce his new message, if he did not want to run the danger of being completely misunderstood even from the start. His whole policy of subterfuge can be entirely explained by the special nature of his ideal of the Messias.

The way Jesus refers to himself, the names with which he expresses the nature of his being, like "Son of Man" and "Son," can ultimately be understood from the half-affirmative, half-deprecating attitude of the Lord towards his contemporaries' expectation of the Messias. These self-designations throw a final, illuminating light upon the reserved manner with which Jesus established his claim to be the Messias. We will therefore devote particular attention to them.

VIII

CHRIST'S CONSCIOUSNESS OF
BEING THE SON OF MAN

The literal meaning of the phrase "Son of Man"

JESUS is fond of calling himself "the Son of Man" (ὁ υἱὸς τοῦ ἀνθσώπου). In the Synoptic Gospels, both nouns always have the definite article. It is never a case of "a son of man," but always "the Son of Man." No other figures ever refer to Jesus as the Son of Man. The name is always the Lord's own designation of himself. It occurs thirty times in St. Matthew's Gospel, fourteen times in St. Mark's, and twenty-five times in St. Luke's. In the Gospel according to St. John the term is found twelve times with the article, and once without (5.27).

Since Jesus spoke Aramaic, not Greek, we have to go back to the Aramaic expression. This can only have been *bar nasha,* or in the dialect *bar enasha.* Philological research shows that *bar nasha* is to be translated by "man." The expression "son" renders a genitive relationship. For example, the phrase in Matthew 9.15, which the King James version of the Bible renders literally as "children of the bridechamber," really indicates some state of belonging to the bridegroom—the friends of the bridegroom, or, as the Douay version puts it, the "wedding guests." Similarly, the phrase "son of the field" means a peasant, and "Son of Man" indicates a relationship of belonging to mankind—or man in general (*homo aliquis*). So Jesus described himself as the Son of Man, or man in general. Strictly speaking, the Greek translation should have run thus: υἱὸς ἀνθσώπου (the Son of a man), because in Greek it is the first of a dual idea that carries the article, and not, as in

Aramaic and Hebrew, the second. So the Greek translation gives a literal rendering of the Aramaic, departing from normal Greek usage—an Aramaicism. In any case, in our exposition we have to keep to the interpretation that "Son of Man" is the equivalent of "Man."

How is this expression to be understood as Jesus uses it? A great variety of explanations have been attempted. Since the second century, the Greek and Latin Fathers of the Church understood it as a reference to Christ's human origin. They too read "man" for "Son of Man," but in doing so overlooked the mystery lying behind the word. F. C. Baur put forward the opinion that Jesus called himself the Son of Man, stressing the baser sense of the term so as to imply that nothing human was strange to him, in deliberate contrast to the exclusive Jewish expectation of a political national Messias. Herder and Schleiermacher defended the interpretation that Jesus stressed the higher sense of the term, so as to proclaim himself to be the ideal man, the highest achievement of pure and noble humanity. The majority of the new interpretations—indeed almost all of them—understand the "Son of Man" in messianic terms. Which of all these explanations is the right one?

The Son of Man in Daniel

We can answer this question only if we have a clear idea of the early history of the expression. As in other instances, Jesus is here taking up a late Judaic use of language. It was the Book of Daniel that first spoke of one "like the son of man." Four great beasts came up one after the other out of the sea. According to Daniel 7.17, they symbolize the four kingdoms that will arise upon earth. Their power will be taken away, and their times of life were appointed them down to the last day. And then the seer continues: "I beheld therefore in the vision of the night, and lo, one like the son of man came with the clouds of heaven. And he came even to the Ancient of Days: and they presented him before him. And he gave him power and glory and a kingdom. . . . His power is an everlasting power that shall not be taken away: and his kingdom shall not be destroyed" (7.13 ff.). And the prophet concludes: "But the saints of the most high God shall take the kingdom: and they shall possess the kingdom for ever and ever" (7.18).

This context should make it clear that by the term "one like the son of man" Daniel intended the people of the saints of the most high God, symbolized and expressed by the "one like the son of man," just as the four beasts were the symbol and expression of the nations that were cast down. But we must note that the symbol does not refer to the historical tribe of the children of Israel, which then as now did not come with the clouds of heaven, but was firmly bound to the earth. It referred to the descent of a new people, a people of saints, which in its entire disposition comes "from heaven," i.e., is supernatural (cf. Isa. 14.14). And the one like the son of man is the original personification and symbol of this new people. As the one like the son of man came even to the Ancient of Days, so too did the people of the saints symbolized in him. It is therefore pre-existent. The Jewish apocalyptic writer Ezra (4.9, 38 ff.) already speaks of this pre-existence, and so does Paul, who refers Isaias 54.1 to Jerusalem: "Rejoice thou barren, that dost not bear" (Gal. 4.26). Daniel's prophecy reaches its climax in the proclamation that in the place of the kingdom of this world, a spiritual kingdom of God would appear, and that this kingdom was in its basic form pre-existent. To what extent is it pre-existent? Late Judaic apocalyptic writings are relevant here. They regarded the one like the son of man not simply as the symbol of the people of the saints, but also as their original representative, and they ascribed to him a personal pre-existence in the presence of the Ancient of Days. He is himself, as Origen was later to put it, the kingdom (αὐτοβασιλεία). The kingdom has its original reality in him. It has already been founded and made manifest in his person. This interpretation is to be found in the symbolic speeches in the Book of Henoch (37–71), which were possibly written before Christ's time (probably between 170 and 160 B.C.). The fourth Book of Esdras, written in A.D. 70 after the destruction of Jerusalem, similarly testifies to the same tradition of the son of man, which must have arisen before that time, for in A.D. 70 the term already had the character of a formula. But neither in Esdras nor in Henoch is the expression "son of man" an attribute of the Messias, i.e., a clear formula of a creed, or an unmistakable dogmatic concept. It is simply one of the many names given to the Messias, and one that is intentionally veiled in the obscurity of mystery, a kind of riddle from which one has to guess that the Messias is meant.

The term "the Son of Man" in Jesus' proclamation

In adopting this usage, Jesus too referred Daniel's vision of the "one like the son of man" exclusively to a pre-existent personal Messias. The "Son of Man" to him is a kind of quotation from Daniel, "man," as it were, personified. Contemporary Jewish apocalyptic writings designated this "man" more precisely as a heavenly being, a being that in pre-existence stands before the Ancient of Days and comes with the clouds of heaven. It has been rightly pointed out (H. Gressmann, *Eschatologie*, 1905, p. 243) that Daniel also describes the angels, heavenly spiritual beings, as "like the son of man." Daniel (8.15) says that Gabriel has "the appearance of a man," and in 9.21 calls him outright "the man Gabriel." The prophet is readily familiar with the connexion between human and heavenly beings. In any case, the figure of the son of man included something supernatural and heavenly.

To what extent did Jesus use the term "Son of Man" in Daniel's sense? Was this the exclusive meaning of his own description of himself? Only a close study of the Gospel texts will solve this problem.

The following observations can be made: The Gospels make a precise distinction between the "Son of Man" in the messianic sense and "man" in the usual sense, even though the meaning of the Aramaic term is simply "man." Frequently the terms "Son of Man" and "man" occur close together in the same context, so that there is a possibility that they might be confused. But they never are. For example, Jesus says (Mark 2.27): "The Sabbath was made for man, and not man for the Sabbath. Therefore the Son of Man is Lord even of the Sabbath." Here the form "Son of Man" occurs only at the point where the issue is raised of Jesus' messianic actions and his sovereign authority in interpreting the law of the Sabbath. Matthew 11.19 shows a similar distinction. "The Son of Man came eating and drinking, and they say, 'Behold [the man is] a glutton and a wine-drinker.' " * The verse does not continue "and they say, 'Behold, the Son of Man is . . .' " The messianic overtones in the words "Son of Man" could not be

* The German Biblical text used by Adam runs: *"Siehe, der Mensch ist ein Fresser und Weinsäufer."* The Douay translation omits "the man is." *Trans.*

brought into the same context as gluttons and wine-drinkers.

The Evangelists, then, were at great pains not to confuse the ideas "Son of Man" and "man," and with deliberate intent. On the other hand, there is something else to be observed about the state of the Gospel texts. The Synoptic Gospels shift between using "I" and "the Son of Man." In parallel passages they interchange these two expressions. They never confuse "Son of Man" and "man," but they do confuse "Son of Man" and "I." For example, in Matthew 16.13, Jesus asks: "Who do men say the Son of Man is?"; while in the parallel passages in Mark 8.27 and Luke 9.22, the question runs: "Who do men say that I am?" In the passages where Jesus first teaches of his suffering, it is the other way round, and the term "Son of Man" is used in Mark 8.31 and Luke 9.22, while the analogous passage in Matthew 16.21 uses the third person. Or again, in Matthew 5.11, when Jesus says, "Blessed are you when men reproach you . . . for my sake." In Luke 6.22, on the other hand, the parallel runs, "Blessed shall you be when men hate you . . . because of the Son of Man."

So Jesus' use of the term "Son of Man" to designate himself is an expression of his sublime consciousness of his identity. Remembering this, the Evangelists take care never to interchange "Son of Man" and "man." On the other hand, sometimes they write "Son of Man," and sometimes, with the same import, "I." The phrase "Son of Man" underlines Jesus' self-awareness, stresses his consciousness of identity.

In what sense does he emphasize this identity? A third observation will give us some help here.

In the three Synoptic Gospels the name "Son of Man" is used in a predominantly eschatological sense, with reference to his Parousia, or second coming. It is also used with reference to the coming suffering of the Messias—in a soteriological sense. There is a third group in which it is simply used to point out the messianic task of our Lord.

The term is used with an eschatological and apocalyptic import in Matthew 24.30 (Mark 13.26; Luke 21.27); "And they [all tribes of the earth] will see the Son of Man coming upon the clouds of heaven with great power and majesty." Similarly in Matthew 26.64 (Mark 14.62; Luke 22.69): "Hereafter you shall see the Son of Man sitting at the right hand of the Power and coming upon the clouds of heaven." The reference to Daniel 7.13, 14 is obvious here. The relation to Daniel is evident also in that the whole idea of the divine dominion in the Lord's proclamation can be referred back to

the Book of Daniel. In this passage in the Synoptic Gospels
the ideas of the kingdom of God and the Son of Man are used
with an eschatological, apocalyptic meaning in exactly the
same way as they are in Daniel. A series of similar passages
points in the same direction: "The Son of Man is to come with
his angels in the glory of the Father" (Matt. 16.27; Mark
8.38; Luke 9.26), etc. In these texts, Jesus' designation of himself as the Son of Man is indicative of his mission to come
upon the clouds of heaven, bringing the kingdom of God down
to earth.

But barely half the passages in the Synoptic Gospels that
refer to the Son of Man do so in this apocalyptic sense. This
needs to be emphasized in face of the eschatological school,
whose main thesis is that the early Christian communities saw
in Jesus nothing but the eschatological figure of the Son of
Man who was to come at the end of time, bringing his new
kingdom. In all three Synoptic Gospels the title "Son of Man"
occurs much more frequently in connexion with our Lord's
prophecies of his suffering, i.e., with reference to his deeds in
the present, not in the future. "And he began to teach them
that the Son of Man must suffer many things, and be rejected.
. . ." (Mark 8.31; cf. Luke 9.22; Matt. 17.9, 12, 22; Mark
9.9, 12, 31; Matt. 20.18; Mark 10.45; Matt. 16.21; Mark
14.21, 41; Luke 22.22; Matt. 26.45). In several instances, the
assumption is that this suffering of the Son of Man is rooted
in the will of God, providentially, and already prophesied in
the Old Testament. "The Son of Man must suffer (as it says in
the Scriptures)" (Matt. 16.21; Mark 8.31; Luke 9.22, etc.).
But on no occasion is there a definite reference to precise
passages in the Old Testament. Only Luke 22.37 reports some
words of Jesus' that expressly refer to Isaias' prophecy of the
servant of God.

In addition to the eschatological passages, and those with
soteriological reference to Jesus' suffering, there is also a third
group in which the term "Son of Man" is used, that simply
throw light on Jesus' messianic authority and mission. "That
you may know that the Son of Man has power on earth to
forgive sins," he says to the paralytic, "arise, take up thy
pallet and go to thy house" (Matt. 9.6; Mark 2.10; Luke
5.24). Here the idea of the Son of Man is brought into close
relationship with the power of the Messias to forgive sins.
Further, there is the significant passage: "The Son of Man
is Lord even of the Sabbath" (Matt. 12.8; Mark 2.28; Luke
6.5). "Blessed shall you be when men hate you . . . because

of the Son of Man" (Luke 6.22). As the Messias, Jesus is persecuted. "For even as Jonas was in the belly of the fish three days and three nights, so will the Son of Man be three days and three nights in the heart of the earth" (Matt 12.40; Luke 11.30). "He who sows the good seed is the Son of Man" (Matt. 13.37). "The Son of Man came to seek and to save what was lost" (Luke 19.10). Similarly Matthew 12.32: "And whoever speaks a word against the Son of Man, it shall be forgiven him; but whoever speaks against the Holy Spirit, it will not be forgiven him, either in this world or in the world to come" (Luke 12.10; Mark 3.28 f.). To deny the Son of Man is a sin, but one that can be forgiven. But what can never be forgiven is stubborn resistance to the judgement of conscience endowed by the Holy Spirit.

*   *   *   *

Now that we are familiar with the text, we can approach the question as to the sense in which Jesus described himself as Son of Man. We are now sure that the expression is to be understood neither in the emphatically sublime sense, as Herder and Schleiermacher would have it, nor yet in the baser sense that Baur suggests. Jesus was not addressing philosophers and humanists. The texts would suggest that by calling himself son of man he wanted first and foremost to claim that Daniel's "one like the son of man" and his kingdom of God had been made manifest. The heart of his claim was that "the sign of the Son of Man" will appear in heaven. On the clouds of heaven he will come with the power and the glory, to set up his kingdom and hold the Last Judgement. Here, his office as *ruler* and judge over all mankind at the end of time is proclaimed. And Jesus decides the fate of all mankind, not simply that of the Jews. Jewish nationalism no longer had any place in this idea. Moreover, it also raised Jesus' claim that the true place and home of the Son of Man was in heaven at the right hand of the Ancient of Days. According to Isaias 14.14, coming upon the clouds of heaven is synonymous with the attribute of divinity. The pre-existent Son of Man will stand *at God's side*. Jesus ascribed this heavenly dignity to himself before the Sanhedrin: "You shall see the Son of Man sitting at the right hand of the Power and coming with the clouds of heaven." The Jewish court understood this claim to divinity, and regarded it as blasphemy deserving death. It is true the Synoptic Gospels do not speak expressly of Jesus' consciousness of pre-existence. This is the message of Paul and John. But by describing Jesus as the Son of Man who will come with the clouds of heaven, they are assuming it. Only such descriptions give the ultimate understanding of Jesus' peculiar expressions "I have come," "I have not come." Jesus is in his essence one who "has come," come from a higher supernatural reality, from the right hand of the Ancient of Days. The expressions are very closely related to the similar ideas of "sending" and "having been sent" in Paul and John (cf. John 4.34: "the will of him who sent me"; Rom. 8.3: "By sending his Son . . ."). The idea of pre-existence, which is explicit in Daniel's image of the Son of Man, is implicit in this "coming."

But Jesus' consciousness of being the Son of Man also contains elements that cannot be explained by the Book of Daniel. He is fond of calling himself the Son of Man when he is speaking of his coming suffering. But Daniel's "one like the son of man" suggests no traces of suffering. Jewish dogma of the time of Jesus had no conception of a suffering Messias, only a Messias of glory. Those visions of the prophets that pointed towards suffering were overlooked by the crude thinking of nationalistic Jewry. But Jesus knows that he is called to suffer. "But how then is it written of the Son of Man that he should suffer many things and be despised?" (Mark 9.12). The expression here would suggest a hint at the man of sorrows in Isaias 53.3, "whose look was as it were hidden and despised." In Luke 22.37, the Lord quotes this passage from Isaias word for word: "For I say to you that this which is written must yet be fulfilled in me, 'And he was reckoned among the wicked.'" Similar references to the man of sorrows can be found in those passages that speak of the service of the Messias. "The Son of Man has not come to be served, but to serve, and to give his life as a ransom for many" (Matt. 20.28; Mark 10.45). The phrase "to give his life as a ransom for many," in the context of "serving," is a clear recollection of the man of sorrows in Isaias.

So we may say that Jesus' idea of the Son of Man is not the exact equivalent of Daniel's. Jesus has rather subsumed Isaias' man of sorrows into his idea of Daniel's son of man. This is his *original* creation, the expression of his own awareness of his nature, going beyond all the prophets, and concentrating their scattered illumination into one consciousness that he is the judge and Lord of mankind, called to rule by his messianic deeds and sorrows, the divine redeemer *in via crucis,* by way of the cross.

So Jesus' consciousness of being the Son of Man is made up

of the following elements: He has come from the side of the Ancient of Days and is called to be judge and Lord for all time. To this extent his proclamation is eschatological. But his achievement as a Saviour also concerns the present, in so far as it is an achievement in suffering and death. To this extent his proclamation is a present message. Jesus knows that he is the Saviour of the world of the present. Thus the expression "Son of Man" corresponded completely to the image of the Messias that he bore within himself, the idea that he would suffer for the sins of men and thereafter be judge over men. In contrast to the ideas dominant in the leading Jewish circles, his ideal of the Messias took him to the side of the Ancient of Days. But at the same time he knows that this supernatural glory will not be fulfilled in the present, but only at the end of time. For him, eschatological expectation has not been suspended; it still persists. However, it has been perceptibly slackened, to the extent that he is conscious of being not only Lord and judge of the future, but also the Saviour of the present who can establish the kingdom of God manifest in all its glory, even in the present, "within you" (Luke 17.21). Quietly and all unnoticed, this process will continue upon earth, like the leaven that works through all the three measures of flour, or the mustard seed that grows into a great tree. It is at work in obscurity, not among the great and the wise of this world, but among the humble, the poor and oppressed. So the radiant future and the grave present meet in the consciousness of the Son of Man. This is precisely what proves the Son of Man to be the coming Lord and judge—that he should in the *present* be the Saviour of the poor and oppressed. The eschatological and soteriological instances are inextricably bound together in the image of the Son of Man. They complement each other.

The Son of Man as a transitional concept

Now we can understand why Jesus was so fond of calling himself the Son of Man. The phrase was a circumlocution for his messianic secret that he was on the one hand the coming king of divine dominion and the judge of the world, and on the other the servant of God, who gave his life as a ransom for many. This was both obscured and revealed in his circumlocution. The strange riddle was meant to draw the attention of those who had ears to hear to his manifestation and his calling.

They were to experience in him that he was at the same time Lord of the future and Redeemer of the present, that the past and the present are one in him, and that his time and his generation will come with the turning of time. He proclaims his awareness of his mission only in hints and guesses. There is an isolated Logion of his: "My secret belongs to me and to the sons of my house" (E. Hennecke, *Neutestamentliche Apokryphen*, p. 7). If Jesus had called himself God from the very beginning of his activities, he would have been stoned on the very first day. If he had called himself the Son of God, he would have turned the thoughts of his contemporaries not towards heaven and the right hand of the Ancient of Days, but to the earth and to man. For, as we shall show, the Jews of his time understood by the phrase "sons of God" any created being, the angels in heaven, or the king and the children of Israel. So Jesus could only hint of his secret, and speak in parables. "He did not speak to them without parables." Without this protective covering of metaphor, his testimony as to himself would have been drowned in the roars of laughter of the crowd. He would really have been casting his pearls before swine. It is very likely that Jesus' own experience did confirm the current saying of the swine who trampled pearls underfoot. "Do not give to dogs what is holy, neither cast your pearls before swine, or they will trample them under their feet and turn and tear you" (Matt. 7.6). And the "swine" did in fact later turn on him and tear him, but not until after he had gathered a band of believing disciples about him who could carry on his tidings.

In this light, we may say that the name "Son of Man" was deliberately chosen by Jesus as a *transitional concept*. The policy of subterfuge forced upon him by his external situation would suggest this transitional idea to him. It persisted only for as long as the disciples were being schooled and trained in his secret. When in fact a believing community was finally set up in the company of the disciples, this expression disappeared from Christian usage. It no longer had any inner justification. The parable was revealed, and the mystery unveiled. The expression no longer was the equivalent of the new experiences. Indeed, from the moment Christianity made its way into the Hellenistic world, it could even be misinterpreted to lead away from Jesus' heavenly mystery. For the Hellenists knew nothing of Daniel, nor of his vision of the Son of Man, nor of the true meaning which it was Christ's original act to unite to this concept. And so this particular designation of Jesus can no longer be found in Paul, nor in Christian writing after him, because this was addressed almost exclusively to the Hellenistic world. Even the Apostolic Fathers no longer used it in the old sense. By "Son of Man," Ignatius of Antioch understands nothing more than Jesus' humanity (*Epistola ad Ephesios,* 20.2); so does Irenaeus later (*Adversus Haereses,* 3.19). Barnabas already expressly rejects it, because Jesus is not the Son of Man but the Son of God (*Epistola,* 12.9, 10). Since Justin (*Dialogus,* 76; 100), the expression "Son of Man" has in Christian exegesis without exception signified only the Lord's human nature. Only a few Gnostic sects, such as the Ophites and the Valentinians, made use of the strange expression to carry their own curious riddles. The moment the belief in God the Saviour had taken root, the idea had outlived its usefulness. The Hellenistic attitude of mind especially, which expressed the mystery of divinity by the idea of the Son of God, not by the Son of Man of Jewish mysticism, found the name completely unfamiliar. Not a few critics have tried to conclude from this sudden disappearance of the term "Son of Man" from Christian literature that the name never came from Jesus originally, but was only introduced later by way of Gnosticism. There is no justification at all for this conclusion; it misjudges the true purpose of the expression, and the peculiar position of Jesus that gave rise to it. The idea of the Son of Man was by its very nature a transitional conception, and could not but disappear when the transition to the new faith had been accomplished.

To sum up: Jesus readily called himself the Son of Man. We have shown that the form of this expression was taken over from Daniel, but that its content goes beyond Daniel. It was Jesus' original act to connect Daniel's idea of the Son of Man with Isaias' image of the servant of God, giving his life as a ransom for many—and this in contradistinction to Jewish apocalyptic writings, which had no conception of a suffering Messias. Two things have been established in Jesus' self-consciousness: he knew he was a heavenly being, who would come with the clouds of heaven, and who had his place at the right hand of the Ancient of Days. In referring Daniel's vision to himself, he gave utterance to his deepest awareness that his proper place, his home, was at the right hand of the Ancient of Days. Without actually putting it into so many words, he assumed the idea of pre-existence. This is the only means of understanding why Jesus affirmed so frequently and emphatically that he had "come." This presumes that he regarded his life as a mission, a descent from above, and that he knew he was in the midst of a mysterious movement leading from heaven to earth and from earth to heaven. Just as the formula for his Parousia, or second coming, runs: "The Son of Man will come . . . ." so the formula for his pre-existence runs: "The Son of Man has come. . . ." This is founded upon the clear consciousness that he has been "sent," that he has come down from heaven as a messenger from the world beyond into this one. This would suggest that Paul was not the first to understand the drama of the Redeemer in terms of the historical course of salvation, nor the first to connect it with an action that is played out first in heaven, then on earth, and finally in heaven again. And it would certainly not appear as if Paul had taken this scheme for the course of salvation from Jewish apocalyptic writings. In the fact that the Jesus of history deliberately preferred to call himself the Son of Man, who would come with the clouds of heaven to redeem the sinful world by his suffering, and set up the new kingdom, he has himself *already established* the scheme of the course of salvation—from heaven to earth, and from earth to heaven. Jesus is one who has his place in heaven at the right hand of God, who has appeared upon earth to sacrifice himself in service for mankind, and who then, returning to the Father, will hold judgement upon mankind and take over the dominion. Paul had no need to go to the Jewish apocalyptic tradition to find this pattern of the history of our salvation. It was already given in Jesus' eschatological designation of himself as the coming Son of Man. This way of regarding the course of salvation was only extended and formulated more precisely by Paul and John in the service of their age and in answer to its questions. Thus the name "Son of Man" as Jesus understood it is for its period the most profound expression of his consciousness that he was the Messias. In its sequence of the Son of Man pre-existent, humiliated, and then exalted, it contained the seeds of the entire history of our redemption.

This brings us to the second element which for Jesus is included in the idea of the Son of Man—the soteriological element of his calling as the Saviour and Messias. The Son of Man came not for the just but for the sinners. He came to seek and to save that which was lost. He knows he is the revelation of the divine mercy and salvation. His mission as the Messias is his mission as the Saviour. This driving-power shines through his entire life, and is not something subsequently read into the picture of the Son of Man. In the synagogue at Nazareth, Jesus already refers the prophecy of Isaias to himself. And the reply he gave to the messenger from John the Baptist is meant to imply the same thing: "The Spirit of the Lord is upon me because he has anointed me; to bring good news to the poor he has sent me, to proclaim to the captives release and sight to the blind" (Luke 4.18 ff.). Later we shall have to show that the Lord's works and deeds as Saviour reached their fulfilment in his death as a ransom for many. By the sacrifice of his own blood, he founded the bond of the new eternal covenant with God: "All of you drink of this; for this is my blood of the new covenant, which is being shed for many unto the forgiveness of sins." Thus the two dominant characteristics of the image of Jesus are united in the Son of Man: his pre-existent being, called to eternal divine dominion, and his calling as the Saviour. Both traits are not isolated, but interpenetrate each other, and shine through the Lord's entire life as the Synoptic Gospels describe it.

But there is yet a third element hidden in the name "Son of Man." It is something so obvious that there is actually no need to stress it, for it is apparent in the expression itself. It is Jesus' human quality. Jesus avoided the title of Messias because he wanted to prevent a political misinterpretation of his mission, but he called himself the Son of Man not only to express his supernatural being at the right hand of the Father and his deeds as the Saviour, but at the same time to say that all this was accomplished within his simple human nature; that for all the glory of his divine secret, he remained a simple man. The two opposing tendencies of his majesty and his lowliness that we observed at the beginning, and which can be traced through all his utterances, come together in the expression "Son of Man." It has two aspects, heavenly and earthly, divine and human. Thus he gave the most striking expression for his time and world of what was nearest to his soul: the consciousness of being a Saviour come down from heaven, a Saviour and judge in the simple garb of a man.

Jesus was particularly fond of calling himself the Son of Man. But on occasion he also called himself the Son. In what historical context can we place this expression? And in what sense did Jesus himself use it? This is the next question that will occupy us.

IX

CHRIST'S CONSCIOUSNESS OF BEING THE SON OF GOD

"Son of God" in the Old Testament

THE expression "son of God" (*bene elohim*) is used in Jewish literature in many senses. In the poetic language of the Old Testament, it signifies first of all the angels, the evil as well as the good. Genesis 6.2, 4, for example, refers to the "sons of God," who united with the fairest of the daughters of men, and begot a race of giants. These are obviously mythological echoes. According to the prelude to Job 1.6, the "sons of God" came to stand before the Lord, and Satan also was among them. According to Job, too, the "sons of God" witnessed the creation. "When the morning stars praised me together, and all the sons of God made a joyful melody" (Job 38.7). In Old Testament usage, the sons of God signify in general all spiritual beings, devils and angels. In this case, we do not accept the mythological interpretation, that these spirits stood in some sort of family relationship with God, as his natural children. For one of the fundamental ideas of the Jewish creed is that Jahve has not wife and child. The spirits are called sons of God simply because they are in God's possession, created by him for his service.

Furthermore, the expression "sons of God" is also applied to the Jewish nation, and in this case the Scriptures make use of the specific name "sons of Jahve," for Jahve is the name of the God of the Covenant; thus the phrase gives expression to the particular dedication of the children of Israel to the God of the Covenant. Jewish thinking was never in the least

143

disposed to misinterpret the term. Deuteronomy 14.1, 2 announces: "Be ye children of the Lord your God [i.e., Jahve],*
. . . Because thou art a holy people to the Lord thy God."
When Moses is told to request Pharaoh to set the Israelites
free, Jahve commands him: "And thou shalt say to him: Thus
saith the Lord: Israel is my son, my first-born. I have said to
thee: Let my son go" (Exod. 4.22 ff.). This description of
Israel as the first-born son of God is very frequent. It always
refers to the chosen people as a whole.

In later Judaic times, the other nations too are regarded as
the sons of God. Indeed, Malachias 2.10 calls God the creator
and father of all mankind. However, Israel remains his first-
born son, his chosen people, his well-beloved. So it follows
naturally that the name "son of God" should also be given to
those persons who are the highest embodiment of the powers
and properties of the nation—the kings of Israel. The king is
the first-born son of God in a special sense. The name is frequently attributed to King Saul in the Books of Samuel. The
Psalms glorify King David in particular as the son of God
and the first-born (18.51; 20.7; 28.8, *et seq.*). In Psalm
88.26 f., God comforts the oppressed king with the words
"And I will stretch out his hand over the sea, and his right
hand over the rivers. He shall cry unto me: 'Thou art my
Father, my God, and the rock of my salvation!' And I will
make him my first-born, the highest among the kings of the
earth."

Ever since Israel had come into contact with the Babylonian
and Egyptian cultures it had shared the belief that the kings
of other nations too were the sons of God. Indeed, it was a
familiar idea of these nations that the king was the son of
God. It was the ancient version of the modern phrase "King
by the Grace of God." In the Egyptian religion, the kings
were the sons of God, and hence supernatural beings, from
their birth. It was said of Ramses II: "On the day of his birth
the heavens rejoiced. The gods said: 'We have begotten him.'
The goddesses said: 'Of us he was born.' " According to this
idea, the gods begot the royal child physically, and directly, in
the form of the king and queen. Even the Israelites could not
escape this ancient belief. Their strict monotheism protected
them from following such speculation to the extent of assuming
a supernatural physical begetting for the royal child. But they
readily accepted the belief that the non-Jewish kings too had

* The Douay translation renders "Jahve" or "Jehovah," the Old
Testament God of the Covenant, by "the Lord." *Trans.*

been called directly by God to be the sons of God, just like the non-Jewish nations, and the evil angels.

But like the children of Israel, the Jewish kings too took precedence. They were regarded as the first-born sons of God. And as the first-born, they had the right of primogeniture—dominion over the world. So it is not strange that Jewish thought should set up the conceptual sequence king>first-born son of God>ruler of the world. We must take this into account in order to understand the religious foundations for the ancient Jewish efforts at world dominion. The second Psalm offers a fruitful commentary on this attitude. The Psalm had no small influence upon the history of the expectation of the Messias, helping to strengthen its political and national tendency; it will be rewarding to look at it more closely. We have already indicated that the Psalms of Solomon, dating from the first century before Christ, were the first to interpret this second Psalm in a messianic sense, and to equate the "Lord's Anointed" with the king who was to come, bringing the Last Judgement, so that from then on the coming king was called the Messias—i.e., the Anointed One. The Psalm begins with the angry question: "Why are the nations in tumult, and why do the people devise vain things? The kings of the earth rise up and the princes take counsel together against the Lord and against the Anointed. . . . He who dwells in the heavens laughs, the Lord laughs them to scorn. . . . 'But I have established my king upon Sion, my holy mountain.' I will make known the decree of the Lord: the Lord has said to me: 'Thou art my son, this day have I begotten thee. Ask of me and I will give thee the Gentiles for thine inheritance, and the ends of the earth as thy possession. Thou shalt rule them with a rod of iron, thou shalt break them in pieces like a potter's vessel.' And now, O kings, understand: be instructed, you who rule the world. . . ." The original intention of the Psalm would seem to be a warning and a threat to the Gentile kings. The mysterious dignity of this new king is meant to fill them with fear. He is the Anointed of God, yea, he is his Son. He has been summoned as the Anointed and the Son of Jahve to bend all kings of the earth beneath his sceptre.

Psychologically, we can well understand how the great religious and political value invested in the king became the nucleus around which expectations of the Messias subsequently crystallized. The greatest hope living within the hearts of the devout and the prophets of Israel was the expectation of a new and glorious age when Israel, the people chosen by God, should rule the world and bring blessings upon it. It is natural that this hope should have been garbed in the idea of a new king who would come, bringing a marvellous renascence of David's glory. It was no great step from the belief that our king is the Lord's Anointed and first-born son, and therefore ruler of the world, to the idea that the kingdom of David was the fulfilment of all prophecies. Like no other, it is clothed in the dignity of descent from God, and made Lord over the entire earth. In the eyes of the devout, the kingdom of itself took on a *messianic* nature, both religious and political. The more the devout were oppressed by the distresses of the present, the more they shifted their expectation of the Messias to the end of time. This will explain how the sequence king>Son of God>Anointed One slowly took on the new significance, that not every king, but only the *king of the end of time* was the true Anointed One, the true Messias and Son of God. On the one hand, the coming of the Messias was understood in a strictly eschatological sense; on the other, it was distinctly political and nationalistic.

The second Psalm appears to have been the point of departure for the new equation: Messias = Son of God = King of the Last Judgement. For here the royal singer testifies: "The Lord has said to me: 'Thou art my son, this day have I begotten thee' " (2.7). It is true, the first certain reference to this Psalm was made in the Psalms of Solomon (17.23 ff.), which were written only a short time after the conquest of Jerusalem by Pompeius Magnus, around the year 63 B.C. As they were very soon lost, and not brought to light again until the seventeenth century, we can hardly regard them as playing an essential or significant part in the development of late Judaic messianism. The Jewish reluctance to utter the name of God also helped to prevent a thorough-going identification of the Messias with the Son of God. However, the fourth Book of Esdras at least testifies that in late Judaic circles the King of the Last Judgement was called the Son of God. But even here, the expression "Son of God" is not a true title attributed to the Messias, even though it occurs quite frequently. In any case, in Esdras the Son of God is a transcendent power, the apocalyptic Redeemer, who is ultimately identical with the "Son of Man."

In Jesus' time, this designation of the Messias (the Anointed) as the king of the last days and as the Son of God was already firmly established. The Gospels give proof of this—for example, the high priest's question (Mark 14.61): "Art thou the Christ, the Son of the Blessed One?" Similar evidence is offered by the men possessed of devils, when they recognize Christ as the Son of God (Mark 3.11; Matt. 8.29; Mark 5.7; Luke 8.28), that in the Lord's time no distinction was made between the concept of the Messias and the concept of the Son of God. The origin of this usage is probably the above-mentioned messianic interpretation of the second Psalm. The Jews followed this Psalm in regarding the "Son of God" only in a *theocratic* sense, i.e., as one specially endowed with God's Grace. His nature was not regarded as divine, but only his calling and mission.

In discussing the usage of the term "son of God" we have established the following: The Old Testament still uses the expression in the broadest sense. It sometimes signifies the angels, sometimes the children of Israel, sometimes the kings of Israel, but always created beings. With the deterioration of Israel's political situation, the devout turned their eyes from the gloomy present with greater yearning to the prophetic promises of a blessed future, and the expression "son of God" was narrowed down to mean the bringer of this fulfilment. When they spoke of the King of the Last Judgement, they thought of the Messias, and called him the son of God. This stage has been reached in the literature written later than the Old Testament canon, especially in the fourth Book of Esdras. But even here the expression is not really a ceremonial title of the Messias. The Jews do not equate the King of the Last Judgement with the Messias and with the Son of God without any further thought of explanation until the New Testament.

This development of the concept "son of God," and in particular the support late Judaic theology found in the second Psalm for naming the awaited King of the Last Judgement Son of God and Christ, leads us to conclude that at that time the Jews by no means ascribed a metaphysical meaning to the expression. The line in Psalm 2, "The Lord has said to me: 'Thou art my son, this day have I begotten thee,' " simply refers to the creation of a special relationship in Grace to Jahve, into which the Jewish kings would be assumed on the day they ascended the throne. The line expressed the supernatural quality of the king's calling, but not of his being. It did not mean to say: Thou art, O King, no longer of humankind, but divine; rather, on the day of your crowning, you entered into a special relationship of love with God. The statement *ego hodie genui te*, "this day have I begotten thee," did not mean that the king had been begotten into earthly existence, but simply into the royal office. The expression "begotten" by God was used at the time as a kind of adoptive formula. The formula was particularly frequent in the Egyptian cultural sphere, though here it was used exclusively in the sense of the supernatural begetting accomplished by the god Ammon in the figure of the king. To the Jewish mind such an idea was impossible. So when the Psalms of Solomon give an expressly messianic interpretation to the second Psalm, all they too imply is that the Messias, by the very fact of his elevation to that state, has been drawn into a particularly close relationship with God—into being the "Son of God." The Jewish mind could have borne no other interpretation. One piece of evidence to support this is the fact that even after Jesus' resurrection there were still certain isolated Judaeo-Christian circles (particularly the Ebionites), who could not give up the conviction that Jesus was the Son of God simply through his elevation in Grace to the dignity of the Messias, but not on account of his divine nature. They held that Jesus was first elevated to his office of Messias only when he was baptized by John, and heard the solemn declaration of God: "Thou art my beloved Son, in thee I am well pleased." The early Christian Feast of the Epiphany, which first and foremost celebrated the baptism of the Messias in the Jordan, would seem to favour this interpretation. There is a very ancient variant of this passage in Luke 3.22 that is significant. In describing the baptism of the Messias, by way of explanation it introduces Psalm 2, and in particular the *ego hodie genui te,* "this day have I begotten thee." This too would seem to assume that Jesus became by Grace the Messias and Son of God only from his baptism in the Jordan.

We may say, then, that at the time Jesus began his public ministry, popular devotion gave to the awaited Christ (the Messias) the additional name of Son of God—but in a theocratic, not a metaphysical, sense. This theocratic understanding included the idea of particular endowment with Grace by God, but excluded the essential divinity of the Christ. Nevertheless a transcendent light played about the figure of the Christ, in so far as he was exalted to that office by God's particular Grace.

The "Son of God" in the Gospels

The question as to the sense in which the Gospels used the concept "Son of God" can be answered only against this background of late Judaic usage. They often use the expression in a purely religious as well as a theocratic sense. The purely religious sense is particularly frequent. In this sense, Jesus promised the peacemakers that they should be called the children of God (Matt. 5.9). Those accounted worthy of the resurrection are praised as the sons of God (Luke 20.36, *et al.*). The concept attains a deeper theocratic meaning when the men possessed of devils hail Jesus as the Son of God (Mark 3.11, Matt. 8.29; Mark 5.7; Luke 8.28). As Jews and true children of their nation, they could not but connect with the idea "Son of God" the belief in Jesus' messianic office. From a psychological point of view, we might say they venerated the Lord out of a strong feeling of the contrast between their own impurity and the holy essence they sensed in Jesus. We might say that their sensible life had already given them an inkling of the divine, the "altogether different." A purely theocratic meaning must also be at the basis of the high priest's question: "Art thou the Christ, the Son of the Blessed One?" (Mark 14.61). As a Jew, Caiaphas' only image of the Messias would be that of the Son of David, summoned by Jahve to be King of the Last Judgement. He was perfectly sure that he had an impostor before him in this carpenter who went among the common people so readily, who broke the Sabbath and the law of uncleanness, and now stood before him as a prisoner. He was quite clear in his mind that this Jesus could not be the King of the Last Judgement. But on the other hand he was equally sure that the Law of Mishnah held that merely to pretend to the title of the Messias was not a crime deserving death. And even when Jesus conceded that he did lay claim to the title of the Messias, Caiaphas could not hope for him to make a confession that would bring death upon his head—i.e., admit some guilt that carried the death penalty. So there is no doubt that whatever his personal conviction that the awaited Messias could only be of human blood, the high priest put a deeper meaning into his question, "Art thou the Christ, the Son of the Blessed One?" than the usage of the time would admit of; there is little doubt that he used the phrase "Son of the Blessed One" in a *metaphysical* sense. Perhaps it was not unknown to him that Jesus had already disputed with one of the Scribes about the purely human origin of the Messias. Then Jesus had posed the difficult question: "If David therefore calls him [the Messias] Lord, how is he his son?" (Matt. 22.45). This would make it seem exceedingly likely that in his question Caiaphas already took the Lord's claim to be the Messias in a deeper sense—not theocratically but metaphysically. We know from the Gospels that Jesus did not reply with a mere affirmative, but made the additional, intensifying comment: "I am. And you shall see the Son of Man sitting at the right hand of the Power and coming with the clouds of heaven." This comment makes his claim to divinity unmistakable. For in the Jewish tradition, only the Godhead himself can come with the clouds of heaven. Matthew (27.43) testifies that the high priests and Scribes mocked Jesus on the cross with the scornful words: "He trusted in God; let him deliver him now, if he wants him; for he said, 'I am the Son of God.'" That the Jewish authorities should have chosen to mock this particular claim of the Lord is proof enough that in their eyes this was Jesus' real crime. This, then, is the situation: The high priest was personally convinced that the Messias would be strictly a human descendant of David, and might be called Son of God only in a theocratic sense. On the other hand, he had reason to surmise that Jesus' claim went far beyond this. Jesus' comment upon Caiaphas' question only confirms his surmise. So the judgement could only be: "'What further need have we of witnesses? You have heard the blasphemy' . . . And they all condemned him as liable to death. . . .'"

Peter's avowal at Cæsarea Philippi, too, must be understood metaphysically, and not just theocratically: "Thou art the Christ, the Son of the living God" (Matt. 16.16). It is true, the two parallel accounts (Luke 9.20; Mark 8.29) present the avowal only in the simpler form: "Thou art the Christ." And we can hardly assume that if Peter had really used it they would have simply ignored the fuller expression "Son of the living God," which is so much a part of their proclamation of the true (metaphysical) Son of God; the phrase here would seem to be the particular property of Matthew, and Peter's avowal in fact to have been only "Thou art the Christ." However, the impression of the Lord's other proclamations had already led the disciples' faith so far that in essentials it towered high above the traditional image of the Messias (cf. Luke

24.19, 21). Only this can give full meaning to Jesus' blessing as he replies: "Blessed art thou, Simon Bar-Jona, for flesh and blood has not revealed this to thee, but my Father in heaven" (Matt. 16.17).

The attribute "Son of God" further appears in the accounts of Jesus' baptism (Matt. 3.13 f.; Mark 1.9 f.; Luke 3.21 f.); in the accounts of his temptation (Matt. 4.1 ff.; Luke 4.1 ff.); and finally in the accounts of his transfiguration (Matt. 17.1 ff.; Mark 9.2 f.; Luke 9.28 f.). In the transfiguration, the voice at the baptism is repeated, and in the temptation Jesus is challenged by the evil spirit to make earthly use of his supernatural powers as Messias. What is first and foremost at issue is the meaning and content of Jesus' claim to be the Messias, not of his claim to divinity. We are not able to elucidate from the text whether in these passages the term "Son of God" already bears a metaphysical meaning. The voice from heaven, "This is my beloved Son," is like a composite assemblage of Psalm 2.7 and Isaias 42.1. Psalm 2.7 reads, "The Lord has said to me: 'Thou art my son,'" while in Isaias 42.1 the Lord says: "My elect: my soul delighteth in him." Originally, both lines refer to the children of Israel, so their original meaning was theocratic. So to apply them to Christ does not necessarily imply that their meaning goes beyond the original theocratic sense, although, on the other hand, the "voice from heaven," particularly, comes close to giving them a metaphysical meaning.

"Son of God" as Jesus' own designation of himself

We may say this: As far as the concept of the Son of God was at all familiar to the Lord's contemporaries, it was not adequate to draw their attention directly to the divine mystery of Jesus. Indeed, it diverted attention *away from* this mystery, for the Jews of the period used the term to describe only created beings. Thus we may understand how it is that our oldest sources, the Synoptic Gospels, do not *expressly* report any occasions on which Jesus described *himself* as the Son of God. Certainly, the name is given to him by others, when referring to his supernatural messianic calling. But he himself refrains from designating himself thus. The expression, to him, was not an adequate description for the precious secret he hid within him. According to Jewish usage, it aligned Christ with man rather than with God. The concept "Son of Man" did to a certain extent reveal his secret, indicating an entity that comes from heaven and sits at the right hand of God. But in the context of contemporary usage, the concept "Son of God" could only disguise it, indeed deny it.

Jesus' silence, then, becomes understandable. However, the Evangelist John tells us that it was not a strict silence based on principle; indeed, Jesus was repeatedly compelled by the peculiarity of his situation to speak his mind on the meaning of the "Son of God." John tells us (9.35) that when Jesus healed the man born blind, he asked him: "Dost thou believe in the Son of God?" Since the man born blind was a Jew, he could only have understood this question to mean did he believe that Jesus was the Messias, specially summoned and chosen of God. In any case, Jesus makes no express attempt to insist upon a deeper meaning of the phrase "Son of God." However, the man born blind appears to sense this deeper, divine quality in Jesus. He questions: "Who is he, Lord?" and Jesus replies: "Thou hast both seen him, and he it is who speaks with thee." And then he cries out, "I believe, Lord." "And falling down, he worshipped him" (John 9.38). He apprehended in Jesus the manifestation of holiness. John 10.30 is still more explicit. Confronted by his enemies, Jesus points to his communion of life with the Father. " 'I and the Father are one.' The Jews therefore took up stones to stone him. Jesus answered them: 'Many good works have I shown you from my Father. For which of these works do you stone me?' The Jews answered him, 'Not for a good work do we stone thee, but for blasphemy, and because thou, being a man, makest thyself God.' Jesus answered them, 'Is it not written in your law, "I said you are gods"?' " Jesus refers to the passage in Psalm 81.6, which plainly calls all the devout "gods." At first glance, this would seem as if he is weakening his claim to be the Son of God in the narrow sense, and saying that his fellowship with the Father was no different from the relationship of any pious Israelite to his God. But in the following verses, Jesus reveals that he has a profounder understanding of his fellowship with God, and distinguishes it from that of the devout Jews. He continues: "If he called them gods to whom the word of God was addressed . . . do you say of him whom the Father has made holy and sent into the world, 'Thou blasphemest,' because I said, 'I am the Son of God'?" (10.35). He distinguishes his own fellowship with God from that of the ordinary devout in maintaining that him alone the Father made holy and sent into the world.

John differs from the Synoptic Gospels in giving us the additional information that when confronted with his opponents, Jesus called himself not only the Son of Man but also the Son of God, striking chords that bade his enemies hearken, and rousing in them the suspicion that he was referring the concept "Son of God" to himself in a special, higher sense. *Only John* makes completely comprehensible what Caiaphas really meant by his question: "Art thou the Christ, the Son of the Blessed One?" He had obviously heard of those allusions of Jesus' which John reports. Jesus' additional comment to his reply, "You shall see the Son of Man . . . coming with the clouds of heaven," confirms Caiaphas' assumption, and brings about his condemnation to death. However, even here we may observe that just as Jesus clearly used the expression "Son of Man" to reveal his heavenly secret only to the pure and the simple among men, and to hide it from the rest, just so there is something dazzling about the expression "Son of God"— apart from the fact that he used it only very rarely. One senses clearly that Jesus wants to avoid exposing his secret to his enemies without good reason. Not until he is confronted with death, not until he stands before Caiaphas' judgement seat, does he speak out. For there is no longer any sense in hiding his secret. His hour was come. It was time to bear witness to the truth.

Jesus' consciousness of being the "Son"

But what Jesus hid from his malevolent opponents, he had already revealed in the intimate circle of his disciples. In calling himself "Son" he revealed it clearly and unmistakably. With his avowal that he is the "Son," the only true well-beloved Son of the Father, we have reached the highest, maturest revelation that Jesus made of himself. Jesus' designation of himself as "the Son" is the culminating point of his consciousness of being the Messias, the final, holiest word that he has to say to us.

He uttered it at a time when his disciples had already drawn nearer him in their growing understanding. And he uttered it at a moment of deep emotion. The seventy-two disciples Jesus had sent out return and joyfully announce that " 'even the devils are subject to us in thy name.' But he said to them, 'I was watching Satan fall as lightning from heaven. . . . But do not rejoice in this, that the spirits are subject to you; rejoice rather in this, that your names are written in heaven.' In that very hour, Jesus rejoiced in the Holy Spirit and said, 'I praise thee, Father, Lord of heaven and earth, that thou didst hide these things from the wise and prudent and didst reveal them to little ones. Yes, Father, for such was thy good pleasure. All things have been delivered to me by my Father; and no one knows who the Son is except the Father, and who the Father is except the Son, and him to whom the Son chooses to reveal him. Come to me, all you who labour and are burdened, and I will give you rest' " (Matt. 11.25–28; Luke 10.21, 22).

This Logion is a *true* utterance of the Lord's. It is to be found in Matthew and in Luke—i.e., in the fund of Jesus' sayings that they have in common, the oral tradition so highly valued by all Biblical criticism. The echoes here of certain Old Testament phrases, particularly of Proverbs, as well as of Paul and John, are by no means proof that this saying is an intrusion from outside into the Gospel of Jesus, and does not originate with Jesus himself, but with the Old Testament, or Paul, or John. Why should it be "suspicious" that Jesus should here make use of phrases from the Old Testament? Indeed, it is the peculiar mark of his way of thinking and speaking that he moves entirely, not only in his parables, but also in single turns of phrase, within the ideas and images of the Old Testament. Even his blessings are largely taken from the Old Testament. And when Paul and John use similar phrases, this is by no means evidence that our saying originates with them. The echo is rather evidence to the contrary, that Paul as well as John was familiar with the thoughts of the Master, and that both were well acquainted with the heart of his proclamation, and faithfully repeated it. In any case, in spite of the similarity of content, our saying is typically distinct from Paul's. For example, it is not in keeping with Paul's way of thinking that Father and Son should be contrasted, and that the meeting of Father and Son should take no account of the Holy Spirit, which brings about the fellowship of Father and Son. And when John uses similar words to repeat virtually the same thought, this indicates only that he has traced and described Jesus' delicate inner life more carefully than the Synoptic Evangelists. In this narrow sense, the observation that the saying is an "artistic metrical form" (E. Norden) is not relevant.

It is not a poem. But it is not strange that Jesus should express himself in elevated language at the moment of such a profound experience—still less so, for in any case such exalted speech is not a rarity in Jesus' mouth. It is sufficient to point out the end of the Sermon on the Mount (Matt. 7.24 ff.), the Beatitudes (Matt. 5.3 ff.), the Lord's Prayer, or the parallels that Jesus draws between himself and John the Baptist (Matt. 11.16 ff.). Norden's attempt to prove that the saying belongs to a "fixed fund of typical religious language" is untenable, for even he fails to demonstrate the existence of a well-established fund of religious formulas, or to point out in current prophetic literature an established literary scheme in which Father and Son have the same reciprocal knowledge of each other. Norden is right only in this one thing: the belief that knowledge of God could be revealed through some mediation was familiar to the Hellenistic world too, and, unlike the Greek attitude of mind, which insists upon rational, intelligible, not revealed knowledge, it is a belief that may be regarded as peculiar to Oriental religious life. The only fixed and typical quality in the saying is the revelatory nature of its cognizance of God, such that the recognition of Father and Son does not take place by way of reason, but from the Father. The particular, intense, vivid way the Son receives his revelation from the Father, and hands it on, and the narrow historical framework within which he utters the saying has none of the colourless abstraction of the Hellenistic maxims. It is a revelation by Christ of his own nature surging up directly out of a precise historical situation.

So we have to do with a genuine, original utterance of the Lord. What is its meaning? There are three great glories with which the Father endows him. "All things have been delivered to me by my Father"—*all* things, all honour and majesty, all authority and power. There is quite simply nothing held by the Father that does not belong to him. It is a word embracing infinities. John the Evangelist supplements this with other claims of the Lord's of a similar kind. "All things that the Father has are mine" (16.15); "all things that are mine are thine, and thine are mine" (17.10); "for as the Father raises the dead and gives them life, even so the Son also gives life to whom he will. For neither does the Father judge any man, but all judgement he has given to the Son, that all men may honour the Son even as they honour the Father" (5.21 ff.).

The second glory lies deeper. It is the source of the first. *"No one knows* the Son except the Father; nor does anyone know the Father except the Son." "To know," in Semitic terminology, signifies a relationship of the closest communion of life. This passage, then, means: No one has such a close communion of life with the Father as the Son; nor has anyone such a close communion of life with the Son as the Father. They are both one single life. The meaning of this passage is closely connected with Christ's saying in the Gospel according to St. John: "I am in the Father, and the Father in me" (14.10). With these words, Jesus sharply contrasts his relation to the Father with that of other devout men. His communion of life with the Father is unique and exclusive. No created being has part in it. It is a unique, eternal relationship, necessary to divine being, far transcending all created relationships, this relationship that makes God the Father of Jesus Christ, and Jesus Christ the Son of the Father. Their existence is rooted in their reciprocal exchange of life and love.

A. von Harnack is reluctant to recognize in this saying such a statement about the being of the Godhead. He would have it that the saying refers not to an eternal relationship necessary to divine being, but to an historical, gradually unfolding immanence, a relationship not of being but only of function. In support of this theory, he calls upon a variant of our text taken over by Justin, Marcion, and Irenaeus, according to which the original ran thus: "and no one has known the Father except the Son; and no one has known the Son but the Father, and he to whom the Son reveals it." Harnack maintains that the use of the perfect tense is an unmistakable indication of a knowledge that is attained to only gradually, in the course of time, and has not existed from eternity. Jesus himself becomes the Son of the Father only by way of a progressive experiencing and recognizing of God as his Father. That he should be God's Son is the result, and not the principle, of this mutual recognition. Jesus knows the Father not because he is the Son, but rather, he is the Son because he and he alone knows the Father. It is not a question of an original essential relationship between Father and Son, but a relation of Son to Father, historically brought into being by Jesus' progressive recognition of God. And so, Harnack thinks, even in the variant the single parts of the saying have been adapted, in so far as prior importance was given not to recognition of the Son by the Father but to recognition of the Father by the Son. This approaches the interpretation that only the free act of the Son brought about the unique recognition of Father and Son.

Harnack's interpretation may be refuted in the first place because the variant he rests his argument upon cannot possibly be original. Indeed, the saying closes with the addition: "and him to whom the Son chooses to reveal him." This addition is intended to hand on to mankind the revelation that had been vouchsafed to the Son. It follows that the previous reference must have been to this revelation vouchsafed to the Son, if the addition "and him to whom the Son chooses to reveal him" is not to be left hanging in the air devoid of any context. If we pay attention to the phrasing, we notice that the stress lies upon "no one" ("nor does anyone know the Father," etc.). It is simply impossible for anyone other than the Son to know the Father. The unique nature of the Son's knowledge of the Father corresponds to the unique nature of the Father's knowledge of the Son ("no one knows the Son except the Father," etc.). Just as the Father's knowledge of the Son is unique and direct, so the Son's knowledge of the Father is to be understood as unique and direct. It is so because Jesus is the Son. He is not the Son because he knows the Father in a unique way; but he knows the Father in this unique sense because he is the Son. The basis for their knowledge is essential, and physical, that eternal relationship that exists between God as the Father and Jesus as the Son. Hence the present tense of the act of recognition is the only one adequate to the context. The reciprocal recognition of Father and Son did not suddenly break through to dawn upon Jesus at any particular point of time in his life, but had eternally existed, because the Father was the Father and the Son the Son. The meaning of the Biblical text is still clearer in the context of contemporary mysticism, which attributed to man only an imperfect knowledge of God. Man is not able to know God fully. It is his part simply to be known by God (cf. 1 Cor. 8.1 ff.; Gal. 4.9). Jesus emphasizes that his relationship to God is quite different. He and he alone has the same perfect knowledge of the Father as the Father has of him. And this knowledge beseems him, for he and he alone is the Son. Similarly, the reality of the Son is not less mysterious to the human eye than the reality of the Father. It is so mysterious that there is only One who may know it, the Father—because he is the Father.

The revelation that Jesus makes in these lines with such

majestic simplicity is identical with those other avowals which
John reports Jesus makes of himself: "I am in the Father, and
the Father in me" (14.10 f.); "Philip, he who sees me sees
the Father" (14.9); "I know mine and mine know me, even as
the Father knows me and I know the Father" (10.14).

This communion of essence of Son and Father gives rise
almost of itself to the third glory that was within Jesus' soul:
"nor does anyone know the Father except the Son, *and him
to whom the Son chooses to reveal him.*" It is the Son alone
who reveals the Father to us. This is the deepest meaning of
his mission and of his message, and of Christianity as a whole:
by way of the Son to the Father. There is no other way to the
Father than through the Son. In this context, too, John recalls
certain additional claims of Jesus. Thomas asks him: "Lord,
how can we know the way?" and Jesus replies: "I am the
way, and the truth and the life. No one comes to the Father
but through me" (14.6).

No critical scruples can destroy this: this saying of Jesus' is
the highest and purest of his self-revelations. It expresses his
own fulfilment, in the high rhetoric of an infinitely joyful
experience. Now the disciples know, first, that all things have
been delivered to him; secondly, that he alone is the Son, and
that he alone stands in a unique relationship of life and love to
the Father; and thirdly, that because he shares all knowledge
with the Father, he alone is the revelation of the Father, and
the way to the Father. This last dictum, that the Son is the
way to the Father, illuminates the modification that the concept of the Messias has undergone in Jesus' consciousness.
Jesus takes over the Jewish idea of the Messias, i.e., the Christ.
Following the prophets, he gives it a spiritual interpretation.
He is the Saviour for the transgressions of mankind, especially
for their sins. But beyond this, he also gives it a metaphysical
interpretation. He raises the idea into the sphere of the divine. And this is exactly what makes him the *Messias: that he
is the Son,* and that as the Son he is the revelation of the
Father's goodness to mankind. This is his mystery as the
Messias, that as the Son he leads mankind to the Father. The
concepts of "Messias" and "Son" fuse into a higher synthesis,
or rather, the "Messias" is assumed into the "Son." Jesus is
God the Saviour.

The Synoptic Gospels tell of only one such solemn self-
revelation of the Lord's. However, they are more concerned
with Jesus' public ministry, whereas John purports to describe the inner life of Christ's soul. John assures us that Jesus

called himself "the Son" not once but many times, especially among intimates. For example, in his conversation at night with Nicodemus (3.17 f.), or when he bade his disciples farewell (14.13; 17.1). But the Synoptic Gospels too give testimony that Jesus frequently called himself the Son, though not in solemn manner. Luke (2.49) reports that strange saying of the child Jesus, which he made to his parents when they were looking for him: "Did you not know that I must be about my Father's business?" The sentence has a deliberate point to it, in reply to his mother's reproach: "Behold, in sorrow thy father and I have been seeking thee." Jesus means to imply: My Father is the heavenly Father who reigns in this temple. I do not belong to Joseph, but to the heavenly Father. All Biblical exegesis explains Jesus' words in this sense. Hardly anyone today repeats the early rationalistic interpretation that Jesus was only saying the obvious—that for every devout person, the temple was the house of his Father. The critics, however, are of the opinion that the cult legend of the community is already at work in this scene in the temple. And yet Luke himself takes pains to emphasize that from the beginning he has carefully gathered together the tradition handed down by eyewitnesses, and has written them down in sequence. The one thing he cannot be charged with is the repetition of mere legends. The simple, thoughtful style and inner truth which the entire account emanates leave no room for such an explanation. Tendentious, special pleading would have approached the narrative quite differently. It would not have been so discreet and tactful, but would have heavily and insistently underlined the divine mystery of the child. We have only to compare Thomas' Infant Gospel with Luke's simple, convincing account. In the light of Luke's report, it would seem that the twelve-year-old already had a clear awareness of his unique relationship to his heavenly Father, knowing that he was his Son in the true sense. Mark gives the further account (13.32) of Jesus' reply to the disciples' question as to when Jerusalem would be destroyed: "But of that day and hour no one knows, neither the angels in heaven, nor the Son, but the Father only." Jesus refers to the Son here as something long familiar to the disciples. So he must already have described himself as the Son to them many times. The parable of the vine-dressers, reported by every one of the Synoptic Gospels (Mark 12.6; Luke 20.13; Matt. 21.37), shows that he had acknowledged himself to be the Son, at least metaphorically, even before his enemies. In this parable,

he contrasts the servants (i.e., the prophets) who were persecuted by the vine-dressers (i.e., the Jews) with the one "beloved Son." His Jewish listeners understood the allusion perfectly well. "And they sought to lay hands on him, but they
feared the crowd; for they knew that he had aimed this parable at them" (Matt. 12.12). It is true, Jesus speaks of the
Son here only as a parable and a metaphor. But he contrasts
it so deliberately with the servants or prophets that a misunderstanding of his nature would be impossible. He is the Son;
compared with him, the prophets are only the servants of the
Father of the house.

We may draw into this context the words used in the accounts of Jesus' baptism and transfiguration, "this is my beloved Son"—which, as we have argued above, could by themselves be understood theocratically. In the light of this parable,
it becomes certain that these words from heaven imply a
unique relationship of Son to Father, which far transcends the
prophets' relationship of servant to master. So we may assume
that these great and holy words that Jesus heard at his baptism and at his transfiguration give utterance to that fundamental experience of the Lord's, which inspired him from his
youth onwards, and for ever more shone like a secret radiance
from out of this message. His enemies' malevolent eyes had
noticed this radiance. Hence their mockery at the cross: "He
trusted in God; let him deliver him now, if he wants him; for
he said, 'I am the son of God' " (Matt. 27.43).

This is the situation. At the time of Jesus, the Messias was
also called the Son of God. Jesus took over the form of this
comparison. He took it over in those circles where it was familiar to his listeners. But he gave it a new, profound sense.
He transformed it into a *metaphysical* expression. In doing so,
he deliberately corrected the Jews' image of the Messias, as a
Christ of earthly flesh and blood, and only endowed by God
with special Grace, just as he had similarly deepened the
concept of the Son of Man by bringing it into connexion with
the servant of Jahve. We can see him directly at work upon
this reinterpretation in his conversation with the Pharisees—
which is also reported by all three Synoptic Gospels (Matt.
22.41 ff.; Mark 12.35 ff.; Luke 20.41 ff.). "And while Jesus
was teaching in the temple, he addressed them, saying, 'How
do the Scribes say that the Christ is the Son of David? For
David himself says, by the Holy Spirit, "The Lord said to my
Lord: Sit thou at my right hand, till I make thy enemies
thy footstool." David himself, therefore, calls him "Lord";

how, then, is he his son?' " Here, Jesus explicitly opposes the Pharisees' ideal of the Messias. His argument is this: If David looks up to his descendant in religious veneration, calling him his Lord, recognizing him as one superior to him in the hierarchy of being, then his descendant, the Messias, cannot be his own human descendant, owing origin and being only to him. The Messias must rather be a being higher than his ancestor, a supernatural being, a being from heaven. Jesus' idea of the Messias rises clearly and confidently above the traditional concept of the Messias. Jesus is full of the thought that the awaited Messias does not belong to the category of the merely human. He cannot merely be the descendant of David.

We repeat: It is Jesus' *original* act, out of his consciousness of his divine nature, that he should have called himself "Son" in a metaphysical sense. Even his malevolent opponents knew this. And because they knew it, they crucified him.

"Son of Man" and "Son"

We may still ask how this claim to be the Son of God is to be reconciled with the transitional idea of the Son of Man. We answer that both concepts are closely related to each other. They point towards each other. The term "Son of Man" is a general indication of the heavenly way of being, of the fact that Christ's true place is at the right hand of the Ancient of Days; at the same time the expression "Son" is a more precise indication of the nature of the relationship between Jesus' heavenly essence and the Ancient of Days. It is the relationship of Son to Father. For the general public, it was enough to indicate Jesus' heavenly origin; it was sufficient to direct the disciples' attention constantly upon his heavenly secret. The disciples were to learn the particular nature of this secret only when they had been schooled and prepared for it. Only when Jesus' proclamation spread, when minds began to break away from him, when hostile groups of unbelievers began to be formed, did the same reverence for his secret call for a clear declaration. As soon as the attention of the world had been drawn to the greater profundity of his claim, there no longer was any purpose to further disguise. Indeed, even the disciples did not receive the decisive explanation until after Jesus' resurrection.

Jesus' consciousness of being the Son as a
  fundamental motive in his life

We may not assume that this consciousness of the Lord's
that he was the Son only flickered up now and again in his
life, just because he gave voice to it only rarely, and then
among his intimates. Rather, it was the hidden motive at the
root of his entire life, and so significant that nothing else can
give full meaning to his life—and especially to his other statements about himself. Jesus' personality loses its mysteriousness,
and becomes clear and transparent, only in the light of his
awareness of being the Son. This is the true solution of the
mystery of Jesus. We have already stressed his statements of
his majesty in the Synoptic Gospels. If they were uttered by
any ordinary man, they would be madness. They achieve their
true place and inner truth only from Jesus' consciousness of
being the Son. Only because the person of Jesus in its inner
reality transcends mere humanity can he range his person and
his proclamation far above the manifestations of previous
prophets and kings. Only now can we understand how much
has appeared in him that is "greater than Jonas," "greater
than Solomon" (Matt. 12.41 f.), and how far all the Jewish
prophets and kings recede before him into the shadows. Even
the greatest of pre-Christian prophets who came in the power
of Elias, even John the Baptist, is "smaller" than those who
have followed Jesus to the kingdom of God (Matt. 11.11 ff.;
cf. John 3.28 f.). Jesus is greater than the entire Old Testament ritual and dispensation which had its culmination in
the temple. "One greater than the temple is here" (Matt. 12.6).
That is why the time of his epiphany upon earth is a time of
bliss and undeserved happiness for all who may achieve it.
"Blessed are the eyes that see what you see! For I say to you,
many prophets and kings have desired to see what you see, and
have not seen it" (Luke 10.24). "Abraham your father rejoiced that he was to see my day" (John 8.56). The time of
his coming will be a blissful, happy time because in Jesus the
source of a new life has been opened. This thought is made
fully clear only in the fourth Gospel, in which the Lord describes himself as the bread of life, the water of salvation, the
light of the world, the true vine, the resurrection and the life.
But the Synoptic Gospels, too, know that with Jesus a new

time of joyful covenant with the Lord has come into being. The parable of the bridegroom who is the Messias belongs in this context. "Can the wedding guests fast as long as the bridegroom is with them?" (Mark 2.18; Matt. 22.2). This saying arises out of the same perception as the parable of the wedding feast in which Jesus is represented as the bridegroom, for whom the heavenly Father celebrates the wedding. The relationship between Jesus and his disciples is the same as the relationship in the Old Testament between Jahve and his chosen people. Jesus is the bridegroom of the new community of faith, the basis of its life, and its joy. There is no doubt that Jesus' claim to divinity lies at the root of this and similar sayings. Otherwise they would be meaningless, indeed blasphemous. They are closely related to other statements of his which maintain that the attitude adopted towards the Lord is decisive not only for Israel but for the whole world. Jesus is the cornerstone which broke to pieces the builders who had rejected it (Matt. 21.42). He is the master of the house who has shut the door to those who would not know him (Luke 13.25). Woe to the unhappy town Jerusalem, for she knew not the hour of her visitation (Matt. 23.37).

A mere awareness of being the theocratic Messias is not sufficient to explain so absolute a claim, nor the enormous passion with which Jesus demands a confession of faith. It is simply necessary for salvation, as necessary as the attachment to God itself. That is why the kind of disciple Jesus requires bears a thoroughly religious stamp. Communion with Jesus is accomplished in the act of faith and love. "Blessed is he who is not scandalized in me" (Matt. 11.6). "Blessed art thou, Simon Bar-Jona, for flesh and blood has not revealed this to thee, but my Father in heaven" (Matt. 16.17). This faith is not only the gift of God but at the same time a task for man, a duty where life and death are at stake. "Therefore everyone who acknowledges me before men, I also will acknowledge him before my Father in heaven. But whoever disowns me before men, I in turn will disown him before my Father in heaven" (Matt. 10.32; cf. Mark 8.38). The faith that Jesus demands is a religious faith, a faith for our salvation. And it is fulfilled in love. The same unlimited surrender that he demands for the Father he also requires for himself. He must be loved more than "father, mother, wife, child, brothers, and sisters," more even than one's own life. With this demand, Jesus stands directly at the side of God, indeed, in the place of God. He demands of mankind the most difficult and the most delicate devotion, which only God himself may demand, and no mere human being. This demand makes it clear that his claim is one of divinity; a purely theocratic claim to be the Messias would not be adequate. Elsewhere in Jesus' life this divinity breaks through in him. It is the true foundation of all his words and deeds. His miracles are not the stale conjurations of the rabbis or the Hellenistic magicians. They are never an end in themselves. They never serve mere show, self-interest, or self-glorification. They serve only to set up the kingdom of God and defeat the realm of Satan. They occur only where there is a genuine readiness for salvation, where the devout are absolutely open to the numinous power issuing forth from Jesus. Jesus' miracles are the expression and confirmation of the divine life working within him. They are not like the miracles of the prophets, which were wrought by calling upon the name of God, but they occur in his own name alone. Not authorization, but authority, yea, omnipotence, is within him. His teaching is as divine as his miracles. Even in externals, it goes far beyond mere human ways of teaching: "He was teaching them as one having authority, and not as the Scribes" (Mark 1.22). And the content is the tidings of the kingdom of God, and the incarnation of the purest, clearest, boldest, profoundest, and sweetest that ever entered human heart. The prophets too spoke of the reign of God with the saints and the just. Even the pagan philosophers knew of love for their enemies. Moses and Buddha, too, spoke of love for mankind. And yet, before Jesus, the religious and moral ideal had at no time and in no place been embodied so vividly, had never entered life so powerfully, as it did in him. His Sermon on the Mount is now and ever will be the highest, purest, most perfect word ever uttered by human mouth. And mankind will never escape this ideal, or go beyond it.

What he taught, he lived, suffered, and died. The supernatural, divine quality that characterizes his doctrine also leaves its mark upon his way of life, his living and dying. He alone may point to himself as an example: " . . . learn from me, for I am meek and humble of heart" (Matt. 11.29). Such words would be unbearable in the mouth of a mere man. Only coming from Jesus, they do not hurt us, for they are spoken from the depth of his being, out of the purest reality, out of a reality that may not be judged after the manner of men.

It can also be heard in his prayers. However filled they are with the deepest reverence for the Father, at the same time his prayers show an unprecedented intimacy and closeness—as close and as intimate as only the prayers of a child to his own Father may be. It is characteristic that in his communion of prayer with the Father, Jesus never includes anyone else. In his prayers he never puts himself on the same level with other men. He does not summon them: "Let us pray," but says: "This is how you should pray." He does not pray, "Thou, our Father," but "your Father," "my Father." This kind of prayer comes from his unique knowledge of being God's child. His piety is also marked by another characteristic: his prayer pours out in joy and thanksgiving and rejoicing. When he prays for something, it is always on behalf of someone else, and no cry of penitence, no *miserere mei*, passes his lips. His prayer is the emanation of his own holy life. He died in doing good for the poorest of the poor, for the sinful, for the sick, for children. Paul can describe his life only as the revelation of "the goodness and kindness of God our Saviour" (Titus 3.4). Human standards fail him when he tries to estimate Jesus' life upon earth. To give voice to the whole truth, he has to have recourse to God himself. Jesus' life is not the goodness and kindness of mere man, but of God alone. Jesus is the only man upon earth who is able to ask his enemies with a clear conscience: "Which of those among you can accuse me of sin?" He does not pray: "Father, forgive me," but "forgive them, for they know not what they do."

At no point in his life is the merest trace of a moral lack, or moral immaturity, or even need for moral development perceptible in him. He is always the same, mature, kindly, true, strong, as a twelve-year-old child in the temple and as a thirty-three-year-old man before Herod. From whatever angle we consider his image, Jesus is always as we in our best moments would wish to be; whether he is blessing the children who are brought to him, whether he is conversing with the Samaritan woman at the well, washing his disciples' feet or comforting Mary Magdalen, calling on the Mount of Olives, "Let this cup depart from me," or affirming in Pilate's face, "Yes, I am a king," he is always austere and simple, and yet virile and proud, reserved and eloquent, full of high seriousness and yet tender as a child, mighty and absolute of will, and yet infinitely indulgent and kind—as the moment requires. His behaviour runs the entire gamut of a spiritual attitude, and every note is perfect, great, mature, heartfelt, and free, always he himself. No mere man has ever been experienced like that. Either this man is just a literary figment of the imagination—

and then the literary art of common fishermen would itself be a miracle and as incomprehensible as their composition—or he is no mere man. He is rather a man in whom the essence of God's holiness is mirrored. He is God become man.

Confronted with this Jesus as he is represented in the Synoptic Gospels, we have no choice. Either he never existed —and in that case we have to reckon with one of the greatest of literary miracles—or he existed as God become man; for mere man cannot exist in such a manner. The divinity cannot be removed from his life and being. This is what makes the image comprehensible, because it gives it its inner truth. It is not something painted externally on the surface. Rather it works through his entire being, his speech and his silence, his tears and his prayers, his miracles, and most of all his death. We say we cannot omit the miracles of Jesus' life without dissolving that life itself. But how much the less can we remove Jesus' consciousness of his divine nature, without dissolving it into an empty fiction. If ever a man existed who really felt and acted as the Synoptic Gospels describe, then it can only have been a man in whom God himself had disclosed his person, and who was united with God in the depths of his awareness. To look for mere man behind his miraculous image would be contrary to all historical analogies, and against any understanding psychology.

The fulfilment in the resurrection of the disciples' belief in Christ

Certain as it is that the Lord's entire life and ministry is a reflection of his divinity, it is equally certain that the disciples accepted these impressions of his divinity only gradually, in a slow unfolding, and not without inner resistance. They were children of the Jewish nation, after all, brought up from childhood in the belief that God hath not wife or child. Only sometimes, only at moments of particularly deep emotion, as once at Cæsarea Philippi, do they pierce through the earthly human garment of the Lord to his divine secret. But generally, they all fell back again into their traditional Jewish ideas, especially when they saw Jesus in the hands of his enemies, suffering and dying. The impression of Jesus' humanity was too strong, and their Jewish inheritance worked on them too powerfully for them to see in the Messias not only the servant of God but the Son of God in the true sense. The Evangelist describes their attitude thus: "Their heart was blinded." Usually, the highest point to which they could exalt Jesus' wise and loving leadership was to trace the power of God in his humanity, to know of his election and unique relationship to God, and to give to this knowledge the highest form of expression at their command, the names of prophet, servant of God, Christ. "Concerning Jesus of Nazareth, who was a prophet mighty in work and word before God and all the people . . . but we were hoping that it was he who should redeem Israel." With these simple words, the disciples of Emmaus themselves describe the sum of all that Jesus was to them (Luke 24.19).

What tore the disciples out of this darkness, uncertainty, and confusion of mind, and suddenly bore them aloft to the mountain of faith in the divinity of Christ, was *the resurrection*. Here we shall discuss only the enormous significance that the experience of the resurrection had for the new faith of the disciples. Later it is repeatedly stressed by the first Apostles, and especially by Peter, that the Lord's resurrection was the ultimate foundation for their faith in the "Lord," in the "Exalted One," who sits at the right hand of God, who sends down the Holy Spirit from the right hand of God, and in whose name alone men may attain bliss. The Kyrie, Kyrie is the first response of their new faith to the tidings of Easter. "The Lord has arisen indeed and has appeared to Simon," the eleven cried to the two disciples as they returned from Emmaus (Luke 24.34). "It is the Lord," John cried out as he saw Jesus resurrected upon the shore of the lake (John 21.7). "My Lord and my God," Thomas avowed when he saw the wounds of the Resurrected One (John 20.28). "Who art thou, Lord?" asked Paul on the way to Damascus (Acts 9.5). If the eyes of the Apostles had previously been dazzled by Jesus' earthly human appearance, they were now the more struck by the elemental impression of his divinity. Now, as they realize the Transfigured One is in their midst, his divine nature becomes the centre of their consciousness, and from now on they apprehend his humanity only from his divinity. For the disciples, their experience of Easter was the *ultimate explanation*, and it brought a decisive deepening of their image of Christ. The old impressions of Jesus' human figure were assumed into the new impressions of his divinity, and filled with them. Forty days the Resurrected One appeared to the disciples (Acts 1.3), and even ate and drank with them (Luke 24.30, 43; John

20.12 f.; Acts 10.41) in a mysterious way quite beyond the
scope of our experience, and the "altogether different" reality
of God became apparent to the disciples. With the compelling
power of his immediate presence, their thinking and feeling
were turned from the earth, and their powers directed towards
the divine Christ. The "kingdom of God," "near at hand" in
the simple figure of the Son of Man, timidly and barely no-
ticeably taking root in Palestinian soil, from now on revealed
itself in the Transfigured One as the "kingdom of God" in that
original, majestic sense which Daniel envisaged—the kingdom
"from heaven." In this supernatural light, Jesus' message lost
for them all earthly traits and all Jewish colouring. It is no
longer a question of disputes with Pharisees and Sadducees;
no longer a question of a greater justice, or the begetting of
the Son of Man, of keeping the Sabbath, of Moses and his
Law. It is a question of the resurrection and the eternal life,
the coming of the Holy Spirit, the forgiveness of sins, baptism,
truth, and Grace. The disciples' gaze no longer clings to Israel,
its temples and sacrifices, high priests and Scribes. Rather the
new flock of the Messias which Peter will have to tend in place
of the Good Shepherd himself is clearly defined—the community of God, the Church, which embraces all nations. The
resurrection transforms the disciples' entire world of ideas,
their spiritual horizon, and their religious conceptions. Their
thoughts and considerations are turned away from the earthly
Jesus in his oppression and lowliness to the divine Christ and
his glory. Their eyes are opened to new insights and tasks, and
with the beating of wings of the Pentecostal Spirit, these new
insights and tasks become a compelling demand, an urgent
command. Only now do they understand what Jesus had once
said to them: "Many things yet I have to say to you, but you
cannot bear them now" (John 16.12). But now, in the inspiration of the Holy Spirit, they no longer regard themselves
as thankful receivers, but as creative begetters, committed
with all their might and all their being to these new experiences, insights, and hopes. A "burden" is laid upon them, as
Paul later says—an unutterable responsibility before God and
man. But the disciples also know that their calling is an unutterable Grace. What the prophets were for the old covenant,
they will be for the new, the bearers of the new spirit of Christ,
the true heralds of his tidings, which move heaven and earth,
"the chosen witness of Jesus Christ." This new faith it is that
moves Matthew and Mark, Luke and John to write their Gospels. It is in the Apostles as they write their letters. It was the

resurrection of the Lord that was the ultimate foundation and seal of the new faith, the belief that Jesus is the Son of God, the divine Christ.

We have gone to the sources to show Jesus' consciousness of his nature. This is the true basis for every Christology. Jesus alone could know what lived and moved within him. He alone could bear witness to his divine mystery. It is understandable that the disciples laboured in their fashion to enter into the richness of this self-consciousness and to describe it with the means and ideas of their time. St. Paul and St. John more than anyone else took on the task of interpreting and illuminating the image of Christ. The Christology of St. Paul and his utterances about the mystery of the Lord are some decades older than those of St. John. So we shall first discuss the Christology of St. Paul, but only to the extent that it attempts to interpret Jesus' own consciousness of himself.

X

PAUL'S INTERPRETATION OF CHRIST'S SELF-CONSCIOUSNESS

The vision of Christ at Damascus

THE foundation of Paul's belief in Christ is his experience of Christ at Damascus. As he himself testifies, God "shone in his heart" then, and kindled in him the recognition that the "glory of God shone on the face of Christ Jesus" (2 Cor. 4.6), and that Christ is the "image" of God (Col. 1.15; 2 Cor. 4.4). This is the true content of his experience of Christ: "knowledge of the glory of God, shining on the face of Christ Jesus" (2 Cor. 4.6). He says expressly that he did not receive it from man, nor was he taught it (Gal. 1.12), but "by a revelation of Jesus Christ" (δι' ἀποκαλύψεως Ἰησοῦ Χριστοῦ). The words "of Jesus Christ," Ἰησοῦ Χριστοῦ, are in the subjective genitive, meaning: I learned it through Christ's revealing it to me, and not from men. Paul's vision of Christ before Damascus is for him the true source of perception, the perception of the Χριστὸς κατὰ πνεῦμα. But this is not to be understood as meaning that Paul learned about Christ only from this manifestation. He learned the historical details of Ἰησοῦς κατὰ σάρκα another way. From the Acts of the Apostles we learn that he had been brought up in Jerusalem as a pupil of the Pharisee Gamaliel (22.3), and that he took part in the stoning of Stephen (7.58; 8.3; 9.1). He must have been acquainted with Christianity very early. Indeed, at that time he would even have been in a position to see and hear Christ in person, for he was in Jerusalem at the same time as Christ was teaching and ministering there, and when he was crucified. In 2

Corinthians 5.16, he himself seems to disclose that he did in fact make use of this opportunity to become acquainted with Christ: "And even though we have known Christ according to the flesh [κατὰ σάρκα], yet now we know him so no longer." In the context, he uses the "we" as the *pluralis majestatis*. This would make it perfectly possible that Paul had known the historical Jesus personally. But all his Jewish nationalism would allow him to see then was the outward humanity of his appearance, and he totally misjudged Jesus' inner, divine essence. It is not out of the question that Paul, the fanatical follower of Gamaliel, might even have been present at the crucifixion and might also have raised his voice to join the cry of "Crucify him." This is what gave him the capacity, which no other Apostle had, of "depicting before your eyes," as he puts it in his Epistle to the Galatians (3.1), the love and suffering of the Crucified One. So he may truly affirm: "We too have known Christ." But he had every reason to add "according to the flesh"—only outwardly, in his historical figure. He was able to extend his historical knowledge of the Lord as he persecuted the Christians "even to the death" (Acts 22.4). Psychologically, we can only think that he must have questioned the Christians whom he was "binding and committing to prisons" (Acts 22.4) about their faith. "It is impossible to imagine that a man like Paul passionately persecuted the Christian faith, with great success too, without knowing or wanting to know anything about this faith beyond the bare fact that these people regarded a certain Jesus who had been crucified as the coming Messias" (Vischer).

The impression Paul received here unconsciously blended with the deep impression of Christ himself he had had against his will. He resisted them with all the force of his traditional ideal of the Messias, which proclaimed only a Messias of glory and not a *Christus crucifixus*. But when Christ appeared to him on the road to Damascus, it was impossible for him to "kick against the goad" (Acts 9.5; 22.8; 26.14). He could resist no longer. What he had struggled to suppress and thrust to the periphery of his consciousness suddenly appeared before his eyes as a mighty reality. "I am Jesus, whom thou art persecuting." The impact must have been overwhelming. Paul sums it up thus: "If then any man is in Christ, he is a new creature: the former things have passed away; behold they are made new!" (2 Cor. 5.17). Six times, Paul and Luke discuss this manifestation of Christ and the radical reversal of his inner life that resulted (Acts 9.3 ff.; 22.6; 26.13 ff.; Gal. 1.15; 1

Cor. 9.1; 15.8). Now he had come to know the true Christ. Now he really did have nothing more to learn. For three years he withdrew in solitude to Arabia. Here, at it were, he accomplished his *exercitia spiritualia,* bringing order into his new impressions, and achieving a complete transvaluation of his former values. No one could help him here, not even the first Apostles, only the Holy Spirit. He himself says (Gal. 1.15): "But when it pleased him who from my mother's womb set me apart and called me by his Grace, to reveal his Son in me, that I might preach him among the Gentiles, immediately, without taking counsel with flesh and blood, and without going up to Jerusalem to those who were appointed Apostles before me, I retired into Arabia, and again returned to Damascus. Then after three years, I went to Jerusalem to see Peter, and I remained with him fifteen days."

The new perception that had dawned upon Paul was the knowledge of the *divine* Christ, "Christ according to the spirit." So important was this knowledge, so completely overshadowing everything else, that any knowledge of Christ "according to the flesh"—purely historical knowledge of his human manifestation—seemed inferior to this supernatural perception. And so the historical name of Jesus recedes in Paul's Christology, and the beginning and end of his proclamation is the dogmatic name of Christ. He is not concerned with the visible, tangible humanity of Jesus, but with his inner mystery and his divine essence.

This is not the place to go into the proof that the manifestation at Damascus was no mere subjective vision or typical case of conversion. Paul does not speak of a new experience that took place merely in his own consciousness. Rather, he represents the events on the road to Damascus as an occurrence that seized him from outside, and compelled him against his will. He had a certain visual impression that was literally *forced* upon his eye from outside. That his vision was not caused by his own will, but was urged upon him, Paul expresses by using not the active but the passive voice in describing it in 1 Corinthians 15.5 ff. "He was seen of Cephas, then of the twelve" * (ὤφθη). Thus Paul distinguishes between this event and his other ecstatic experiences, which he *never* adduces as proof of his faith in Christ, and the nature of which he deliberately leaves an open question (2 Cor. 12.2 ff.). Only the encounter before Damascus does he regard as equivalent to the mani-

* King James Authorized Version. The Douay translation has: "He appeared to Cephas, and after that to the eleven." *Trans.*

festations of Christ that had been granted the disciples. It alone legitimizes his claim to be an Apostle. "Am I not an Apostle? Have I not seen Jesus our Lord?" (1 Cor. 9.1). The Apostle's own statements are quite unequivocal here. And the earnestness of his new way of life would be hardly comprehensible psychologically if he had not been overwhelmed by an objective experience that came to him against his will and contrary to all the ideas he had held till then. As a witness of Christ, Paul is very close to the first Apostles, although not an eyewitness of the life, death, and resurrection of Jesus as they were. For it is likely that he had known the historical Jesus—"according to the flesh"—in person, and in any case had been able to correct and extend his historical picture from what he had heard from the Christian prisoners. And he had "seen" Christ "according to the spirit" just as the disciples had seen him. He had been directly and personally moved by him. He saw the glory ($\delta\acute{o}\xi\alpha$) of God on his face.

Religious history's attempts at an explanation

This automatically puts an end to those theories that have tried to explain the faith in Christ of the Apostle to the Gentiles purely "naturally"—i.e., according to historical evolution. Above all, the historians of religion have taken it upon themselves to explain Paul's Christology as the product of a logical *process of thought,* a progressive clarification by the Apostle of the truth of the messianic picture of the first man in Jewish apocalyptic literature, which had been described in the Psalms of Solomon, the metaphorical speeches of the Book of Henoch, and in the Apocalypse of Baruch. This is largely Brückner's thesis. Other historians, like Windisch, maintain that Paul was influenced by Hellenistic philosophizing. In Hellenistic Jewry, the figure of the Jewish Messias had already merged with that of the Hellenistic "wisdom" ($\sigma o\varphi\acute{\iota}\alpha$). In his heart Paul had taken issue with these possibilities, and in his struggle on the road to Damascus had reached the full conviction that this "divine man" and this "wisdom" had appeared in Christ. The appearance of Christ before Damascus was only a reflection of these inner conflicts.

What can we reply to this? Above all we must emphasize that neither the "divine man" nor the "wisdom" is central to Paul's Christology. Its centre is rather the certainty:

"Christ is the Lord," "the image of the Father." Moreover, all
Paul himself is aware of is that he was led to this Christ on
the way to Damascus. He never gives any indication that before his conversion he had brooded and struggled over a certain ideal of the Messias. All he bore within him were impressions of the historical Jesus. He had no conception of a late
Judaeo-Hellenistic eschatological Christ. Indeed, this Christ
lacks exactly what for Paul was most important and decisive:
his death for our salvation and his resurrection. The *Christus
passus et crucifixus* is something totally foreign to Judaeo-
Hellenistic thought. So the Apostle too felt his conversion as
a "new creation," a catastrophe that came upon him and compelled him to pledge his entire ministry for this *Christus passus*.

Biblical criticism has come more and more to recognize that
Paul could not have attained to his faith in Christ by way of
late Judaic ideas. It has, instead, attempted to discover the true
source of his Christology in the Hellenistic mysteries. These
critics draw attention to the fact that the Apostle's image of
Christ bears very little trace of the historical Jesus. His image
of Christ might therefore arise from ideas outside the Jewish
sphere. They contend that what Paul says of Jesus is at root
a myth, to which Jesus has contributed only the name—the
myth of the dying and the resurrected divine Saviour. Gunkel
was the first to offer this interpretation, and a number of historians followed him. Wendland maintains that Paul's Christian
mysticism is largely determined by the mysticism of Oriental
religions of salvation. Reitzenstein would have it that Paul was
completely dependent upon the religious ideas of the Oriental
Gnostic religions of salvation. Reading Paul's Epistles, he feels
constantly the mental climate of those ideas familiar to him
from the mystery religions.

We have to admit and, indeed, encourage the thought that
in formulating and proclaiming his Christology Paul should
have made use of those ideas and expressions understood by his
contemporaries. He had to look for aid to those schemes and
images that he could assume in his listeners, those among them
who had been adherents of the mystery beliefs. So it is hardly
surprising that we should observe in his writings expressions
and turns of phrase that were at home in the Hellenistic mystery theologies. The concepts truth, life, rebirth, illumination,
can be found in Paul's thought, just as they can in the mystery religions. But it is a dubious assertion to maintain a similarity of content as well as of form. This is where the mytho-

logical comparison fails us. What do we know of the mysteries, their structure and their meaning? Searching for an answer, we realize that all we have are fragments, scattered notes and indications here and there, that have only subsequently been put together by the historian into a unified picture. Moreover, most of these indications come down to us from the time after Christ. We do not know what the mysteries originally signified; perhaps they were originally sheer nature myths, devoid of any ethical or religious content, only later taking on an ethical meaning by contact with Christianity. In any case, there is proof that the Christian influence was strong at the time of the Emperor Julian. Julian the Apostate wanted to reanimate the old myths by blending them with Christian thoughts. But how little contact they did in fact have with Christian ideas, a brief glance at the Isis and Mithras mysteries will make clear.

We learn from Apuleius of Madaura (b. *circa* A.D. 130) that the religious community of Isis was divided into two groups, the *advenae,* who took part in the religious service, and the true adepts, who had dedicated themselves for life with an oath to warlike service for the goddess. These latter consisted only of those who had been summoned by the goddess in a dream. They were instructed by the initiates in the "tradition" (Paradosis). The initiate was to them their "spiritual father." The instruction was followed by a bath of purification and baptism. After a fast and strict abstinence lasting ten days, the novice was conducted by the high priest to descend into the "adyton"; i.e., he wanders through the subterranean chambers which symbolize the realm of death. Apuleius describes this journey into the nether world thus: "I went as far as the confines of death. I reached Proserpine's threshold. And after I had traversed all the elements, I went back again. At midnight I saw the sun with bright, white, radiant beams. I came face to face with the higher and the lower gods. Right close to them, I worshipped." The initiation represented a journey through the beyond, through the night of death to the light of the upper gods. During this journey the novice must go through twelve transformations in twelve different garbs during the twelve hours of the night. At last he has been removed into a new life, he is reborn, *renatus, ro formatus.* At sunrise he is decked with the garment of heaven and is crowned with a wreath. So adorned, he is set upon a pedestal before Isis as the sun-god, and is worshipped by the members of the cult as the "image (εἰκών) of God. At a solemn feast, he celebrates his "birthday," *natalitia.* Then he goes back into the world, leaving the garment of heaven behind him in the temple. He is not garbed in it again until

his death. This raiment holds and brings about the "illumination" (φωτισμός).

If we compare these rites with Christian custom, we find
not a few similarities: the obligation to do war service
(*militia*), bound by a kind of oath (*sacramentum*), which is
similar to our baptismal oath; the novice's instruction in the
tradition, or Paradosis, by the spiritual father; the baptism at
the end of the instruction, and the description of the new life
as "rebirth and illumination." We are unable to establish
which of these rites are truly pre-Christian. It is possible,
indeed very likely, that a great deal was borrowed from Christianity. But there is also the thought that Paul and the first
Christians among the Gentiles borrowed the external rites
from the mysteries. Apart from these common factors, however, there are certain essential differences precisely in the
image of the Saviour. Isis, like Osiris and the other mystery
gods, is not a "Saviour" in the sense that she consciously took
it upon her to suffer for the sins of her devotees. Rather, these
mystery gods were themselves in need of redemption, and
experienced suffering and rebirth through a destiny that fell
upon them against their own intent. So *they* do not redeem
the novice. Rather, he redeems himself, following them by a
kind of imitation magic. The redemptive blessing does not
penetrate to their spiritual being. Their lives are not animated
by the gods' saving powers. Even after the initiation, the
adept remains completely on his own, and goes on living his
secular life without further thought. Only in death does he
receive divine being with the garment of the mystery. This
would seem to be a purely external cult of deification. The adept
does not really enter with his soul into communion with the
Saviour, but is himself directly transformed into the god of
the cult. He himself becomes Isis and Osiris. The entire cult
has a pantheistic, monistic meaning. It lacks the decisive
element—the figure of God incarnate, the mediator who will
take the faithful up into himself and unite them with the
Godhead. And this mediator is missing because he is not
necessary to the pantheistic assumptions that dominate the
mysteries. The divinity, indeed, does not strictly belong to the
world beyond, but is rather a representative of this world.
Which is why the adept can be immediately deified.

The Mithras cult is more relevant to Paul's mysticism than
the Isis mystery, so we will adduce this, too, as a comparison.
No doubt Paul had opportunity enough to become acquainted
with the cult in his native town of Tarsus, where it flourished.
It is true the Mithras mysteries began to spread only in the
second century after Christ. So we must be exceedingly
cautious, because Christian ideas might easily have made their
way into these rites. We are no longer able to ascertain how

the cult appeared originally. But this much seems certain: the novice had to go through seven stages of initiation (analogous to our seven ordinations). These stages of initiation were symbolized by masks which the novice had to wear at the mystery rites. They were masks of the raven, the hidden one, the soldier, the lion, the Persian, the course of the Sun, and finally the Father. The masks of the lion, the Persian, and the course of the Sun reveal the Persian origin of the mystery. The adepts called one another "brother." There were no sisters, because women had no access to the mysteries. The sacramental rites included a baptism with water and honey, branding with a sign (χαρακτήρ—analogous to the seal of our confirmation), and a sacred repast of bread, water, and wine. These sacramental rites were introduced by a series of ordeals intended to test the courage of the novice. As in the cult of Isis, these mysteries took place in crypts, which were adorned with pictures of the stars and the elements of the world. Stage by stage, the novice had to ascend through the seven portals of this world of the spheres until he finally reached the true divine image of Mithras himself. Cumont, whose knowledge of the Mithras cults is the deepest there is, gives this description of the ascent (*Textes et monuments*, I, 322): "When the neophyte had gone through the entrance hall of the temple and descended the steps of the crypt he would see before him in holiness, splendidly adorned and illuminated, the venerated image of Mithras the bull-killer standing in the apse, and then the monstrous figures of Kronos, the lion-headed, heavily decked with the attributes and symbols of the mystery whose meaning was still hidden to him. Those taking part in the ceremony knelt on either side on stone benches, prayed, and collected themselves in the dim light. Lamps arranged around the choir threw a vivid light upon the faces of the gods and the priests, who, garbed in strange apparel, received the new converts. The unexpected play of lighting, carefully managed, would startle his eye and mind. The religious rapture with which he would be seized endowed these rather childish spectacles with a terrible appearance. The dazzling deceptions that confronted him appeared to him as real dangers, over which his courage triumphed. The potent wine he took roused his senses and confused his reason. He murmured conjurations, and they summoned divine manifestations before his imagination. In his ecstasy, he imagined he was exalted beyond the bounds of the world. After his transports, he would repeat, like Apuleius' adept: 'I went as far as the confines of death.' "

The mere description of these mysteries is sufficient to demonstrate the great difference between them and the Christian mystery. In the Mithras cult, as in all similar cults, everything is directed towards impressing the senses, which causes the religious historian to call them aesthetic religions of redemption. In Paul's doctrine of the sacrament, there is no echo of Mithras to be found at all. The seven ordinations of Christianity, which recall the seven initiations of Mithraism, were as yet unknown to Paul. His teaching of baptism with water is innocent of any idea of honey, and at root signifies a baptism into the death and resurrection of the Lord. His feast is no ordinary repast, but communion with the flesh and blood of Christ. His confirmation is purely spiritual, and has no need of branding. And Paul knows nothing of the essential part of the Mithraic rite—the course through the spheres of heaven. The centre of his faith and ritual is a figure totally unknown to the Mithraic mysteries—the figure of God the Son, the Saviour who suffered and was resurrected. The Mithraic liturgy has no conception of this soteriological motive; in these cults, redemption takes place through the adept's own powers, through maintaining his personal courage in face of all the cosmic and daemonic dangers that threaten him. He has to struggle to achieve his own salvation.

*   *   *   *

To sum up, we might outline the distinction between Paul's soteriology and the mystery myths as follows. The cult of the mystery religions was always founded on a nature, or astral, myth. Hence the union of the adept with God was a magical identification of natures. The adept became the god himself. In contrast to this, the New Testament teaching refers to an historical event for our salvation, and to him who died for our sins. So in Paul's doctrine, mystical union is never identification of natures. The Apostle knows nothing of any deification, but only of a commitment in faith and love to the mediator who unites us to the Godhead. So the objects of the dedications in each case are different. In the hour of initiation, the adept of the mysteries gazes upon the gods of heaven and of the nether world. "To see the universe" (πανοπτεύειν πάντα), the highest vision, is the adept's longing. But the confirmed Christian knows that now he sees only as in a mirror. He is transformed not by seeing but by believing. Because the ancient mysteries were concerned with a magical union of natures, sin to them consists in entanglement in the world of matter. Redemption accordingly means liberation from the bonds of the destiny of one's nature, from the blind machinations of fate (εἱμαρμένη). Sin is understood as something natural, besmirching with cosmic dust, and hence with transitoriness. Hence ethical and religious obligations are foreign to the pagan mysteries. It is true, strict demands were made on the devotees of Isis and Mithras too. But fundamentally they are nothing but the cults' decrees for purification—for example, abstinence from certain foods, sexual enjoyment, sleep, etc. This essential difference between the religions is also mirrored in their use of language. The language of the pagan cults knows nothing of the key word of Paul's soteriology: εἶναι ἐν Χριστῷ, "in Christ, with Christ." It is true they speak of "becoming God" (ἐν θεῷ γίνεσθαι), or of "entering into God" (ἔνθεον εἶναι). But this is something achieved only in ecstasy, and never a permanent state. Paul speaks of sharing in the crucifixion and resurrection of Christ. The mysteries speak only of being free of death (ἀποθανατισμός) (cf. A. Dietrich, *Mithrasliturgie,* 12.5; 2.8; 4.8).

Historical traits in Paul's figure of Christ

There is a considerable distinction, too, between the Hellenistic and Paul's Christian redemption mysteries. However, the historians of religion still believe that Paul's image of Christ at least is to be explained as a borrowing from the mysteries, because, unlike the image of Christ in the Synoptic Gospels, it bears completely unearthly, supernatural, divine characteristics. Indeed, Paul does know Christ "only according to the spirit," and not Jesus "according to the flesh." Almost all earthly colours have faded away in his picture. There is no longer any smell of the earth about it. The historians argue that it has become a purely mythical figure, as in the mysteries.

Is this true? Is the Apostle to the Gentiles aware only of the divine Christ? Or does his "Christ according to the spirit" also bear earthly, purely human traits, marked in with the clear, sharp lines of history, as they are in the Synoptic Gospels? This is the question that will occupy us first. Only when we have decided this may we proceed to evaluate the Apostle's Christology in detail.

Indeed, Paul does stress the spiritual, divine Pneuma in his Christ, but for all that, his picture of the Lord never dissolves into a purely mythological figure. The strict and solid lines of history and historical reality still endow it with the particular stamp of true humanity. Paul knows and describes the outward historical framework of the figure of Jesus. Jesus was born "of woman" (Gal. 4.4), "of the offspring of David" (Rom. 1.3). He knows some of the Lord's brethren (1 Cor. 9.5; 15.7; Gal. 1.19; 2.9,12). He knows the twelve disciples (1 Cor. 15.5). But his most detailed account is of Jesus himself, especially of his suffering and resurrection. His entire system of thoughts is anchored in the historical facts of Jesus' crucifixion and resurrection. "Before their eyes" (κατ' ὀφθαλμούς), the Apostle depicts Christ's crucifixion to his Galatians (ἐσταυρωμένος, Gal. 3.1). This "depiction before their eyes" (προεγράφη) he intends as an urgent and solemn proclamation. He wants to point his finger, as it were, to the Crucified One, and make the picture vivid and tangible. His formulations are evidence that he took over the main part of the early Christian tradition—the facts of Christ's death, burial, resurrection on the third day, and his appearance before Cephas. But beyond that, the Apostle also knows of the other occasions when Christ resurrected appeared to the faithful—once to the eleven disciples, then to five hundred brethren at once, most of whom still survive, and to James and all the Apostles together. This history of the passion and the resurrection he regards as one of the chief elements of Christianity (ἐν πρώτοις) to be passed on to them; and this he does, seeking support in other accounts (ὃ καὶ παρέλαβον), closely dependent on the succession of eyewitnesses (1 Cor. 15.3; cf. Acts 13.27 ff.). Paul knows very well that he is on firm historical ground. To him, the Kyrios is not a divinity hedged around with legend, but a God who became man, and this humanity has been caught and described in its entire course through history. Just as he recounts the history of the passion, Paul also tells of the last supper, of the betrayer, and of the arrest of Jesus "on the night in which he was betrayed." He knows that Jesus had to endure mockery (Rom. 15.3). As if he had himself seen the crucifixion, he never wearies of describing the sufferings of Christ and the griefs of his calling. It is the Christian's task to bear the sufferings of Christ (τἀπαθήματα τοῦ Χριστοῦ, 2 Cor. 1.5), and become like him in the fellowship of his sufferings (κοινωνία τῶν παθημάτων). He himself declares that he bears the marks of the Lord Jesus in his body (τά στίγματα τόυ Ἰησοῦ, Gal. 6.17). And just as he recounts Christ's passion and resurrection, he also recounts his conflict and struggle. When in Romans (5.15; 18.19) he contrasts the first Adam with the second, who by his obedience made good the disobedience of the other, he leaves room for the entire content of the history told in the Synoptic Gospels. Behind their parallels, the Synoptic picture of Christ rises, with the smell of the earth, his prayers, his struggles, and his suffer-

ing. In the image of Jesus, Paul recognizes the ideal of holiness.
Jesus was without sin (2 Cor. 5.21). He possessed "holiness of
spirit" (Rom. 1.4). And Paul has as sharp and detailed an idea
of the doctrine and message of Jesus as he has of his historical
person. Paul does not talk merely in general terms about the
early Christian tradition from which he derives his historical
information. Rather, he quotes single sayings of the Lord almost word for word, and they ring true and original when he
cites them. He follows Mark's account of the Last Supper (1
Cor. 11.23 ff.), and he is the first witness to testify that Christ
understood it in the sense of a perpetual foundation. In for-
bidding divorce, he calls unmistakably upon a saying of the
Lord's (1 Cor. 7.10; cf. Matt. 19.8). Similarly, he quotes
Jesus' dictum that nothing is of itself unclean (Rom. 14.14;
cf. Mark 7.15), and recalls an isolated Logion, whose content
alone survives in the Synoptic Gospels (Matt. 10.10; Luke
10.7): "So also the Lord directed that those who preach the
Gospel should have their living from the Gospel" (1 Cor.
9.14). A literal quotation of Jesus' sayings is also to be found
in Romans 12.14: "Bless those who persecute you; bless and
do not curse." The sentence recalls Matthew 5.44 ("Love your
enemies . . ."), but there is no doubt that it is original.

Paul is also familiar with Jesus' vocabulary. He knows it so
well that he reports maxims of the Lord's which the Synoptic
Gospels do not mention. From close comparison of the accounts of the Last Supper it would seem that he already had
a collection of sayings of Jesus in his hands. In his earliest
writing, the first Epistle to the Thessalonians (4.15), he relies
upon the "word of the Lord" when he talks of those who will
survive until the coming of the Lord. Jesus' words to him are
the highest authority. "The Lord directed," "the Lord commands" (1 Cor. 9.14; 7.10; cf. 12.25; Gal. 6.2; 1 Tim. 5.18).
In the Acts of the Apostles (20.35) he reminds the Ephesian
presbyters that he had taught them that they should "remember the word of the Lord Jesus." In Galatians 6.2, and in 1
Timothy 5.18, he describes the law of Christ as the absolute
standard. And in 1 Thessalonians 4.2 he observes that he had
given the faithful precepts "by the Lord Jesus." He constantly
reminds his congregations that he was handing on definite traditions (παραδόσεις, 2 Thess. 2.15; 3.6; 1 Cor. 11.2) and
definite doctrines (διδαχή, 2 Thess. 2.15; Rom. 16.17; Eph.
4.21; Col. 1.28; 2.7). He wants to pass on only what he has
received. Paul had a precise dogmatic tradition before him of
the words of Jesus.

But it is not only single maxims of the Lord's that the Apostle knows and turns to good account. Paul more than anyone else has most faithfully presumed and shared the entire spirit of Jesus' doctrine and its dominant ideas. For example, Jesus' important words about the kingdom of God. The kingdom of God is mentioned outside the Gospels only once in the second Epistle of St. Peter (1.11), and twice in the Epistle to the Hebrews (1.8; 12.28). In contrast, St. Paul uses the concept of the kingdom of God frequently, whether he is speaking of a kingdom of God already with us in the present (Rom. 14.17; 1 Cor. 4.20; Col. 4.11), or of one that is to be fulfilled only in the future (1 Cor. 6.9, 10; 15.20; Gal. 5.21 *et al.*), or where he calls the kingdom of God quite simply the kingdom of Christ (Col. 1.13; 2 Tim. 4.1, 18). And just as he takes up the concept of the kingdom of God, Paul too is the one who again and again makes use of that other central idea of Jesus' teaching: of how we are the children upon earth of God, our Father in heaven. The Christian spirit, freely calling as child upon father, which cries Abba, Father (Rom. 8.15; 2 Cor. 3.4 ff.; 3.17; Gal. 4.6 *et al.*)—the tenderest and deepest of Jesus' teaching is also the tenderest and deepest of Paul's. Just as Paul faithfully preserves Christ's theological doctrine, so he also preserves Jesus' moral tone and mood. Of course, he cannot, like Jesus, speak with that absolute authority that comes of Christ's messianic awareness—"but I say unto you . . ."—but he knows he is "the servant of Christ," and his moral imperative accordingly sounds every bit as categorical as the Lord's, especially at the end of his Epistles. It is true that for the achievement of morality he presupposes inspiration by the Holy Spirit. His ethics have an absolute supernatural foundation. One can act morally only out of a commitment to Jesus, and not of one's own strength. But this supernatural foundation is also an essential trait of Christ's message, for Jesus' moral demands too assume commitment to his person, and fellowship with him as a matter of course. The kingdom of God in the Lord's teaching too is a "planting" of the Father, a heavenly gift, and it is up to the master of the house alone to decide what he will pay his vine-dressers in the vineyard. And Paul is also a "pupil" of Jesus Christ with respect to the warmth of spirit and urgency of heart with which he proclaims his teaching. "Thou shalt" in Jesus' mouth is different from Hellenistic, and particularly from ancient Stoic, ethics; it is not an imperative of the intellect, but of the heart, or rather of the whole man. The love and serene unselfish joy of the heart at doing good is the basic tone of Jesus' teaching, but it is also to be found in Paul. "The Apostle's language is never richer, warmer, more enthusiastic than when he is speaking of love, renunciation, and resignation, of service and endurance. Romans 12 is never wearied of depicting the various forms of love, and in 1 Corinthians 13 Paul praises love in a dithyrambic tone so glowing, rapturous, and enthusiastic, that there has never been his like before or since" (J. Weiss). Who taught Paul this paean of love? We have only to read the thirteenth chapter of the first Epistle to the Corinthians to learn the answer. Love "is not self-seeking, is not provoked; thinks no evil, does not rejoice over wickedness, but rejoices with the truth; bears with all things, believes all things, hopes all things, endures all things." It "never fails."

No longer are these simply the thoughts of Jesus, it is Jesus of Nazareth himself whom Paul is painting for us here with the delicate brush of human love. When we recall that Paul's proudest description of himself is as the "herald," the "Apostle," the "servant," the "minister," of Jesus Christ, then it seems monstrous to try to deprive him of the very thing that is his all: his knowledge of Jesus, the Christ.

The significance of Paul's experience before Damascus for his image of Christ

There is no trait in Paul's image of Christ that is not illuminated by his encounter with the Exalted One before Damascus. That he should straightway recognize Christ as the "divine man" came to him from his overpowering experience on the way to Damascus, and not from Jewish apocalyptic literature or the Gnostic Persian myth of the first man. This experience brings home to him that Jesus, whom up till then he had regarded as mere man, and had persecuted, is now garbed with the "glory" of heaven, and is a heavenly man. The expression "the heavenly man" (ὁ ἐπουράνιος), or the similar formulation "the second man from heaven" (ὁ δεύτερος ἄνθρωπος ἐξ οὐρανοῦ, 1 Cor. 15.48), or the third turn of phrase "the one man" (τοῦ ἑνὸς ἀνθρώπου, Rom. 5.15), is to be entirely understood from his experience before Damascus. For this revealed to him that the one who had previously seemed merely man had in truth come down from heaven, and was a heavenly being. Moreover, it is certain that Paul knew Jesus'

description of himself as "Son of Man," even if he does translate "Son of Man" literally as "Man" (Rom. 5.15; 1 Cor.
15.21; Eph. 5.31). This can be seen from the messianic interpretation in 1 Corinthians 15.27 of Psalm 8, which speaks of
the Son of Man. Paul's designation of the Lord as "the Man"
has a messianic meaning. And the honorific title of "the Lord,"
too, which occurs so frequently in Paul's Christology, is also
to be explained from his experience before Damascus. Did he
not cry, "Who art thou, Lord?" (Acts 9.5), and, "Lord, what
wilt thou have me do?" As a Hellenist he was familiar with
the title "Kyrios." And so it came involuntarily to his lips when
at the height of day the light shone from heaven and a voice
cried, "Saul, Saul, why dost thou persecute me?" Is it strange
that Paul, who addressed Christ as the Kyrios when he saw him
for the first time, was never to forget it, and was to make it
one of the keywords of his proclamation? And similarly with
Paul's doctrine, "the Lord is the Spirit" (ὁ δὲ Κύριος τὸ
Πνεῦμά ἐστιν, 2 Cor. 3.17). On the road to Damascus it was
revealed to him that Jesus no longer existed in earthly lowliness, but was spiritualized and transfigured, and radiant with
the splendour of God. The impression of spirit transfigured
was so strong that he was never afterwards able to image
Christ otherwise than as a spiritual power. And when he
pondered—and he never ceased to ponder over it—that from
his mother's womb, and out of the midst of his persecutions
of the Christians, this transfigured Lord had drawn him to
him, all he could do was yield to him with passionate love
and regard the true content of his life as "being in Christ"
(εἶναι ἐν Χριστῷ).

The heart of his personal experience, accordingly, was this:
The Jesus of the Christians is the true Christ, the heavenly
man, the true Lord, and the Transfigured One. These are already the essentials of his entire Christology. The heavenly
spirituality of being in Christ become man from then on was
bound to be the core of his Christology. The idea of a human
Jesus walking the earth necessarily receded before this new
image. He delighted in developing the idea of the heavenly
Christ out of the language and philosophical resources of his
age. If he wanted to tell his contemporaries what had been
revealed to him in this Christ, he would have to use their own
ideas and means of expression. Accordingly, he made use of
terms known to him from the mysteries: rebirth, life, illumination. This too is where the influence of contemporary ideas
can be traced in his Christology. But even so, it is not as if the

essentials of his image of Christ could have been affected by
them. This was not possible because, after all, Paul was not
the only witness and Apostle of Christ. Even though he did
receive his new faith from Christ himself, and not by way of
the first Apostles, the disciples, it was quite natural that in
offering a conceptual formulation of this faith he should hold
fast to the terms of the early Church, ultimately to the fundamental ideas of Jesus' message itself.

Paul's proclamation and the first Apostles

This brings us to the second source of his understanding of
Christ. We know that Paul certainly came into conflict with
the first disciples over practical questions, but never over questions of a theological nature, and certainly not over problems
of Christology. When he writes in 1 Corinthians 15.11 to the
congregation, "Whether then it is I or they [i.e., the first
Apostles], so we preach, and so you have believed," he is
testifying that in preaching about Christ there is no difference
between him and the first Apostles. They all preach of Christ
arisen. This agreement can be demonstrated even in detail.
Paul is conscious that Christ's death for our salvation belongs
to "the first doctrines" of the Christian tradition. He expressly
draws attention to it. "I delivered to you first of all what I
also received, that Christ died for our sins . . . according to
the Scriptures" (1 Cor. 15.3 f.). The reference to the Scriptures
(κατὰ τὰς γραφάς) makes it certain that the early community had already related Isaias' prophecy of the man of sorrows
(Isa. 53) to their image of Christ. A comparison of this passage with the system that is implicit in Paul's sermon at Pisidian
Antioch (Acts 13.16 ff.) makes it clear that in his proclamation of Christ he was using established forms which he had
not invented for himself, but had taken over from early Christianity. In the sermon, Jesus appears as the Christ in whose
suffering, death, and resurrection the Old Testament prophecies
are fulfilled (cf. especially J. R. Geiselmann, *Jesus der Christus*,
1951). Today we come increasingly to recognize that the
Apostle had found the images and symbols he used to describe
Christ's suffering—the image of the Paschal Lamb, ransom,
atonement—already present in the early Christian proclamation, and had taken them from there. As early as the first
Epistle of St. Peter (1.2), a liturgical formula already refers

to the "sprinkling" of the congregation with the blood of Christ, to redemption "with the precious blood of Christ, as of a lamb without blemish and without spot" (1.19). One is tempted to regard these images as already common property of the early Christian faith. The Epistle to the Hebrews is the clearest and most decisive expression of Christ's death for our salvation. All these phrases of the expiatory ransom through the blood of Christ are ultimately rooted in the Lord's own words that he would "give his life as a ransom for many" (Matt. 20.28; Mark 10.45). Of the Last Supper the Apostle expresses the same thought in liturgical formulation: "This is my blood of the new covenant which is being shed for many unto the forgiveness of sins." From this we may say that what Paul taught about the person of Christ and his death for our salvation was already part of the established fund of the Christian proclamation. What he experienced himself before Damascus was confirmed by the common Christian tradition. So Paul's Christology is by no means a foreign borrowing. We remain upon early Christian ground.

Thus we have created the basis for a detailed analysis of Paul's interpretation of the mystery of Christ. What was Paul's doctrine concerning Christ?

The theological content of Paul's faith in Christ. Christ's divinity according to Paul

One thing is certain: that Paul, like the Synoptic Evangelists, equated Christ and God. He was summoned to Christianity, he maintains, by God; and yet in the same breath he describes the Christians as "called to be Jesus Christ's" (Rom. 1.6), or called to be "a slave of Christ's" (1 Cor. 7.22). The acceptance of such a summons in faith is accomplished through God (Rom. 14.3) but equally through Christ. The service of God is the service of Christ (1 Thess. 1.9; Gal. 1.10; Rom. 14.18, et al.). He refers his own Apostolic office now to God (Gal. 1.15; Col. 1.25, et al.), now to Christ (2 Cor. 5.20; Rom. 1.5; Phil. 3.12). He is an Apostle "by Jesus Christ and God the Father" (Gal. 1.1). The Apostles are all servants of God (2 Cor. 6.4, etc.), but also servants of Christ (1 Cor. 3.5; 2 Cor. 11.23, et al.). The Holy Spirit is at one moment the Spirit of God (1 Cor. 2.10; Rom. 8.9) but also the Spirit of Christ (Gal. 4.6; 2 Cor. 3.17; Phil. 1.9, et al.). In the Apostle's eyes, God and Christ are merged in an inextricable union. The equation God = Christ is the presupposition of his message. Accordingly, words that in the Old Testament refer to God he applies without further ado to Christ (2 Thess. 1.8 f.; 1 Cor. 1.31; 2 Cor. 3.16, *et al.*). His declaration in Romans 14.6 ff. is typical of this kind of usage: "He who eats, eats for the Lord, for he gives thanks to God. And he who does not eat, abstains for the Lord, and gives thanks to God." Here "God" and "the Lord" are easily used as interchangeable expressions.

This manner of expression proceeds from Paul's fundamental idea that *God is revealed to us in Christ*. "For God . . . has shone in our hearts, to give enlightenment concerning the knowledge of the glory of God, shining on the face of Christ Jesus" (2 Cor. 4.6). The glory of God, God's own peculiar radiance (the *Kabod* of the Old Testament), shines upon the face of Jesus Christ. Christ is thus the "image of the invisible God" (εἰκὼν τοῦ Θεοῦ ἀοράτου, Col. 1.15), "the image of God" (2 Cor. 4.4), "the image of his substance" (Heb. 1.3). In the Hellenistic mysteries, the adept himself became the "image" of the cult god, but for Paul only the mediator is the image of God. Knowledge of the divine essence of God's ways with mankind can be achieved only by Christ. "For in him dwells all the fullness of the Godhead bodily" (ἐν αὐτῷ κατοικεῖ πᾶν τὸ πλήρωμα τῆς θεότητος σωματικῶς, Col. 2.9), which is to say, the fullness of the Godhead has been caught up in the human appearance of Jesus. Accordingly, Christ is "in the form of God" (ἐν μορφῇ Θεοῦ, Phil. 2.6); he is "equal with God" (τὸ εἶναι ἴσα Θεῷ). When Jesus entered this world of time, God showed "by sending his Son" (Rom. 8.3) that he was his "own Son" (Rom. 8.32).

In this connexion, the question arises whether Paul actually and expressly called Christ "God." Or did he only describe him as the "Son of God"? In Romans 9.5 he appears to have made the ultimate and absolute evaluation of Christ. The other passages that seem to be relevant here are of a different order. When in 2 Thessalonians 1.12 the Apostle prays ". . . that the name of our Lord Jesus Christ may be glorified in you, and you in him, according to the Grace of our God and the Lord Jesus Christ," he is not speaking of an individual person. Here as elsewhere, Paul is equating God and the Lord Jesus Christ (cf. 1 Thess. 3.11, 13; 1 Cor. 1.3; Rom. 1. 7), so that the "and" is to be understood only enumeratively. He is referring to God the Father and Jesus the Christ. This is most likely also the case in Titus 2.13. There, Paul writes: "We live

. . . looking for the blessed hope and glorious coming of our great God and Saviour Jesus Christ," and by the "great God" he can imply only God the Father. The "glorious coming of this great God" is Christ, for he is after all "the brightness of his glory and the image of his substance" (Heb. 1.3), "the image of the invisible God" (Col. 1.15). It is the habit of Paul's idiom to describe Christ as the glory of his Father. In the Gospel according to St. John, too, Jesus is described as a "glory as of the only-begotten of the Father" (1.14). The meaning of the passage in the Epistle to Titus, then, is this: We live looking for the coming of Christ. This Christ is the glory of the great God, and our Saviour. This is supported by the evidence of Romans 9.5: "For I could wish to be anathema myself from Christ for the sake of my brethren . . . from whom is the Christ according to the flesh, who is, over all things, God blessed forever, amen." Following this text, the Christ according to the flesh is identified with the God blessed forever. Some editions of the text put a period or sometimes a colon before the qualifying clause, so that it becomes an independent sentence, a closing phrase of this kind: "the God over all things be blessed forever, amen." This variant would certainly be in accordance with Paul's customary idiom, in which the Father alone is placed "above all things." Cf. Ephesians 4.6: "one God and Father of all, who is above all, and throughout all, and in us all." But the context of Romans 9.5 would seem to require a comma, not a period, in front of the appended clause, and would thus give undisguised expression to Jesus' Godhead. In any case, this explanation is linguistically possible, and has the support of the oldest original texts as well as of the Vulgate. But even if this version was not tenable, this would not affect the Apostle's fundamental idea that the fullness of the Father's Grace has been revealed to us in the human figure and corporeal manifestation of Christ. Paul constantly finds new phrases to express this basic idea: ". . . the love of God, which is in Christ Jesus" (Rom. 8.38); "the overflowing riches of his grace in kindness towards us in Jesus Christ" (Eph. 2.7); "the grace of God which was given you in Christ Jesus" (1 Cor. 1.4); "God . . . who has blessed us with every spiritual blessing on high in Christ" (Eph. 1.3). This would make Christ the Grace of God incarnate, God's fatherly love become man. When Paul does reserve the name of God for the Father alone, and he usually refers to Christ as "the Lord" in distinction to the Father, this is because he always has in mind Christ *become man*, who, in his humanity, is "lesser" than the Father, as John puts it. But Paul also takes pains to stress that this Christ become man also shares directly in the divine substance. Indeed, as we have seen, he is "like God," and "God's only-begotten Son."

Christ the Kyrios

Paul's most adequate expression for this divine mystery of Christ is the name of "Kyrios." In the entire Judaic literary tradition before Paul, this name never once occurs as a description of the Messias. It is reserved for God alone. The Septuagint, the Greek version of the Old Testament, always uses the title "Kyrios" to designate Jahve himself, and refrains from using his true name. It means Jahve, in so far as he is outwardly revealed. In applying the name "Kyrios" to Jesus, Paul is once again demonstrating that to him Jahve and Christ are in essence identical. Jahve and Christ are so closely related in his way of thinking that it is frequently uncertain whether by the term "Kyrios" he means God or Christ (e.g., 1 Thess. 1.8; 3.12; 4.6; 2 Thess. 2.13; 3.1, 5, 16).

It is proper that Christ as the Kyrios should be worshipped as divine. The Apostle prays to Christ just as he does to God: "May God our Father and our Lord Jesus direct our way unto you. And may the Lord make you to increase and abound in charity towards one another" (1 Thess. 3.11, 12; cf. 2 Cor. 12.8 f.). The "Maranathâ" of 1 Corinthians 16.22 is a prayer to Jesus, "Lord, come." Similarly, Paul declares that when the faithful pray to Christ, they "call upon the name of our Lord Jesus Christ" (1 Cor. 1.2; Rom. 10.12 f.). As God's goodness revealed, Christ is the fountain of all Grace and bliss. Paul begins his Epistles by commending his people to the "Grace and peace" of God and Christ. He closes them with an appeal to the "Grace of our Lord Jesus." Elsewhere, too, he frequently speaks of this Grace (2 Thess. 2.16; Gal. 1.6, et al.). It is the Grace that Christ bestows upon us through his Holy Spirit. Christ possesses "the power of God" (2 Thess. 1.7; 1 Cor. 1.24, et al.). It is poured over the Apostle like the *Shekinah* of God (2 Cor. 12.9). Christ enables the Apostle to journey to his congregations (1 Thess. 3.11; 1 Cor. 4.19; 16.7). But his mysterious, divine power can also be harsh and terrible. The Lord punishes and chastises even in this life (1 Cor. 11.32). But he can also bless and heal. He can avert sickness

(2 Cor. 12.8). Christ guides all hearts (2 Thess. 3.5). He increases the Christian's charity (1 Thess. 3.12). He comforts and strengthens our hearts in every good work and word (2 Thess. 2.16), and guards us from evil (2 Thess. 3.3). And so the Christian rejoices in Christ (1 Cor. 1.31; 2 Cor. 10.17; Phil. 1.26, *et al.*) just as he does in God (Rom. 5.11). Thus, as the fatherly goodness of God becomes man, Christ is the Kyrios, the exalted object of worship, the divine power and source of all Grace and bliss, but also of all damnation.

The Christological speculation of St. Paul

These fundamental ideas of Pauline Christology bear the marks of Paul's particular clarification of the relationship between Christ's divinity and his humanity. The basis of his speculation is the conviction that *Christ is the pre-existent Son of God*. He takes Christ's pre-existence so much for granted that he himself never sets about proving it, but presupposes it in all his arguments. The figure of Christ consists in the super-historical personality of Christ. In his vision at Damascus, Paul experienced Christ as the Kyrios—i.e., as the *Deus revelans*. Paul's belief in the pre-existence of Christ is a conclusion drawn directly from his belief in the divinity of Jesus. To explain the Pauline doctrine of pre-existence, there is no need for us to refer, for example, to the contemporary Judaic idea that such great elements in the history of their salvation as Moses, the temple, the tabernacle, or the children of God should have existed eternally in the divine ordination, because the ultimate in achievement must have been the absolute of divine intent. Paul had no need of these sublime speculations. The knowledge that Christ was the divine Kyrios for him necessarily involved Christ's pre-existence. There are eight passages in his Epistles where he puts this quite clearly. "When the fullness of time came, God sent his Son" (Gal. 4.4). The expression "sent" indicates that Jesus already possessed a divine mode of existence before he took on fleshly form. So Paul says "by sending his Son in the likeness of sinful flesh" (Rom. 8.3); "how, being rich, he became poor for your sakes, that by his poverty you might become rich" (2 Cor. 8.9). "Though he was by nature God, [he] did not consider being equal to God a thing to be clung to, but emptied himself, taking the nature of a slave, and being made like unto men" (Phil. 2.8).

Being pre-existent, Christ, is *the first-born of all creation* (Col. 1.15), and thus above every creature. "For in him were created all things in the heavens and on the earth, things visible and things invisible, whether Thrones, or Dominations, or Principalities, or Powers. All things have been created through and unto him" (Col. 1.16, 17). "For us there is only one God, the Father from whom are all things, and we through him" (1 Cor. 8.6). This faith in Christ's pre-existence gives rise to the conclusion that for Paul what is originally given in Christ is his divinity; this is his profoundest reality, supporting and dominating his created being, this is what truly makes the person of Christ. He is one and the same eternal Son of God, through whom are all things, who was sent in the fullness of time in the likeness of sinful flesh, and who finally, by his resurrection, when with his death on the cross the bonds of sinful flesh fell away, "was foreordained Son of God by an act of power" (Rom. 1.4). In all three stages of being, before creation, in human form upon earth, and at the right hand of the Father in heaven, the Son of God remains the basis of Christ's various modes of being. In all the stages of his sacred history, there is only one single self, which remains the same. It is always the same, the pre-existent Lord. Paul does not recognize a double identity in Christ. He does not distinguish between a natural and an adopted son, like the Nestorians. There is only one self in Christ—the Son of God. What is the relationship between divinity and humanity in this self? Is Christ's humanity subsumed into his divinity, as the later Monophysites would have it, or does it preserve its own integrity?

Paul never tires of stressing the *complete humanity* of the Lord. On two occasions (Rom. 5.15; 1 Cor. 15.21 f.) he draws a parallel between Adam and Christ as the two types of humanity. The importance of this comparison is precisely in the complete identity of the first and second Adam. Paul designates Christ as man with all the emphasis with which he calls him the Son of God. "For there is one God, and one Mediator between God and men, himself a man, Christ Jesus" (1 Tim. 2.5). This man Christ Jesus is described more exactly out of his concrete Jewish circumstances. He is born of woman, thus coming from the earthly world, and was born under Jewish Law (Gal. 4.4). He is of the seed of Abraham (Gal. 3.16) and of David (Rom. 1.3). He became "a minister of the circumcision" (Rom. 15.8) and, like other members of his people, performed the Mosaic dues and obligations.

What is the relationship, in Paul's speculation, between this true "man" Jesus and the Son of God, or, more precisely, his divine self? Philippians 2.6–11 gives us a clear insight into Paul's view. In this passage, which possibly takes its starting point in an early Christian liturgical hymn, the Apostle, it is true, does not intend to give explicit teaching on the connexion between the two natures in Christ. His intention is rather to draw us to humility by pointing out how Jesus became man, but this very absence of any dogmatic intent makes what he says in this passage particularly valuable. Here, too, Paul takes Christ's pre-existence as his starting point. "Though he was by nature God, [he] did not consider being equal to God a thing to be clung to, but emptied himself, taking the nature of a slave, and being made like unto men. And appearing in the form of man, he humbled himself, becoming obedient to death, even to death on a cross. Therefore God also has exalted him and has bestowed upon him the name that is above every name, so that at the name of Jesus every knee should bend of those in heaven, on earth and under the earth, and every tongue should confess that the Lord Jesus Christ is in the glory of God the Father." What Paul wants to stress here is the depth of Christ's humility. This was proved in his humiliation in becoming man. Before his existence upon earth, Christ was "in the form of God" (ἐν μορφῇ Θεοῦ). He was, adds Paul, so much upon the side of God, and not of creation, that he "did not think it robbery to be equal to God"—i.e., he was compelled to regard being equal to God as his original, innate right. Christ was originally by his nature equal to God. And yet he did not obstinately and forcefully hold on to this mode of being. Rather, he "emptied" himself of it (ἑαυτὸν ἐκένωσεν) when he took upon himself its opposite, the nature, or form, of a servant (μορφήν δούλου λαβών). This, to the Apostle, is the astounding quality of Christ's humility: that he should have "emptied" himself of his divine mode of being, and entered upon an earthly, human existence. This word "emptied" illuminates the peculiar nature of Pauline Christology. It is clear that the Apostle had often brooded upon how the pre-existent divine being could come to us as a mortal man. In doing so, he had already touched upon the Christological problem in the narrower sense—the problem of how divinity and humanity are united in Christ. His solution of the problem was in this "emptying." Who emptied himself? The heavenly pre-existent being Christ. Indeed, only he is under discussion. So the basis of the new mode of being remains the pre-existent self of the Godhead. Of what has Christ emptied himself? Of the "nature," or "form," of God. The stress here is not upon the prominence of divinity but upon the form of divinity. Christ has emptied himself not of divine existence but of "being equal to God"; he has divested himself of his divine garment, of his divine splendour, of those divine characteristics that are proper to God, and by which he proclaims himself as God, that divine form of glory to which he would by nature have had a claim. This is the astounding thing about Christ's becoming man, that the selfsame Christ, equal to God, has exchanged the garment of divinity for the apparel of a servant. In other words, in the process of incarnation, the heavenly pre-existent being suspended the fullness of his divine qualities, his omniscience, his omnipotence, his infinity. The place of these divine qualities is now taken by the purely human qualities and attributes of the servant. The result of the incarnation is that the selfsame being, previously a divine form in heaven, is now upon earth, but working its divine being exclusively in human fashion, by means of human qualities and capabilities. This is not a transformation of divinity into humanity, but rather the contrary: the divine glory is suspended, so that only the humanity is visible. If we translate this thought of St. Paul's into the language of theology, this is what it implies: The divinity in Christ is and remains the *principium quod* of his earthly activity. But in the place of his divine nature, his human nature becomes the *principium quo,* through which Christ works upon earth. So it is wrong when many theologians, like Anscar Vonier in his book *The Personality of Christ,* see a "psychological miracle" in the fact that Christ could suffer and die, and thus assume that Christ's humanity, on account of its connexion with the Godhead, could not have suffered and died if God had not constantly, miraculously "suspended" the effects of divine power upon his humanity. It is the same view as was already put forward by Hilary of Poitiers, and shows dubious signs of following in the direction of Monophysitism. For according to this view, Christ's human nature would not be the same as our human nature, not like our servant's garment, but specifically different from it on account of its constant connexion with the divine self; i.e., it would be a new and different nature, in the sense of the later Monophysites. But this very point is what makes the incarnation unique: that from the beginning the divine self is divested of all pretensions to glory, in the process of becoming man. It is not as if, having become man, he continued on principle to maintain these claims, and at every human action had to perform a separate miracle to make it a purely human one. For Paul, the miracle of his humiliation is precisely that he did not simply put on the outward appearance of the servant's garb, but wore it in reality with all its consequences. Of course, even after this speculation, it is still certain that Christ's pre-existent heavenly identity stands behind all his human acts. Everything that he acts and suffers he achieves as the heavenly Christ. It has the character of the absolute. So, strictly speaking, within the Pauline speculation we must say that we encounter Jesus' divine mystery only in the earthly form of its human frailty. Or, in theological terms, the human nature is the instrument, the organ, through which Christ's divine self works. To this extent, the theologians speak of an *instrumentum conjunctum*.

If we look forward from the point of vantage offered by St. Paul's dogma to the Christological disputes of the coming centuries, we see clearly that Nestorianism is not Pauline. For it destroys the unity within Christ's person of his divinity and his humanity. It denies that all Christ's modes of being are supported by the selfsame, pre-existent heavenly self. It teaches that there were two selves in Christ, a divine and a human. But Monophysitism and Monotheletism, too, are not Pauline. For they would have the Incarnate One work not by means of his servant's form but by his divine form. The Church's dogma alone reproduces in sharp formulations the true Pauline doctrine, that Christ is one divine person in two natures, but that the divine nature does not subsume the human. The human nature rather preserves all its qualities, its natural will as well as its natural way of taking effect.

The ideas in the Epistle to the Philippians are also expressed in the Epistle to the Romans in terse but pregnant phrases. As we turn our attention to it, the Pauline Christology is rounded off for us in a complete unity, a survey of Christ's essence, pre-existent, earthly, and post-existent. Unlike the Epistle to the Philippians, the Epistle to the Romans is from the start speculation, an attempt to understand in conceptual terms the mystery of Jesus. According to this Epistle, he is the Son of God, the Christ prophesied in the Old Testament. Because he is the Son of God, he is from the beginning and before all time possessed of a "spirit of holiness" ($\pi\nu\epsilon\tilde{\upsilon}\mu\alpha$ $\dot{\alpha}\gamma\iota\omega\sigma\acute{\upsilon}\nu\eta\varsigma$). This spirit of holiness is identical with the divine nature. Historically, we encounter this Son of God in two modes of being

and revelation. On the strength of his descent from David
(ἐκ σπέρματος Δαβίδ), he is for us the Son of God "according
to the flesh"—i.e., the Son of God in human frailty (corresponding to the servant's garb in the Epistle to the Philippians); and on the strength of his resurrection (ἐξ ἀναστάσεως
νεκρῶν), he becomes for us "the Son of God by an act of
power" (υἱὸς Θεοῦ ἐν δυνάμει). He has his being as the Son
of God from his spirit of holiness; his being as the "Son of
God according to the flesh" he has from the seed of David;
and his being as "the Son of God by an act of power" he derives from his resurrection from the dead. Christ exalted no
longer means the garb of a servant. His humanity too is transfigured and deified. He is "the Son of God by an act of power,"
which corresponds to the passage in the Epistle to the Philippians: "Therefore God also has exalted him."

To sum up, we may say that the basic scheme of the Pauline
Christology is this: Christ is the Son of God, real, pre-existent,
and sharing in the creation of the world. In order to redeem
mankind, God sent him down to earth. As the Redeemer he
wore the garb of a servant. In doing so, he emptied himself,
divested himself of the divine garment—i.e., the attributes of
God in so far as they are outwardly visible. By his resurrection, he once more donned the garment of God, and fulfilled
the redemption.

To Paul we owe the first systematic Christology. He reveals
to us Jesus' pre-existent divinity as the principle uniting and
supporting his being and working, and forming his person.
Paul's doctrine of Kenosis makes it comprehensible how the
Son of God could suffer and die for our redemption.

John the Evangelist attempts to interpret the mystery of
the Lord from a quite different approach, not from the point
of view of Judaic speculation, but solely out of the impressions of his own great experience and with the delicate means
of Hellenistic culture.

XI

JOHN'S INTERPRETATION OF
CHRIST'S SELF-CONSCIOUSNESS

ST. John's commentary comes as a welcome supplement to St. Paul's proclamation. His horizon is wider. His questions arise not from a mind that has been trained in the school of Gamaliel the Pharisee, but from the depths of his humanity as a whole, hungering and thirsting after righteousness. His ideas and concepts belong to mankind in general, and not only to the rabbinical tradition. There is something at once majestic, radiant, and profound in the picture of Christ he draws for us. John's Christology is not frozen into a rigid system, but is full of tenderness and the warmth of life.

The characteristics of the fourth Gospel

Decisive proofs for the authenticity of St. John's Gospel are found in the Biblical introduction. Ever since Heinrich Müller established the rules for composition in the Semitic languages as distinct from the Greek, we have had a standard at our disposal by which we have been able to test the language of St. John's Gospel. Müller himself was compelled to admit, "to his own considerable surprise," that the laws of strophic construction apply to the Gospel according to St. John in the same degree as they do for the prophets, the Sermon on the Mount, or the Koran. There is no longer any doubt as to the Semitic nature of John's language. In addition, John's Gospel has the support of the entire ancient Church, Western and Oriental; it is vouched for in particular by Irenaeus, the pupil of Polycarp, who was already a mature man at the end of the first century, and thus belongs to the witnesses of the second generation; he is joined by Theophilus of Antioch and the author of the Muratorian canon—and these are all men with a sharp ear for distinctions of style. It cannot be proved from the testimony of Bishop Papias that John had been executed long before the end of the first century. At the time of the Council of the Apostles, Paul calls him one of the "pillars" of the Christian community (Gal. 2.9), and Eusebius of Cæsarea informs us that John went to Ephesus, and died there (*Historia Ecclesiastica,* 3.28.6). Certainly there is a significant difference between John and the Synoptic Evangelists. The scene of their story is Galilee, while John's takes place in Jerusalem. They put the main stress upon the actions of Jesus, while John emphasizes his words. Their style is vivid and concrete; John's is abstract and allegorical. However, John's Gospel is indispensable for the understanding of the Pharisees' hostility to Jesus and his condemnation to death, and of the interpenetration of divinity and humanity in Christ. John supplements the Synoptic Gospels in essential points. The acceptance of John's Gospel among the early Christian communities, in spite of its difference from the three others, can be explained only by the strength of the Apostle's own authority, which was legitimation enough for his Gospel. His use of the Hellenistic doctrine of the Logos in his Gospel can be sufficiently explained by the traditional account of his departure from Jerusalem for Ephesus, where Hellenistic ideas were firmly rooted. In any case, they were not unknown in Galilee. The distinction of styles is not an absolute one.

John and Paul

John's manner of describing the mystery of the Lord is characteristically distinct from Paul's; on the other hand, they are at one on certain essential points. Paul and John—in their youth they were both passionate souls, with fiery, excitable spirits. They were both for all or nothing What their heart once seized upon became for them the one sole thing of value, to which all else was subordinate. All their thinking was bent on embracing this one great good in a majestic, sweeping vision. They are, however, distinguished most of all by their difference in temperament. Paul's passion is storm-tossed, unruly, defiant. It breaks out in violent explosions. His sentences

come rushing from his pen in leaps and bounds, allowing him
no time to put them in order. The power of his restless mind
thrusts such an abundance of thought and experience into
them that the framework of his phrases bursts apart under the
strain. John's passion is turned inwards. There is a warm glow
deep within him. The eyes of his soul contemplate a great and
holy image hidden there, and they never weary of gazing in
wonder upon this glory of God incarnate; they never weary of
searching out the beautiful and the best to give adequate expression to the beauty they have seen. The fire of St. John is
quiet, lambent, and gentle; the fire of St. Paul is darting, blazing, scorching. This distinction of personality is further increased by the very different paths they took in their development. The one reached Christ only by way of a terrible inner
crisis. He had to make his way by violence across insuperable
heights, and over dizzy abysses. He may have cried "Crucifige"
beneath the cross. He certainly guarded the garments of St.
Stephen with fanatical hatred, and rejoiced at every stone that
struck the martyr. He never tired of hunting out the Christians
and imprisoning them. And then finally there came the hour
that cast him to the ground and drew from him the question:
"Who art thou, Lord? Lord, what wilt thou have me do?"

In contrast, John spent his youth on the quiet shores of the
Lake of Gennesaret. This was where the first spark of God fell
into his soul, when he heard the Baptist preach. And this spark
grew into a great and holy flame when the Promised One himself came. "Behold the Lamb of God!" They were days of
solemnity and rejoicing when he sat with the bridegroom as
his attendant, and might rest upon his heart. More than anyone else, he saw deep into the innermost life of the God-man.
He heard words so delicate, so profound and gentle that his
tongue stumbled when he tried to reproduce them, and he
had to begin afresh to recapture all these nuances. Not one
of the Apostles or the Evangelists traced the spiritual life of our
Lord with such tenderness and such self-surrender, or described it with such sympathy as he. This sympathy is so tactful and profound that we are tempted to think that no simple
fisherman from the Lake of Gennesaret could possibly have
written with such delicacy. And yet in John's Gospel there is
the one Logion of the Son to whom all things have been delivered by the Father, which is also reported by Matthew and
Luke, that proves that the true Jesus, the Jesus of the still
hours, who did not pander to the mob in the streets, really did
speak as John recounts. If we want to know how Jesus spoke,

not as a public preacher on the streets or at the lakeside, but as a friend among friends, as a bridegroom among the attendants, we must turn to John. He has made Jesus' manner of expression so much his own that his own style merges into Jesus' style, and in reading his Gospel there are times when one can no longer be certain whether it is Jesus who is speaking, or the disciple whom he loved. And because John, made ready by the Baptist, came to recognize and love his highest good in Jesus while still a passionate young man, everything that is not Jesus is petty and pitiful to him. His Gospel is full of sharp contrasts between what his master affirmed and what he denied. Heaven and earth, above and below, God and the devil, light and darkness make up the two worlds between which the decision lies. John knows no mediation and no transition. What does not belong to Jesus belongs to the devil and his domain.

There is a third factor distinguishing the two Apostles. At the time Paul wrote his Epistles, the Christian mission was only in its very beginnings. Apart from the first Christian community at Jerusalem, there was only a small Hellenistic-Christian community flourishing in Antioch. The world of Western culture was still closed to Christ. The new religion came out into the open timidly and hesitantly. And the old husk held on obstinately to the young shoot, and would not let it go. Hard work was needed to clear away room for the young life. Sharp attack was necessary, even if it meant pulling up the roots and tendrils away from the old mother tree that had nourished it. It was unavoidable that many a thorn should remain clinging to the work of the reformer. Hence the rabbinical element in Paul's theorizing. And in addition there was the Hellenistic Gnosis with its legends of aeons, angelic powers, and elemental spirits. Like a tough weed, it threatened the tender plant of Christianity from the moment it had been transplanted into the Hellenistic garden. So the new struggle arose, for the true Kyrios against the false gods of Gnosticism. In this dispute, Paul had no alternative but to make use of Hellenistic ideas and concepts to make his new message comprehensible to these circles. Hence the Hellenistic elements in St. Paul's Christology. So St. Paul's life was full of conflict and struggle for the true understanding of Christ. In face of the Jewish view of the Messias as man, and the Gnostic cult of the Kyrios of the Hellenistic mysteries, Paul was compelled to describe Christ as the true Lord, the head of the dominions, principalities, and powers, the man from heaven. His theology has its essential centre in Christ, not in Jesus, for it strives to grasp the mystery of Christ from God, from his heavenly origin. Which is why Paul has none of John's interest in the historical details of the life of Jesus, and why he regards the incarnation as limitless humiliation, as Kenosis. His vision is concentrated upon the miracle of God "emptying" himself, and does not pay sufficient attention to the aura radiating from the spirit of holiness, creating the person, and casting its light upon the humanity of Jesus.

St. John is utterly different. When he wrote his Gospel, towards the end of the first Christian century, the first hard pioneer work had in essentials been achieved. The enormous strength of Paul's mission had established the new Christianity in the Jewish as well as in the Hellenistic world. He placed Christ's divinity so emphatically at the centre of the Christian faith that, in the context of Hellenistic Gnosticism, there was the danger of regarding it as the exclusive element, and denying the humanity of Jesus. Which is why John is solicitous to present and illuminate the *humanity* in Christ too. "I write of what was from the beginning, what we have heard, what we have seen with our eyes, and what we have looked upon and our hands have handled: of the Word of Life" (1 John 1.1). In opposition to Gnostic Docetism, he emphasizes the fleshly nature of the Logos. "And the Word was made flesh" (John 1.14). He does not regard the Logos as simply pre-existent, but as also united with human nature (ὁ λόγος σὰρξ ἐγένετο).

We must also note that when John wrote his Gospel, he was no longer in the full power of his prime. He was an old man, who saw himself remote from things and men, especially from the struggles of the day. He is filled with the eternal, timeless essence of the Christian message. His Gospel has been purified of the accidents of time. All the persons and events in his portrayal have a timeless quality. They are like a window opening onto eternity. His Christ is always the same timeless eternal One in his pre-existence, his historical manifestation, and his postexistence. The Son of Man is "in the bosom of the Father" even when he is ministering upon the earth. The angels of God hover about his head even in Galilee and Jerusalem. Unlike Paul, John does not regard Jesus' humanity as something opposed and strange to his divinity; he does not regard it as a humiliation, but as a *transparency* and a revealing of the divine. Christ's divine glory shines through his humanity. Any dualism in the image of Christ is vanquished. Paul had eyes only for the divine Christ. To him,

Christ's humanity was the crass antithesis of his divinity. John had eyes—and love—for his humanity too. To him, it became the symbol of Christ's divinity. Not only Christ's human nature but also its ministering and suffering became for John the transparency of the divine. Indeed, John sees the divinity shining precisely in this human activity. The miracles are not so much marvellous deeds of the Messias, intended to rouse men to faith, as the essential aura of his divinity—its "sign" (σημεῖα, 2.11; 3.2; 4.54 et al.). His first "sign," according to John, takes place in Galilee. The miracles are, as it were, detached from their concrete historical circumstances, and presented in their essential significance. Thus the Lord's multiplication of the loaves points to the bread of heaven; his waking of Lazarus, to the resurrection of the dead; his healing of the blind, to the light of the world. However much John individualizes the separate characters, he has conceived them less as individuals than as the personified symbols of eternal powers and motions. The Lord's keenest opponents are designated quite simply as "the Jews" (2.20; 5.16, et al.). The Jewish nation is no longer divided into classes and groups, into Pharisees and Sadducees, but is collectively regarded as the symbol of the hatred of the world for our Lord. God's redemptive intention is no longer related to the Old Testament—which is rather referred to as "your law" (13.34; 15.12, et al.)—but to Jesus' commandment of love. In comparison with Christianity, Judaism is nothing but a mere episode. Unlike the Synoptic Gospels, John's account of Jesus' suffering and death does not present the torment and execution of the innocent, but Christ's triumphant victory over death—that Christ who said, "It is consummated." He does not write of Jesus in struggle, but of Jesus in victory, of Christ triumphant. The eschatological expectation of the future disappears. The "glory of God" is already present in Christ. "We have seen his glory." Instead of the apocalyptic speeches of his second coming in the Synoptic Gospels, John gives us Jesus' farewells, in which he speaks of the present. Instead of the scene in Gethsemane, he gives us Christ's pontifical prayer. While Paul hoped to possess Christ in the future, John already did possess him, and that was the basis of his hope (G. Kittel). Similarly, John has no trace of the vivid images and parables of the Synoptic accounts; everything accidental, earthly, and historical disappears. Jesus, our life, our bread of heaven, the light of the world, the vine, the Good Shepherd—these are the motifs of St. John's Gospel. Everything in our Lord's life is conceived in its essence, and illuminated with the light of eternity. This is concentrated into the confession: "And the Word was made flesh, and dwelt among us. And we saw his glory—glory as of the only-begotten of the Father—full of Grace and of truth" (John 1.14).

The Christology of St. John

The new addition that John made to the Pauline interpretation of Christ's self-consciousness stands out against this background of the special character of his Gospel. In fundamentals, John is in agreement with Paul, above all in the avowal that Christ is a divine person and pre-existent; but he stresses that Christ is also truly human, and in his humanity redeemed us. Christ's peculiarity is that he is the "Son." Where Paul expressly called him God's "own Son" (Rom. 8.3, 32), the Evangelist calls him his "only-begotten Son" (μονογενής, 1.18; 3.16). He borrowed this name from the Gnostics, whom otherwise he repudiated. In John, as in Paul, this Son is the pre-existent creator of the world (3.31; 16.28; 17.5, et al.). But there is already a slight variation here. In accordance with his contemplative cast of mind, unlike Paul, John does not make a distinction in time between the various stages of revelation, but describes them as a self-revelation of the Logos. Before this world was, the Logos is. "In the beginning"—which is the counterpart of the *"in principio"* of Genesis—the Logos was with God, and all being was brought about through him. Not only inanimate but also animate being is from him. For "all things were made through him" (1.4). Through the Logos, this life, conscious, spiritual life, occurs in every place that opens itself to his light. "The life was the light of men" (1.5). It enlightens "every man who comes into the world" (1.9). And every man who receives this light will become a child of God (1.12), born of God. Thus, becoming more and more all-embracing, the Word of God became incarnate in the world. Finally, the Logos entered humanity, and became flesh. The prologue to the Gospel according to St. John is a hymn to the working of the Logos through the entire cosmos. Paul too is aware of Christ's pre-existent working (1 Cor. 10.3 f.). But it is only an influence upon the children of Israel. Paul goes deeper only in the Epistle to the Colossians. In Christ, "all things hold together." But where Paul makes only isolated allusions, John has a clear, unequivocal doctrine. There has been nothing in the world or in the entire history of mankind that does not have its life and truth from the Logos. He is the only true revealer of God.

The term "Logos" is used to express this broad universal vision. John found it in the concepts of his world. The Babylonian belief in Marduk, the Egyptian cult of the dead, the Jewish doctrine of Memra, and especially the ideas of Plato, Philo, and the Stoics—these were all familiar with this most fruitful word "Logos." John took it over because it expressed the universal, all-embracing quality of the divine revelation. In thus giving voice to the power of revelation of the living Christ, a living concrete personality, his doctrine of the Logos became something peculiar to him alone, something specifically Christian, so that from then on all it had in common with the non-Christian Logos was just the name. For, unlike the non-Christian systems, the "Word" is not an impersonal attribute of God, or a divine power subordinate to the highest God, but the concrete revelation, in personal form, of God himself.

As the Logos, Christ is the Word of God uttered into the world; he is God revealing himself, the *Deus revelans*. This revelation of God had its most perfect expression and conclusion in Christ's becoming man. Christ's humanity is the true place where the Father communicates with mankind through his Son. Christ's humanity is so bound up with the Godhead, and involved in it, that divinity and humanity in Christ can be distinguished but never separated. When John speaks of the Logos, he thinks of this Incarnate One whom he had looked upon and handled with his hands (1 John 1.1). To him, the union of Christ's divinity and his humanity is so close that it cannot be any closer. It is closer for John than for Paul. Even during his earthly existence, Christ is in the bosom of the Father (*in sinu Patris*). "I and the Father are one" (John 10.30). "Dost thou not believe that I am in the Father and the Father in me?" (14.10; 10.38). "Glorify thy Son, that thy Son may glorify thee" (17.1). Whoever knows Christ knows the Father; whoever sees him sees the Father (14.7 f.). "All things that the Father has are mine" (16.15). During Jesus' earthly existence, Father and Son are in constant interchange of life, a perpetual fellowship of love. "You shall see . . . the angels of God ascending and descending upon the Son of Man" (1.51). In the consciousness of this communion, Jesus can even say: "Before Abraham came to be, I am" (8.58). For Christ incarnate, there is only a now, an eternal present, being in the Father. His consciousness of being one with the Father is unequivocally expressed in his words: **"And no one has ascended into heaven except him who has descended from heaven: the Son of Man who is in heaven"** (3.13). This "being in heaven" is not anything historical, past or done with, but something constant, perpetual. This inextricable interpenetration of God and Man in Christ gives rise to what later theology was to call the *scientia visionis,* the direct vision of divine essence through the incarnate Logos.

This again shows the difference in the way the two Apostles evaluate Christ's incarnation. Paul looks so directly at Jesus' divine nature that his theorizing seems to be unaware of its radiance and influence upon his human nature. Under this aspect, he regards the human nature as something so wretched and lowly that in comparison with the divine nature he can understand it only as Kenosis, Christ's complete self-divesting and self-emptying. True, the divinity remains the profoundest identity, the true self of the Incarnate One. But it is something static, something endowing human actions with the character of absoluteness only to the extent that they are actions of the pre-existent Son of God. But the divinity does not flow over and through Jesus' humanity. This humanity is rather a prison wall, preventing the divine light from shining through. To this extent we may call Paul's Christology *dualistic,* because it sets up a certain contrast between divinity and humanity in Christ. But John's intuitive genius achieves what Paul's theoretical powers had left undone. He is called to do so in a particular sense. Had he not seen with his own eyes "the glory of the only-begotten of the Father," "full of Grace and of truth"? So he and he alone is in a position to give us a psychology of the God-man—i.e., show us the interacting of divine and human powers in Christ. Which is why he more than any other stresses that not only the pre-existent and exalted Jesus was filled with the divine consciousness, dwelling in an eternal present, but the historical Jesus also.

So for John, Jesus' entire earthly ministry is bathed in a divine lambency. Even the Lord's earthly life and ministry radiates his "Doxa." There is no word in English to render this "Doxa" exactly. In the Old Testament "Kabod" signifies that which has, or imparts, weight or importance; in the case of God, it means the force of his appearance (particularly in thunderstorms), Jehovah's mighty revelation in Israel, more closely, the fiery clouds which symbolize it (Exod. 24.15 f.; 40.34 f., *et al.*). In the New Testament, "Doxa" is the mark of the divine world as distinct from the earthly, God's proper mode of being and manifestation. Paul attributes this Doxa to the Christ of glory (2 Cor. 3.18; 4.6; 1 Cor. 15.40). But John sees it shining *in Jesus' earthly life* too. We do best to translate "Doxa" by "glory" or "majesty." This is the *majestas Domini,* the glory of the Lord, which, according to John, is visible in Jesus' earthly being too. This is why he clings with such a brooding love to the Lord's humanity. Paul has eyes only for the heavenly Christ. It is true he has known Jesus "according to the flesh," but "now he knows him no longer." This is why, as we have shown, Paul lays remarkably little stress upon the historical traits of his image of Christ—although it is still too much of an exaggeration to say that Paul's Christ is a mystical experience and not an historical reality. In contrast, John never wearies of contemplating the earthly image of the Lord. *The Word was made flesh.* This is what he meant his Gospel to testify. Having spoken in the prologue of the pre-existent mode of being of this Logos, and of its incarnation in the world, he uses all the resources of the language to develop this theme. In the Jewish idiom, the word "flesh" signifies man in his imperfection and weakness. John chooses this expression to strengthen the paradox: the Logos, which from the beginning was with God, and was the life upon earth and the light of men, has become flesh, the epitome of transience, the absolute opposite of everything divine. The Evangelist is concerned with this very contrast. For Gnostic Docetism, taking its starting point in the dualism of Platonic and Hellenistic thought, had found the flesh of Jesus repugnant, and set up the doctrine that his body was mere outward appearance. Which is why John puts it as the *thema probandum* at the apex of his Gospel: the Logos really and truly did become flesh. And he plays a variation on this idea by adding "and he dwelt among us"; the Greek term has the meaning "and he pitched his tent among us." The Evangelist is probably thinking of the ark of the Covenant with the *Shekinah,* or of the "descent" of which the Scribes speak, and by which they mean the glory of God revealing itself to mankind. It is his pleasure to point to the radiance of this divine glory in Jesus' earthly life. This is why he portrays Jesus' words, actions, and sorrows in such a way that they can be understood only as a revelation of the divine glory. And, of course, this does not prevent him from giving an account that is historically true. We are indebted to this particular Gospel for a number of historical events in Jesus' life that go unmentioned in the Synoptic accounts. We learn the exact day of the Lord's death, the decisive reason for his condemnation to death. We hear of his burning thirst on the cross, of his tears over the dead Lazarus, of his care for his mother standing at the foot of the cross, of his special love for John (to express this the Evangelist uses the word φιλεῖν, not ἀγαπᾶν, i.e., the word that signifies a very profound and personal affection). Like Luke, John pays special attention to the life of Jesus' spirit. In doing so, he brings us humanly very close to Christ. He makes it *possible for us to experience him*. One of the strongest supports for the Apostle's historical reliability is that for all his pains to emphasize the glory of the Logos, he never falls into the Hellenistic error of the Kyrios cults; he never portrays the Lord as a god wandering the earth, exalted high above all earthly clay, exulting in his own divinity. On the contrary, he portrays the Lord as One who has become man, and who in his human consciousness knows himself to be absolutely *dependent* upon the Father, declaring: "The Father is greater than I" (14.28). And just as John draws his picture of Jesus true to history, he also portrays the other characters more sharply than the Synoptic Evangelists do—more so, even, than Luke: Martha, Thomas, Mary Magdalen, Caiaphas, Pilate, Peter, and the disciple whom Jesus loved. In the Lord's conversations and sermons, he presents the struggle between the opposites more powerfully and profoundly than we shall ever find it in the Synoptic Gospels. He sketches in the mood of the masses (7.11 ff.; 11.55 ff.). He has the art of tersely outlining a situation (cf. 13.30; 20.19). This is not to be explained, as in Luke's case, who even uses technical terms, by a possible imitation of Greek narrative style, or even of Greek drama. Rather, we can sense the original power of a man of rare "liveliness and talent" (Kittel) and one who to his last line is full of the overwhelming certainty that he himself has gazed directly upon the eternal Word.

So John's picture of Christ is the most *consummate* that revelation has vouchsafed us. Later Christian theology had nothing essential to add to it. All it did was to clarify, conceptualize, and systematize into an ordered Christology what John had described with simple directness. In the following chapters we shall discuss in greater detail the Christology that came after the New Testament.

XII

THE INTERPRETATION OF
CHRIST'S SELF-CONSCIOUSNESS
BY THE EARLY FATHERS
AND THE SCHOLASTICS

SURVEYING the speculation of the early Fathers upon the mystery of Christ, we may recognize three stages in its development: the Christology of the Apostolic Fathers, the Apologists, and the theology subsequent to the Council of Nicaea.

The Apostolic Fathers

It is not difficult to understand why the Apostolic Fathers did little to interpret the Christological problem in the narrow sense; they were fully occupied with cherishing and protecting in the hearts of men the great new thing that was Christianity, and its faith in the Son of God become man. So what they had to say about the mystery of Christ was only a *paraphrase,* more or less detailed, of the Christology of the Bible. Some held more closely to the terminology of St. Paul, others to St. John, or they drew their formulations from both. St. John's pupil, Ignatius of Antioch, and the Epistle to Diognetus clung closely to the Johannine version; while Clement of Rome and the Pseudo-Barnabas are clearly followers of St. Paul. But even they are not completely faithful to the phraseology of their models. Clement follows the Epistle to the Hebrews in calling Christ "the image of divine majesty." And, like Paul, he commends humility by pointing out that the Lord Jesus Christ, the "sceptre of God's majesty," did not come in glory, although it was in his power to do so, but in lowliness (16.2). And Barnabas, with Paul's doctrine of Kenosis in mind, declares that man, who "could not bear the light of the fleeting sun, certainly would not endure the sight of essential glory, which is why Christ took on human nature" (7.2). Following St. John, Ignatius describes Christ as the Logos who was with the Father in eternity and was in recent times made manifest, who issued forth from the Father, and was with him, and had returned to him (*Epistola ad Magnesios,* 6.1; 7.2). "We have a physician, and he is flesh and spirit, begotten and unbegotten, God become flesh" (*Epistola ad Ephesios,* 7.2). Like his master John, he opposes the Judaic Christian Docetae, and stresses the true humanity of Jesus most emphatically. All the fundamental truths of Christianity—Christ's death for our salvation, his resurrection, and our redemption—stand or fall with the truth of his humanity. Docetism denied the power of Christ's crucifixion, the hope of resurrection, and the martyrdom of those who died for their faith. But Ignatius also uses Paul's terminology to confess: "This—Christ—is truly of David's line according to the flesh; and Son of God according to the will and the power of God" (*Epistola ad Smyrnenses,* 1.1). He is the New Man and, as such, takes all of those ready for salvation up into himself and makes of them his body. The Epistle to Diognetus in particular is strongly marked by the influence of St. John. Christ is the Logos sent into the world; the beloved, only-begotten Son of God, who was from the beginning and evermore shall be; who is for all time born anew in the hearts of the faithful; who enriches the Church and endows it with Grace (11.3; 10.2). This makes comprehensible the accusation levelled by the pagans at the Christians that they worshipped a crucified man. In reply, the Fathers did not maintain that what they worshipped in Christ was only the Logos; they held fast to the doctrine that in the Crucified One they worshipped the Son of God.

The first traces of a primitive Christological speculation can be perceived in the Shepherd of Hermas. Like the later Apologists, Hermas too thinks in terms of a duality, not a trinity. It is true he is familiar with the idea of the three divine persons and, indeed, mentions them. But in his terminology, the third person of the Godhead, the Holy Spirit, is blended with the Son of God. To him, the Son is the Spirit of God working in the world. This Spirit of God is great and immeasurable.

Every creature has been wrought by it. It fills the Apostles and the teachers, the Church and the faithful. In becoming man, it was united with the human form of a servant (δοῦλος). Mary was visited by this Son-Spirit. It takes up its dwelling in this human figure (δοῦλος). And as this human figure, this δοῦλος, acts in accordance with the divine Spirit dwelling in it; as it is obedient to it even unto death, so it too is raised to the status of Son of God. Hermas shows the first traces of what was later to become the Christology of Adoptionism and Nestorianism—the separation of the two Sons, the natural and the adopted, in Christ. But even Hermas insists that the divine Son-Spirit dwells in Christ the man, i.e., that it descended into the figure of a man, a servant. It is possible that his conception was influenced by Gnosticism. The Hebrew Gospel, which was written before the third century A.D., describes how the maternal power of the Holy Spirit descended upon Jesus at his baptism and made him the Son of God. The Ebionite Gospel and the Gnostic Gospel according to the Egyptians from the second century have a similiar content.

The Apologists

Hermas is the transition to the second stage in the development of a systematic Christological doctrine, to the Christology of the Apologists Justin, Irenaeus, Hippolytus, Tertullian, and others. Where the Apostolic Fathers were only the faithful witnesses to the Biblical proclamation, the Apologists make the first hesitant attempt at conceptualizing and *interpreting* the Biblical annunciation of Christ with the aid of the dominant philosophy of the age. In the third and fourth centuries, this was Neo-Platonic and Stoic. According to its doctrine, God is absolutely transcendent. He has no relationship at all to the world. In order to explain the creation of the world, some concept of a *mediator* between God and the world was needed as the creator of the world. This concept of God led Christian thought to define the Logos after the fashion of Subordinationism, i.e., as the divine being standing between the remote transcendent God and the world, as a mediator between the two. Because in this way the Logos is dependent upon its relation to the world, it entered into the temporal mode of being at least in the sense that its whole full essence came into being and received the designation "Son of God" only with the creation, or with Christ's incarnation. Previously it had been present only, as it were, in embryo. The spirit of the age favoured this Subordinationist doctrine, which left its mark even upon Origen and the earlier Alexandrine school, even though they laid decisive stress upon the divinity of Jesus and its consubstantiality with the nature of the Father. This thought persisted until the Council of Nicaea (325), and, as far as the Holy Spirit is concerned, even afterwards. The influence of contemporary thought was not overcome until the Cappadocian Fathers, and not ultimately until Augustine and after him John of Damascus.

However, the Apologists did good service. Their finest achievement was their unfailing belief in the Lord's metaphysical status as the Son of God; and by their very clarification of John's concept of the Logos they prevented Christ from being ranged on the side of creation, and his status as the Son of God from being understood in ethical and theocratic terms after the fashion of the Judaeo-Christian Ebionites or the Dynamistic Monarchians. They finally overcame the theocratic image of the ancient Judaic Messias.

The second achievement of their theorizing was in their concept of the Logos. Unlike the Stoics, they regarded it not simply as a cosmic principle but as the means of the revelation of our salvation; they regarded it as the creative founder of a new relationship to God, who as the Logos is indeed immanently at work in all men and at all times, but who has bound himself in an utterly unique union to human nature in Christ. Their Logos was at the same time Redeemer, and the bringer of all truth and Grace. The cross was an essential part of this image. St. Justin Martyr (d. 165) already placed Jesus' death for our salvation at the heart of his theorizing (*Dialogus cum Tryphone,* 13.40; 54, *et al.; Apologia* 1.32, 50), and Irenaeus (d. 202) dealt with Hellenistic Gnosticism, which denied Jesus' true humanity, and with the Judaeo-Christian Ebionites, who regarded Jesus only as a man endowed with Grace, in emphasizing that an understanding of our redemption required the avowal both of Jesus' divinity and of his humanity (*Adversus Haereses,* 3.16 f).

This soteriological estimation of Jesus' humanity led the Apologists to broach the question of the relationship between Christ's divinity and his humanity; they were already posing the Christological problem in the narrow sense. That is their third achievement. Irenaeus, who deduced the doctrine of the two natures from the idea of redemption, also emphasized to the Gnostics the unity of the divine person. "One and the same is Jesus Christ, the Son of God, who through his suffering has reconciled us to God" (*Adversus Haereses*, 3.16, 19). He describes the union of God and man in Christ as a commingling, a *commixtio*. This expression survived for a long time in Christological speculation, although it did not entirely exclude a Monophysite interpretation. Even Augustine still speaks of a *"commixtus Deus homo,"* but not without adding a *"quodammodo"* (*De Trinitate*, 4.20, 30).

This expression *commixtio* still left a considerable vagueness, until it was expounded with greater precision by the keen dialectician Tertullian. He is the true creator of the phrase *"conjunctum in una persona,"* which was later to be established as the classic formula by Pope Leo I. In opposition to Praxeas the Patripassian, he maintained that "we see in Christ a double status of being, which are not blended with one another, but united in one person, the God and the man Jesus. And in this union, the characteristic properties of each substance are preserved" (*Contra Praxeam*, 27). This is the essential achievement of African theology, especially of Tertullian: that as early as the third century it should have solved the Christological problem—at least as far as the terminology is concerned—in a precise formulation, and thus have given the Roman Church the weapons to dispose of all the Monophysite and Nestorian interpretations. What Tertullian understood by *persona* is explained to us by his follower Hippolytus. In dispute with Noëtus he declares: "The flesh by itself could not persist [ὑποστάναι] without the Word, because it had its existence, its being [τὴν σύστασιν] in the Word" (ch. 15). According to this it is the person that gives to the human nature its independence and autonomy. The Logos takes on the human nature in such a way that it becomes its own. No longer does it subsist by itself, but it belongs now to the "I" of the Logos. This assertion of Hippolytus' really anticipates the result of the coming disputes. But a gradual clarification was not achieved, as I have already described, until the disputes with Arius and Apollinaris, on the one hand, and with Nestorius, on the other.

Later Theologians

The culminating point of the Christological debates, and hence of the development of Christological dogma, came with the debates between the schools of Alexandria and Antioch. It will be remembered from an earlier chapter that the Alexandrians always put the greater stress upon the unity of the divine Logos, while the school of Antioch emphasized the duality of the two natures, and the true humanity of Christ.

A brief glance at the theology of the Cappadocian Fathers will show that obscurities continued to persist in Christological theorizing above and beyond the actual Scholastic tradition and its encumbrance by the old received patterns of thought. The Cappadocian theology in particular demonstrates how important for Christological speculation a clear and unambiguous terminology would have been.

It is true, in the struggle against Arianism, St. Basil had tried to define the concepts nature (φύσις) and person (ὑπόστασις) in order to describe the relationships of the three persons of the Trinity within the Godhead. By "nature" he wanted to describe the general, common (τὸ κοινόν) quality of the individual, and by "person," its particular, individual quality (τὸ καθ' ἕκαστον). But his distinction was applied only to the Trinity, not to Christology. So in this latter field, at least, the old confusion of ideas still persisted.

Of course, these Fathers wanted to testify faithfully to the traditional faith in Christ. Just as they clung decisively to the unity of the divine person, so they also taught the duality of natures. Gregory of Nazianzus, for example, says: "Although in Christ there are two natures, God and man, the latter being in turn body and soul, there are not two sons or two Gods . . . that of which our Saviour is made is two distinct things [ἄλλο καὶ ἄλλο] but not two distinct persons." He means to say that there is only *one* self in Christ, which supports both natures (*Epistula ad Cled.*, 1.3). Gregory of Nyssa wrote against the Arian Eunomius and against Apollinaris. Like the Alexandrians, he too speaks of a union "of nature," indeed of a "mixture" (κρᾶσις), and does not scorn to illustrate this mixture of divinity and humanity in Christ by the metaphor of the drop of vinegar that disappears in the ocean (*Adversus Apollinarem*, 42). His *Oratio Catechatica* seems to follow the

Apollinarian tendency when he compares the interconnexion of divinity and humanity with the union of soul and body in man (ch. 11). However, he himself has scruples about this comparison. For body and soul in man make up only one nature. And the conclusion might be that in Christ too there would be only one nature, the divine. He cannot find any way out of this difficulty, and so falls back upon the "mystery." The so-called Athanasian Creed, which probably developed in southern Gaul in the sixth century out of the terminological tradition of the interpretations of the symbol of Union, also makes use of the comparison of the union between body and soul. The explanation of the symbol of Union, *sicut anima rationalis et caro unus est homo, ita Deus et homo unus est Christus,* came very close to the false interpretation that the divinity and humanity in Christ were united into one nature, like body and soul in man.

The concept of the unity of person, *unitas personae,* was firmly rooted only in *Western,* not in Oriental, theology. Which is why Oriental theorizing remained uncertain and undecided not as far as the content of the doctrine is concerned but in its terminology. When it referred to a unity of substance, it meant a unity of person. In recognizing the *unitas personae,* Western theology ensured the duality of nature. Tertullian is not the only one to speak without reservation of a *conjunctio* of the Godhead and Jesus the man. Jerome and Augustine favour this expression too. The Christology of St. Hilary (d. 366) betrays certain unmistakable Alexandrine features. This great Bishop of Poitiers, the Athanasius of Western theology, regarded the divinity of Jesus as the starting point of all Christology. To him, Jesus' humanity is such a strong antithesis to his divinity that they plainly cannot be coordinated side by side. Rather, the incarnation takes place in such a way that the Logos divests itself of all its divine attributes and approaches us only in its humanity. He emphasizes the subordination of Christ's humanity even more strongly than St. Paul, inasmuch as he ascribes to Christ not the ordinary common human nature, but a heavenly body, *caeleste corpus (De Trinitate* 10,18, 17). So Christ was possessed of a transfigured body, not the frail mortal frame that is ours. With this theory, Hilary draws very close to the views of the Monophysite Severus of Antioch.

The other Western theologians—Victorinus, Zeno, Ambrose, Jerome, for example—clung faithfully to the terminology established by Tertullian. On the one hand they referred to the *homo* Jesus, and on the other to a divine person in Christ. Ambrosius and Jerome, who were contemporaries of Apollinaris, wielded their pens decisively against him. To what end should Christ have taken on mere *caro* or *anima irrationalis,* when such a shell would be incapable of sin, and hence could not be redeemed? *Illud ergo pro nobis suscepit, quod in nobis periclitabatur* (Ambrose, *De incarnationis Dominicae sacramento,* 60; Jerome, *In Epistolam ad Galatas,* 1.1). This soteriological principle, which Irenaeus had already stressed, was the constant point of orientation for their theorizing. They said to themselves: If Christ redeemed man in his entirety, then the Logos must have taken into itself everything that required redemption. Their principle was still: *quod non est assumptum, non est sanatum.*

Towards the end of the fifth century this stage of development had been reached: In the East as well as the West, the two natures in Christ were maintained. East and West, Apollinarianism and Monophysitism had been completely conquered. East and West, the principle was that the union of both natures in Christ was not accidental but essential. But there was no agreement, especially in the Orient, about the concepts nature, hypostasis, person (φύσις, ὑπόστασις, πρόσωπον). The *persona* of Western theology in the Greek rendering πρόσωπον did not signify the autonomy of a nature, but a being's outward mode of appearance, the mask, as it were, under which it appeared, something completely external, not its innermost, deepest principle of being; on the other hand, the Greek expression for "person," "hypostasis," was translated by the Latin Fathers with the Stoic term *"substantia,"* so encouraging the suspicion that the ideas of the Greek Church were Monophysite in tendency. And in fact, to the extent that the Greeks did take over the inheritance of Alexandrine theology, they were always inclined to deify the humanity of Jesus.

Leontius and Boethius

It was Leontius of Byzantium who finally clarified the Christological terminology for the Eastern Church. He lived in the second half of the sixth century, but little that is certain about his life has been handed down to us. However, he himself tells us that in his youth he favoured Nestorianism. Gradually he turned to the orthodox doctrine. He was convinced that the decisions of the Ephesian symbol of Union on the one divine person in Christ, and the Council of Chalcedon's doctrine of the two natures, which had been played off against one another by the Nestorians, did not at bottom contradict each other. He dedicated his penetrating studies to demonstrating their agreement. He saw at once what was needed: a clear, conceptual definition of nature (φύσις) and person (πρόσωπον). Systematically he attempted to determine the content of these two concepts. The result of his philosophic studies was this: It is characteristic of the person (πρόσωπον) that it exists autonomously and is not communicable; in contrast, mere nature, physis (φύσις), is communicable. Such a nature can never exist without a person as its bearer. It is never impersonal (ἀνυπόστατος). But this bearer of the human nature can also be an extraneous person if the extraneous person is divine and creative. This was precisely the property of God, that in accordance with the decision of his free will, he could immerse himself in his creation, even down to the last possibility, down to a personal union, to the extent of taking upon himself a nature not his own, so that it belongs to him, and his divine person becomes its bearer. So as well as impersonal being (ἀνυπόστατος) there is also the state of "being in a person" (ἐνυπόστατος), that peculiarity of being in which an extraneous nature does not exist autonomously (καθ' ἑαυτήν) but only in the Logos-self, into whose personality it has been assumed.

Another philosopher, Boethius, carried out a similar task of clarification for the Western Church at roughly the same time as Leontius. In his work against Eutyches and Nestorius, *Liber de persona et duabus naturis contra Eutychen et Nestorium,* he gives independently of Leontius a precise translation of the Greek expressions (οὐσία, οὐσίωσις, ὑπόστασις, πρόσωπον), together with their carefully developed definitions. His conceptual definition of *persona* has been adopted into the fund of theological formulations: *persona est naturae rationalis individua substantia.* Unlike Leontius, he also and rightly stresses that, as well as incommunicability (*individua*), rationality and hence freedom too are the essential definitive factors of human nature. Even a crystal can be a mere *individua substantia.* So Boethius penetrates still further. The individuality of the substance that goes to make up the person would have to be incomparably more distinctive and exclusive than the substance of some material element. It would have to be a spiritual substance. For only in spiritual being is that absolute tendency towards autonomy, towards the ultimate intensification, to be found, which is the mark of personal being. So only a spiritual essence can be a person. It is distinguished from mere nature because such a nature has no need to be either *individua* or *spiritalis*.

We may say that roughly at the same time Leontius in the East and Boethius in the West finally clarified the terminology of Christology. This established the foundation upon which the Council of Constantinople in 553 could propound the dogmatic truth, that the union of divinity and humanity in Christ is strictly hypostatic. It is ἕνωσις καθ' ὑπόστασιν or, in the Latin translation, *unio hypostatica* (Denzinger, 220). The Council of Chalcedon had already used this formula when it taught that in Christ the two natures, divine and human, were united into a "unity of person and hypostasis" (εἰς ἓν πρόσωπον καὶ μίαν ὑπόστασιν).

This dogma of a strictly hypostatic union of divinity and humanity in Christ is a guarantee that the Logos does not just impart to the human nature the divine nature and with it the divine properties. It simply gives it its independence, its autonomy. For the incarnation is an assumption of the humanity *not* into the divine *nature*, but into the divine *person*. So the concept "person" simply gives utterance to an ontological instance: autonomy. In comparison with this, "nature" is the dynamic field of power. Hence theology designates nature as the *principium quo*, the agent, and person as the *principium quod*, the subject of the union.

From then on, speculation moved along quieter ways. It is true the monk and the philosopher had not yet said the final word. Only the formulation, not the content it referred to, had been adequately clarified. Even when the terminology of the article of faith—Christ is one divine person in two natures— had been secured, the question could still arise—indeed it had to: What is really meant by this hypostasis, this being a person? What does the divine person in reality give to the humanity of Jesus? Or does it perhaps deprive his human nature of something? What is its function as a person?

Theological speculation has certainly never been so bold as to claim that this terminology has brought it a complete understanding of the hypostatic union. Rather, this is a mystery in the strictest sense of the word, a *mysterium quoad substantiam*. Even after revelation, reason will not be able to lift the last veil. We are confronted here with a purely supernatural fact that has and can have nothing analogous to it within the world of our experience. No creature, no angel, would be capable of taking up into itself a nature not its own in such a manner that it would become its nature, and still preserve its own peculiar properties. This can be accomplished only by God, the Lord of nature himself. And even in the divine ordinance, the hypostatic union is something totally unique. For the union of Grace, and God's personal indwelling within the human soul, are not, like the hypostatic union, a substantial union of man with God, but an accidental sharing in the divine essence. Thus quite simply the hypostatic union is beyond comparison and beyond conception. It cannot be grasped by knowledge, only by faith. When St. Paul speaks of "the wisdom of God, mysterious, hidden . . . which none of the rulers of this world has known" (1 Cor. 2.7 f.), and contrasts it with the wisdom of this world sought by the Greeks, he is ultimately referring to the incarnation of the Son of God. His subsequent words, in particular, are relevant: "For the Spirit searches all things, even the deep things of God . . . the things of God no one knows but the Spirit of God."

But even though human reason will never be able to reach a complete understanding of the mystery of the incarnation, it is nevertheless capable of demonstrating its inner possibilities before the eyes of critical thought. It is the task of theological speculation to expound the content of the concept of one person and two natures, of the unity in the duality, in such a way that all opposition to its metaphysical possibility is forced into silence.

The first attempt to demonstrate this possibility was undertaken by the theology of the early Schoolmen.

XIII

THE INTERPRETATION
OF CHRIST'S SELF-CONSCIOUSNESS
IN LATE SCHOLASTIC AND
POST-TRIDENTINE THEOLOGY

THE GREAT question posed by Scholasticism was this: How is the inner constitution of the God-man to be conceived? What, in concrete terms, does the formulation mean: The self of the Logos is the unifying principle of divinity and humanity?

Assumptionism

The first theory that attempted to probe the depths of this question was what is known as Assumptionism. Its object was to contrast the real process of God's having become man with the equally real process of one man's having become God, and to explain the incarnation by this same divinization. The divinization took place by means of the assumption. The divine person takes up, or assumes into itself, the mere man of body and soul. This assumption is so close and so powerful that it creates a complete identity between the man assumed and the divine person assuming him. God's incarnation, then, means this: The Word of God is embodied in the man; the man Jesus is the visible manifestation of the invisible Word of God. The man Jesus, taken up into God, is selfsame and identical with the God that takes him up. This is the great miracle—that the selfsame person should at the same time be identical with two entities having different modes of being. Christ is at the same time the one and the other, *aliud et aliud*. He is both, *utrumque*. So he is not composed of body, soul, and God, but of body and soul alone. Both elements of his human nature are so closely united with the self of the Logos that Christ can be regarded as the humanized Logos. From this it may be concluded that the humanity assumed into the divinity is in possession of everything that the divine person by nature possesses: omniscience, omnipotence, and so on, not by its own nature, but by virtue of this mighty assumption into the person of the divine Word—by Grace.

The Habitus *Theory*

In contrast to Assumptionism, there is the doctrine known as the *Habitus* theory. This takes its starting point not in man but in the immutability and unchangeability of God. The divine being cannot be transformed into a new one, and so it cannot become a being that is both God and man at the same time. It cannot assume anything new into its immutable being. And so the union of divinity and humanity cannot possibly be an identity of the two; they can persist only side by side; it is only a relationship of one nature to another. The divine Word possesses the humanity as a man might possess a garment. When putting on apparel, we do not become the apparel, but are merely apparelled. And thus God too does not become man, but only puts on the garment of humanity (*humanatus est*). Hence the name "*Habitus* theory." According to this theory, the union of God and man in Christ would be far less close than the union of body and soul in Christ's human nature, for the latter is a union of nature and substance, while the former is not. But in this way, Christ would disintegrate, because his human parts would be far more closely interconnected than his humanity and his divinity. To meet this objection, the advocates of this theory were compelled to make the union of body and soul less close, and the union of divinity and humanity more so. The natural union of body and soul had to be diminished. And so they said: The Logos is not united to the human nature as such in its entirety, but with its single parts, with its body and its soul separately. This would mean that the process of incarnation took place thus: Before the body and soul of Christ were united into a human nature, the divine person joined itself to the human body, as yet still separate, and to the human soul, as yet also separate. Thus the original elements in the figure of Christ were a body joined to God and a soul joined to God. Christ did not become man in the same way as other men, by the union of body and soul, but by the indissoluble and supernatural union of the Logos on the one hand with the human soul, and on the other with the human body. The conclusion to be drawn from such a theory is that even during his death Christ would have been just as much man as he was during his life or after his resurrection. For he would have already become man because the divine Word had taken upon it the garment of the human soul. The second conclusion is still more dubious: As a man, Christ is in no way a person, he is not *aliquid,* someone, anyone, at all. For he is not apparelled in human nature as such, but only in the separate parts of the human nature. So the incarnation does not create a new essence. No new being is added to God, only an external, though indissoluble, possession. Christ is called man, not because he is man in essence, but because he possesses the two essential parts of man, body and soul, *velut indumentum,* as if he were apparelled in them.

It has been assumed that this strange theory first originated with Abelard. This is not so, for Abelard advocated the Subsistence theory, which we have still to discuss. But Hugh of St. Victor does seem to have approached it. At least, he certainly teaches that in the three days of his death, Christ was not only truly God but also truly man, for his body and his soul, each independently, preserved its union with the Godhead. So in fact he does appear to have advocated the view that the divine Word was not united to the human nature as such, in its entirety, but to its separate elements. This theory was a threat to one of the fundamental ideas of Christology, the doctrine that Christ became truly man. Pope Alexander III repeatedly described it as an irregular doctrine, *prava doctrina,* and finally in 1177 expressly repudiated it.

The Subsistence Theory

Where Assumptionism had its origins in St. John, the *Habitus* theory went back to St. Paul's Epistle to the Philippians. The third theory current in early Scholasticism, the Subsistence theory, also had its roots in St. John. In contrast to the view that Christ, God incarnate, was made up of body and soul, like the rest of mankind, they put forward the theory that Christ the man was made up of body, soul, and divinity. Christ became man only because the created human essence, human nature, received a supernatural support and bearer, the divine person. Christ has within him on the one hand the universal substantial essence that we all, as men, have in common. But on the other hand he also has within him the divine nature. And these essences are borne and supported by the Logos. This theory is based upon the naïve realism of the early Scholastic Platonists, for whom every essence already truly existed before it was realized in phenomena; the universal is prior to the thing, *universale ante rem*. According to this assumption, human nature as such would be in Christ, who as the Logos supports this just as he does the divine nature. Thus in reality Christ is a synthesis of two natures, *persona composita*. Now it is true this synthesis is infinitely higher than a mere natural synthesis. For where, in the ordinary course of things, every nature has its one corresponding support, in this case there are two natures having one single support, for the person of the divine Word carries both the divine and the human natures with equal immediacy. It did not assume some individual human nature, born of Mary, but a universal human nature, *natura universalis*, that all men have in common. Through the self of the Logos, "mankind-in-itself," as it were, becomes this one concrete man. As we see, this Subsistence theory distinguishes between the form of the nature (*subsistentia*) and the subject of this form (*subsistens*), which betrays that it was one consequence of the theories of Gilbert de La Porrée, who was indeed a most extreme realist. The same point of view is put forward still more clearly by the anonymous *sententiae divinitatis*, among others.

The interpretation of Jesus' self-consciousness by post-Tridentine theology

The influences of these three theories, by which early Scholasticism attempted to comprehend the mystery of the hypostatic union, persisted into High Scholasticism, even though no special attention was paid to them. The *Habitus* theory gradually died away. It was not until after the Council of Trent that late Scholastic theology turned to the task of clarifying and deepening the two other theories, mostly with the aid of such Aristotelian concepts as essence and existence. The question it was confronted with was this: What is the function of the Logos as person? If it is the Logos that gives Christ's human nature its autonomy and incommunicability, its *perseitas*, what is more precisely the addition that it makes to the human nature in doing so? Or perhaps it takes something from it, to give it concrete form? What does the person of the Logos accomplish, in order to bring about the union of Jesus' complete and undiminished humanity with his divinity? How does it bring it about that both natures, although they are entirely unchanged, *substantiae completae,* nevertheless make up a unity of substance? This question probed after the ultimate basis of unity in the constitution of the God-man.

Clarifications in terminology

The Church has not pronounced a decision on the question, so theological opinions upon it are free. As in the dogma of the Trinity, here too it is a question of the fundamental concepts of nature and person. Before we go on to evaluate the solutions theologians have offered, we must reach an understanding of these fundamental concepts.

"Nature" is the essence of a thing—what makes a being what it is. More precisely, "nature" is the essence of a thing in so far as it is the principle of its functioning, of its peculiar activity and passivity. It answers the question *quid?*—what?

The person asks who?—*quis?* It is defined as the *hypostasis rationalis,* the spiritual self. Literally, the concept hypostasis implies an autonomy, a self-sufficiency, a "standing-in-itself." The hypostasis as an autonomy is thus distinguished from the accident, which subsists in something other than itself; in Scholastic terms the accident is an *ens in alio,* whereas the hypostasis is an *ense in se.* As a thing-in-itself, however, it cannot be a merely intellectual being, but must also have an individual concrete reality of being. In other words, the hypostasis cannot be a *substantia secunda,* as Aristotle puts it; it cannot be a mere generic concept. It is an individual, concrete substance —in Aristotelian terms, *substantia prima.* This concept of autonomy (*inseitas*) thus does away with the accidental on the one hand, and the merely abstract and intellectual on the other. It is essentially a concrete substance, for example, this stone, this Cephas. However, there are also substances, for example, the human body, or the arm or foot of an organism, which are certainly concrete and individual, but are not entire in themselves, and attain their whole being only by being united with another concrete substance. These are called *substantiae incompletae.* So as well as the concept of autonomy, *inseitas,* the concept of hypostasis also requires that of *integritas,* organization as a whole. The hypostasis must be a *substantia prima completa.* But even then the complete concept of hypostasis has not yet been reached. There is a possibility—and in Christ it became a reality—that a complete individual substance, such as Christ's humanity, however closed and independent its being, nevertheless might in fact lose this closed autonomy because it is integrated into a higher substance. In this case, it is no longer an hypostasis, because it receives its definiteness and completion not in its own being but only in a higher being. So for the concept of hypostasis to be complete, it is also necessary that this last possibility of an ordination of being towards a higher hypostasis should be excluded, that the hypostasis should be "totally in itself," or entirely autonomous. In this sense, Scholastic terminology speaks of a *totietas in se,* or a *perseitas. S*o the concept of hypostasis includes three things: the *inseitas,* the *integritas,* and finally the *totietas in se,* or *perseitas.* As such a closed and autonomous whole, it excludes any kind of synthesis or composition; it is incommunicable, unique, and unrepeatable (*incommunicabilitas*). In positive terms, it is a closed entirety, with an independent autonomy. The mark of the hypostasis is this very quality of a *closed* being. That is why it is defined as *substantia prima, integra, tota in se.*

A purely formal evaluation of what gives the complete substance this incommunicability would be to call it *subsistence.* Subsistence is that mode of being, *modus essendi,* which gives to the substantial essence its incommunicability.

Only now have we reached a definition of the concept "hypostasis." But, even a crystal can be this kind of hypostasis. How is this to be distinguished from a "person"? Something new must also be added—*rationalitas,* the faculty of reason. The person is the *hypostasis rationalis.* The person arises only when the incommunicable, autonomous substance is also a spiritual, rational substance, only when it has that independent spiritual possession of its autonomy which is the basis for the development of a consciousness of self-sufficiency. It is true, being a person does not condition one's actual knowledge of one's own autonomy, but it certainly conditions one's capability of reaching this consciousness, this conscious self-possession. This faculty of reason, this *rationalitas,* is what transforms the hypostasis from a purely static, dead, frozen *toteitas in se* into one that is dynamic, spiritual, profound. The autonomy of being becomes an autonomy of self-possession, the faculty of self-consciousness. So person cannot be separated from intellectuality. The person is necessarily *sui juris,* subject to law, and, being subject to law, bears the responsibility of the activities of its nature. It is not as if the *rationalitas,* although a characteristic of the "nature," had no effect upon being a person. Because it is a question of a spiritual rational being, the autonomy is *in ipsa ratione hypostaseos* intensified, to the extent that only then is its independent self-possession and self-belonging fully realized.

Using this terminology, the theologians sought to answer the question of the ultimate basis for unity in the constitution of Christ.

The solution of the Thomist school

Fundamentally, their solution depends upon the position taken up by the various schools of thought within the Church with regard to the relationship between person and nature, and essence and existence. They are all agreed that the distinction between person and nature, essence and existence, is not merely a logical, but above all a virtual, distinction, that is, one founded upon fact (*cum fundamento in re*), even though such a distinction is not readily to be established in the concrete reality of phenomena. A virtual distinction is one that becomes apparent only after thinking about certain given facts. The question that divides the various schools of thought within the Church is rather this: Is the distinction between person and nature simply a virtual one of this kind, or is it more profound, is it a substantial distinction, as between one thing and another? If the latter, then the "existence as a person" can in substance be detached from the human nature. This nature would remain undiminished, *integra,* even if it had no person. In this case, the Logos would be united to the human nature by the simple suspension of the human existence as person, or, more precisely, by the suspension in the very act of union of the human mode of subsistence, while its place would be taken by the divine existence as person. According to this theory, the union takes place by way of subtraction; the being of the person is subtracted from the human person. The real point of unity is, then, what the Logos puts in the place of the suspended and withdrawn human mode of subsistence, that is, the autonomy of the second divine person, or, in Scholastic terms, the divine *esse existentiae*. This doctrine was mainly put forward by the Thomist school founded by the Dominican Bañez (d. 1604), which was based upon certain fundamental doctrines of St. Thomas Aquinas. His view was that its union with the self of the Logos caused the human nature to give up its own mode of subsistence, its own peculiar mode of self-possession and self-belonging. It no longer belongs to itself, but to the self of the Logos. This is where it has its ultimate resting place, its proper autonomy. The independent sense of identity, which transforms ordinary human nature in general into an individual concrete man, is attained in an infinitely higher sense by the human nature that is integrated into the identity of the Logos. Being thus assumed into the absolute autonomy of the Logos, it appropriates to itself the Logos' absolute power of reality and might of existence. It no longer exists in and by itself, but by this power of existence of the Logos. And thus the *unio in persona* becomes more profoundly a *unio ad esse, ad existentiam*. This is possible because in the Thomist scheme a real distinction persists not only between nature and person but also between essence and existence; they are distinct as potency and act, the mere possibility of being and realized being, are distinct. Hence the humanity of Jesus is able to receive the absolute power of reality of the Logos, as well as its personality. The Logos extends its divine power of being to it, and takes it up in its might. Its own power of existence, its own *existere*, is of itself suspended or, rather, assumed into the absolute and autonomous reality of the Logos.

The advantage of the Thomist explanation is in its ability to establish the closest unity of the humanity of Jesus with the person of the Logos without in any way diminishing or harming the human nature itself. But in depriving the human nature of its highest and ultimate stage of existence, the *esse existentiae*, it is inadequate. Its opponents are in a position to maintain that Thomism does in fact diminish the human nature; they have only to regard this *esse existentiae* as the essential characteristic of nature and essence, and to assume that person and nature, essence and existence, are only virtually distinct from each other, and not detachable from each other. On the other hand the Thomist theory appears to divinize the human nature in so far as its existence is also the existence of the Logos. Since in the Logos existence is identical with the divine nature, the conclusion would not be far to seek that the human nature came into possession of the divine essence as well as the divine existence.

The solution of Duns Scotus

The sharpest refutation of the Thomist explanation came from Duns Scotus (d. 1308) and his school. Duns Scotus taught that the nature and person and the nature and existence of created things are not really distinct, but rather that their separation is only virtual. And therefore the assumption must be made that in Christ there is, as well as the two natures, also a dual mode of existence, human and divine, created and un-created. Where, then, does Scotus locate the point of unity of the two natures in Christ? If the human nature of Jesus does not exist in the eternal existence of the Logos, but possesses a human existence, what joins it with the Logos in a substantial union, what is to be understood by the existence as person which the human nature has from the Logos? Duns Scotus has recourse to the following explanation: To the created person-ality, being a person is something wholly negative. To the creature, it simply means the *negatio dependentia actualis et aptitudinalis*. Being a person simply means that the created being does not belong to another subject either in fact (*inde-pendentia actualis*) or potentially (*independentia aptitudinalis*). Every individual rational nature is thus without any further ado and without the approach of another substantial perfection a person, as long as it remains belonging to itself, and is not united to any higher hypostasis. The moment a created being united to a higher hypostasis is released from this higher hypostasis, it would promptly return to being a person again. In the created being, its being as person is something purely negative, a state of not-being-dependent, or of not-being-po-tentially-dependent. In contrast, however, it is something posi-tive in God, because God, as an entity in himself, an *ens a se,* is the absolute autonomy of all being. This autonomy is his nature. It is the source of his abundant perfections. If this definition of the person of the Creator is applied to Christ,

Scotus' theory would argue that the human nature, in being assumed into the unity of person of the Son of God, would lose its being as a person in so far as it loses its actual and potential independence, its *independentia actualis et aptitudinalis*—i.e., to the extent that it is no longer independent. It loses nothing positive but only its negative independence and incommunicability with regard to another hypostasis. By means of God's omnipotence, a human nature is integrated into the divine person "after the fashion of a part." This integrated part, however, with the exception of its lost independence, preserves the fullness of its specific human mode of being, and thus its human existence, which is an essential part of this specific mode of being. There is only one person in Christ, but a dual existence. Unlike the Thomist theory, Scotus does not regard the being as person as a real *modus subsistendi*, which would be the addition of a positive reality to the human nature; it is something negative, freedom from all dependence. And in so far as human nature loses this independence to the Logos, this Logos is its person, endowing it with its own incommunicability and autonomy. The existence itself belongs as a positive mode of being not to the identity as person but to the human nature. This is how it preserves Christ's humanity, even in the hypostatic union. To this extent we must say that Christ's humanity is no longer an independent human person, in so far as it has surrendered its independence to the Logos. But by virtue of its nature, it exists through its own created existence, and not through the uncreated existence of the divine Word.

The advantage of Duns Scotus' theory is that it preserves Christ's full humanity in every conceivable form. The identity of our nature with Jesus' humanity, the ὁμοούσιος ἡμῖν, is consistently maintained. But we have doubts about its depletion of the concept of person. St. Thomas Aquinas, whose authority Duns Scotus too recognizes, describes "person" as the "most perfect in the entire nature"—he is referring to what subsists in a rational nature (*Summa Theologica*, I, qu. 29, a. 3). Now this expresses something absolutely positive: the autonomy. This autonomy is primary; the independence is only secondary, since the autonomy is its prerequisite. A further weakness in Duns Scotus' conception is that it is unable to say clearly what really does inextricably unite divinity and humanity in Christ. The union does not bring about the slightest change in the human nature of Jesus. Similarly, the Logos also remains unchanged in every respect. So what really takes place in the hypostatic union? After all, the God-man is a substantial essence, a substantial synthesis of the divine and human natures. But how can a substantial essence arise if nothing substantial takes place in either part of the synthesis? Scotus would reply: The true union is brought about by the absolute and immutable will of God, an all-embracing transcendental power. It is God's will that this concrete human nature should belong not to itself but to the Logos. And God's almighty will has its effect. So we may conclude that its only correlative can be a substantial union.

As we shall see, this divine will remained in all it wrought strictly transcendent. Scotist thought is disposed to ensure this transcendence of the divine and supernatural in every respect, unlike Thomism, which recognizes the immanence of the divine. Because the divine will that constantly integrates the humanity of Jesus into the Logos is entirely transcendent, it can be known only by faith. So the incarnation is purely the object of faith. There is nothing in the miracle that has its place in the world of experience. On the strictly empirical level of experience, Christ in his human figure appears just like the rest of us. Only our faith has any knowledge of his divine mystery.

The Scotist and Thomist doctrines

The theory of supernatural and divine transcendence at the bottom of Duns Scotus' doctrine is the stamp of his entire system, just as on the other hand Thomism is marked by the contrasting doctrine of the immanence of the divine in things earthly. This is the crucial point where, in our judgement, the two schools clearly part company. To mention but a few points: Catholic doctrine holds that there was a union of God and man for the act of salvation, God's Grace on the one hand joined with man's free will on the other. Now in the Thomist system, this would imply that there was an absolutely supernatural quality in the mere movement of Grace from God to man, something that belongs to God alone, which is called the *qualitas fluens*. This is the true principle that elevates our human actions, our unconscious moods and awarenesses, up to good, and to acts of Grace. On the other hand, in the Scotist system, the divine movement of Grace would remain strictly transcendent in its entire course. It arouses our unconscious experiences and awarenesses for good from above, without in any way entering into human spirituality, or the complexity of human action. In this scheme, the *gratia praeveniens* is identical with the unconscious inclination towards good. Similarly, the two schools are distinct in their attitudes towards sanctifying Grace. According to Thomism, its essence lies in a supernatural *infusio*, in endowing us with a *habitus supernaturalis*, which is the true source from which our supernatural acts, of love of God, and so on, issue forth. According to the Scotist system, on the other hand, the supernatural source of this love of God remains strictly transcendent. On the empirical level of experience, all that is given is the spiritual depth of our sense of God, the purely human attitude of love of God. Only our faith knows that this love is wrought by God. So sanctify ing Grace and love are one and the same thing. And the same conditions apply to the two doctrines of the sacrament. Catholic dogma holds that in the symbol of the Eucharist, form and material are conjoined into a sacramental unity. In the Thomist system, this outward symbol itself is supernatural, a power of God, a divine movement of love which, because of the *potentia oboedientialis* peculiar to every being, fills the symbol of the Eucharist with life and the power of Grace. In the Scotist system, on the other hand, God's act of Grace remains strictly transcendent even here. All that is given on the empirical, visible level is simply the visible symbol itself; it is our faith that assures us that it is the symbol of Christ, and therefore will work our salvation. The same distinction is present in the two schools' doctrines of predestination, their concept of the Church, and so on. But even these few examples have shown us that in the Thomist view the supernatural, holy, and divine is something that breaks through this world of ours, subject to time and space, and all things in it, and transfigures them. They are all symbols, because they are related to the divine; they are numinous not simply on account of their causal origins (*quoad principium*), but also in their very being (*formaliter*). This is particularly clear in the Thomist concept of the Church. In its view, the Church is that *corpus Christi mysticum* which in all the orders is essentially, physically permeated and transfigured by the spirit of Christ. Thus, as an institution for our salvation (*in se*) it is supernatural. In the Scotist view, the divine activity takes place in pure transcendence. Only faith has any knowledge of it. All that is empirically given in the Church is purely human. The Church is supernatural only to the extent that it has been caused by God's will to salvation (*quoad principium*), but not in its earthly being. And so in the

Thomist view of Christ, too, the purely human, natural being of Christ is so penetrated and animated by the divine power of the Logos that its true reality is the same as that of the Logos. But in the Scotist view, the Logos and its activities remain strictly transcendent. All that is to be seen and experienced of Christ the man is purely human. Only our faith knows that in his metaphysical depths this man Jesus belongs not to himself but to the Logos.

The solution of the Molinist school

The Scotist doctrine was revised, or rather deepened, by certain theologians who were adherents not so much of the Scotist school as of Molinism. They were mostly members of the Society of Jesus. Tiphanus, Franzelin, and Pesch maintain that the Logos assumed complete human nature in the further sense that not only the individual human existence but also the being of the human person belongs at least virtually to the human nature. The person, then, is not negative, but something positive. But it is only virtually distinct from the nature. The moment the humanity of Jesus would be released from the hypostatic union, it would be able to exist as a separate created being, in its own power, and be a person. Nothing is taken away from Christ's human nature by its assumption into the Logos. Whatsoever belongs to human nature forms part of it even after the incarnation. Hence the Thomist theory of subtraction is untenable. What has happened in the incarnation is simply that the selfsame intact human nature has been assumed into the divine hypostasis, and that from this moment on it no longer belongs to itself but to the Logos. But in this process the human personality is by no means completely cancelled out. Because it belongs to the human nature, it is still there, virtually, and is not extinguished or destroyed by the divine person, but assumed into it. This assumption does not imply the destruction of the human self, but its exaltation. In Scholastic terms, it is not a *defectus ad imperfectum,* but a *profectus ad perfectum,* a tremendous transfiguration into the divine. This process of perfection is possible because human nature, like every created nature, on account of its *potentia oboedientialis,* is ordinated towards union with the divine. The hypostatic union is the fulfilment of the deepest longing that lies like an undeveloped seed in created nature, the longing for the most real union and unity with God. This is why there is nothing in any way unnatural about the process of incarnation. Indeed, it is much rather the fulfilment of what the Creator from the beginning planted in nature as its ultimate culminating potentiality.

The solution of Suárez

It was Suárez (d. 1617) who put forward a theory mediating between the two opposing conceptions of the Thomist and Scotist schools. He too follows Scotus in the doctrine that nature and existence are in reality the same, and that therefore in Christ a dual existence is to be assumed. So the point of unity of the two natures in Christ cannot lie in the uncreated existence of the Logos, as the Thomist theory would have it. To this extent, Suárez follows the Scotist school. But he labours to avoid the evil conclusions that would arise if the Scotist principles were applied unmodified to Christology. To this end he makes use of the Thomist distinction between person and nature. Certainly nature and existence can be separated only conceptually. But person and nature can be distinguished in reality, *realiter*. Existence as person brings with it its own peculiar reality, distinct from that of nature. This reality is to be conceived after the fashion of modal accidents. In distinction to absolute accidents, modal accidents are those conditions of being (*quidditates*) that could not be conceived as existing without having a substance as bearer. They are the necessary forms of appearance of a substance. Such modal accidents, for example, would be the form, the figure, the movement, of a body. They are not mere relationships, because they are real effects of real activities, and are themselves in turn the causes of real effects. Movement, for example, is a real factor in the production of speed, just as is the mass of a body. The reality that makes of nature a person is to be conceived after the fashion of these modal accidents. Only this reality would not be an accidental mode, but substantial, because its ultimate perfection is rendered in autonomy, in substantiality. According to Suárez, this would make a person out of nature only by adding to nature the *modus per se existendi,* the mode by which nature itself has its autonomous existence, the *modus substantialis.* And thus the person is not, as Scotus assumed, something negative, but a positive perfection, since it is not yet contained in the individual nature as such. This was the way by which Suárez tried to improve Scotus' concept of the person. By the hypostatic union of Christ's human nature with the Logos, whereby the Logos appropriates the human nature to itself and becomes its bearer, it loses its natural *modus substantialis.* It gives something up, something certainly real, but not its *existentia,* as the Thomists would have it, not the highest stage of its ordination in being, but simply a mode of being, the *modus per se existendi.* And the place of this natural mode is taken not by the eternal mode of being of the Logos itself, as the Thomists would have it, but by a new mode created by divine omnipotence, the *modus unionis,* which binds the two natures together. This new mode too is a *modus substantialis,* and it contains the basis of unity of the two natures in Christ. The rôle played by the eternal will of God in the Scotist system is in this case taken over by something real, created, the *modus unionis.* This is a rejection of the Thomist explanation, which acknowledged the ultimate basis of Christ's unity in the *"existere."* Here, we have a bond of unity that is not uncreated but created, the supernaturally created *modus unionis.* This disposes of the danger of divinizing Christ's humanity. Suárez attempts to improve upon Scotus by giving up his negative conception of the being of the person as *independentia,* and ascribing to it a positive created reality. This brings the further advantage of being able to establish a positive bond of unity in Christ in so far as the union of both natures is not brought about by the will of God alone, but also by means of the real, supernaturally created *modus unionis,* which takes the place of the natural *modus per se existendi* that has been abolished in the incarnation, and which by this very substitution inextricably unites the human nature with the Logos. Suárez believes that this gives him the advantage over Thomism, for in his system Christ's human nature is not directly taken up into the divine existence and essence, and thus divinized, but preserves its own relative autonomy and its peculiar characteristics as a created being.

The objection to Suárez's theory is that, given his presuppositions, the concept of a *modus substantialis* is not tenable. Suárez does not assume any real distinction between essence and existence. And so existence is already given with nature. The conclusion then would be that the *modus per se existendi* of which Suárez speaks cannot be a mode of substance, but only of accident. For in Scholastic ontology, everything that is a subsequent addition to being is an accident, *Omne, quod sequitur ad esse rei, est ei accidentale* (Thomas Aquinas, *Summa contra Gentes,* 1, 22). Now, it is true, in the case we have been discussing there does not seem to be any justification for the objection. If we assume that the being at issue here is divine being, then it cannot be said of it that its mode of subsistence is a "subsequent addition." Rather it is already included in divine being, indeed, it is the culmination of divine being. So Suárez's theory does in fact appear to have cleared away all doubts that could be raised against the Thomist and Scotist conceptions. Objections to Suárez's theory itself are only of a terminological nature, for the expression *modus substantialis* is an unusual one in Scholastic usage.

Psychological understanding of the mystery of the incarnation

The multiplicity of theories by which theology has tried to approach the mystery of the incarnation is a fresh testimony to the truth that the incarnation is a *mysterium stricte dictum* that cannot be solved, even after revelation. However, they allow us a glimpse into the possible ways in which the incarnation might be realized. They bear witness at least to the inner possibility of this mystery. But however difficult the ontological structure of Christ's constitution may be, psychological understanding of it comes very easily. We have abundant examples of how another person is capable of entering into our own life and making it his own; indeed, how our own life can be possessed by the other person, and lose itself in him entirely. With an invisible but mighty power, the beloved makes such a claim upon the lover that the lover no longer belongs to himself, but to the beloved other. The rhythm of the beloved's life pulses in him, and assumes his own identity. How much stronger the supernatural love of God and Christ is than any natural love is shown by this kind of incarnation in the lives of the saints and the devout, the *homines religiosi.* When St. Paul says, "Christ is my life," "it is not I that live, but Christ liveth in me," he is saying that his own natural self has been completely absorbed by the divine self dwelling within him, and has been taken up into it. Christ is his truest, deepest self, the life of his life. This process of incarnation is wrought in the humanity of Jesus with incomparably greater intensity than in the experience of natural and supernatural love. Because Christ is one with the Godhead, not accidentally, but in substance, his human self-consciousness as well as his human self has been assumed into the divine consciousness so completely that they are aware of this union with the divinity in every respect; this divine consciousness takes first place within him, and all his human feeling, thought, and volition are accomplished only in the closest intercourse with this divinity. "I and the Father are one." Jesus' humanity has given up the knowledge that it belongs to itself, and belongs to the living God, which, as the Logos of the Father, takes on and possesses its human doing and being, so that it can only conceive of itself as the organ or instrument of the Logos. We have already pointed out that it was above all St. John the Evangelist who described how real and close this interpenetration of God and man was in Christ, and who taught us to understand Jesus' humanity as the transparency of the divinity in Christ. Although the incarnation of God in Jesus the man is so difficult to explain completely, or even tentatively, in ontological terms, at least we are able to approach it with our psychological understanding and sympathy. We are in some manner able to experience it, and to that extent we are able to illuminate and deepen our own faith in the mystery of Jesus.

Now that we have discussed the inner foundations for the unity of the hypostatic union, we shall turn to observing the separate parts that go to make up the synthesis of the incarnation, first the divinity, and then the humanity in Christ.

XIV

THE HYPOSTATIC UNION AND THE DIVINE NATURE OF CHRIST

IN HIS classic *Epistola dogmatica ad Flavianum,* Leo the Great expounded the Church's dogma of the duality in Christ's unity so clearly that all the bishops gathered at the Council of Chalcedon in 451 were carried away, and cried with one voice: *per Leonem Petrus locutus est,* Peter himself has spoken through Leo's mouth. Taking Leo's epistle as its basis, the Council defined not only the one person and substance, *una persona atque substantia* (ἓν πρόσωπον καὶ μία ὑπόστασις), but also the two natures unconfused, immutable, indivisible, inseparable, *duae naturae inconfuse, immutabiliter, indivise, inseperabiliter* (ἀσυγχύτως, ἀτρέπτως, ἀδιαιρέτως, ἀχωρίστως). We shall first discuss the divine nature in Christ in its relationship to the Trinity.

The incarnation of the second divine person

It is an article of faith (*de fide*) that only the *second person* of the Trinity became man. In opposition to the Patripassians, who ascribed the incarnation to the Father because they thought they were compelled to assume only one divine person, the Church's creed called upon the testimony of the Scriptures and the early Fathers, and demonstrated that the Trinity as a whole did not enter into the hypostatic union, nor yet the first or third person of the Trinity, but only the second person. The question immediately arises: Does not the consubstantiality of the three divine persons (they are not indeed substantially separable from the divine nature) mean to imply that the incarnation of the second person necessarily drew the other two divine persons in its wake? This conclusion seemed so inevitable to the Nominalist Roscelin (d. after 1120) and the philosopher Günther (d. 1863) that they abandoned the consubstantiality of the three divine persons in order to avoid the necessity of ascribing the incarnation to the Father and the Holy Spirit as well as to the Son. To this extent they were adherents of tritheism, which splits the divinity up into three separate persons, and denies their common substance. We shall not be far from a solution to our question if we follow the Church's definition of the relation of the person to nature. According to this, it is the person that first gives a substance its autonomy. It had already been decided by St. Thomas Aquinas with a simple *"distinguo."* He distinguished the effective principle of the incarnation and its goal, or object (*terminus*). The object of the union of both natures can be only a divine person, and not a divine nature. For what the incarnation is intended to effect is after all the unity of the divine person in two natures. Only the person gives the autonomy. And the substantial being of Jesus' humanity attains its end and its fulfilment only in the autonomy of the second divine person. Hence it is only one of the three divine persons, and not the triune divine substance, that in the incarnation can give the human nature its autonomy. The divine nature too exists with inner necessity only through the absolute autonomy of the three divine persons. It is not the divine nature that is the ultimate bearer, but the three divine persons in their relationship to one another. Thus Christ's humanity is not assumed into the unity of the divine nature, but into the unity of the divine person. The function of the Logos towards the human nature is purely ontological, and not dynamic. For all it shares of the divine substance with the human nature is its autonomy. The union is strictly hypostatic. So the object of the union can be only a divine person. The divine nature can also be described as the object of the union only to the extent that it has assumed the human nature in *persona Verbi*. It belongs to the human nature only *ratione personae Verbi,* only through the autonomy of the second person.

Though the object of the union can be only one divine person, its effective principle belongs to all *three persons* together. This is the express doctrine of the Fourth Lateran Council (1215): *Dei filius Jesus Christus a tota trinitate communiter incarnatus.* For it is through the power of the divine nature that the hypostatic union is wrought. This is the *principium quo* of all divine works (while the person, on the other hand, is the *principium quod*). All God's external works belong to the divine nature. For that which is not person in God, that which strictly speaking does not give the Godhead the autonomy of the Trinity, belongs to the divine nature. The real difference of the three divine persons is relevant only to the divine life within the Trinity. Outside the Trinity, the triune God works as the one omnipotent God, through the unity of his nature. So we must say that the hypostatic union takes place actively, to the extent that it is an *incarnare*, an act of incarnation brought about by all three divine persons. It is an *opus Dei ad extra*, an act of the divine essence. On the other hand, it is passive to the extent that it is an *incarnari*, a state undergone by the second divine person, and belonging to him alone.

The grounds for the incarnation of the Son

But why is the second divine person the object of the union, rather than the first or the third? Human reason is unable to illuminate the most profound sufficient reason. It can only show that the incarnation was most fitting for the Son alone. The Son is the eternal Word of the Father, the expression in personal form of his being, the quintessential personal form of all the divine ideas according to which the world—and man in particular—was created, *similitudo exemplaris totius creaturae*, the pattern and likeness of all creatures. The natural and supernatural image of man was formed after him, who was the likeness of the Father. And so it was fitting that when this image formed in the likeness of the Son was distorted by sin, it should once again be renewed and re-established in the Son, the eternal Word. If the creation was accomplished by means of the Word, and in its likeness, then it is fitting that the new creation should also be accomplished by the Son, and in his likeness. This is related to the idea that Christ is God's Son in a unique, physical sense. As far as the purpose of the new creation was to re-establish in man redeemed his filiation to God, to elevate him to the status of God's adopted son, it was fitting that the very person to restore man to this filiation and exalt him to be the son of God should have been the eternal and consubstantial Son of God himself. So we maintain that it is fitting that the Logos alone, as the image of all human and created perfection, and on account of its mysterious filial relationship to the Father within the Trinity, should have been the divine person to restore mankind to its lost likeness and filiation to God.

This may give us some modest insight into the supernatural motive for the mystery of the incarnation, and into those thoughts of God's that caused Christ to become man. When we speak of Christ's mediation, the first thing that comes to mind is his function of reconciling sinful mankind to God. But this function is only one single impulse in the entire idea of divine mediation. Essentially, it is rather the communication of the marvellous closeness of *God's union with his creation*. And the reconciliation of created beings is only one instance within this. As man, Christ is one with mankind; indeed with the entire created world, at whose head he stands. As God, he stands in a union of substance with his Father, from whom he comes, and with the Holy Spirit, in which he encounters the Father. Standing in the world, one with the world, he towers up into the very heart of the Godhead, he is God himself, one with the Father and the Holy Spirit. And so in his person, he draws the world up into the very neighbourhood of the eternal Father, while on the other hand he emanates over the entire world the union he has with his Father. He binds God and his creation into such a close reciprocal relationship that he cancels and overcomes not only every abyss between God and his creation but also the infinite disparity that separates them by their very natures; Christ conquers not only religious and ethical remoteness but also ontological distance. The God-man cancels out both the infinite remoteness of mere created being and the infinite remoteness of sinful being. So Christ is the substantial bond which brings together the most disparate antinomies. The Lord's sublime prayer that mankind "may be one even as we are one: I in them and thou in me; that they may be perfected in unity" is perfectly fulfilled in the God-man (cf. Scheeben, *Mysterien des Christentums,* pp. 350 f.).

The peculiar significance of the incarnation

This makes it easy to understand the number of theologians who follow the Scotist doctrine in maintaining that the incarnation could have taken place *even without Adam's fall,* and quite independently of it. It has its end in itself. It is the most sublime fulfilment of Paul's words: "In him we live and move and have our being." If we were to recognize God as he is, in the innermost necessities of his being, then the incarnation would appear to our astounded eyes as God's most radiant revelation, in the added sense that it is the freest expression of his innermost essence, freely willed and outwardly wrought by the infinite power of his life and love. This inner beauty and sublimity of the mystery of the incarnation helps us to understand why the German Idealist philosophers (such as Fichte, Schelling, Hegel) described this very idea of the God-man as the "profoundest insight," and made it the basis of their philosophic speculation. It is true their interpretation of the idea has a pantheistic twist: for them, Jesus' significance consisted in the fact that he had led man as a species to the consciousness of the divinity of his humanity. In contrast to this, Christianity cherishes the certainty that just as no new development ever comes from the species as a whole, but only from single personalities, so the great new thing that was made manifest in Christ—especially the idea of God made man—was accomplished and fulfilled in one single man, Jesus of Nazareth, and not in the species man. However, these interpretations of the Idealists are testimony enough to the abundance of truth and value that lies within the Christian message, "*et Verbum caro factum est.*"

Now that we have thrown some light upon Jesus' divine nature under the aspect of the hypostatic union, we shall proceed to discussing that union in its relationship to the humanity of our Lord.

XV

THE HYPOSTATIC UNION AND THE HUMAN NATURE OF CHRIST

The integrity of Christ's human nature

WE have already pointed out that Pope Leo's *Epistola dogmatica ad Flavianum,* which was later confirmed by the Council of Chalcedon, stresses the proposition that the assumption of Christ's humanity into the person of the Logos took place without in any way diminishing the peculiar properties of either nature, *salva proprietate utriusque naturae et substantiae*. This expression was repeated in the dogmatic decision reached at the Council of Chalcedon. As we have learned, it was originated by Tertullian. By way of commentary, the Council added the explanation that the self-same Christ was contained unconfused and immutable (*inconfuse, immutabiliter*) in both natures. This decision was levelled against Eutyches, who defended the doctrine that both natures were transformed into the divine, which implied a unity and a homogeneity in the nature of Christ (μιά φύσις). Like Gregory of Nyssa, Eutyches made use of the metaphor of the sea and the drop of vinegar to illustrate his doctrine of transformation. Just as a drop of vinegar poured into the sea will take on the nature of the sea, just so the human nature was transformed into the divine. So Christ was certainly made up *out of* two natures originally, but after the union he no longer persists *in* two natures, but only in one. This Monophysite heresy recalls the Indian myth of the god Krishna, who has the power to transform himself into men, or even into beasts. There were other Monophysites, particularly Severus of Antioch (d. 538), who did not advocate this virtual transformation of human into divine nature, but maintained that the union brought about the formation of a new, third commingled nature that embraced both the divine and the human natures. Or they assumed at least that the unchanged humanity and divinity in Christ were so closely compounded that they made up one single "composite" nature, just as body and soul together make up the one human nature.

It is not necessary to refute the various versions of the Monophysite doctrine in the light of revelation. We have already advanced sufficient proof that the Holy Scriptures and the early Fathers maintained that both natures preserved their own integrity, and were not commingled, even after the incarnation. As we have seen, the image of Christ derived from the Synoptic Gospels, and from the Scriptures previous to them, stresses the humanity of Jesus. The very fact that the incarnate Logos remained truly human is the premise from which we conclude his capacity to suffer, and his power to save. The Fathers emphasized again and again that if Jesus' humanity were to lose the complete integrity of its nature, its "naturality," it would not be able to redeem our own nature in its entirety. Irenaeus of Lyons (d. 202) had already established this principle. Gregory of Nazianzus gave it the following formulation: "What is taken away from the human nature remains unredeemed. Only what is united with the Godhead is also redeemed" (*Epistola* 101). Besides the testimony of the Fathers, the very fact that our nature *was* redeemed in its entirety is a further warranty that a complete individual human nature persisted in the Incarnate One, and that Christ's humanity did not in any way dissolve away into the divine nature.

Philosophical objections to Monophysitism

We intend here to throw some light on the philosophical objections to Monophysitism, because they help to clarify the Church's formulation of the dogma and reveal the keen dialectic at its foundation. Monophysitism is a metaphysical impossibility, because it violates the concept of God—the infinity and immutability of God. A finite nature can certainly receive its autonomy and personality from the infinite divine person, but it can never be commingled into becoming one with the divine nature. As long as the infinite is to remain so, the finite can never be absorbed or compounded into it. Two orders of being confront each other here, and they are simply not comparable. There is no operation that will transform nought into a positive number. Jesus' humanity, as a created contingency, is this kind of nought in comparison with the absolute being of God. But the concept of God is destroyed even by the more moderate theory of Severus. The Antioch theologian assumed that, by analogy with the human soul in the body, Christ's divinity would be the forming principle, the *forma substantialis,* of Jesus' humanity. In this way, this humanity of Jesus' would no longer remain pure humanity, but would have become divine humanity, a new and specifically different nature. But this theory too is a metaphysical impossibility. For God, who is infinite, can never be the *forma substantialis* of a finite nature, as the soul is the *forma substantialis* of our body. The infinite quite simply surpasses the bounds of the finite in every way. There is no single point in the chain of being which the infinite and the finite have in common. And so divinity cannot join with humanity to form a third nature, because this would be a denial of the distinction between the infinite and the finite. Both parts of the new compounded nature would have to belong to a new order of being, and either the infinite would have to become finite or the finite would have to become infinite.

The Monophysites appeal for support to the expression "mixture" or "compound" (κρᾶσις), which is frequently used by the early Fathers. But in doing so they misinterpret patristic usage. Those Fathers, such as Irenaeus, Tertullian, Augustine, and Cyril of Alexandria, who speak of a *"commixtio,"* are perfectly clear that they advocate the continued integrity of both natures. They use the expression "compound" or "mixture" simply to stress the fact that the two natures come together in one divine person, and that the closest interpenetration of both natures is thereby achieved. What they mean is the circumincession, which we shall discuss later.

The Monophysite theologians also made frequent use, for their own ends, of the patristic allusions to the analogy of the union of body and soul in man; body and soul in man together make up a human nature, and, analogously, divinity and humanity could be united in Christ into a new divine-and-human nature. Even the Athanasian Creed made this simile. But in fact it was intended only as a simile, and nothing more. In one respect the comparison was exceedingly apt. Like the divinity and humanity in Christ, body and soul in man are also compounded into one unity of subject, into one individual person.

And just as the unity of body and soul is not merely moral but also physical, that is, given by the nature of both substances, just so the unity of divine person and human nature in Christ is not merely moral and accidental but substantial. Moreover, like Christ's humanity and divinity, man's body and soul too remain after their union essentially different substances. And just as the divine Logos is the higher and dominant principle, possessing the human nature and endowing it with its ultimate perfection, just so is the soul the dominant principle in man, animating the body, and granting it a part in its spiritual life. But notwithstanding all these similarities between divinity and humanity in Christ on the one hand, and soul and body in man on the other, the differences are not to be overlooked. Divinity and humanity are *substantiae completae,* while body and soul are *substantiae incompletae.* Divinity and humanity together could never form a third nature common to them. On the other hand, the union of body and soul produces one single nature. Furthermore, the soul is the *forma substantialis* of the body. But, because the divine nature is infinite, it can never be the substantial form of a nature that is finite. Finally, body and soul are thus real parts of the human whole. Divinity and humanity, on the other hand, can never be regarded as parts of the God-man, for of course divinity can never be a part.

The duality of Christ's will and his exercise of will

More important than the proof of Christ's unimpaired humanity for our assessment of his inner life is it to establish in theological terms the conclusion that can be drawn from his duality of nature. This conclusion is the dogma of Christ's duality of will, and the duality of his exercise of will. For reasons of ecclesiastical politics, Sergius, the Patriarch of Constantinople, attempted to win over the Monophysites, and after the year 620 defended this formulation: "There are two natures in Christ, but only one will and one mode of activity" (ἓν θέλημα καὶ μία ἐνέργεια). This proposition was very soon repudiated at the Vatican Council in 649 under Pope Martin I. And later it was condemned by the dogmatic Epistle of 680 sent by Pope Agatho to the Emperor Constantine. This was confirmed by the Sixth General Council at Constantinople in 680–81, which promulgated the following doctrine: "We acknowledge in Christ two physical wills and two physical activities without separation, without transformation, without division, and without commingling." This definition alone is enough to make clear that the question at issue is not the moral unity of both natures, not whether Jesus' human will was, or could ever be, at variance with the divine will—for that was the very thing that made up the sanctity of Jesus' human will, that it should always be freely in harmony with the will of God. What was rather at issue was exclusively the question of the physical freedom of the wills and their activities, whether in fact after the incarnation two wills were present in the incarnate Logos, and whether the human exercise of will was able to take effect after the human fashion, in complete freedom. Holy Scripture gives a clear and unambiguous answer to this question. Christ himself speaks expressly of his human will, and contrasts it to the divine will. He prays on the Mount of Olives: "Father, if it is possible, let this cup pass away from me; yet not as I will, but as thou willest" (Matt. 26.39; Luke 22.42). And in the Gospel according to St. John, Christ's words have a similar tenor (6.38). "For I have come down from heaven, not to do my own will but the will of him who sent me." Jesus' human will knows what infinities separate it from the holy will of God. That is why Christ prays to the Father. Christ is not only the object but also the subject of prayer. He himself prays. And sometimes this prayer comes from the depths of his desolate humanity. "My God, my God, why hast thou forsaken me?" (Mark 15.34). When the Gospels speak of our Lord's humility, and his reverence towards the Father, they are describing Jesus' purely human ways of exercising his human will. While the early Fathers emphasize the duality of natures in Christ, they are also indirectly—and sometimes expressly—stressing his duality of will. The only exception seems to be Pseudo-Dionysius the Areopagite. In fact, he seems to regard the conative powers of the God-man to be a specific kind of striving, unique and peculiar to God incarnate. Although he lived around 500, at the time of the Monothelete disputes he was regarded as a pupil of St. Paul, and the Monotheletes made use of his doctrines in this sense. In his Fourth Epistle, Dionysius makes this striking remark: Christ's divine activities were not wrought in divine fashion, nor his human activities in human fashion, but he exercised "a certain new activity," the activity of God incarnate, both divine and human (θεανδρικὴ ἐνέργεια), or theandric. The expression "both divine and human" (θεανδρικὴ) derived from Origen, who was the first to speak of the "God-man" (θεάνθρωπος). The Monophysite theologians interpreted this strange proposition to mean that the divinity and humanity in Christ composed a kind of new nature, as body and soul did, and that the activities of this compound theandric nature were peculiar and special activities. They understood that the moving principle in Christ was exclusively the divine will. The human will was purely passive in its relationship to it. It was simply a passive instrument in the service of the divine will. What distinguished Christ's human will from the ordinary will of the rest of mankind was that it should be entirely assumed and solely activated by the divine will. According to the Monophysites, Dionysius leaves no doubt that the real initiative for Christ's actions is to be ascribed solely to the divine will of the Logos. But this interpretation of the Monophysite theologians does not entirely coincide with what Dionysius really taught. The Father simply meant that because Christ's two natures subsisted in the one divine person of the Logos, their volition and way of acting alike should be ascribed to this one divine person. So he does not derive the new quality in Christ's willing to a unity of nature and a commingling of both wills in Christ, but to the unity of person, and the uniqueness of the divine bearer of these two wills. According to the principle: *actiones sunt suppositorum,* that is, all activities are to be ascribed to the self that commits them, all Jesus' activities, divine or human, are true activities of the self of the Logos. For this self is the *principium quod,* the agent or subject, of all the Lord's activities. But to the extent that these activities of the self of the Logos are accomplished only through the medium of Christ's humanity, that is, to the extent that this humanity is the *principium quo* of the Logos' activities, Dionysius believed he should describe them all as actions that were truly divine and human, or theandric (θεανδρική). Obviously, this is not directly relevant to our problem of whether we may establish two wills and two modes of exercising them in Christ. Dionysius is not calling the autonomy of both wills into question, but only emphasizing that the Lord's purely human activities belong to the Logos, and to that extent are theandric activities. Later theology too had no quarrel with this formulation. But it did attempt to distinguish the single activities of the incarnate Logos not only under the aspect of the divine person, the *principium quod,* but also under the aspect of the dual nature through which they were wrought, the *principium quo.* The kind of activity, after all, is determined not by the person, but by the nature from which the activity proceeds. Only the nature determines the *quale,* the kind or sort of act. And so ever since St. Thomas (*Summa Theologica,* III, qu. 19, a. 1 ad 1), Scholasticism has come to distinguish three kinds of activity in Christ. Firstly, the purely divine acts. These are the actions brought about by the Logos before its incarnation—for example, the creation. They were wrought exclusively by the divine nature as the *principium quo.* In distinction to these, there are the purely human acts. These are the actions which, by their very character, belong exclusively to Jesus' human nature, actions like seeing, weeping, suffering, and so on. These actions can be called theandric only in so far as their subject is the second divine person. Their *principium quo* is solely the human nature. The third kind of activity in Christ consists of those actions which are in fact accomplished by the Logos through the divine nature, but in such a way that in doing so he makes use of his human nature as an instrument. This is the category in which the miracles primarily are ordered. To the extent that these are supernatural in substance—for example, the raising from the dead—Christ can accomplish them only because he is God. But he works them with the help of his humanity—for example, when he says to the dead girl, "Talitha kumi," or when he touches the blind man's eyes with spittle. These activities are divine and human in the true sense.

We may conclude from this classification of Jesus' activities that Christ could also accomplish purely human activities, and did in fact do so. Even after the hypostatic union, his human will preserved its own peculiar properties and its own play of movement. This will was by no means impaired; it was by no means the passive object of volition. The psychological laws governing the course of the human will and its activities continue to function with complete self-sufficiency and independence even in the incarnate Son of God. And thus a psychological assessment of Jesus' inner life is made possible.

The freedom of Christ's human will

The most important conclusion to be drawn from the character of human volition is this: Christ's human will was *free,* as free as anyone else's human will. But we must be careful to set clear limits to the concept of human freedom. It is of the essence of human freedom that human volition should remain true to its innermost nature, that is that it can freely, unimpeded from without or within, strive to attain its specific object or not. The specific object of volition is what it regards as "good" or "valuable." Volition is, by its very nature, directed towards good. In theological terms, value is the formal object (*objectum propter quod*) of volition, just as truth is the formal object of our rational disposition, and beauty the specific object of our aesthetic disposition. That being which is so constructed as to strive for the objectively valuable, unimpeded by outward compulsion or inner susceptibility, and in the conscious affirmation of its own fundamental tendency, is in the most consummate sense free. This freedom is a "sweet necessity," as St. Augustine puts it. In this sense God is uniquely and absolutely free, because in the conscious working of his being he is in no way impeded by influences that are not divine, and because from within he affirms his own most perfect being as the highest value. Similarly, the angels and the saints in his Grace enjoy a relatively consummate freedom. For to be free means to affirm and fulfil the tendency of our being towards the objectively valuable, unimpeded from within or without. This freedom from external compulsion (*libertas a coactione*) and from inner constraints (*libertas a necessitate*) is essential to human volition, if it is to be exercised as a free activity. But on the other hand, the freedom to strive after what is of no value to its nature, to strive for what is objectively worthless (*libertas contrarietatis*), is not essential to volition, indeed, it is even a defect in it. When the human will strives after something that is only apparently valuable to it, only in its imagination, but not objectively, not in reality, it is clearly a will directed towards a false goal out of a false motive, a will that is a breach with the objective tendency of its being. This is a volition that is fundamentally unnatural, and an abuse of freedom. In this connexion, we will later establish that because of the hypostatic union, Christ was not liable to this abuse of freedom. The true freedom of his will lay rather only in the direction of what is objectively valuable. This is where he was free to choose and not to choose (*libertas exercitii*), and to choose one thing or another (*libertas specificationis*). This freedom of moral will is an essential premise of Jesus' power of redemption. By inwardly affirming what his divinely illuminated thought acknowledged to be objective good and the will of the Father, and by appropriating it to himself, and fulfilling it for the Father's sake, he endowed his action with a moral value, and made it an action of merit. Only his freedom and his responsible decision made him the *causa meritoria* of our justification (The Council of Trent, sess. 6, cap. F). Only this can explain his claim to a divine reward for what he has wrought: "I have glorified thee on earth; I have accomplished the work that thou hast given me to do. And now do thou, Father, glorify me with thyself, with the glory that I had with thee before the world existed" (John. 17.5). Jesus' greatest moral strength and his concentrated affirmation of the Father's will is revealed in his suffering submission. "He humbled himself, becoming obedient to death, even to death on a cross" (Phil. 2.8). Jesus expressly stresses his freedom of volition. "No one takes it [my life] from me, but I lay it down of myself. I have the power to lay it down, and I have the power to take it up again" (John 10.18). John the Evangelist in particular is concerned to point out our Lord's divine glory even in his suffering, and he stresses this sovereign freedom of Christ's moral will in the passion. The Synoptic Gospels underline how Jesus submitted to his Father's will that he should drink the cup of sorrows only after an inner struggle, only after conquering the reluctance of his own natural desires. But John deliberately stresses that even this struggle was suffused with the triumphant awareness that "I lay down my life for my sheep" (John 10.15). In John's view, there was not a moment in our Lord's inner life when he would not have affirmed his Father's will, the *summum bonum* of his striving, with all the power of his own volition. The Evangelist does not hide the distress in Jesus' soul that caused him to cry out: "Father, save me from this hour." But it is significant that he immediately follows this appeal with another: "No, this is why I came to this hour. Father, glorify thy name" (John 12.27, 28).

Christ's incapability of sin

This absolute freedom of Jesus' human will necessarily led to a unique *moral unity* of the divine and human will in Jesus. The physical duality of Christ's will was cancelled out into a consummate moral unity. In his Epistle to Sergius, Pope Honorius had this moral unity in mind when he explained, "We acknowledge one will in our Lord Jesus Christ, because what was assumed by the divinity was certainly not our guilt, but our nature. It assumed our nature in the state in which it was created before we sinned, and not in its corrupted state after our sin." With these words, Honorius meant to imply that Jesus' human will had not been corrupted by original sin, and that therefore he could never be at variance with the will of the Father. His human volition was animated by one purpose—the fulfilment of the Father's will. Obviously, Honorius did not recognize the problem that came to the fore in the Monothelete disputes, or he did not want to recognize it, and so he forbade any discussion of the problem of the two energies or activities at all. Such a question, he maintained, had no support either from the Bible or from ecclesiastical tradition. By this command, he aided the growth of the new Monophysite heresy, and was therefore excommunicated.

It is hardly necessary to give express reasons for the moral unity of the two wills in Christ from revelation. After all, it was Jesus' task to do the Father's will. "Thy will be done on earth as it is in heaven"—this is the very heart of his message. John tells us that he declares: "I seek not my own will, but the will of him who sent me" (5.30). On the Mount of Olives his created being, the natural instincts of his human nature (*voluntas ut natura*), protested against the terrible shape the Father's will threatened to take for him, and he begged, "Father, let this cup pass away from me." But even then, his heroic magnanimity made him add: "Yet not as I will, but as thou willest" (Matt. 26.39; Luke 22.42). He prayed to be saved from suffering, but only under the condition that this should coincide with the Father's will. However much his natural volition (*voluntas ut natura*) might instinctively turn to animal self-preservation, his moral volition (*voluntas ut ratio*) was subordinate to the will of the Father. His natural instincts protested against suffering and death as a physical evil. And his moral volition to a certain extent admitted this protest. This is why Augustine describes it as *ratio inferior*. But to the extent that it was not one with the divine will, it was overcome by the *ratio superior* of his free moral decision, and subordinated to the will of the Father. So Scholastic theology distinguished three wills in Christ's prayer on the Mount of Olives: the commanding will of the Father; the protesting will of Christ's animal nature; and the freely obedient, moral will of the Lord.

If we probe to the roots of this absolute moral unity of the two wills in Christ, we shall ascertain that its first immediate cause was the independent movement of the human will. Like all the movements of created beings, this independent movement too is brought about by the physical influence of the divine first cause. God as the creator and support of all being is the cause of this independent movement's taking place in complete freedom, corresponding to the free causality of the creator. But the independent movement of Christ's will towards the Father was simply *incapable* of departing from this course; every possibility that Christ's volition might oppose the working of God was excluded. This *incapability of sin* (*impeccabilitas*) was the necessary result of the inclusion of Jesus' human will in the hypostatic union. To put it more clearly, in fact, Jesus never consciously acted against the will of the Father. This inability to sin, *posse non peccare*, he derived from his moral freedom. But above and beyond that, he was incapable of sin, *non posse peccare*, and this he derived from his substantial relationship to the Logos. The theological schools have various explanations for this *impeccabilitas* brought about by the incarnation, which we shall discuss later. But on principle we may already accept the fact that because Christ's human nature had its autonomy in the divine person, his human will too was so much the possession of the self of the Logos that it was metaphysically unable to break out of the sphere of the divine will. It was the second divine person that gave our Lord's human nature its autonomy, and at the same time it was the Son that was the subject and support of all our Lord's human acts. This was why it was a metaphysical impossibility for the human will ever to deviate from the divine will. Otherwise we would be confronted by the inner impossibility that he who was God and the essence of sanctity was capable of sin.

But how is this incapability of sin to be explained? How can it be reconciled with the freedom of Christ's human will?

The Scotists' doctrine posits an *impeccabilitas externa*. They would have it that an external factor, divine Providence, preserved Jesus' will in advance from any fall. Indeed, according to the Scotist view, Jesus' will would in fact be capable of sin, like any other human will, for his human nature is human in every respect; and even if actual sin does not belong to human nature, the potential capability of sinning certainly does. And Jesus too possessed this capability. But his efforts were watched over and cared for by God's provision so powerfully that any fall was out of the question from the start. As we may see, the Scotist theory preserves the freedom of Jesus' human will in every respect. Pope Paul V expressly ensured its doctrine against the accusation of incorrectness, or even heresy. For however much it stresses Jesus' complete humanity, it still achieved the essential thing the theologians were concerned about: it acknowledged and preserved the *impeccabilitas* of his human volition. It is easy to see that this theory of Duns Scotus' is a direct conclusion from his view of the inner constitution of God incarnate.

In contrast to Duns Scotus' doctrine, Thomism advocated an *impeccabilitas interna*. According to this view, Jesus' humanity existed only through the Logos, so his human will too could exist only through and in the Logos. So his will is constructed and predestined in such a way that he himself in his peculiar structure and disposition is the most perfect human instrument of the Logos—so perfect that he is absolutely incapable of sin. Because Jesus' human will receives its existential being from the Logos alone, it possesses only those psychological potentialities and faculties that are directed towards the good, the best, the divine, and no capability of sinning at all. So in the Thomist view, Christ's freedom of human volition was not absolute, but had certain limits. The underworld of sin is out of his range. But according to Thomism, his scope in the realm of good is so much the more inclusive and intensive. Because he is free to will and not to will (*libertas exercitii*), Jesus is able to commit or omit a morally good action. He is able to undertake the healing of the sick, or not, speak or hold his peace, pray or not pray. And because he is free to will one thing or another (*libertas specificationis*), he is able to make the independent decision whether he should heal all ten lepers or only the one grateful Samaritan; or whether he should make his mortal journey to Jerusalem at once, in keeping with the wishes of his "brethren," or wait until his hour had come. So according to the Thomist theory, Jesus' human will was completely free to do good. The rhythm of his soul was a movement between the good and the better. It was the freedom of the saints and the angels, the existential affirmation of all that is holy and divine.

Jesus' freedom in face of his suffering

From this point of view, how are we to regard the freedom of Jesus' human will when confronted with his passion? If Jesus' will was so constructed that he was able to strive only after the good and the best, and if on the other hand he clearly acknowledged that it was his Father's will that he should die for mankind, is it still tenable to speak in Thomist terms of his sorrowing submission and the meritoriousness of his suffering? After all, Jesus knew that the prophets, Isaias especially, had all foretold his death for our salvation. Time and again he reminds us: "It is written that the Son of Man must suffer." So Jesus' human consciousness was confronted with a "must," the express will of his Father. But if his own will tended according to its very nature towards the consummation of this his Father's will, how can we still speak of any freedom or meritoriousness in his own will to suffer? Scheeben regards this problem as a crucial difficulty. He tries to clear it away by regarding the freedom of God incarnate as a kind of freedom that cannot be compared with ordinary human freedom. Its specific quality lies precisely in the fact that Jesus' moral will is not the will of an ordinary man, but the will of the Logos. But does this not take us back to the Monophysite error of Severus, who called Jesus' human nature a specifically new one, a compounded nature different from ours?

The Thomist view does not provide us with a complete solution to this problem. We might, however, mention one or two points that make this enigma less burdensome to the Thomists.

One thing is certain: that Jesus' death for our salvation was from eternity determined in the divine ordinance. Because this divine ordinance concerned the ways of God in the outward world (*quoad extra*), it belonged not only to the Father but equally to the Son and to the Holy Spirit, in short, to the *unus Deus*. So God's divine ordinance that the Messias must suffer and die also belongs to the Logos. Therefore, the Messias' prayer known as *Speravi, speravi* (Psalm 39.7; Heb. 10.5 f.) should not be ascribed to the Logos, as many Church Fathers have done, but only to his human consciousness and human will. "Therefore in coming into the world he says, 'Sacrifice and oblation thou wouldst not, but a body thou hast fitted to me: In holocausts and sin offerings thou hast had no pleasure. Then said I, "Behold, I come—(in the head of the book it is written of me)—to do thy will, O God." ' " St. Basil was of the opinion that this prayer of the Messias presupposed some task imposed upon the Logos by the Father, but the kind of task that is not given to the Logos as if he were a slave (δουλικῶς), but as a father would give it to his son (υἱκῶς). In reality, when the Epistle to the Hebrews refers to this prayer, it does not have the pre-existent Logos in mind, but the Logos incarnate. It belongs to Jesus' human will. Following this, so much is certain: The suffering and death of the Messias was ordained in eternity by God, the *unus Deus;* the Logos had a part in this decree just as the Father and the Holy Spirit had. Furthermore, it is also certain that Jesus knew of this even in his human consciousness. This consciousness was permeated with the certainty that he was confronted with suffering and death. "It is written that the Son of Man must suffer." When Peter tries to dissuade him from his thoughts of suffering, he calls him Satan, who does not mind "the things of God." Thirdly, it is certain that for Jesus' human consciousness, the fulfilment of the divine will was a categorical imperative every bit as forceful as any other commandment of God's. His moral conscience had no freedom of choice in the sense that he could ever have withdrawn from this decision of God's will, which he recognized so clearly. Such a flight from the will of God would have been impossible to his moral conscience. Jesus had no *libertas contrarietatis* here or elsewhere. A fourth certainty may be concluded from this: The freedom with which Jesus acquiesced to the passion was specifically the same freedom with which he always acquiesced to the clearly acknowledged will of God. Because his human intellect was filled and permeated by the absolute wisdom and goodness of his Father, to a degree that we mere mortals may never attain, here too his human will could make its complete and unreserved affirmation out of its innermost freedom, although the circumstances under which this will might take shape were as yet unknown to him. It was a free and unreserved, inward affirmation of the Father's will. The freedom with which he uttered it was the same freedom with which he always affirmed the Father's will. By the power of his own volition, his moral will was forever bound to the Father's will. This was the personal freedom Jesus had in mind when he declared: "No one takes [my life] from me, but I lay it down of myself." For his affirmation of the Father's will came entirely of his own free personal decision to do his Father's will in everything. His incapability of sin secured immutably only the *goal* of his way, which was the fulfilment of the divine will. That he went his way as he did was for his human freedom to decide.

In the course of his passion, whenever Jesus found himself in a new situation demanding a renewed effort of will, he was able, and was compelled, to renew this affirmation of his Father's will, made on principle and out of his innermost personal freedom, on the empirical level. Or, more precisely, the empirical experience of his passion was a constant challenge to the initiative of his will to suffer. He must surely have had some anticipatory knowledge of the suffering that was awaiting him. On three great occasions he prophesied to his disciples about his coming sorrows. But to know a thing in theory is quite different from experiencing it in practice. After his experience upon the Mount of Olives, Jesus was able and was compelled to renew his position towards the Father's will constantly at every station of the cross, and so constantly preserve the freedom of his volition even when confronted with the ultimate terror.

Our conclusion is this: Jesus' clear awareness that his suffering as the Messias was the will of God could in no way prejudice the freedom of his decision—it could have as little effect as the knowledge of any other divine decree would have on the freedom of his moral action towards that decree. What distinguished his freedom from ours was simply the fact that it was not a *libertas contrarietatis*. But Jesus had no psychological apprehension of this fact—that it was impossible for his will to depart from the divine will. Metaphysically, it was certainly impossible for him to sin. But this metaphysical factor in his incapability of sin lay *beyond* his human consciousness. It is to be strictly distinguished from the psychological factor that he always clung faithfully to the will of the Father. He had no psychological means of knowing of his metaphysical incapability of sin. For such knowledge would have impeded the heroic ardour with which he exercised his freedom. All theologians are agreed that Jesus' humanity lacks the supernatural illumination and energy of God's absolute vision, in so far as it would have diminished the merit of his suffering or rendered it impossible. So he could not have had any direct, unfailing, supernatural certainty of his metaphysical incapability of sin either. This certainty issued from the power of his own natural human will alone.

This enables us to affirm that within the bond of the hypostatic union the human will was not merely passive; it was not a lifeless instrument upon which the Logos played at will. It was *active,* and *independent.* How sublime the divine synthesis is can be seen precisely in the human nature's independence. It is as mighty and all-embracing as it is gentle and tender. The closeness of its union with the divine self of the Logos never weakened the autonomy of human volition, not even in the question of Jesus' human freedom. This volition too preserved the *proprietas* of created being. So even from the Thomist point of view we may understand the extent to which even an *impeccabilitas interna* might make a truly free action on the part of Jesus' human volition possible. The solution of this problem is incomparably easier from the Scotist theory of an *impeccabilitas externa*.

The beginning and the duration of the hypostatic union

We may now return to our main problem of the relationship of Jesus' humanity towards the hypostatic union. We still have to answer the question: At what point did the miracle of the hypostatic union have its beginning in our Lord's humanity? How long did it last? How was it related to the personal, meritorious activity of Jesus' human will? This is the question that probes into the beginning, the duration, and the ultimate cause of the hypostatic union.

It is part of our dogma that the hypostatic union began at the moment when Christ's human nature was conceived, when God's triune creative power begat the Lord's human nature in the Virgin's womb. This is not to say that this generation of the human nature preceded the union with the Godhead, and that the union with the Logos took place only afterwards. The generation of Jesus' human nature was rather brought about by the power of the union, by the act of assumption into the divine person. All the Creeds of the Church are one in reciting: *qui conceptus de Spiritu Sancto, natus ex Maria virgine*. There was no moment when Jesus' humanity existed without being hypostatically united with the self of the Logos. We have already discussed the view, put forward by the Judaeo-Christian Ebionites in particular, that the divine principle did not descend upon Jesus' humanity until his baptism, and that this baptism was the hour of birth for his epiphany upon earth. As long as Christology remained undeveloped, this view raised its head now and again even in ecclesiastical circles. They were inclined to refer the words of the second Psalm, "this day have I begotten thee," to the commencement of Christ's career as the Messias, and not to the beginning of his natural life. The Nestorians referred it to the divine Pneuma's act of indwelling within Jesus the man. This presupposition could be the basis of avowing Christ as the God-man, but it would mean that there would be two selves within him, a divine and a human self, and the union would depend upon the meritorious works of the human self, and would be a merit, and not pure Grace. We can see here how closely Nestorianism and Pelagianism approach each other.

Our analysis of Jesus' self-consciousness has shown that from childhood Jesus knew himself to be the Son of the Father according to his nature. When his mother reproaches him, "Behold, in sorrow thy father and I have been seeking thee," he rejoins, "Did you not know that I must be about my Father's business?" His description of himself as the Son of Man is a sufficient indication that he was conscious of his pre-existence. Jesus knew that he was the Saviour coming from heaven to set up the kingdom of God upon earth. Paul and John were both perfectly clear in their doctrine of his pre-existence as the Son of God. And Matthew and Luke furnish express testimony that the pre-existent Son of God was already incarnate in Mary's womb. This belief in Jesus' pre-existence was a common part of the Christian tradition from the very beginning. Both Ignatius of Antioch and Clement of Rome are completely at home in the ideas of Paul and John. Later Fathers of the Church expressly oppose the Ebionite doctrine that the divine Pneuma did not descend upon Jesus before his baptism. For example, Gregory of Nyssa says, "As the man first came into being, the divinity became one with him" (*Adversus Apollinarem*, 53). Leo the Great made it his urgent teaching, "*natura nostra non sic assumpta est, ut prius creata, post assumeretur, sed ut ipsa assumptione crearetur*" (*Epistola* 35.3).

Origen too ascribed pre-existence to Christ's soul, and put forward the view that this soul had from eternity existed in union with the Logos even before the conception of the body. But he was building upon the false assumption, originally deriving from Platonic thought, that pre-existence was the property of all human souls. So in 553 this doctrine was repudiated by the Synod of Constantinople, with the agreement of Pope Vigilius.

The supernatural conception and the birth of Jesus according to Matthew and Luke

To be completely clear about this, let us look more closely at the accounts given in the New Testament of the supernatural conception of Jesus. The Gospel according to St. Luke gives us a detailed description of the annunciation (1.26–39).

It reaches its culmination in the angelic tidings: "The Holy Spirit shall come upon thee and the power of the Most High shall overshadow thee; and therefore the Holy One to be born shall be called the Son of God" (1.35). And the account concludes with Mary's reply: "Behold the handmaid of the Lord; be it done to me according to thy word" (1.38). This is Luke's description of Mary's experience. Matthew too gives us an account of Jesus' supernatural conception, but this time not from Mary's point of view, but from Joseph's. Because Joseph was disturbed that his betrothed was blessed with child, and in his distress was minded to put her away privately, an angel of the Lord appeared to him in a dream and said, "Do not be afraid, Joseph, son of David, to take to thee Mary thy wife, for that which is begotten in her is of the Holy Spirit. And she shall bring forth a son, and thou shalt call his name Jesus; for he shall save his people from their sins" (1.20 f.). Jesus' genealogy, which is set down from different traditions by both Matthew (1.1–18) and Luke (3.23–38), gives some help in interpreting the supernatural conception. Without going into a discussion of the variations in the tradition (some assume that the account Luke gives is of Mary's descent), we may point out what they have in common: in both, Jesus is represented as the legally recognized son of Joseph, the descendant of David. In Matthew's account, the line of the generations stretches from David to Abraham. Luke extends this line back to Adam, in keeping with Pauline theology, to show that Adam and Christ are the two original created types of mankind. There is apparently a contradiction here between Jesus' supernatural, unfathered conception and his descent from the line of David, but this is resolved in Matthew's tendency to describe Jesus' relationship to David's line as legal and not natural, brought about by his adoption by Joseph. Joseph recognized him and accepted him as his child even while he was still in Mary's womb. His true father is God alone. Jesus did not have an earthly father, but only an earthly mother, Mary. This is expressed in Matthew's account of Jesus' descent when he writes: "And Jacob begot Joseph, the husband of Mary, and of her was born Jesus who is called Christ" (1.16). This text has been disputed, as we possess it in many variants. One of them runs as follows: "And Jacob begot Joseph, who was betrothed to Mary the maid. She bore Jesus, who is called Christ." The reference to "the husband of Mary" (Matt. 1.16), and hence to a bond of marriage, is lacking here. Jesus was born unfathered from the betrothed Virgin Mary. Now this variant was obviously intended to stress the *spiritual* character of Jesus' conception as much as possible, and to exclude any possibility of an earthly, natural origin. This tendency towards spiritualization puts this variant close to Tatian and his *Diatesseron*. Theodoret (*Compendium Haereticarum Fabularum*, 1.20) recalls that, in his *Diatesseron*, Tatian cut out the genealogies and everything else that might point to the birth of our Lord from the seed of David. So it would seem that our variant might be influenced by Tatian. The third variant has a different tenor. This is the one that is welcomed by the opponents of the miracle of the incarnation. It runs as follows: "Jacob begot Joseph. Joseph, to whom the virgin Mary was betrothed, begot Jesus, who is called Christ." In this passage, Joseph is referred to as Jesus' true father. But it is remarkable that the text nevertheless speaks of the *Virgin* Mary, and that she was merely betrothed. We might well think that if the author of this variant seriously wanted us to regard Joseph as Jesus' real father, he would have had to omit the expression "virgin" as well as the reference to her betrothal. For if Joseph is Jesus' real father, the reference to Mary's state of virginity is simply meaningless, and so is the reference to her being Joseph's betrothed, for it was Jewish law and custom that the affianced bride should live as a virgin, and might not yet live in wedlock. So we are justified in concluding that in this variant we have to reckon with a very clumsy editor. Vogels' speculation is probably correct—that the editor deliberately tried to do away with the influence of Tatian clearly apparent in the previous variant, and therefore called Joseph Jesus' father, but without meaning to imply that Jesus was naturally begotten. His use of the expression "begot" was figurative, just as Matthew and Luke used it figuratively in one or two places in their genealogies. Be that as it may. This variant cannot in any way be regarded as clear and unequivocal evidence that Joseph was Jesus' natural father. If it really does contain a polemic thrust against the influence of Tatian in the previous text, then it certainly cannot be the original one. The genuineness of these variants is disputed even with the evidence of textual tradition by such distinguished commentators as Tischendorf, Westcott, Hort, Nestle, and Vogel.

The uninterrupted duration of the hypostatic union

Next we shall inquire as to the duration of the incarnation. It is dogma that the hypostatic union will never come to an end. On the other hand, it is not dogma, but *sententia certa,* that the hypostatic union was never interrupted. With reference to the latter, there were certain Gnostics and Manichees who assumed that the divine Pneuma left Jesus at the beginning of his suffering. As late as 418, the monk Leporius maintained that at Jesus' death, at least, the divinity departed from our Lord's body, if not from his soul. He based this argument upon Jesus' cry of grief upon the cross, "My God, my God, why hast thou forsaken me?" (Matt. 27.46). There were even some Fathers of the Church, such as Ambrose, Hilary, and Epiphanius, who were inclined to this idea. This was the only way they imagined that the utter depth of Jesus' suffering could be understood. Contemporary theology declares it is its "certain" opinion that in the three days of his death Jesus was no longer a living man, but that his body still belonged to the hypostatic union. They refer to St. Paul's words in his first Epistle to the Corinthians, *"Dominum gloriae crucifixerunt,"* "they . . . crucified the Lord of glory" (1 Cor. 2.8). This would imply that it was not our Lord's humanity, forsaken by God, that suffered, but "the Lord of glory." In any case, the Crucified One remained part of the hypostatic union even in his death, body as well as soul. But those Fathers of the Church who have confronted this problem—Gregory of Nyssa and Augustine, in particular—maintain above and beyond this that our Lord's dead body too remained in union with the Godhead, because it showed itself to be incorruptible. They are right in understanding the cry of the Crucified One to mean that Jesus saw he was destitute of all divine aid, but not of the divine presence.

Late Scholastic theologians were tormented by the question whether the blood shed on the cross left the hypostatic union with the self of the Logos. The Franciscan theologians of the fifteenth century maintained that this was so, while the Dominicans denied it. In 1464 the problem was disputed for three days before Pope Pius II, but with no final decision. As far as contemporary theologians are concerned with this thorny problem, the majority have come to the decision that only the blood that was reunited with the body in the resurrection remained in union with the self of the Logos while body and soul were separated. The blood that is now and again to be seen preserved in ampullae is no longer part of the hypostatic union, even if it were the real blood of our Lord, and not that well-known blood bacillus *prococcus prodigiosus*.

We now proceed to the second question, whether the hypostatic union will ever come to an end. Origen betrays the extent to which he is a Hellenist and a follower of Plato in his view that the Lord would be divested of his body at the Last Judgement. To Origen, the body is something unspiritual and unworthy, and so he cannot imagine that this body could remain in eternal union with the divine spirit. In order to repudiate any possible inferiority of the Logos, Bishop Marcellus of Ancyra (d. 374) went so far as to maintain that at the end of time the Logos would be divested of all human nature, including the human soul. This was opposed by the proposition of the First Council of Constantinople in 381: *"cujus regni non erit finis."* Origen's view was repudiated in 553 at Constantinople. The dogma is supported by clear statements in the Holy Scriptures. The angel Gabriel announced to Mary: "The Lord God will give him the throne of David his father, and he shall be king over the house of Jacob forever; and of his kingdom there shall be no end" (Luke 1.32, 33). The doctrine of the Church Fathers followed this. Christ's incarnation would persist even in his transfiguration, because it is founded in his special position as the head and mediator of the universe. When St. Paul declares (1 Cor. 15.28), "When all things are made subject to him, then the Son himself will also be made subject to him who subjected all things to him, that God may be all in all," he is referring to the fact that the Son's active mediation as the Messias, which now upon earth is constantly taking up new saints into his holy body and extending the kingdom of Christ, will come to an end at the Last Judgement. Then Christ's messianic reign will be over. It will be succeeded by the reign of God.

Grace as the ultimate cause of the hypostatic union

We have still one question left to answer. What is the basis of the hypostatic union? Is it founded upon the merits of Jesus' humanity, or is it pure Grace? Should we refer the assumption of Jesus' human nature into the self of the Logos back to some meritorious action performed by that human nature and foreordained by God's omniscience, so that the humanity might claim its union with the Godhead as a kind of right? Or is the hypostatic union in every sense the unmerited Grace of God? As we have already shown, the primitive Christology of the Shepherd of Hermas established a causal relationship between the assumption of Christ the man into the filiation of God, and the consummate act of obedience, the probation of the "human servant" Jesus who dwells within the spirit of the Logos. Similarly, Nestorius based his doctrine of the two Sons of God upon the doctrine of probation. Christ's human self earned its union with the divine self because it demonstrated its obedience in life and in death. Contrary to Nestorius' doctrine of probation, it is regarded as *sententia communis* that the hypostatic union was in the full sense of the word *pure Grace* given to Christ's human nature, an unearned, supernatural gift of divine love. This is why theology refers to a Grace of union, *gratia unionis*. Logically speaking, it was impossible for Jesus' humanity to earn or deserve or merit its assumption into the divine Word, for before the union, of course, it did not exist at all. A causal relationship between Jesus' human probation and the union of divinity and humanity could be understood only by calling upon the concept of a *scientia media,* which was later used by Molina. This would offer the interpretation that God had foreordained this probation of Jesus' human will in eternity, and brought about the temporal realization of the union of the humanity with the Logos on the basis of this eternal prevision. It is certainly conceivable that this was the precise reason why God chose this concrete human nature for the union, because he had from eternity foreseen that it would exercise its free will perfectly. But in objection to this, the question immediately rises as to what necessary reason God could have for uniting this nature with his second person, taking into consideration its foreordained probation, in a way that in essence transcends every other supernatural relationship between God and his creation, and every other supernatural form of union that had been granted to other saints. This is not a question of an accidental union with the Godhead, as in the case of other men endowed with Grace, but a substantial union. In human terms, why was not God satisfied with ranging Jesus' humanity in the highest rank of the saints, as he did the Immaculate Virgin, on account of the foreordained sanctity of her person? Why did he translate Jesus' humanity into an entirely new and unique order of being, the hypostatic union? What was his purpose? If our reply is because from eternity God foreordained that Jesus' humanity should work together with divine Grace in a unique mode, then even this unique co-operation does not serve to make the prodigious miracle of the hypostatic union comprehensible. An infinite amount still remains that no activity of any created being, even under the mightiest influence of Grace, could ever merit or earn, and that is the elevation of this one creature out of its natural mode of existence, and its translation into the unity of the personal being of God. Only the infinite fullness of the divine essence is able to communicate divine being, and this is its sovereign action. The achievement of a mere creature cannot be intensified to such a degree that it surpasses the bounds of created being and claims the right to be assumed into the autonomy of the Logos. And so, however perfect we may conceive Jesus' humanity to be, it can *never earn* the hypostatic union on its merits. True, it would certainly be possible for God to foresee in eternity the pure and holy activities of Jesus' humanity, and for him thus to have predestined it to join in the hypostatic union. Then it would have been in the name of divine justice, and not as an act of God's free love. In this case too it would be a union of free Grace (*gratia unionis*). But all the same, it would still somehow be bound up with the foreordained merits of Jesus' humanity. And so this possibility too yields before the infinite miracle of the incarnation. This miracle penetrates so far into the depths of the divine substance, so deep into his mercy, wisdom, and omniscience, that it would be presumptuous for us to seek its foundation in created being. This is an act of God alone.

This throws new light upon the relation of our dogma to the Christian concept of Grace. The Christian concept of Grace is nothing but the application of the Christian concept of God. Because God alone is the essence of perfection and holiness, the effort of any created being to attain to God is conceivable only because it has been previously affected by God himself. Just as no created act comes about in the order of cosmic being without having been metaphysically supported and brought about by God, just so in the order of supernatural being no efforts towards the highest are possible that have not first been anticipated by the Grace of eternal sanctity and love. And so even the most consummate moral behaviour would be just an empty stammering, as long as it were not dominated in its totality by the Grace of the eternal God. So the empirical concrete humanity of Jesus is the purest work of God's Grace, the most sublime work of art formed by the All-Holy from the stubborn material of humanity. And the elevation of this work of art into the sphere transcending every mode of created being, into the circle of God's own life, is even more intensely God's personal act alone, pure Grace. It was St. Augustine, profoundly moved, who pointed to this miracle of love: *Natura humana sine ullis praecedentibus bonorum operum meritis Deo Verbo est in utero virginis copulata* (*De Trinitate*, 15.26).

If we wish to formulate the *gratia unionis* more precisely in Scholastic concepts, we must describe it as *uncreated, substantial Grace*. For the gift it makes to Christ's humanity is the autonomy of the Son of God. And so it is an eternal Grace, because it is identical with the personal being of the Son of God. And it is a substantial Grace, because it is the highest and most perfect substance, the Logos itself, that endows the human nature with its autonomy.

*   *   *   *

We have thrown some light upon the mystery of the hypostatic union in its peculiar properties, in the innermost foundation of its being, in its relation to the Trinity, and in the effect of this mystery upon the humanity of Jesus. But every thought we have uttered has made us realize that all our human speech is mere stumbling. To understand the hypostatic union would mean to understand God. Even here we cannot get beyond merely metaphorical concepts. But we are able to ascertain as much as we need for our own religious life. We have attained the apperception that in Christ we are confronted with the personal revelation of God, that he is the highest and holiest Word that God ever uttered into the world, and that all the boldest dreams and sublimest longings of mankind are united in him. The riddle of existence, and with it its narrowness and gloom, are solved for us in the Incarnate One. Christ lifts us out of the limitations and imperfections of our sinful nature up into the infinite breadth of the divine life. Our own life too draws its ultimate meaning and definitive form from the same pattern upon which St. Thomas based the divisions of his *Summa Theologica:* from God—to God—through Christ—in God.

We shall now go on to discuss the consequences that rose directly from the hypostatic union. As the first consequence, we shall take the Christological Perichoresis, or circumincession, that is, the profound penetration of Jesus' humanity by the presence of the triune God; and then we shall go on to discuss what is known as the *communicatio idiomatum,* the reciprocal exchange of divine and human properties in the God-man, and so we shall learn the right way of speaking of the mystery of Christ.

XVI

CIRCUMINCESSION AND THE
COMMUNICATIO IDIOMATUM

Trinitarian and Christological Circumincession

WE are familiar with the concept of perichoresis, or circumincession, from the doctrine of the Trinity. The Latin Fathers of the Church speak of *circumincessio,* and the late Scholastics of *circuminsessio*. It would be a mistake, however, to confuse the Trinitarian and the Christological concepts of circumincession. The Christological circumincession is not a mere reflection of the Trinitarian, but its *complement and counterpart*. For where the Trinitarian circumincession takes its starting point in the unity of nature, the Christological circumincession reverses the process and takes its starting point in the unity of person. Just as in the life within the Trinity three divine persons inhabit one selfsame nature, just so in God incarnate two natures inhabit one person. In formal terms, the concept of circumincession applies to both cases, because in each it is a question of a reciprocal compenetration and the closest community of life. But the content of the two circumincessions is different. Circumincession in the Trinity starts from the permanent possession of a common nature and reaches its climax in the active animation of this possession of a common nature by the three divine persons. The Christological circumincession has its starting point in the unity of the divine person. It has its basis in the hypostatic union which is the substantial union of Jesus' humanity with the second divine person. It reaches its climax in the effective compenetration of both natures by the activity of the incarnate Logos. The one divine person of the Logos permeates the human nature as it does the divine, because it possesses it as its own. It dwells within it, but in such a way that it never subsumes this human nature into itself, devouring or destroying it.

Since the power uniting and binding the two natures is the Logos alone, and does not also proceed from the human nature, it is an error to speak of a mutual compenetration (*compenetratio mutua*), or a reciprocal indwelling. It is only meaningful to say that the humanity is dominated and inhabited through and through by the Logos and its divine nature. The Christological circumincession can thus be defined as the inhabitation of Jesus' humanity by the Logos, or simply as *the presence of the triune God in Jesus' humanity*. But the peculiar characteristics (*proprietas*) of the human nature remain unimpaired by this permeation with divinity, rather as the glass through which the morning sun shines remains glass, without being transformed into the sun. This circumincession is presented very vividly in the Gospel according to St. John in Jesus' Logion: "I and the Father are one; who knows me knows also the Father." This circumincession is the foundation and reason why the two natures in Christ do not confront each other as strangers, but work together so that divine-and-human actions are brought about in Christ.

For a psychological view of Jesus' inner life, it is clear that however much each nature preserves its own properties in Jesus himself and in his human consciousness, they are not strange and unknown to each other, lying side by side in separate compartments; rather, they *interpenetrate* each other. That is, the divinity of the Logos, or more precisely the divine nature that is substantially identical with the Logos, streams and flows through Christ's humanity too, and Jesus' human consciousness is really aware of this presence of the triune God in his human life. Only in this consciousness could he say, "I and the Father are one." On the other hand, we must not forget that even in this mysterious interpenetration of both natures, the divine nature, the triune God, remains strictly transcendent. It is not as if it were a power immanent in Jesus' humanity, forming it from within; it is not as if it were therefore comparable with the human soul, which forms the body. The divinity does not enter into the organization of the humanity like the causality of some created being. It strictly preserves its own peculiarity, its "utter difference." Its effect upon Jesus' humanity is the same as the effect of the Creator himself upon creation. Certainly, God is omnipresent as the creator *quoad substantiam.* For "in him we live and move and have our being." And yet his presence there is "altogether different" from the presence of a created secondary cause in creation. He is always and still "altogether different," and "strictly transcendent." In his working, he never declines into a secondary cause, a purely inward causality. This is related to the fact that this permeation and penetration of Jesus' humanity is not brought about directly by the Logos alone, not by way of the natural emanation of the power of the Logos, but it issues forth from the presence of the triune God, according to the free decision of God's will. It does not happen as it were of itself, out of the necessity of its nature, as water flows from the spring, or flowers grow from their root. Certainly, the union in one person of human nature and Logos does mean that this human nature is filled and animated by God's presence in a special sense, and that it is in a special sense empowered to attain to supernatural deeds, knowledge, and experience, above all the direct contemplation of God. But this endowment with Grace does not follow naturally and necessarily upon the presence of the Logos, but that of the triune God. And because in his outward acts this God is free, it is brought about in each case by a separate decision of this ever-present triune God, whenever, according to God's eternal Providence, Christ's humanity requires supernatural gifts to bring about his work of redemption. Therefore it is wrong to conceive these supernatural miracles wrought by Jesus as the immediate and necessary emanation of the Logos alone. In that case the hypostatic union would no longer be made up of an *assumptio humanitatis in personam divinam,* as dogma teaches, but of an *assumptio in naturam divinam.* All the divine powers and properties would have to flow without any hindrance into Jesus' humanity. But in reality, the human nature receives from the Logos nothing but its self-sufficiency and autonomy. All the supernatural powers and properties, such as actual sanctifying Grace, and especially the supernatural charismatic powers of working miracles, or of God's absolute vision—all these are given to the Lord's human nature by the ever-present triune God, out of his free love and goodness, just as the Christian receives all his supernatural blessings from the triune God alone according to the decision of his free will. So between the eternal Word and Christ's human nature, there stands the *free will of the ever-present triune God* as the effective power of all the sublimity and holiness working in that humanity. This presence is the result of the presence of the

Logos. This is why the first proclamation of the early Apostles constantly uses these phrases: "God has made both Lord and Christ, this Jesus whom you crucified" (Acts 2.36); "The god of Abraham, the God of Isaac, and the God of Jacob, the God of our fathers, has glorified his Son Jesus" (3.13; 2.14, 32; 5.31). It is always the living triune God (ὁ Θεός), and not the second divine person by itself, that endows Christ's humanity with its messianic powers. So when the early Fathers compare this interpenetration of the circumincession, this permeation of the human nature by the divine, to a glowing iron, or to light shining through glass, we must not forget that they are only similes, which are apt only in one respect, but not in all. Because God is transcendent, he can never be integrated into the organization of mere finite powers, as if he were the inward causative power of these finite powers.

The communicatio idiomatum

It is only against this background of circumincession that the Church's doctrine of idioms can be understood.

By the *communicatio idiomatum* (ἀντίδοσις τῶν ἰδιωμάτων ἢ ἰδιοτήτων) we understand the reciprocal exchange of divine and human attributes in the God-man. This exchange is not of a merely external, moral kind, simply founded upon a moral relationship, in the sense that we might ascribe divine properties to Jesus' humanity, in the same way as a husband's property can be attributed to his wife. This was how the Nestorians understood the community of idioms. In their view, the divine properties were not transferred to Christ's humanity in any substantial, physical sense, but as one self might claim the property of a second self bound to him in love. But the exchange is furthermore not physical in the sense that the divine and human properties might coincide, that the divine properties of the Logos might be ascribed without any hindrance to his human nature, and vice versa. Jesus' humanity is not assumed into the divine nature but into the divine person. This exchange is rather the *transference* of human characteristics to the *self of the Logos that forms the person,* the issuance from one support, the Logos, of both divine and human properties at the same time. The properties of both natures might be emanated only by the one divine person supporting both natures, and not separately by one of the two natures themselves. Since Christ is both truly God and truly man, his divine person, the bearer of both natures, can be named after both natures. I can speak of the Logos; but I can also speak of the son of David. In both cases, I am referring to the same self, the Logos, and therefore I can attach human predicates to the person named after the divine nature, and divine predicates to the person named after the human nature. For example, I can say, "God's only-begotten Son died on the cross." And on the other hand, I can say, "The Son of David is the Creator of the universe." Each time I am referring to the self-same person, the self of the Logos. The Apostles were already making use of this *communicatio idiomatum*. Paul, for example, writes, "He has not spared even his own Son, but has delivered him for us all" (Rom. 8.32); "they . . . crucified the Lord of glory" (1 Cor. 2.8). John uses similar phrases: "[God] laid down his life for us" (1 John 3.16). And vice versa: "And no one has ascended into heaven except him who has descended from heaven: the Son of Man who is in heaven" (John 3.13). Towards the end of the fifth century a passionate dispute arose on account of the formulation first used by Proclus of Constantinople: "One of the Trinity was crucified," because it was interpreted and used by Peter Fullo, the Bishop of Antioch, in a Monophysite sense. Literally, there is no doubt, this is correct. Its recognition was expressly demanded at the Fifth Council of Constantinople in 553. But when the Theopaschites—so called because they "made God to suffer"—added to the ancient triad referring to the Trinity, *sanctus Deus, sanctus fortis, sanctus immortalis,* the extra clause, *qui crucifixus est pro nobis,* the intention could no longer be orthodox but Monophysite. For in this clause, the word *"crucifixus"* no longer referred to the divine person but to the triune divine nature.

Since the *communicatio idiomatum* is founded upon the unity of the divine person, it can never be used *in abstracto* of both natures. For example, I cannot say, "The divine nature suffered." But I can say, "The Logos, the only-begotten Son of the Father, suffered." I cannot say, "Christ's humanity is omnipotent." But I can say, "Christ the man is omnipotent." Only when the person is also named, can the properties of the other nature be ascribed to it. For only the person bears the conjunction of both the divine and the human attributes. For the same reason I cannot say, "Jesus' humanity is the Logos," because this humanity is not the *identity* of the Logos, but its *possession*. But I can certainly identify the divine person with the divine nature, because they are neither of them substantially different. So I can say, "The only-begotten Son is the divinity." However, I cannot say, "The only-begotten Son is the humanity," but only, "The only-begotten Son possesses the humanity."

Negative expressions too, such as "God is not dead," are to be avoided in the *communicatio idiomatum*, because they do not admit of a narrow determinative sense, but allow of a number of interpretations, and lead to misunderstandings. For example, if I say, "Christ is incapable of suffering," the proposition is only partly correct, in so far as it refers to the divine nature. But if it meant the incarnate Christ, it would be the Manichaean heresy.

We may put forward the rule that only *positive* formulations may be used, uniting *one concrete factor with another,* because the person is necessarily given with the concrete. I can never combine one abstract factor with another (Jesus' human nature, for example); and I can combine an abstract with a concrete factor only when the abstraction refers not to the human but to the divine nature.

In keeping with the rules for the *communicatio idiomatum,* I can also say, "Christ the man is the natural Son of God." For in this concrete formulation, Christ the man is the divine self of the Logos described according to his human nature. Indeed, John also gives us a similar assurance: "[The Son of Man] who has descended from heaven: . . . [and] who is in heaven" (John 3.13). Hence, it is a dogma of our faith that Christ the man is worthy of our adoration. But since this is something that has been partly denied, and party misinterpreted, it will require a more thorough discussion.

XVII

THE ADORATION DUE TO CHRIST'S HUMANITY

In this context, by "adoration" we mean the *latria* which is fittingly paid to God alone, as the Lord and Creator, and is based exclusively upon our dependence upon God as his creatures. Consequently, we do not mean the mere cult of veneration (*cultus duliae*) which is paid to created beings—the saints, for example. Something of its proper meaning is preserved in the root of our word "adore," from the Latin *adorare*, to address, to pray to, and hence to worship. But the Latin *adorare*, and its Greek equivalent προσ-κυνεῖν, have acquired several additional meanings. In ecclesiastical and Scholastic usage it is simply a generic concept, and its particular meaning can be ascertained only from the context. We shall first discuss the dogma that the same adoration is due to Christ the God-man as is due to the Logos himself, so that in our act of worship we may not separate the Manhood from the Godhead in Christ, and worship only the Godhead. The Council of Ephesus opposed Nestorius, who held that in Christ only the Logos should be worshipped, with its definition that both natures in Christ should be worshipped, *una adoratione* (μία προσκυνήσει), *cum propria ipsius carne* (καθὸ γέγονε σὰρξ ὁ λόγος). So it is the Church's dogma that the same adoration is due to the God-man as such, as to God or the Logos.

The adoration due to Jesus Christ the God-man

In the Gospel according to St. John, Christ himself requires that the same homage be paid to the incarnate Son as to the

Father: ". . . that all men may honour the Son, even as they honour the Father" (5.23). In John's usage, the word "Son" always refers to the incarnate Logos. Paul establishes it as a commandment of God "that at the name of Jesus every knee should bend of those in heaven, on earth, and under the earth" (Phil. 2.10). The Apocalypse of St. John (5.12) makes a similar declaration: "Worthy is the lamb who was slain to receive power and divinity and wisdom and strength and honour and glory and blessing." The Epistle to the Hebrews (1.6) refers to Psalm 96.7 with a similar intent: "And let all the angels of God adore him." The pagan Pliny bears witness to the worship of Christ when he reports that the early Christians sang hymns to Christ as it were to God, *"carmen Christo quasi Deo"* (*Epistulae*, 10.96). There are a number of apocryphal writings, those precipitates of popular piety, that bear witness to this worship, for example, the *Acta Petri*. And some of the testimonies of the martyrs do so too, such as the *Martyrium Polycarpi* (21) and the *Martyrium Carpi* (41). On the other hand, however, solemn liturgy preserves the main axiom that one should not pray directly to Christ, but rather pray through Christ to the Father. Origen goes as far as actually to *forbid* prayer to be addressed directly to the Incarnate One. "One may not pray to him who is himself the subject of prayer" (*De Oratione*, 15.1). But this is not the faith of the Church giving voice, but only the particular theorizing of one theologian whose Neo-Platonic views led him to posit an absolute antithesis between divinity and humanity in Christ, and thus repudiate any homage paid to his Manhood. Not until the development of theology had established the union in one person of Jesus' humanity with the self of the Logos was the ground prepared for a speculative foundation for the worship due to Christ's humanity. The later patristic dispute with Nestorius came to a conclusion quite opposed to Origen's: that the Logos had entered into a substantial union with Jesus' humanity, and that after this incarnation he was no less the true Son of God than he was before. St. Cyril of Alexandria comes forward as the classic interpreter of the patristic faith when he declares against Nestorius, "We do not pray to the man bearing the divinity" (θεοφόρον ἄνθρωπον), "but to the God become man" (ἐνανθρωπήσαντα Θεόν).

The adoration of Christ's humanity in the hypostatic union

So it is dogma that we should worship the God-man. There is a second proposition that is not strictly regarded as formal dogma, but certainly as *fidei proximum:* On account of the hypostatic union of Christ's humanity with the Logos, it too is to be reverenced with *latria,* the adoration due to God, *in itself, though not for its own sake.* The object of worship in this case is not the God-man as a whole, but his humanity alone, but then only in its connexion with the Logos. To understand this proposition correctly, we must not forget that this Church dogma would not have Christ's humanity worshipped for its own sake (*propter se*) but in itself (*in se*), in its hypostatic bond with the Logos. His human nature is simply the object of worship (*objectum materiale*), but not the motive or, in Scholastic usage, the formal object (*objectum formale*) of worship. The motive and formal object is exclusively the Logos, the Godhead. It would be sheer idolatry to offer *latria* to Christ's humanity for its own sake. But since early Christianity did not pose this question with such precision, we cannot find any express confirmation for our dogma in the early theologians. However, the early Church's actual worship of the God-man does at least *imply* the dogma that worship was due to his humanity. We know that Origen consciously opposed such adoration of the Incarnate One. To him the object of worship is the Logos *in forma Dei,* not *in forma servi.* Later Fathers point out that to worship the Logos after his incarnation is possible only by venerating the Logos in and through his humanity. The human nature is the Logos' earthly, visible manifestation, which alone gives us some intuitive grasp of him. In this sense, Athanasius writes emphatically (*Epistola ad Adelphium,* 3): "We certainly do not worship a created being. That is an error made by Arian heretics and heathens. But we do worship the Lord of creation, the incarnate Logos of the Godhead. For although the flesh itself is something created, it has nevertheless become the body of God. We do not worship this body in such a way as to separate it from the Logos, nor worship the Logos in such a way as to tear him out of his flesh. Who would be so ill-mannered as to say to the Lord: 'First come forth from out of the flesh, that I may worship thee.' " The Fathers took up the same position against the Apollinarian objection that the worshippers of Jesus' humanity were idolaters of man and idolaters of flesh (ἀνθρωπολάτραι, σαρκολάτραι); and from the worship of Christ's humanity they drew the conclusion that the true body and blood of Christ must be worshipped in the Eucharist, because it is no ordinary body and blood but the Sacred Flesh and Blood of the Logos. St. Augustine and St. Ambrose in particular require the worship of the Eucharist: "Because Christ walked the earth in this very flesh, and gave us this his flesh to eat . . . not only do we not sin when we worship it, but we sin when we do not worship it" (*peccamus non adorando*).

Of course our question and our reply would be very different if it were a matter of Jesus' humanity by itself, and not his humanity in its union with the Logos. In this sense, the theologians have raised the question whether Christ's humanity might be venerated for its own sake as the saints are, in a *cultus duliae,* or as the Blessed Virgin is, in a *cultus hyperduliae,* which would simply be addressed to the created perfection of Christ's Manhood. The Thomists and Suárez in particular emphasize that such a hyperdulic cult would be admissible. But the majority of theologians who are not adherents of Thomist thought object to it, and rightly so, for such a worship could very easily be misinterpreted as introducing a dualism between the self of the Logos and the humanity in Christ.

The dogmatic foundation for the worship of the Sacred Heart

One direct consequence of our introductory proposition that Jesus' humanity in its union with the Logos may be worshipped in itself, though not for its own sake, is the further dogma that *single parts of Jesus' entire humanity,* such as his Sacred Heart, or his five wounds, are also to be worshipped. This axiom is regarded as *conclusio theologica.* Just as the humanity cannot be physically separated from the Logos, neither can its single parts. They belong to him. The human heart is the Logos' heart, and the five wounds his wounds. And so we do right to speak of a worship of Christ's body and blood, his holy wounds, his head in its crown of thorns, and his heart. Here too the object of adoration (*objectum formale*) is God alone. But in so far as these parts of the human body belong to the Logos, they are the object of worship (*objectum materiale partiale*). The Logos subsists in them.

This gives us an understanding of the homage paid in particular to the Most Sacred Heart of Jesus. It was first initiated by St. Margaret Mary Alacoque (d. 1690) and was encouraged by the Popes and especially by the Jesuit order until it spread far and wide in Christendom. On August 26, 1856, Pope Pius IX elevated the Feast of the Sacred Heart of Jesus into a general Church festival. At the turn of the century, in 1900 Pope Leo XIII promulgated a solemn dedication to the Sacred Heart of Jesus to take place in all churches in Christendom. In 1794, Pope Pius VI had published the dogmatic bull *auctorem fidei* in which he defended the orthodox nature of this worship against the Jansenists and the Synod of Pistoia, which branded the adoration of the Sacred Heart as "new-fangled and erroneous, or at least dangerous." But it is sufficiently ensured by the worship due to Jesus' humanity as a whole. Here too, however, we must not forget that although Jesus' heart may be worshipped in itself, it may not be worshipped for its own sake (*non propter se*). The heart is venerated with *latria* more than any other part of Jesus' humanity. This may be explained from the common tradition that regards the heart as the concrete symbol of the true source and motivating force of the entire hypostatic mystery, the love of God's Son. In all the languages of the world, including the languages of the Bible, the heart is regarded as the organ and symbol of love. It is true, modern physiology has shown that the sensible feelings of love are more probably to be located in the ganglia, rather than in the heart. However, it is still true that popular human sensibility still interprets the heart as the symbol of love, and it is still true that even physiologically the increased intensity of love is perceptible in an increased beat of our heart. So there is an inner reason why the Church should have chosen the heart rather than any other part of Christ's humanity for our worship, to give us a concrete symbol of Christ's profoundest mystery, his incarnate love. An abundance of love towards God and man, a fullness of devotion and magnanimity, has sprung from this adoration of Jesus' Sacred Heart. It is, to be sure, conceivable that this mode of veneration may hold something repugnant especially to an outsider, and it may threaten to materialize religion. This danger is present if the devotion does not go beyond the *objectum materiale* and press forward to the inner life of the Lord, of which it is the concrete symbol. What this adoration of Jesus' Sacred

Heart means is our encounter with Jesus' inner life, so that we too may enter and share his innermost feelings, purposes, and emotions. In worshipping Jesus' Sacred Heart we should never forget that it is only the illustration of something much deeper, the Lord's inner experience. When the beggar kisses the hand of his benefactor, because this hand symbolizes the bounty and liberality of his patron, this homage paid to the hand really signifies homage to the benefactor himself. In the symbol of his heart, we pray to Jesus himself, who gave his heart's blood for our salvation.

We have discussed the consequences of the incarnation that concern the relation of Jesus' humanity to his divinity. In the following chapters we shall scrutinize the psychological effects of the incarnation in detail. The most sublime effect is the ethical perfection of our Lord's human nature.

XVIII

THE ETHICAL PERFECTION OF CHRIST'S HUMANITY

THE ethical perfection of Jesus' human will has a dual significance; it means both his freedom from sin and the fullness of God's life within him, which is love.

Jesus' perfect sinlessness

It is dogma that Christ's soul was entirely without sin; it was free from original sin, from concupiscence, and all personal sins.

The Decretal of Pope Eugene IV, *pro Jacobitis*, of 1439, expressly promulgates Christ's freedom from original sin. *Qui sine peccato conceptus . . . peccata nostra delendo solus sua morte prostravit.* This freedom from original sin also brings with it freedom from the compulsions of the body, from evil concupiscence (*fomes peccati*). In 553, the Fifth General Council at Constantinople defined this freedom from concupiscence against the doctrine of Theodore of Mopsuestia, who had maintained that Christ's humanity was inwardly susceptible to temptation. It was St. Paul in particular who, for soteriological reasons, stressed the inviolate nature of Christ's flesh. According to him, the Son of God assumed real flesh from the seed of David. But this real flesh is not identical with the sinful flesh of historical man, for Christ knew nothing of sin (τὸν μὴ γνόντα ἁμαρτίαν, 2 Cor. 5.21). To that extent, Christ's human flesh is only a flesh that has been formed after the image of sinful human nature. God sent "his Son in the likeness of human flesh" (ἐν ὁμοιώματι σαρκὸς ἁμαρτίας,

Rom. 8.3), "as a sin-offering" in order that he might in his purity condemn "sin in the flesh." This purity is rooted in Christ's entire human nature, not simply acquired, and for Paul is the first great premise for Christ's power to redeem us. Only because he was related to human nature on the one hand, but on the other not related to human sin, was he able to lead all those who followed him in faith back to purity and holiness. Even in those passages where Paul parallels Adam and Christ, Christ's original purity is the decisive presupposition for his comparison. For in contrast to the "earthly man" (ἄνθρωπος ἐκ γῆς χοϊκός), Christ would not be the "man of heaven" (ἄνθρωπος ἐξ οὐρανοῦ) if he were not in his entirety a new principle of holiness and purity (Rom. 5.15; 2 Cor. 5.21; 1 Cor. 15.47). Certainly Christ had the same flesh as Adam, and not a *corpus caeleste* in St. Hilary's sense. But he was unique in that within this selfsame flesh he bore no stain of sin. St. Peter stresses this very purity from all sin when he describes Jesus as "a lamb without blemish and without spot" (1 Peter 1.19). John emphasizes the same thing when he calls Christ the Lamb of God "who takes away the sin of the world" (John 1.29). The Epistle to the Hebrews is emphatic that Christ is "innocent, undefiled, set apart from sinners" (7.26). All these statements are made in the fullest sense of the words, and bear absolute witness to more than Jesus' actual purity or the certainty that he could never in his historical life be guilty of any sin; they also stress that by his very nature he was without sin. For to the early Christian proclamation, this purity of nature was the guarantee that Jesus could actually redeem us, because he and he alone was the "Pure One." So it was not simply that Christ did in fact live his life without sin. He also had no inclination to sin. There was no tinder to kindle into concupiscence in him. Early Christian theology was so utterly certain of this sinlessness of Jesus that some of its spokesmen —such as the Apollinarians and the Monenergists—would rather doubt the full integrity of Jesus' human nature, and maintain that Christ's humanity had no human will, than acknowledge any disposition towards evil in him. Accordingly, the temptations of Christ reported in the Gospels are not the outward reflection of certain processes within Jesus' soul, as though they had arisen from the desires of Jesus' nature; they were quite literally insinuations of absolute evil, suggestions from the devil coming from without. If we do not want radically to distort the moral image of Jesus, we cannot evade such real attempts on the part of the devil. It is characteristic of

Christ's moral disposition that his command should be "Be-gone, Satan!"

This gives rise to a further question. Even if Jesus were not accessible to evil from within, could he not be seduced to evil from without, as Adam and Eve were, and fall prey to sin in this way? Did he in fact ever submit to such a temptation?

It is *de fide* that Christ *never* committed even the slightest *personal sin*. The Council of Ephesus condemned those who taught that Jesus the man—*qui peccatum omnino nescivit*—atoned for his own sins rather than for ours alone (c. 10). The Council of Chalcedon declared that Christ was like unto us in all respects except sin, *absque peccato*. Even before his birth, it was announced that the mark of Christ's holiness was his personal purity from sin. "The Holy One to be born shall be called the Son of God" (Luke 1.35). We have already shown that wherever and whenever we encounter Jesus in the Gospels, he is always the Spotless One, the Pure, the Valiant, the Magnanimous, the Kindly. This is a picture so noble that we are virtually compelled to conclude that it must have been impossible for these simple Scribes, true children of a narrow, puritanical Pharisaism, to have created out of their own imagination such a great, radiant, free image of humanity, if they had not encountered it in the flesh. We learn from Ottilie, Goethe's daughter-in-law and intimate, that in his family circle the aged poet of Weimar used to praise "the glory of Christ with a growing emotion, which became ever more solemn, ever more passionate." In conversation with Eckermann (March 11, 1832), Goethe vowed that "from Christ's person there issues forth a radiance of such majesty, and of such divinity, as could only be the appearance of the Divine upon earth. . . . I bend before him, as the divine revelation of the highest principle of morality. . . . However far our spiritual culture may advance, however great the natural sciences may grow in extent and profundity, however much the human spirit may spread as it lists, it will never go beyond the majesty and moral culture of civilization, as it can be seen glimmering and glowing in the Gospels." In his *History of the Popes* (Eng. tr., London, 1896, v. I, bk. 1, p. 3) Leopold von Ranke says of Christ, ". . . we may safely assert that nothing more guileless, or more impressive, more exalted or more holy, has ever been seen on earth than were his life, his whole conversation, and his death. In his every word, there breathes the pure spirit of God. . . . The records of humanity present nothing that can be compared, however remotely, with the life of Jesus." To appreciate

Jesus' moral nobility in all its uniqueness, we have only to cast an honest eye upon ourselves and our fellow men. Those of us who daily experience how difficult it is to be really good, how easily even the slightest cause can upset our moral balance, how subtly self-interest insinuates itself into all our actions, even the holiest; those of us who honestly and soberly scrutinize ourselves in the mirror of our conscience will apprehend that Jesus' sinlessness is something absolutely new, without any analogy in ordinary humanity.

Objections to Jesus' moral perfection

We have spoken of Jesus' innate substantial purity, illuminating the whole man, and of the incomparable beauty with which the ethical ideal of all ages and cultures has been made manifest in him. But in considering his life more closely, certain doubts arise that conflict with this impression. Are we not saying too much when we regard him as the incomparable, inachievable zenith of all ethical cultures? In the present day particularly, there are voices to be heard that would dispute this moral perfection, and point out that Jesus was human, all too human too. They rest their arguments upon Jesus' words "No one is good but only God" (Mark 10.18). Jesus addressed these significant words to the rich young man, because he had called him "Good Master." Clearly, he refused to be called good. Had he perhaps recognized inadequacies in his own being? But in this case he surely had his eye not so much on himself as upon the infinite perfection of God. And precisely because he was closer to God than any other creature, he saw deeper than our human eye into the depths of divine holiness. His human feeling was overawed by the sight of this glory, which stood like an overwhelming light before his soul. Jesus could see this light more clearly than any other man. But be that as it may. In any case, this passage does not tell us anything decisive against Christ's moral perfection.

But does not Jesus' human life manifest many peculiarities and characteristics that we might well describe as weaknesses, or at least as an imperfect moral disposition? When he cleanses the temple, whip in hand, is he not driven by sudden anger? Is he not hard and unloving in many of his judgements of man? Does he not call the Pharisees a brood of vipers (Matt. 12.34), hypocrites (15.7), an evil and adulterous generation (16.4), like unto blind fools and whited sepulchres (Matt. 23)? He calls Herod, his ruler, a fox (Luke 13.32). He dismisses the Canaanite woman with the harsh words "It is not fair to take the children's bread and cast it to the dogs" (Matt. 15.26). He rages even against the defenceless fig-tree, because it bore no fruit, "for it was not the season for figs" (Mark 11.13 f.). With reference to Jesus' cleansing of the temple, Rasmussen even speaks of a fit of frenzy, and Loosten observes of the curse upon the fig-tree, "The way in which Jesus vents his ill-humour upon a defenceless tree can only be explained as the discharge of intense mental tension, and is quite plainly senseless. This senseless excitement points to an abnormal disposition, be it called epilepsy, or paranoia, or manic depression." Just as this striking irritability of Jesus seems to betray a moral infirmity, indeed a certain ethical blindness to values, something morbid and abnormal, so does his lack of family feeling. Jesus makes the demand that one should hate one's own family. The words of the twelve-year-old to his own mother in the temple in Jerusalem sound cold and distant. So does his reply to Mary's request at the marriage at Cana, "Woman, what is that to me and to thee?" (John 2.4). And when Mary wanted to speak to him, he refused to see her, with the hurtful question, "Who is my mother and who are my brethren? . . . Whoever does the will of my Father in heaven, he is my brother and sister and mother" (Matt. 12.48; Mark 3.33; Luke 8.21). And in doing so, his indication of his disciples might seem to imply that Mary, his real mother, did not do the will of the Father. Similarly, when the woman from the crowd glorifies Mary, "Blessed is the womb that bore thee," he rejoins most distressingly, "Rather, blessed are they who hear the word of God and keep it" (Luke 11.27). In this rebuke, too, there seems to be a hidden reproach directed against Mary, as if in Jesus' view she did not hear the Word of God and keep it. He reveals a total and most extraordinary disregard for any family feeling when he commands the young man who asks to be allowed to bury his father first, "Let the dead bury their dead, but do thou go and proclaim the kingdom of God" (Matt 8.21; Luke 9.60 ff.). Does not this show a terrible lack of *pietas*, a transgression of the fourth commandment, "Honour thy father and thy mother, that thou mayest be long-lived upon the land which the Lord thy God will give thee"?

We shall first discuss Jesus' alleged irritability, the apparent excitability and vehemence of his nature. This is the very point where the deep meaning of the Christological dogma of Jesus' true, complete humanity is so profoundly penetrating. Jesus' humanity is not an empty abstraction, not something purely formal and generalized, like the general type of man; through and through it is concrete and individual (*natura individua*), the most distinctive personality that ever appeared upon earth. The divine hypostasis took not a jot of its peculiar nature from this humanity, but rather gave it its sharpest distinction. From a purely psychological point of view, this humanity is characterized by an enormously powerful will. Jesus knew what he wanted. He knew it as no one else did. In his entire public ministry, as it is presented in the Gospels, we cannot point to a single moment when he pauses to consider, or where he reflects, or where he takes back any word or deed. From the beginning he appears as a finished, mature man. And at every moment, in every sermon, every time he heals the sick, in his circle of friends or confronted by his enemies, he always shows this same accomplished maturity. This can already be seen in the concentration of his diction, heavily charged with the power of his will, "I have come," "I have not come." The enormous certainty of his volition constantly blazes forth from his speech. Jesus was all will, and it was an urgent, passionate will. It would be totally wrong to imagine the Lord, after the fashion of some effeminate painters, as the embodiment of mildness and softness, of a sort of weak and wilted virtue, or to compare him, with Nietzsche, to "a mimosa, the sensitive plant." In Jesus, on the contrary, there is something choleric. What he says and wills proceeds out of a concentrated strength, an urgent activity, indeed, sometimes out of genuine passion and agitation. His words are loaded with energy. "Begone, Satan," he banishes the appearance of the tempter in the desert (Matt. 4.10). "Get behind me, Satan, thou art a scandal to me," he commands Peter (Matt. 16.23). "I never knew you, depart from me, you workers of iniquity" is what he will say to those who have done no good to his brethren upon earth (Matt. 7.23). His parables, too, breathe out this urgent, stormy agitation of his character. It is not only the still and silent spirit of meekness and gentleness that dwells in them. They are full of the roar of thunder and the flash of lightning too. Take the parable of the weeds, for example. "Therefore just as the weeds are gathered up and burnt with fire, so will it be at the end of the world. The Son of Man will send forth his angels, and they will gather out of his kingdom all scandals and those who work iniquity, and cast them into the furnace, where there will be the weeping and the gnashing of teeth" (Matt. 13.41

ff.). To describe God's punishment, Jesus takes from profane life the most brutal, the most painful, the most cruel images. Obviously, this proceeds from an attitude that is completely dominated by the Old Testament *ira Dei*. This is the Messias of the wrath of God, not a Messias surrounded by children and flowers. The feeling behind the parable of the net is also in this vein (Matt. 13.47 f.). It closes with the words: "The angels will go out and separate the wicked from among the just, and will cast them into the furnace of fire, where there will be the weeping and the gnashing of teeth." The same wrathful judgement brings to a close the parables of the wise and foolish virgins, the talents, and the sheep and the goats (Matt. 25). In the parable of the unmerciful servant (Matt. 18.23), his master, finally, "being angry," "handed him over to the torturers until that he should pay all that was due to him." And in the parable of the marriage feast of the king's son, the king became "angry," and sent out his armies to destroy the murderers and burn their city. And when he returned afterwards to the marriage feast, and "saw there a man who had not on a wedding garment," he was speechless with wrath, and commanded, "Bind his hands and feet and cast him forth into the darkness outside, where there will be the weeping and the gnashing of teeth!" (Matt. 22.13). And in the parable of the prudent and the unfaithful stewards (Luke 12.42), the master returns unexpectedly, and will cut the wicked steward "asunder and make him share the lot of the unfaithful." There is no doubt, the world of feeling and emotion that gave birth to these parables was full of a mighty passion. There is no trace of any feeble sentimentality. And Jesus' attacks and judgements upon the Pharisees! They are ablaze with the passion of the Messias' divine wrath. "Woe to you, Scribes and Pharisees, hypocrites! because you devour the houses of widows, praying long prayers. For this you shall receive a greater judgement . . . blind guides, who strain out the gnat, but swallow the camel! Woe to you Scribes and Pharisees, hypocrites! because you clean the outside of the cup and the dish, but within they are full of robbery and uncleanness!" (Matt. 23.14, 23). We must bear in mind that these Pharisees whom he attacks so sharply were the reigning caste in Jewry, and the Jewish people regarded them as the spokesmen of the true faith, and the irreproachable representatives of the church; and the Scribes were the teachers of all Israel, the recognized religious authority of the devout. But in face of these authorities, Jesus did not show blind obedience or spinelessness, but honest valiance, the pride and defiance of a clear conscience full of the awareness of God. As he utters these words, we can only imagine our Saviour with eyes blazing, lips trembling, cheeks aglow.

From this we may conclude that Jesus' humanity, the heart of his human volition, was no mere abstraction, no mere generalized human form; through and through, it is personal and individual, sharp-edged, as much and more so than in any other towering personality in the history of the world.

This is the background, this is the mood and the attitude, this is the unbending will to do the Father's bidding for the Father's glory, against which we may understand all those actions and utterances of the Lord that appear so incomprehensible, indeed, morbidly exaggerated, to the average man, because of their mighty ethical ardour, their hard, unrelenting sense of the good. If the average man were right, there would be no ethical passion or wrath, no sacred anger at baseness and abjectness, that was not morbid. This inward irritation at what is obviously evil *belongs to the moral nature of man.* When the Pharisees gave him no reply to his question, "Is it lawful to do good upon the Sabbath?" he looked at them "full of anger." It was holy wrath. The man who does not in his heart protest against obvious baseness, and does not passionately try to suppress it whenever he can, is not a moral man. The more purely and intensely someone is sensitive to good and evil, the more sharply and decisively his feeling will be expressed. So Jesus' infinitely pure and high-minded spirit more than any other would react to every baseness and wickedness with a bitterness without like or peer. And this was aroused especially by the Pharisaical type. Theirs was the exact opposite of the kind of devotion Jesus meant. The devotion of the Pharisees was a devotion fettered to the Law, which never made its decisions and actions out of the sovereign freedom of a conscience kindled by God and penetrated with his love, but out of a servile submission to the letter of the Law, and the rigidities of each single paragraph. It was an external, legalistic devotion. This type lacked the very values that Jesus sought and proclaimed—the inner truth and alertness of conscience, purity, love, and righteousness. Jesus knew how relentless and cunning these narrow-minded legalists were in their persecution of his works, just as they stifled all inward, personal life, all the divine Pneuma in the name of the Law. It was an act of moral self-assertion to refuse to come to terms with this brood of vipers, and ruthlessly unmask them. That is why he uses such hard words: hypocrites, brood of vipers, adulterous generation. These were words of moral wrath, trembling with a passion for the true, the pure, and the holy. On the other hand we know from the Gospels that Jesus attacked the Pharisees only as a type, and not their single representatives. Whenever he perceived a search for truth and a sense of religion—as he did in Nicodemus, or Simon the Pharisee—he was as gentle and kind as he was to the children, the sinful, and the sick.

This mighty feeling for the true, the pure, and the holy also explains the purification of the temple. An outrageous lack of religious modesty and spirituality, the exploitation of religious institutions for the ends of business, the ugly confusion of religion and the service of Mammon, came forth to meet him with offensive vigour in the courtyard of the Temple. Business here was carried on in the very face of the All-Holy One, taking advantage of the long-suffering of the simple devout. This was no "fit of frenzy," but moral action animated by the purest zeal for the majesty of holiness, when Jesus ruthlessly destroyed this simoniac abuse of religion. And at the same time it was the act of the Messias. By casting out the money-changers from the temple, he publicly demonstrates his domination over the temple. "One greater than the temple is here." Driving the money-changers out was a commentary upon this saying. The old covenant is over. The new temple is rising, where the Father may be worshipped in spirit and in truth. The casting out of the buyers and sellers was a veiled messianic prophecy, the proclamation of the dawning kingdom of God.

Christ's cursing the fig-tree, too, ceases to strike us as strange when we appreciate its profound *symbolic* significance. It must be seen and appreciated against its background of messianic prophecy. It was regarded as the true prophetic style, indeed the true messianic style, to proclaim the prophetic tidings of the Messias, and their new, utterly different, exciting, and revolutionary nature, by paradoxical and apparently incomprehensible deeds. The very paradox of the deed was intended to draw attention to the prophet and his revolutionary works. To the disciples, it is precisely the bitter incomprehensibility of the apparently meaningless cursing of the fig-tree that is the Messias' way of expressing the terrible curse hanging over Israel, the fig-tree that remained unfruitful in the good season as in the bad. It must have struck the disciples all the more strongly, since it was not yet "the season of figs" when the Lord expected fruit of the fig-tree. He was reminding them that execration and barrenness were the final fate of every unfruitful life, Jerusalem's above all, and that God demanded fruitfulness at every time, inopportune, opportune, in season and out of season. Obviously, this cursing was meant to impress the disciples. Jesus' passion loomed large on his horizon. For three years he had given of his best in Corozain and Bethsaida, as he had in Jerusalem, and now his reward was death upon the cross. The fate of the fig-tree must have brought home unforgettably to the disciples that Jerusalem's unfaithfulness and spiritual barrenness were the cause of its fall. This miracle was one of the few miracles with a purely symbolic significance, which otherwise are to be found only in John; it is really more of a sign in the style of the Old Testament, more of a σημεῖον than a miracle. When Baumann objects to this miracle especially because it harmed the many who later went hungry beneath its boughs, there is no point in wasting words on such simple-mindedness. If these spirits had created the world they would certainly have seen to it that exactly enough apples and figs and nuts grew upon trees for mankind to eat its fill.

Jesus' alleged lack of family feeling, as well as his irritability, is also the direct expression and precipitate of his *heroic* disposition, turned towards God. We may assume that only a total blindness towards God would dare to regard this lack of family feeling as a morbid symptom of disease. Certainly Jesus did preach hate towards one's family, but it was that kind of hate whose reverse side is the greatest love. It is the same hate as he commands us to direct against our own soul—the absolute denial of animal sensuality as our ultimate purpose, and its absolute subordination to the highest purposes of spiritual life. "Hate" here means to value something as secondary to the highest good. In Jesus' sense, it means to sacrifice the earthly and the sensual, if the interest of the highest good, the kingdom of God, should demand it. In this sense, indeed, the soldier must hate even his own life. In the hierarchy of value, natural human sympathy is subordinate to love for the *summum bonum*, the highest good. Jesus' conversation with his mother at the marriage at Cana sounds harsh only to our ears. But it did not sound harsh to the Jews of his time, for the phrase "What to me and to thee, woman?" was a customary formulation. What Jesus really meant to say was just: What you want is not our affair, but the affair of my Father, and his hour. I may act only "when my hour is come." Obviously, Jesus' human consciousness had not yet been informed as to the moment when he might work his first miracle, and take up his messianic ministry. It was not until his human consciousness and human volition turned at his mother's behest to question the Father that he learned in inward contemplation that now his hour was come. So even on this early occasion, Mary already showed herself to be the interceding mediator, for it was at her intercession that Jesus' first miracle took place.

His apparent rebuke of the woman's praise of Mary, "Rather, blessed are they who hear the word of God and keep it," really arose from the same attitude as made him give the command to hate father and mother. It was directed against the cult of sheer animal sensuality, and stressed that everything human and sensuous must receive its value and worth from the supersensuous and the divine—even bodily motherhood. Mary became his true mother not only because she bore him in her body but because she bore him dutiful to the Word of God. It is significant that Luke, who reports this apparent rebuke of the Lord's, should also record Elizabeth's words to Mary, "Blessed is she who has believed" (Luke 1.45). The same fundamental attitude made Jesus refuse to receive his mother and brethren at Capharnaum. He was at the turning point of his messianic ministry, immediately before his last journey to Jerusalem, and the cross. That was no time to be absorbed in family cares, and justify himself in face of these cares. His Father's will was sharp and clear before him, and only those who could make this will their own, as he did, were mother, brother, and sister to him. If this behaviour of Jesus' indicated a morbid disposition, then all heroism has something morbid about it. For such heroism cannot be carried out without courageously pushing aside this or that family wish, however justified it may be in the narrow perspective of the family. Moreover, this situation tells us that Mary too, just like other men and women, had to walk her way in the *darkness of faith*. Certainly she had the deep and secret knowledge that in Jesus she had given birth to "Sanctity," and that her child would be called Son of the All-High. But more she did not know. For her, there was still a long way to go from this knowledge to faith in the metaphysical Son of God. And the road was longer still to the belief that this Son would die upon the cross. In suffering and silence, she had to make her way right up to her son's cross, questioning, lamenting, daring, until at Pentecost the light of the Holy Spirit entered her soul and illumined it. Many of the Church Fathers, such as Origen, Basil, and Chrysostom, imagined that the incident at Capharnaum was to be interpreted in the sense that Mary doubted in her son. But they overlooked the fact that Mary's anxieties in this time were only the proper expression of her maternal love, and so there can be no question of sin. Only her purposes were confined to the narrow frame of humanity. Jesus alone knew of the divine intent. Which is why he harshly refused his mother's request.

Jesus' reply to the young man, "Let the dead bury their dead," points in the same direction. It was a reminder to the disciples who were with him not to put temporal responsibilities before eternal; and at the same time it was a test of the new disciple's strength of will, intended to prove whether he was strong enough to bear the great sacrifices that were to come. Time was short. So Jesus wanted to impress upon the new disciple that he did not belong to the dead and their ministry, but to the living. Not lack of love, but heroic magnanimity, pulses in these words and deeds of the Lord. They are a radiant witness to his valiant and heroic soul. The Gospels testify that, despite his high aims, he nevertheless felt true and profound human love, like none before or since. Even on the cross, did he not think with love of his mother, and does he not stand as Caritas Incarnate before the eyes even of the most sceptical criticism? It was from him that mankind learned for the first time what true love was, that it is sacrifice even unto death, yea, even unto death upon the cross.

The positive sanctity of Jesus

The idea of Jesus' sanctity includes a positive as well as a negative element. His human volition was not simply free of sin, but as holy and perfect in its roots as a man can be. Theologians distinguish this sanctity into sanctity of substance (*sanctitas substantialis*) and non-substantial sanctity (*sanctitas accidentalis*). By *substantial sanctity* the Thomists mean that the sanctity of the Logos is substantially embedded in Jesus' humanity through the hypostatic union. They maintain that because our Lord's human nature is united in one person with the self of the Logos, Jesus' human soul possesses *in substantia,* in his entire substance, the sanctity of God. Even if Jesus' human soul were conceived of as denuded of all created sanctity and all sanctifying Grace, it would still be bound to give forth infinite joy on account of its union in one person with the substantial sanctity of God's Logos. The Scotists contest this, and rightly so. As we have already established, it is not in accordance with the rules of the *communicatio idiomatum* to connect an abstraction with an abstraction in Christ, and, for example, ascribe divine omnipotence to the Lord's humanity. It is equally improper to predicate this humanity with the sanctity of God. It is not that the humanity appropriates the Logos, and its substantial sanctity to boot, but the other way round: the Logos appropriates the humanity. Otherwise, it would not be far to the Monophysite error that the Logos imparted to the Lord's human nature not only the self-sufficiency of his person but also his divine attributes. And so the theological opinion of the existence of *sanctitas substantialis* in our Lord's humanity is *wrong*. Following the *communicatio idiomatum,* we may certainly say: Jesus the man was in possession of *sanctitas substantialis,* in so far as Jesus the man is the Logos who is in possession of the humanity. But it is not correct to say: Jesus' humanity is in possession of the substantial sanctity of the Logos. For all that is appropriate to it is only the self-sufficiency of the Logos, but not his divine nature.

We may, however, agree all the more decisively with the entire body of theology that puts forward the *sanctitas accidentalis* of Jesus' humanity. Jesus' human soul possessed love of God and man in the highest degree. As far as a human vessel is capable of receiving the abundance of eternal Grace, Christ's soul is permeated with it. According to the divine dispensation, sanctifying Grace is that created form by which a created being is holy. From the point of view of God, it is the planting of a germ of divine life in the human soul, it is a new and supernatural principle of life, enrapturement with God, animation by the love of the Holy Spirit. From the point of view of man, it is the spirit of surrender to God and man, intimacy with the divine. In so far as this spirit of perfect surrender kills all selfishness and brings the right orientation in height and breadth towards God and man, it implies the fullness of all divine and moral virtues, faith, hope, and love, the seven gifts of the Holy Spirit on the one hand, and the four cardinal virtues and their train on the other. Sanctifying Grace is God's most intimate exchange of life and love with the human soul, it is the kiss of love. It is *propositio theologice certa* that Christ's human soul possessed the highest degree of all sanctity that a created being is capable of, and that his sanctity even surpassed that of the angels. And so the Church has never actually formulated dogma on this subject, probably because it has never been seriously disputed. Only once, when Abelard maintained that the spirit of God's filiation in Christ did not admit that the spirit of the fear of God should persist in him, the Church indirectly took a firm stand, and repudiated this view. So we may hold fast to the view that as a whole man, Christ bowed before his Father in the spirit of fear, and that his attitude was full of adoration and awe. So we are justified in speaking of devotion in Jesus, because he was not, after all, a god walking upon earth, but the God-man, God Incarnate. His religious life was quite specifically no different from ours. Indeed, it was so very similar to ours that we may regard Christian devotion as an extension and continuation of Jesus' devotion (cf. Galtier, *La religion du fils*). So it is not necessary for us to recapitulate the cloud of witnesses for Christ's *gratia creata*. When John (1.14) declares, "We saw his glory—glory as of the only-begotten of the Father—full of Grace and of truth," he has said everything. Luke (2.52) expressly instructs us that the abundance of this Grace developed parallel to the unfolding of Christ's human consciousness. "And Jesus advanced in wisdom and age and Grace before God and men." This "advancing," or "increasing," as it is sometimes rendered (προέκοπτε, Luke 2.52), signifies in New Testament usage a progression, or development. This is not to say that the wealth of divine Grace was poured out upon Jesus only gradually, for Jesus was from the beginning the well-beloved Son of the Father. Only his human receptivity grew with this blessing of Grace. As he developed in body and soul, his human self opened itself to this blessing correspondingly. So Luke was able to speak of a constant advance in Grace. It was not the Evangelists' intention to describe the abundance of Christ's created Grace in detail. Their first concern is to illuminate his divine majesty. But in pointing to this godliness, they cannot help but describe the miraculous reflection cast upon the human soul by its intimate union with the self of the Logos. So the dominant passion in the life of Jesus' will was the passion for his heavenly Father. The eternal God was never more rapturously or more passionately worshipped and adored upon earth than by Jesus. No one could call to his Father in heaven as he did from his earliest youth to his very last breath. "Did you not know that I must be about my Father's business?" was what he said as a boy in the temple. "It is my part to do the will of my Father," the mature man avowed in the midst of the struggle. "Father, into thy hands I commend my spirit" was his dying cry upon the cross. His Father's name is the high hymn of his love, which his holy lips constantly sing to his Father—on the quiet mountainside and in the public market, at the murmuring lakeshore and in the stillness of his chamber. And no one heard the answering voice from heaven with such a full response, "Thou art my beloved Son." If we allow the picture of Jesus at prayer, as the Gospels describe him, to work upon us, we will have the impression that his prayer, his conversation with God, was the tenderest, gentlest, most delicate activity of his human soul. "When thou prayest, go into thy room and, closing thy door, pray to thy Father in secret." Jesus said this out of his own practice, and his own style of prayer. With locked doors and in the stillness of his room, he met with his Father. The Evangelists also tell us that Jesus liked to withdraw to lonely mountain heights, and spend whole nights in prayer. And he did not pray, like the heathen, with many words. As far as his prayers are recorded by the Evangelists, we can really feel the inward emotion and intense concentration with which he uttered them. "Abba, Father, all things are possible to thee. Remove this cup from me; yet not what I will, but what thou willest" (Mark 14.36). "My God, my God, why hast thou forsaken me?" Even this appeal is a prayer in the Lord's sense, for it is a conscious quotation from the 21st Psalm, in which these words are put into the mouth of the Messias (Matt. 27.46). His other prayer upon the cross is likewise brief and urgent: "Father, forgive them, for they do not know what they are doing" (Luke 23.34). "Father, into thy hands I commend my spirit" (Luke 23.46). The most delicate movements of an infinitely sensitive and infinitely warm spiritual life are here concentrated into a single cry. Jesus' prayers were his most powerful experience of God's Grace, the profound restoration of his soul in the love of the Father. It was out of the depths of this experience of God's Grace that Jesus girded his will. From quiet prayers he advanced to valiant deeds in the Father's service. This is the point where the bitter heroism of his love for God breaks through. His declaration, "The kingdom of heaven has been enduring violent assault, and the violent have been seizing it by force" (Matt. 11.12); and his rejection of any uncertain groping, and hesitant second thoughts—"no one, having put his hand to the plough and looking back, is fit for the kingdom of God" (Luke 9.62); "for which of you, wishing to build a tower, does not sit down first and calculate the outlays that are necessary" (14.28)—all this, austerely and bitterly, his own life vouched for. For his human volition, too, the kingdom of God was like a treasure, which one would give one's all to purchase. For the sake of that pearl of great price, the kingdom of God, of his own free will he led a life of poverty. "The foxes have dens, and the birds of the air have nests; but the Son of Man has nowhere to lay his head" (Matt. 8.20). For the sake of this pearl, he utters those strange words of the "eunuchs who have made themselves so for the sake of the kingdom of heaven. Let him accept it who can" (Matt. 19.12). For the sake of this pearl, he can regard the terrible death on the cross as something radiant and holy. "The Son of Man is to be betrayed into the hands of men, and they will kill him; and on the third day he will rise again" (Matt. 17.21). And this mighty love for God can become so gentle and meek when it is transformed into love for mankind. He felt so closely united to mankind that his love for the Father and for man flowed together in one stream. It was indeed the great achievement of the new ethic he brought that he did not simply add love of mankind to the other commandments as one more precept, but set it up as *the* new commandment. His love was meant for man as such. All other religious, social, and even ethical limitations fell before it. The Father lets his sun dawn and his rain fall upon the good and the wicked, the just and the unjust. Whenever Jesus senses a true longing for salvation in the Canaanite woman, in the publican, in the whore, in Nicodemus the Pharisee, he lavishes all the wealth of his Saviour's love. It was Jesus' love for man that first discovered the true man. Amidst the hurly-burly of national, religious, and ethical prejudices, it rediscovered the gold of true humanity. And thus his heart belongs above all to those whom the spirit of the age had deprived of full human worth—children, sinners, the poor. "Let the little children come to me, and do not hinder them, for such is the kingdom of God" (Luke 18.16). "Blessed are the poor in spirit, for theirs is the kingdom of heaven" (Matt. 5.3). "Son, thy sins are forgiven thee" (Mark 2.5). "Amen I say to thee, this day thou shalt be with me in paradise" (Luke 23.43).

It is the task of the Christian moralist to describe the thousandfold radiance of Jesus' love of God and his neighbour, and to show in detail how his fundamental passion of divine love is manifested as tenderness in one case and as vigour in another. On the one hand he commands, "Judge not the speck in thy brother's eye," and on the other he teaches his followers to pray, "Forgive us our debts as we also forgive our debtors," and yet again he warns, "Let the dead bury their dead." If we scrutinize all the delicacy and tenderness in our entire ethical culture, from Lao-tse and Buddha to Epictetus, we shall find that all this delicacy and tenderness is but a quiet murmuring in comparison with the mighty and overwhelming hymn of heroic love which Jesus exemplifies. In his image God's Grace has virtually gone to the limits of its potentialities. We cannot imagine that anything might be added to it. "The goodness and kindness of God our Saviour appeared," rejoiced St. Paul (Titus 3.4). Whoever has sensed, even remotely, this inward beauty of Jesus' humanity, will never more escape him. "Jesus the great sun can never be lost by anyone who has once been illuminated by his rays. We can never forget him. We can deny him, but that does not change anything. He is buried even in the most beclouded heart. And it can happen any moment that he will arise again" (Hans Carossa).

The Grace of Christ as gratia capitis

Theologians use the concept of *gratia capitis* in order to establish the vital connexions between Christ's life of Grace and the life of Grace of the believing Christian, and to set up the life of Grace of Christ's humanity as the true source of all true Christian life. Following St. Augustine's doctrine of Christ as the head of the Christian body, Peter Lombard had already distinguished between the Grace of the union and the *gratia capitis* that emanates from Christ as the head of the Christian body. Following this, Peter of Poitiers put forward the doctrine of the *gratia capitis,* as did William of Auxerre in his *Summa Aurea.* From them the formulation *gratia capitis* came into theological usage.

Certainly, Christ's abundance of Grace is first and foremost his own personal attribute. But Christ does not live his rich life for himself alone. He is the head of mankind, and mankind is in need of redemption. All blessings proceed from this head to the members that are united with it in one body. "And of his fullness we have all received, Grace for Grace" (John 1.16). On account of the circumincession, the presence of the triune God permeates Jesus' human willing and doing so intensely that his human nature, without giving up one jot of its own characteristics, becomes the concrete location, the point of contact, at which we come into direct apprehension of the divine Grace. And thus his humanity is our *caro vivifica.*

To that extent, the humanity of Jesus Christ is called the *sacramentum conjunctum*. It is that place in the human structure at which the blessing of Grace from the triune God enters into mankind. We have "no other means by which we may become blessed, but through the name of Jesus." In him and through him, the triune God blesses us, and there is no other blessing. Because the blessed soul of the Incarnate One is formed in our image, we are enabled to experience this Grace abounding. He becomes our Grace, our life. We are able to draw our life's strength from Christ as directly as the grape draws it from the vine. And so the entire sacred life of Christianity is nothing more nor less than *Christ working in history* (*totus Christus*), as Augustine constantly says. In believing mankind, in the blessed inhabitants of heaven, in the patient dwellers in Purgatory, and in the devout upon earth, *Christus totus* presents himself in living form. There is no prayer that rises to heaven that does not rise out of the fullness of his life. There is no sacrament offered that does not bear his blessing. And to this extent we must say that Christ constantly perfects himself in his saints. The "whole Christ" is thus not only the God-man alone, but the God-man united in Grace with those he has redeemed. These are his Pleroma, his fullness. The "whole Christ" will thus attain to his full consummation only when the Son of Man descends from heaven. As long as the Parousia has not yet come, he is a Christ who is still becoming. Seated at the right hand of the Father, he gathers in all the redeemed natures and cultures to him, by means of the *gratia capitis*, until the whole Christ is perfected. He accomplishes this his sanctifying activity especially in the sacraments. Hence they are called *sacramenta separata*. Only when the last saint is gathered in will the whole Christ reach his consummation, and the kingdom of heaven be realized on earth. Only then will he give back his power to the Father. The time of the Messias will be succeeded by the time of the Trinity.

Theology has a formulation for this idea of the inner dependency of all the blessings of mankind on the fullness of Christ's Grace: Christ's human nature is the *causa instrumentalis*, or *instrumentum conjunctum*, of the Godhead in bestowing Grace upon mankind. There is no Grace flowing down upon mankind that was not appropriated through mankind by Jesus' humanity. So this humanity of the Lord's is our true sacrament, the visible sign ministered to us by the Grace of the Holy Spirit. And so we may conclude that Christ in his humanity is possessed of the *potestas excellentiae,* the

power of initiating sacraments, and thus of relating his blessing and Grace to a simple outward symbol. Thus he is the
author of all sacraments.

From the ethical perfection of Jesus' humanity we shall now
turn to its intellectual perfection. This is the second effect upon
Christ's humanity that was brought about by the hypostatic
union.

XIX

THE INTELLECTUAL PERFECTION OF CHRIST'S HUMANITY

OUR question here is one of the most difficult problems in Christology, largely because there have been no heresies on this issue to compel the ecclesiastical office into precise formulations about Christ's knowledge.

The hypostatic union did not bring about any apotheosis or deification of Christ's human nature, such as occurs in heathen mythologies. But it did produce a divinization, a union of the inviolate and undiminished humanity with the divine Word, so close and intimate that all Jesus' purely human actions have the Logos as their subject, and are to be ascribed to him. So we may conclude that the proper attribute of Jesus' humanity and its religious knowledge is the highest and most perfect that in this respect can be imagined of humanity. There is absolutely no reason why our Lord's understanding and knowledge should be thought imperfect. Rather, it is bound to exhaust all the potentialities of human knowledge with regard to our salvation. Indeed, it is *a priori* conceivable, and completely probable, that because the self of his humanity is the Logos, and because Jesus the man had his substantial being in the supernatural and divine, supernatural sources of his knowledge might spring up within him, so that in addition to his *perfect natural understanding* in matters of salvation he would also possess a *perfect supernatural knowledge*. We shall discuss this later on. But whether the perception of Jesus the man be natural or supernatural, it remains a knowledge within the figure of humanity. For the instrument through which the Logos utters its perfect knowledge remains a human instrument, the human faculty of perception—physiologically, the functioning of the human brain. So the peculiar way in which the God-man reveals himself to us, even when the origin of his knowledge is supernatural, is still human. It bears the peculiar characteristics of humanity and created being. First, we shall discuss Jesus' purely natural understanding.

Jesus' natural knowledge

As *natural* knowledge, attained by the powers of his own human nature, this is a knowledge achieved by way of the senses. Sense-perception, and then the power of abstraction (*intellectus agens*), are the requisites for conceptual thought. According to Aristotelian and Scholastic epistemology, it is this power of abstraction that extracts the essence (*species intelligibilis*) from the visible appearance of things, conveyed by the senses (*species sensibilis*). For its part, this essence abstracted from the sensible appearance of things fertilizes the passive intellect awaiting conception (*intellectus possibilis*), and helps it to the inward utterance and inward birth of the concept, the idea. So the natural process of thinking in Jesus' humanity is a thinking that does not advance intuitively, by the simple contemplation of the essence of things, but *successively*, by way of sense-perception to abstraction, *per visibilia ad invisibilia*. This abstractive thought is of its essence. It takes place in a succession of acts. The Holy Scripture expressly testifies to this successiveness when it speaks of an "advance," or "increase," in Jesus' knowledge. "And Jesus advanced in wisdom" (Luke 2.52). The Epistle to the Hebrews (5.8) declares that although Jesus was the "Son," he "learned obedience from the things that he suffered" (ἔμαθεν ἀφ' ὧν ἔπαθεν τὴν ὑπακοήν). So there was a *progression* in his experience of suffering, an increasingly deep penetration into what God wanted of him. The more Jesus came into contact with the outward world, and with the sensible appearances of things, the richer were the impressions that he could store up in his soul. One day he would learn by experience, through the sense-impressions he received, what a vine was; on the next day what a mustard seed might be. His perception of nature grew from day to day. Jesus' parables, which are almost all taken from the life of nature, tell us that his eye caught the smallest of the small, the sparrow on the rooftop, the pearl on the ocean bed, the lily of the field. And similarly his knowledge of men increased. One day he would become acquainted with men who previously were unknown to him; and on the next he would compare them one with another, and apprehend their outward and inward differences. His knowledge of men, as it can be seen in his confident, self-assured dealings with publicans and sinners, and with the Pharisees, reveals a profound penetration into the secrets of the human soul. Only a penetrating understanding of human nature can explain his words to the Jews, when they bring the adultress before him, "Let him who is without sin among you be the first to cast a stone at her," or those other words of his, "Why dost thou see the speck in thy brother's eye and yet dost not consider the beam in thy own eye?" And we can also observe a certain progression in the Lord's understanding of himself. When the Epistle to the Hebrews assures us that Jesus learned obedience from the things that he suffered, it indicates that he came to understand the sorrowful experiences that he was increasingly compelled to make in proclaiming his tidings, with a more profound and vivid awareness of their mysterious connexion with his Father's will. The Evangelists are one in their account that on the day of Cæsarea Philippi, when Peter first avowed him to be the Christ, he "began" (ἤρξατο) also to speak of his suffering. Now it is certain that from the beginning, ever since his human consciousness first awoke and he felt himself to be the well-beloved Son of the heavenly Father, Jesus also knew in advance that his calling was one of suffering. For it was written in the prophets that the Son of Man must suffer in order to enter into his glory. But at the beginning it would seem that this suffering loomed before his soul obscurely, imprecisely, as an inevitable destiny. At first he did not know its details; he had no idea of when his suffering would begin, nor the particularly terrible form his execution would take. Only when he arose to make his pilgrimage to Jerusalem, the centre of orthodox Jewry, only as opposition to his message increased, and hostile groups were formed against him, and attempts on his life were made, only then did his natural understanding attain the knowledge through experience (*scientia experimentalis*) that his death for our salvation was near. So Jesus learned the details of his passion only by way of his advancing personal experience in immediate contact with his situation, which daily grew more critical. Scholasticism thus gives this increasing knowledge by way of experience the name of *scientia experimentalis,* or *scientia acquisita.*

The co-operation of natural and supernatural modes of perception

At this point we must of course observe that Christ's natural, acquired knowledge went hand in hand with a higher mode of perception; that is to say, his human intellect assimilated and appropriated the insights proceeding from this higher, Grace-given perception with an increasing consciousness. We can demonstrate that in the life of Jesus' soul there dwelt, side by side, and *inextricably interfused, two modes of perception, human and supernatural.* The knowledge gained from the world of outward and inward experience is there. But it is equally certain that a supernatural perception, gained from the immediate vision of God, is also at work. There is what is known as the *scientia visionis,* which we shall now discuss.

St. John the Evangelist, the Apostle whose main concern it is to demonstrate the divine glory even in the poor human life Jesus led, draws our attention to the co-operation of these two modes of perception, natural and supernatural, in two distinct passages: at the marriage at Cana, and before Jesus begins his ceremonial journey to Jerusalem. When Mary points out to him at the wedding, "They have no wine," he replies: "What wouldst thou have me do, woman? My hour has not yet come" (2.4). Mary clearly does not take this reply to be an outright refusal, for she immediately says to the attendants, "Do whatever he tells you." She understood the Lord to say that in principle he was prepared to help, if and when it was the Father's will. By explaining, "My hour has not yet come," Jesus was saying that in his human consciousness of the Father's will he was not at that moment clear whether he should begin his ministry of salvation then. But in the same moment as Mary came to him with her request, he brooded within him on the Father's will, and from the dependency of his human consciousness upon the self of the Logos he reached the clear perception that this was the awaited hour. And so he wrought this first of his signs, "here at Cana," "and he manifested his glory" (2.11). To this extent we may say that by her intercession for the young wedded pair, Mary first released in Jesus his exact understanding that his hour had come. She brought about the first result of his awareness of his calling, and showed herself to be a mother for Jesus too, and not simply for the wedded couple.

John 7.6 portrays a similar co-operation between Jesus' natural understanding and his supernatural vision of God. Just as the Jewish Feast of Tabernacles was at hand, Jesus was in Galilee. His brethren urged him, "Leave here and go into Judea, that thy disciples also may see the works that thou dost" (7.3). Then Jesus replied, "My time has not yet come, but your time is always at hand . . . go up to the feast, but I do not go up to this feast, for my time is not yet fulfilled." So at this moment, Jesus did not feel any inner impulsion to begin his journey. He knew perfectly well that in his enemies' stronghold he was bound to meet his death. But the Father's will was not yet clear enough before his soul for him to make the dangerous journey to Jerusalem as yet. But just as his mother's request at Cana had opened his human consciousness to the illumination pouring in from God, so did the advice of his brethren on this occasion. Jesus' soul turned questioning to the Father, and the answer came that he must go up to Jerusalem, even now. And thereupon he really did go up to the feast, but after his brethren had already left, at first "not publicly, but as it were privately" (7.10). "But afterwards he went up into the temple, and began to teach" (7.14).

Following this testimony of St. John, we must establish that Jesus' consciousness of his calling in respect of external details, which he learned by way of experience, was increasingly clarified under the influence of his supernatural perception, the *scientia visionis*. Of course, his acquired knowledge remained the foundation. Just as in the realm of Grace his nature remains the foundation upon which Grace built, so in Jesus' understanding it was the perception natural to his humanity, and acquired from his experience, that was the foundation for the decisions of his will.

It is also the final opinion of St. Thomas that Jesus' acquired knowledge was increased in this way. In his *Commentaria in Libros Sententiarum* (III sent. dist. XIV, a. 3; dist. XVIII, a. 3), he explained Jesus' knowledge by way of experience as a *scientia per accidens infusa*, that is, a knowledge of the outside world which has flowed directly from God. On the other hand, in the *Summa Theologica*, the product of his mature mind (III, qu. 9, a. 4), he writes, "Nothing that God planted in our human nature was wanting to the human nature assumed by the Word of God. Now it is manifest that

God planted in human nature not only a passive but an 'active intellect' (*intellectus agens*). . . . The proper operation of the active intellect is to make intelligible species in act (that is, to develop the essential forms of things, the *species intelligibilis* out of the *species sensibilis*) by abstracting them from phantasms. Hence . . . it must be said that in Christ there was acquired knowledge, which some call empiric. And hence, although I wrote differently . . . it must be said that in Christ there was acquired knowledge, which is properly knowledge in a human fashion."

Of course this acquired knowledge of Christ's must have been more perfect in extent and depth than it is in us ordinary men. For the power of his mind was not broken or debased by sensuality or passion, which has been the case with us ordinary mortals ever since Adam's fall. Indeed, we are incapable of any process of thought that is completely impersonal and pure, and in no way determined by our emotions. The more impure these feelings in us are, the more cabin'd, cribb'd, and confined is our thought; the purer it is, the freer it will be. And so Jesus' thinking must have been incomparably more mobile, more elastic, and more certain than the thinking of fallen man. For he was not oppressed by the prejudices and fantasies of the world around him. He was born of a virgin, from Mary his mother, who conceived him without original sin. And so his intellect too was pure and clear. And thus in his humanity, too, Jesus was a born teacher, a master of thought and word; "and the crowds were astonished at his teaching; for he was teaching them as one having authority, and not as their Scribes and Pharisees."

In the light of Jesus' advance in empirical knowledge, it is hardly surprising that Jesus should constantly be asking *questions* of the world around him, although "he himself knew what he would do" (John 6.6). And so in the country of the Gerasenes he asked the man possessed by devils, "What is thy name?" (Mark 5.9). At Capharnaum he asked his disciples, "How many loaves have you?" (Mark 6.38). He questions the Father of the possessed boy, "How long is it since this has come upon him?" (Mark 9.20). There is no need at all to regard these questions as purely didactic, as many theologians do, intended to inform not Jesus himself but others. As a true man, he could ordinarily acquire his empirical knowledge only by purely human means. And so his questions are quite fitting. And where he questions, he also *marvels*. The answer of the Gentile centurion, "Only say the word, and my servant will be healed," made Jesus marvel. "And when Jesus heard this, he marvelled, and said to those that were following him, 'Amen, I say to you, I have not found such great faith in Israel'" (Matt. 8.10; Luke 7.9). Here he strengthens his awareness that he had come to save all men, by the precise experience of having found men, even among the Gentiles, who were more ready for salvation than the Jews.

In conclusion, we may say this: From the fact that Jesus was perfect man, with a human soul and human understanding and volition, we may conclude that his perception of the outward world of experience was made in the form of purely human apprehension, by way of sense-perception: and that he assimilated it by means of his human intellect. And this of itself brought with it an increase in his empirical experience and knowledge. Whoever disputes this raises the suspicion that he favours a disguised form of Monophysitism and ultimately that he misinterprets the hypostatic union as an assumption of Christ's humanity not into the divine person but into the divine nature, and into the fullness of all its divine powers and properties.

The scientia visionis of Christ

However, as we have already observed, in addition to this purely human, natural mode of perception, Christ also possessed a supernatural mode of knowing. Theology describes this latter kind as the *direct vision of the divine essence,* the *scientia visionis.*

There are two points here that we must bear in mind. Firstly, the truth that the hypostatic union does not signify assumption into the nature of the Logos, but only into his person. What the Logos gives immediately and absolutely to the Lord's humanity is simply its self-sufficiency, but not the perfection of its divine being—its omniscience, for example. However, if Jesus' human soul nevertheless possessed a direct vision of God that went infinitely beyond natural knowledge, this knowledge was still not directly brought about by union with the Logos, but rather by the presence of the triune God within the Logos, who endowed our Lord's human nature with Grace, according to the free decision of his most holy will. That is the second point we have to bear in mind. So we have to regard this immediate vision of God on the part of Jesus' humanity as an act of Grace, freely made, on the part of the triune God. For the external acts of the triune God are always made in sovereign freedom.

What, more precisely, does this *scientia visionis* consist in? At heart, it is no more nor less than the vision of the Logos, to which Jesus' human nature belongs; it is his theandric consciousness of identity. If Jesus knew that his identity was divine, he can have attained this knowledge only through an especial, free act of Grace on the part of the triune God, only because the triune God opened Jesus' human consciousness at its zenith to the direct contemplation of his divine personality, and thus elevated his human consciousness into the sense of identity of the Logos. Since all that Jesus' humanity received from the Logos was only the divine identity and person, but no knowledge of this identity, and since on the other hand such a knowledge of his divine identity would be indispensable and absolutely necessary to him, we can only conclude that when the triune God endowed him with the incarnation, he also gave him the knowledge of this incarnation as soon as his human consciousness was sufficiently mature to understand the union.

In establishing this primary content of Jesus' vision of God, its actual existence at once becomes clear. M. J. Scheeben (*Handbuch der katholischen Dogmatik*, bk. 3, p. 183) rightly discovers that the relationship between this vision of God on the part of Jesus' humanity and the hypostatic union is so close and so necessary that its absence would be far more miraculous, or rather, far more incomprehensible than if the influence upon Jesus' soul of the sanctity brought by this vision of God were to cease with the passion. In any case, says Scheeben, "for Christ's soul, the intuitive perception of the divine person to which it belongs is the only fit and worthy form of theandric self-consciousness. For in this self-consciousness, Christ's soul is bound to recognize that it subsists in the divine person. . . . It is difficult to understand how some modern theologians, in spite of having the right concept of the hypostatic union, are still reluctant to admit this; and they hardly realize that their very reluctance endangers the concept of the union itself. For if Christ's soul does not itself see into the divine person, he must be conscious of his identity only by abstracting from his personality, or by imagining that he is a (human) person in his own right. In any case, without this contemplation of the self of the Logos, the hypostatic union would not achieve that form of life which is proper to it as a union of spirit and spirit."

If we maintain that Christ's human soul received its self-sufficiency from the Logos, there can be no doubt that it also had most certain knowledge of this. So the vision of God on the part of Jesus' humanity is a necessary inference from the mystery of the incarnation. Jesus' human soul is bound to know more than merely its human characteristics; it must also be acquainted with the ultimate that is rooted in those characteristics, its own divine identity. So if it is clearly conscious of its divine personality, it must have an *intuitive vision into the essence of the Logos* in which it subsists. But if it had a direct vision of the Logos itself, then we should be justified in concluding a vision into the essence of the living God himself. For the Logos, the second divine person, is substantially identical with the divine nature. The vision of the Logos therefore necessarily implies an immediate vision of the divine nature, of the triune God; it thus implies the *visio beatifica*. It was St. John the Evangelist who stressed this. Jesus himself explicitly stresses his precise insight into his filial relationship to the Godhead. "If I have spoken of earthly things to you, and you do not believe, how will you believe if I speak to you of heavenly things? And no one has ascended into heaven except him who has descended from heaven: the Son of Man who is in heaven" (3.12 f.). "Amen, amen I say to you, the Son can do nothing of himself, but only what he sees the Father doing. For whatever he does, this the Son also does in like manner. For the Father loves the Son, and shows him all that he himself does. And greater works than these he will show him . . ." (5.19, 20; cf. 7.29; 8.55). In the Synoptic Gospels, too, there is a quiet hint at the active interchange between Jesus' human soul and the Father. This is the famous Logion in Matthew and Luke, which we have discussed earlier, "All things have been delivered to me by my Father; and no one knows the Son except the Father; nor does anyone know the Father except the Son, and him to whom the Son chooses to reveal him." This "no one" implies the exclusiveness of the exchange of knowledge between Christ and the triune God. In Semitic usage "to know" means an intimate and active communion of life between two living beings. The exclusiveness of the knowledge of Father and Son is founded upon Jesus' filiation. Only because Jesus is the Son, he knows the Father as no one else does. This makes it very difficult to understand how certain theologians could ever have doubted this mysterious fact. The only explanation could be that the early Fathers never promulgated an express dogma on this mystery, because they were afraid of transferring divine characteristics to Jesus' humanity—that is, of Monophysite tendencies. On the other hand, the Schoolmen's subsequent interpretations of this mystery became completely immoderate, and paid all too little attention to the limits which bound Jesus' human nature and his messianic mission.

The limits of the visio beatifica

These limits show that the *visio beatifica* of Jesus' humanity was a specific vision peculiar to him alone; for it had its particular limitations. The first limitation it has in common with every creature's vision of God, which is the limitation of created being. As a created being, Jesus' soul could apprehend the divine essence only after the fashion of all creatures, only with the aid of the *lumen gloriae,* and only as far as a created being is capable of comprehending the divine at all. And so its vision of the Godhead is not as clear and comprehensive as God's own comprehension of himself. The vision of God of Jesus' human soul is not comprehensive, it does not grasp God totally and at once in a single act, *simul et totaliter.* It grasps God only partially and in successive stages, *successive et partialiter.* To this extent, Jesus' human soul is only potentially, not actually, only *in potentia,* not *in actu,* confronted with the abundance and totality of the vision of God. The Scotist Frassen does right to emphasize (*Scot. Acad.,* 1720, v. VII, p. 450): *Probabilius est, intellectum Christi non videre omnia quae Deus videt scientia visionis, sed dumtaxat aliqua idque non actualiter, sed habitualiter.*

The second limitation of Jesus' human soul is peculiar to Jesus alone. It is drawn by his messianic task and mission. Jesus' redemptive powers are rooted in the moral freedom with which the work of redemption is fulfilled. If the vision of God of Jesus' humanity had been absolutely unconfined, it would set certain limits to this sovereign freedom, for it would have imposed an inner compulsion upon Jesus' human volition, like a *necessitas interna* restricting all freedom. On the other hand, it would have poured such an abundant measure of bliss upon the emotional life of Jesus that his soul would have lost all sensitivity to human suffering, and he could never have been the Lamb of God who gave his life for our sake. His suffering would be only the appearance of suffering, and the heresy of Docetism would not be far to seek. And so the vision of God of Jesus' humanity must be restricted even with regard to his volition and his feeling, it must be a *visio partialis,* never extending so far as to affect Jesus' moral freedom or his capability of suffering. Where Scholasticism did not follow Duns Scotus, it overlooked both restrictions upon Jesus' vision of God.

The objects of the visio beatifica

To what, in detail, was this vision of God directed? This question inquires after the *object* of Jesus' specific vision of God. Above all, it is certain that if Jesus' human soul, within the limits just discussed, directly contemplates the being of God, it must also within the same limits be capable of perceiving *all the potentialities* that belong to the divine being. For the infinite realm of possibilities is identical with the being of God, and the infinite abundance of ideas that belongs to it. So Jesus' soul must have been capable of surveying all the possibilities of his actions pertaining to his messianic mission, and of making his decisions accordingly. We say that, potentially, it has access to all the possibilities that are necessarily implied in the being of God. And, actually, it is able to make use of them at the moment when this is required by his peculiar messianic task, his office as redeemer and judge. If we may call this survey of all possibilities "knowledge," then we can speak of a relative omniscience on the part of our Lord's human soul. It is omniscient because in principle it comprehends everything that God knows. And it is a relative omniscience because it is given only potentially, only according to its capabilities, and put into action only successively, from one case to the next, according to the decision of Jesus' free will.

But what of Jesus' knowledge of reality, all the processes of nature and history, in heaven and upon earth? The realm of the real is not necessarily identical with the realm of the possible. Rather the two are separated by the free decision of God to realize this thing or that out of the infinite realm of the possible. For only what God wills is realized. *Ipse dixit et facta sunt.* So it does not necessarily follow from the direct vision of God of Jesus' soul that it will have knowledge of all reality. This would make it conceivable that Jesus had no knowledge of when the Day of Judgement would be. But if nevertheless he did know this day, and anything else in reality—within the limitations we have discussed—he did not owe this to his direct vision of God by itself, but to a new, fresh, free decision of will on the part of the triune God. Whether this is the case, we can learn only from revelation. The Holy Scripture does not make a direct statement on our question. But we can conclude indirectly from St. John that Jesus' human intellect must have been capable of knowing all reality, within the limitations drawn for him. For John does not make any exceptions to what the Son "sees the Father doing." "For whatever he does, this the Son also does in like manner" (John 5.19). And the Logion in Matthew and Luke that we have already quoted is similar testimony: "All things have been delivered to me by my Father; and no one knows . . . the Father except the Son." So in principle Jesus' knowledge seems to be just as unlimited as the Father's. St. Thomas' declaration is brief and concise (*Summa Theologica*, III, qu. 10, a. 2): *Nulli intellectui beato deest, quin cognoscat in Verbo omnia, quae ad ipsum spectant. Ad Christum autem et ad ejus dignitatem spectant quodammodo omnia* ("Yet no beatified intellect fails to know in the Word whatever pertains to it. Now to Christ and to his honour, all things to some extent belong, inasmuch as all things are subject to him.")

Jesus' knowledge of the day of the Last Judgement

This compels us to find an answer to the great problem posed by no less a one than Jesus himself when he expressly assures us in Mark 13.32, "But of that day or hour [the Last Judgement] no one knows, neither the angels in heaven, nor the Son, but the Father only." According to this, there is at least one fact in the future that is unknown to Jesus—the hour of the Last Judgement. Who is right here? Jesus or the theologians? Jesus, or the Holy Office, which on the seventh of June, 1918, published a decretal declaring, firstly, that one may not deny Jesus' *scientia visionis* in a public lecture; secondly, that one may not publicly dispute the doctrine of Jesus' relative omniscience; thirdly, that one may not publicly maintain that the assertions of certain modern theologians of Jesus' limited knowledge are equally justified as the Scholastic view that our Lord's knowledge was unlimited.

If in answering this question we had only the choice between Jesus and the theologians, we should know at once whose side to take. Where Jesus speaks out clearly, it is the theologians' task to interpret, not to misinterpret. And where they obviously misinterpret, we must for Jesus' sake refuse to follow them. Moreover, we know that the decretals of the Holy Office, even when they are confirmed by the Pope *in forma communi,* are by no means infallible. With particular reference to the decretal in question, P. Dieckmann, S.J., pointed out that the Office only forbids lecturing in public upon the opposing opinion, but does not forbid private inquiry into the problem, and that there is certainly the possibility that this decree of the Holy Office will one day have to be corrected.

What is the situation in our question? It is striking that although Jesus avers that the Son has no knowledge of the Day of Judgement, he nevertheless expressly declares in John 5.27 that *the Judgement is in the hands of the Son.* "And he [the Father] has granted him power to render judgement, because he is the Son of Man." According to Matthew 7.21, it will be the Son who says to the damned, "Depart from me, you workers of iniquity." According to Matthew 13.41, "The Son of Man will send forth his angels, and they will gather out of his kingdom all scandals and those who work iniquity, and cast them into the furnace of fire." According to Matthew 19.28 ff., as well as the Son of Man, who "shall sit on the throne of his glory," the twelve Apostles too will "sit on twelve thrones, judging the twelve tribes of Israel." And according to the mighty picture of the Last Judgement that Christ depicts in Matthew 25.31 ff., the Son of Man surrounded by all his angels will appear as the king of the new kingdom, and separate the sheep from the goats, according to whether they gave him to eat when he was hungry, or not. St. Paul too describes the Incarnate One as our judge. "For all of us must be made manifest before the tribunal of Christ" (2 Cor. 5.10; cf. 1 Thess. 4.6; 1 Cor. 4.4). This would *a priori* make it remarkable that the Son of Man should not have known the hour of the Day of Judgement. Are the theologians really misinterpreting a clear statement of our Lord's, or are they rather offering the correct commentary on his words, and ensuring them against dangerously false interpretations? That such a misinterpretation was possible, and had been feared in the very earliest days of Christianity, can be seen from the fact that in several manuscripts, the Gospel according to St. Matthew omits the perilous saying about the Son's ignorance. And so in Matthew the Logion is already to be found in a completely straightforward form: "Of that day and hour no one knows, not even the angels of heaven, but the Father only" (Matt. 24.36). In fact, in the subsequent period, this saying of our Lord's underwent great distortion in the hands of the Arian heretics, and even now it is often adduced to destroy the incarnate mystery of Jesus. With reference to this passage, the Arians attempted to find a basis for their main thesis that the Logos was a created being. Here was the proof that the Logos was the *Deus inferior,* lacking the Father's omniscience, and ignorant of the Day of Judgement. They interpreted the Logion as referring to the divinity of Jesus, the Logos. This was the first great misunderstanding the theologians were called upon to resolve. In their first attack on the Arians, they evidently did not proceed with a sufficiently precise dialectic. In order to deny ignorance on the part of the Logos, the divine person, they ascribed it to Jesus' humanity. And so the anti-Arian Fathers, primarily Athanasius, Basil, Gregory of Nazianzus, and Cyril of Alexandria, arrived at the thesis that it was not the Logos, but only Jesus' human soul, that was ignorant of the Last Day. And they did not reflect any further on the psychological difficulty of whether it was conceivable that the selfsame identity should be at the same time knowing and unknowing.

The second misunderstanding of the Logion, in a certain sense even more dangerous than the first, made its appearance with the Deacon Themistius Calonymus of Alexandria. He was a Monophysite, and a spokesman of the heretics known as the Agnoëtae. According to their view, Christ's nature was neither purely divine nor purely human, but he possessed a new compound nature which was distinguished from the divine nature precisely by this ignorance of the hour of the Last Judgement. Themistius and his followers took this Logion of the Son's ignorance as the foundation for their Monophysite view of the Lord's compound nature. It was no longer sufficient for orthodox theology to oppose this by simply removing the ignorance from the Logos and ascribing it to his humanity. For Themistius maintained that not only was the Logos ignorant, but also Christ in his entirety, the synthesis of Logos with the human nature. To cut the ground away from under this proof, the Fathers were compelled to probe the question whether Jesus' words of the Son's unknowing were to be taken literally, or whether they admitted of another interpretation. If this unknowing had to be ascribed to the entire, actual Christ, it became difficult, indeed impossible, to range the God-man in the same line as the omnipotent God. The theory of Jesus' compound nature could not be decisively overcome from this position.

Finally, it was a Christological interest of the first degree that enabled the most skillful opponent of the Agnoëtae, the Patriarch Eulogius of Alexandria (d. 607), to demonstrate that Jesus' humanity too was completely free of error, because it was united with the omniscient Logos, itself completely incapable of error; thus he was able to brand as a heresy the doctrine that the concrete Christ within the hypostatic union had no knowledge of the Last Judgement. Pope Gregory the Great praised Eulogius in two epistles, and in doing so gave an explanation of the passage in Mark which was significant for its theological interpretation. He distinguished between the humanity of Christ which was joined with the Logos in the hypostatic union, and the humanity of Christ that is conceived as detached from the Logos. On the basis of this distinction he established: *in humanitate,* that is, in the concrete hypostatic union, Christ possessed the omniscience of God; but not *ex humanitate.* Christ's humanity by itself has no knowledge of the Last Judgement. When Christ declares he does not know when the Last Day will be, he is speaking *more humano,* out of his human disposition. Since Gregory the Great, the fact can no longer be shaken that the concrete God-man had an *unlimited knowledge.* This is expressly formulated in proposition 34 of the new Syllabus. It rejects the modernistic assertion that it is historically untenable and contrary to all sound moral sense that Christ should have had unlimited knowledge, and yet should never have communicated anything of it, either to his disciples or to posterity. There were a number of Greek Fathers of the Church, such as Leontius of Byzantium, Sophronius, Patriarch of Jerusalem, Maximus of Constantinople, and John of Damascus, who shared the view of Eulogius and Gregory.

To sum up: Christ declares that even the Son does not know the day of the Last Judgement. On the other hand, the Ecclesiastical Office assures us that the Son does know the day of the Last Judgement, for he knows everything *in Verbo,* in the Logos in which his humanity subsists. And this assurance is based not on any superficial or unrealistic theorizing, but upon the Church's solemn care for the preservation of Christ's incarnate mystery. How can this antinomy be solved? Three different interpretations have attempted a solution. The one put forward by the anti-Arian Fathers, that Jesus' unknowing belongs to his humanity within the hypostatic union, is no longer acceptable since Gregory the Great. A second, equally untenable theory was put forward by Origen and his successors. They ascribed the Lord's ignorance to the mystical Christ, the Christ whose body is the Church. In content, this explanation amounts to the same as the third theory. Hilary, Augustine, and Gregory the Great assumed that by these words Christ meant only to say that his knowledge was *not communicable to his disciples.* As the Messias, it was not his part to reveal this knowledge. In itself, this is a useful explanation. But it must avoid giving the impression that Christ was deliberately disguising the truth, making a kind of mental reservation. Christ was too upright for anyone to impute such an equivocation to him. His yes meant yes, and his no meant no. So we must assume that the entire situation in which he said these words to his disciples was such that the disciples too could understand the sense in which he implied his unknowing. Mark does not give us any details of the circumstance in which the Lord uttered these words. However, the assumption would seem to be confirmed by the observation that on that occasion the disciples certainly did understand the Lord's meaning. It is a fact that in other contexts, too, Jesus speaks of "not knowing." But he does not mean it in the strict, literal sense; it was rather, as it were, a didactic ignorance implying the absence of any wish to know. According to Matt. 7.22 f., he will say to the damned, "I never knew you" (οὐδέποτε ἔγνων ὑμᾶς). The context makes it clear that in fact he knew the damned perfectly well. They will say to him, "Lord, Lord, did we not prophesy in thy name, and work many miracles in thy name?" Similarly in the parable of the ten virgins, Jesus says to the foolish virgins who wish to be admitted at night, "I do not know you" (οὐκ οἶδα ὑμᾶς, Matt. 25.13). But since these foolish virgins belonged to the bridegroom's closest acquaintance, there is no doubt he must have known them very well. When he speaks of his unknowing, he really means his unwillingness to know. Moreover, it may be observed that after our Lord's resurrection, his disciples asked him whether he would not in the glory of his resurrection restore the kingdom to Israel. And he gave them the significant reply, "It is not for you to know the times or dates which the Father has fixed by his own authority" (Acts 1.7). Being the Messias, on this point he has no revelation to make to the disciples.

It is true that even this interpretation leaves open the question whether this passage in Mark 13 does not present a conscious concealment on the part of our Lord. He seems to behave as if he did not know the day of the Last Judgement, although he really knows it. Why does he not say outright, as he did after his resurrection, "It is not for you to know the times or dates"?

We therefore prefer the following explanation. As we have already established, relative omniscience is proper to our Lord's human consciousness only *secundum potentiam,* not *secundum actum.* Because Jesus' human soul belonged to the self of the Logos, all knowledge is objectively and in principle available to it. His possession of it was potential. Every time his messianic mission made it necessary, he could draw with the cup of his human intellect from the infinite spring of divine wisdom. But because in each case this knowledge was due to a free act of Grace on the part of the triune God, Jesus could not, and might not, make arbitrary use of it, but only "when his hour had come," at its most profound, when his Father's will required it. Usually, it remained potential knowledge, and not actual knowledge. It remained in his unconscious, hidden beneath the threshold of his daylight consciousness. Only when his hour was come, could and might he by way of contemplation realize this potential knowledge given him by Grace into his actual consciousness. Now it was the Father's will, as Christ resurrected expressly declared (Acts 1.7), that the day of the Last Judgement fixed by his authority should remain unrevealed. It was a reservation on the part of the triune God. Therefore the Lord refused to reflect upon the day and the hour and to call his potential knowledge into realization. His Logion in which he says he did not know the day of the Last Judgement is thus to be taken *literally.* In fact, he did not know the Last Day, for "the Father has fixed [it] by his own authority."

*　　　*　　　*　　　*

Our solution of the problem proceeds from the Scotist assumption that Jesus' human soul possessed only the capacity for the *scientia visionis,* but that he would use this capacity—

in fact, did use it—only from time to time, according to the declared will of the Father—when his hour had come.

Jesus' expectation of the end

Now the assertion that in his humanity Christ had no knowledge of the Last Day is already hostile to the hypostatic mystery. But even more harm is done by the other idea, that Christ's knowledge of the Last Day was *positively false,* and that he lived in the illusion that the Last Judgement was immediately at hand, and that he built his entire message upon this illusion. Since Jesus was fully man, it would be quite conceivable that as a child of his time he might cherish certain ideas of the age, even if they were wrong. That our knowledge should be determined by the age we live in is the lot of man, and Jesus was wholly man. But it is a very different state of affairs when, as the moderns would have it, this false historical knowledge is made the basis and turning point of Jesus' entire message, as if he had constructed his entire proclamation upon this one illusion.

Among Catholic theologians, it has been Tyrrell, Loisy, and Schnitzer, in particular, who have thought they were compelled to ascribe to Jesus this error concerning his Parousia. In this work, *Hat Jesus das Papsttum gestiftet?* (Augsburg, 1910), Schnitzer writes (p. 27): "Jesus' sky is lit by the blood-red sun of evening. The dark idea of the looming end of the world allows no clear joy to dawn at the speedy death of the consecrated things of this world. The end draws near. The Judgement is at the gates. The Lord may appear at any moment for the last decisive struggle. There is no place here for petty cares and distracting anxieties when the heart is full of the one great urgency! If the end is near and the Lord is girded, what need of a Church, a Pope? Because Jesus was convinced that the end was near, he could utter his blazing cry, 'Repent, for the kingdom of heaven is at hand.' He could make his harsh demand, 'If thy right hand is an occasion of sin to thee, cut it off,' 'Let the dead bury their dead!' That was why he was conscious that he had come to proclaim the great new thing that was to come. His own mystery would be fulfilled only when the great thing that was to come made its appearance in the heavens. That is why all he has to say is aimed at the immediate present, and is provisional in character. Jesus does not think of setting up a great foundation, the Eucharist, or Repentance, or Baptism, or the Church, because in his consciousness all this was unnecessary. The end of the world was at hand. Why establish such permanent institutions?" It is clear that from this kind of starting point it will be impossible to discuss any theandric self-consciousness in Jesus. He is nothing but a visionary, clinging to an *idée fixe* determined by the age he lived in, the illusion that the end of the world was due in the immediate future. Schnitzer, and other modernistic Christologists similar to him, base their views in essentials upon the statements of the eschatological school. What texts does this school refer to? In his great eschatological sermon, common to all three Synoptic Gospels (Matt. 24.1 ff.; Mark 13.1 ff.; Luke 21.5 ff.), the Lord recounts various calamities as the sign of his coming. Among the abominations is the desolation of holy places, and the appearance of false Christs and false prophets. Then Jesus continues, "But immediately after the tribulation of those days" (εὐθέως δὲ μετὰ τὴν θλίψιν, Matt. 24.29) there will come mighty catastrophes among the stars. The sign of the Son of Man will appear in heaven, and his angels will be sent out with a trumpet, "and they will gather his elect from the four winds" (v. 31). This passage would make it appear that Jesus related his coming very closely in time with the destruction of Jerusalem. This interpretation is strengthened by another utterance of Jesus', which is also reported in all three Synoptic Gospels (Mark 13.30; Matt. 24.34; Luke 21.32): "Amen I say to you, this generation will not pass away till all these things have been accomplished." Another remark of the Lord's makes it clear what he means by "this generation": "Amen I say to you, there are some of those standing here who will not taste death, until they have seen the Son coming in his kingdom" (Matt. 16.28; Mark 8.39; Luke 9.27). According to this, Jesus would seem to have been of the opinion that there were some among his contemporaries who would live to see the end of the world. This opinion would have been erroneous, and apt to discredit our Lord's entire proclamation. What can be said about it, from the point of view of an unprejudiced evaluation of the entire Gospel picture in general, and the texts we have quoted in particular?

1. It is certain that Jesus' message had a marked eschatological tendency. Its climax is the proclamation of the coming of the kingdom. The heart of his sermon expects the

final settlement to be brought by the end of time. The Beatitudes are made with an eye to future rewards: "Blessed are they who hunger and thirst for justice, for they shall be satisfied." His parables make it a duty that mankind should be prepared for the great things that are to come. His parables of the talents, the wise and foolish virgins, the unjust steward, the marriage feast, all transfer the true reckoning, the resolution of tension, to the end of the world. Jesus' message is eschatological in the sense that the kingdom of God will appear not in this age but in the future, "on that day." The good fish will not be separated from the bad, the sheep from the goats, or the wheat from the tares, until the Last Judgement. Those are the last words that he has to say to the Jews: "They will see the Son of Man coming upon the clouds of heaven with great power and majesty."

2. But Jesus' proclamation does not imply that the kingdom of heaven is to be expected only in the future. Its consummation and outward glory are certainly reserved for a future aeon. But its foundations are laid in the *immediate present*. The powers of this kingdom are being planted even now. Luke takes over Mark's version of the great eschatological sermon without any omissions, and thus most certainly does not offer any theology of mediation, nor does he try to water down the eschatological ideas, as Loisy would suggest (*The Gospel and the Church,* Eng. tr., New York, 1912). The same Luke records a Logion of the Lord's which confirms the presence of the kingdom of God within the hearts of the faithful. The Pharisees ask Jesus, "When is the kingdom of God coming?" The question we are concerned with was being posed in all manner of ways. The Lord replies, "The kingdom of God comes unawares" (or: "not with observation"). The Greek expression μετὰ παρατηρήσεως is a metaphor taken from sailors' usage. It means observation of the stars during an ocean voyage. So from this it would seem that the appearance of the kingdom of heaven cannot be perceived and observed from outward signs. In this sense, the Lord continues, "Neither will they say, 'Behold, here it is,' or 'Behold, there it is.' For behold, the kingdom of God is within you" (ἐντὸς ἡμῶν ἐστίν, Luke 17.21). This "within you" is understood to mean that the kingdom of God already exists within the world of the Jews, but unknown and unregarded. There is no need to await it as an outward manifestation. Invisible as yet, it is among the Jews here and now. Its powers are as yet still hidden, like the leaven that invisibly works through the entire

dough. It is not a geographical or racial concept. It does not correspond to the children of Israel, nor yet to any outward community, such as the Church. Its bounds are drawn by the conscience alone. There where the new, good men, the disciples of Jesus, are to be found, is the kingdom of heaven. With these words, Jesus describes the kingdom of heaven as a spiritual power immanent in this world, revealed not by outward observation but invisibly within the conscience. This reveals the real point of Jesus' message, his emphasis on inward spirituality, his fundamentally moral and religious position. The kingdom of heaven is the kingdom of the love of child for father, and the warmth, vigour, and love that spring from this love. This is the very characteristic of Jesus' message that is overlooked by the eschatological school. In their view, the Lord must have gazed fixedly upon the one point, the end of the world. But if we look at the fundamental thought animating Jesus' sermon, we shall find that Jesus' main purpose was the inner world of the good, clear conscience. His lifelong struggle against the Pharisees arises from his fundamental intentions for the inner life. This is why he condemned all outward show and Pharisaical pride of achievement, "all that is seen and praised by man," because it was hostile to the essence of religious subjectivity, which was his greatest concern. His intent as a teacher comes of itself with his other fundamental concept of the "Father." This is what ultimately gives meaning to his message of the kingdom of God. It is not fit and proper to interpret his proclamation of the kingdom of God from late Judaic, eschatological, apocalyptic writings, but rather from his own central concept of the Father and the message of filial love and spirituality that accompanies it. His words of the inwardness of the kingdom of God, which Luke alone hands down to us, are not due to any particular "theology of mediation" on the part of the Evangelist, but are anchored in the heart of Jesus' own message, rooted in his ethic, whose end is the immanence of the kingdom of God.

Christ emphasizes this immanence so strongly that in comparison the eschatological and transcendent tendencies in his proclamation of the kingdom of God pale into insignificance. Indeed, scarcely half the texts in the Synoptic Gospels referring to the Son of Man have an eschatological meaning. The other half refer to his ministry of salvation in the immediate present. His eschatological expectation refers to the future only to the extent that it also *includes the present.* For precisely by reminding and warning man's conscience in the present, and by preparing him for the ultimate decision of the Last Judgement, Christ proclaimed himself to be the Lord and judge of the future. The immanence of the kingdom of God is emphasized so strongly in the Gospels that there have been a number of Protestant theologians, such as Ritschl and Harnack, who have regarded this immanence as the foundation of Jesus' entire message, and are inclined to assume that the eschatological texts are supplementary insertions, "apocalyptic writing by a Jewish hand" (Wellhausen). But this conception, too, goes too far. Jesus' doctrine was not one of pure immanence, just as it was not one of pure eschatological transcendence. It was both: filial love of the Father planted in the hearts of the faithful would bring about the blossoming of the great kingdom of God that one day would come. The parables of the sower and of the mustard seed achieve their ultimate significance from this double meaning. They do not describe the kingdom of God as a divine act that suddenly breaks forth in all its power and glory, but a gradually maturing life, as yet still hidden in secret, and present only in delicate seeds; but one day it will grow and become a large tree, and the birds of heaven will dwell in its branches. We must hold fast to this: Jesus does not stand in the line of the apocalyptic writers, but in the line of the prophets; in particular, he follows Daniel, who regarded the coming kingdom, or rather its descent from heaven, only as the final stage in the history of the kingdom of God.

Whenever Jesus is questioned about the day or hour when the kingdom will come, he declines to answer. He ends his great eschatological prophecy with the significant Logion, "But of that day and hour no one knows, not even the angels of heaven, nor the Son, but the Father only" (Matt. 24.36). Jesus is not simply refusing to give further details of the coming Parousia. He is also quite unambiguously declaring that he does not know (we have already established that his unknowing was only actual, of the moment, and not potential). He only wants to emphasize that the Parousia will come. There is no point in asking when it will come. The Lord shows the same reluctance after his resurrection to say anything about the day and hour of the Last Judgement. When the disciples ask him whether he will restore the kingdom to Israel, here, too, he answers with a refusal. "It is not for you to know the times or dates which the Father has fixed by his own authority" (Acts 1.7).

His parables reveal that perhaps that day and hour might

be postponed until far into the future. The parable of the
weeds among the wheat (Matt. 13.24 f.) takes a long time
for granted before "the blade sprang up and brought forth
fruit," until the time of "harvest" comes, when the servants
will root out the weeds. The parable of the talents gives us
the picture of a man who embarks on a long journey, and
first entrusts the administration of his property to the hands
of his servants. During this time, the zealous servants "traded"
with the talents that had fallen to their share, until they had
increased them twofold. "Then after a long time" (Matt.
25.19), the master returned and settled accounts with his
servants. The parable of the wise and foolish virgins expressly
emphasizes that the bridegroom was so "long in coming that
they all became drowsy and slept. And at midnight a cry
arose, 'Behold, the bridegroom is coming'" (Matt. 25.5–6).
The marriage feast of the king's son is similarly delayed
(Matt. 22.2 ff.). On two occasions the king sends out his
servants to summon the guests: "But they made light of it,
and went off, one to his farm and another to his business,
and the rest laid hold of his servants, treated them shame-
fully, and killed them." Then the king sent his armies to
punish the evil-doers, and burn their city. Thereupon the king
sent out his servants for a third time: "Go therefore to the
crossroads and invite to the marriage feast whomever you
shall find. And now at last the marriage feast was filled with
guests." All these apparently eschatological parables assume
a very long time of waiting. When Jesus taught them, he obviously did not have in mind that the Parousia should come
very shortly, but that it would be a long time before the
end broke upon the world.

Just as Jesus is clear in his indications that he will not
come until after a long time of waiting, so he is clear that
when he does come, it will be *suddenly* and unexpectedly.
This is probably the key to our understanding of the early
Christian belief that the Son of Man would come very soon.
It was easy enough for the early Christians to interpret his
promise, "The Son of Man will come suddenly," to mean,
"The Son of Man will come immediately." The entire age was
vibrant with the belief that the new era was about to dawn
at any day or hour, and so it was psychologically disposed
to understand Christ's words of his sudden coming as the
proclamation of his immediate coming. All the terrors of persecution helped to increase their passionate desire for the
second coming, and to interpret in Jesus' words what they

so much desired. And so we may understand why there was no crisis of faith among the early Christians when hopes were disappointed as the end of the world did not come about. The eschatological expectation existed only in the popular faith, but not in the Church's proclamation of salvation. And so, as the millennium did not come, the belief died out of its own accord, without any great disturbance of spirit. In the second Epistle to the Thessalonians, we hear only the faintest echo of these eschatological expectations. While the first Epistle of St. Peter still warns, "The end of all things is at hand" (4.7), the second Epistle (3.8) recalls "that one day with the Lord is as a thousand years, and a thousand years as one day." The Evangelists themselves admit of no doubt that the Lord did not originally speak of the immediate coming of his Parousia, but that it would come suddenly and unexpectedly. He closes his great eschatological sermon with a warning that throws a great deal of light on his true meaning. "Watch, therefore, for you do not know at what hour your Lord is to come. But of this be assured, that if the householder had known at what hour the thief was coming, he would certainly have watched, and not have let his house be broken into. Therefore you also must be ready, because at an hour that you do not expect, the Son of Man will come" (Matt. 24.42 ff.). According to Luke's account, our Lord stresses the suddenness of his second coming, as well as the uncertainty as to its hour: ". . . at an hour that you do not expect, the Son of Man is coming" (Luke 12.40). "For as the lightning when it lightens flashes from one end of the sky to the other, so will the Son of Man be in his day" (17.24). "Like a snare" (21.35), and "like a thief in the night" (12.39), the Son of Man will appear. "Watch, then, praying at all times, that you may be accounted worthy . . ." (21.36).

But how can this explain those utterances of Jesus' which we quoted at the beginning of our discussion, that the judgement would take place immediately after the destruction of Jerusalem (Matt. 24.29) and that "there are some of those standing here who will not taste death till they have seen the Son of Man coming in his kingdom"? We shall first discuss the great eschatological sermon, and its main proposition, "Immediately after the tribulation of those days"—that is, immediately after the destruction of Jerusalem—there will be mighty catastrophes among the stars, and then will appear the sign of the Son of Man in heaven. What is the meaning of this

apparent adverb of time, "immediately"? The sermon first recounts the disasters that will herald the coming of the Son of
Man. The tribulations begin when false Christs arise (Matt.
24.5). Then nation shall rise against nation (v. 7). The disciples will be "hated by all nations" (v. 9). But the Gospel
shall be "preached in the whole world" (v. 14). This will be
followed by the abomination of desolation in the holy places
(v. 15), and again by the appearance of false Christs with
signs and wonders (v. 24). Only then, hard upon them
(v. 29), shall there be mighty catastrophes among the stars,
and the Last Judgement. The very enumeration of these disasters makes it clear that a considerable time will pass between the fall of Jerusalem and the coming of the Son of Man.
It will be heralded by international wars, world wars. By
their very nature, these will last for many years. Christianity
will be preached "in the whole world." This is something that
assumes centuries. Christians will be "hated by all nations"
—this requires still more time, if this hate is to be understood as the reaction of evil to the profound effectiveness of
the Christian idea. So we are confronted with a difficulty. On
the one hand, Jesus enumerates disasters that require long
periods to develop in, and in any case cannot be unfolded
within the space of one generation. On the other hand, he
leaves no doubt that the Last Judgement will come in "this
generation," and some at least will live to see it.

The most immediate explanation of this difficulty would be
that the Evangelists, imprisoned in the errors of their age,
had read their own false views into Jesus' words; it might be
assumed that the error was not the Lord's doing, but the
Evangelists'. But this interpretation cannot be reconciled with
the dogma of inspiration. So Catholic commentators prefer
the explanation that our Lord's utterances in this speech are
to be interpreted as a *prophetic vision,* and that his "immediate coming" is not to be regarded in a chronological, historical
sense, but as part of the course of salvation. Jesus and his
tidings were seen in the perspective of the prophets. This
would comprehend all the temporal disparities in one logical
unity, and arrange the details not in historical sequence but
in their place within the context of the course of our salvation. Within this context, the fall of Jerusalem acquires primary significance in the history of salvation. For it is not the
fall of any ordinary town, but the fall of the old covenant,
divine judgement upon the first-born of Jahve, because they
did not know the time of their visitation. In Jesus' prophetic

view, the fall of Jerusalem signifies the first act of the judgement of the world, the true introduction of the looming Last
Judgement. To Jesus, the town's fall was already part of the
great new thing that came unawares into the world with his
mission, and will reach its fulfilment in the Parousia of the
Lord. And because the fall of Jerusalem, the overture to the
Last Judgement, would take place within this generation,
then, indeed, many of Christ's listeners would be witness to
this judgement. Whether the end of the world would follow
immediately upon the fall of Jerusalem was an historical
question that did not occur to the Lord; he was concerned
exclusively with the essential connexion between the fall of
Jerusalem and the end of the world. This gives us an un-
clouded understanding of the term "immediately" in the great
eschatological speech, as well as of the expressions "this generation" and "some of those standing here" who will live to
see the Parousia. The Evangelists' "immediately" is not to be
understood as a *true adverb of time*. Rather it serves as an
extension of the prophetic tone, and is intended to illuminate
the inner connexions between the events Christ pictures and
the Parousia of the Son of Man. This is why Mark lays hardly
any emphasis upon the expression at all, but uses the customary phrase "in those days" (13.24). With the simplifica-
tion "and then," Luke ascribes all the events to "the times of
the nations" (21.24). To sum up: 1. Jesus repeatedly states
that it is not up to him to establish the time of the Last Day.
He gives sufficient indication in a number of parables that
there will be a long time of waiting before he comes to judge
the world. 2. The highest peak of his entire message is the
foundation of the kingdom of God by preparing men's hearts
for the greatness that is to come. The kingdom of God is immanent as well as transcendent. 3. What Jesus wants to stress
to the disciples is not that the Lord is about to come soon,
but that his coming will be sudden and unexpected. 4. In his
prophetic view, the very miracle of his appearance, the
epiphany of the Son of Man, with all the upheavals that such
an appearance will bring about in the world, including the fall
of Jerusalem, is already a partial impulse towards the judgement of the world, and his second coming.

THE WORK OF CHRIST

We are redeemed by Christ because he is the way to the Father. By his message of eternal truth he redeemed man's erring thoughts. By his Grace and love he redeemed man's will, weakened by sin. By his incarnate nature, he redeemed our fallen nature in all its associations. These are the new powers of redemption: Christ's tidings, Christ's Grace, and Christ's incarnate being. We shall first discuss the redemption of human thought. This is the way of truth, along which Christ leads us to the Father.

XX

REDEMPTION FROM ERROR AND SIN THROUGH CHRIST

The redemption of human thought

JESUS was clearly conscious that he had been sent from the Father to be as a guide to the blind, and as a light in the darkness. The Gospel according to St. Matthew in particular places our Lord's consciousness of his mission as a teacher well to the fore. Jesus is the great teacher who, like a wise householder, draws "old things and new" out of his store. This pedagogic mission of the coming Messias is clearly foretold in the Old Testament. God says to Moses, "I will raise them up a prophet out of the midst of their brethren like to thee. And I will put my words in his mouth: and he shall speak to them all that I command him" (Deut. 18.18). In his first speech at Nazareth, Jesus himself refers to one of Isaias' sayings: "The spirit of the Lord is upon me, because the Lord hath anointed me. He hath sent me to preach to the meek, to heal the contrite of heart" (61.1). He knew that this prophecy was fulfilled in his own person. And so he does nothing to prevent the Jewish people from regarding him as a teacher and prophet (Matt. 16.14; 21.11, *et al.*), or his disciples from referring to him quite simply as "master," or "teacher" (διδίάσκαλος). "You call me Master and Lord, and you say well, for so I am" (εἰμὶ γάρ, John 13.13). He regards himself as the only true Master, or teacher. "Neither be called masters; for only one is your master, the Christ" (Matt. 23.10). The rabbis are false teachers, blind and foolish. They bind heavy and insupportable burdens, and lay them on men's shoulders, for they will not bear them themselves, and so they shut the kingdom of heaven against men. Matthew in particular constantly stresses the Lord's unique didactic mission, in contrast to the false teachings of the Pharisees. In the Gospel according to St. John, too, Jesus' task of redemption through truth is thrown into sharp relief. "I am the light of the world" (8.12). "I am the way, and the truth, and the life" (14.6). "If anyone thirst, let him come to me and drink. He who believes in me . . . from within him there shall flow rivers of living water" (7.37, 38).

This consciousness of being the teacher, and the redeemer from error, cannot be separated from our picture of Jesus. When Pilate, that child of an age devoured by scepticism, asks him, "Thou art then a King?" rejected of the world, a carpenter in chains, he replies with sovereign confidence, "Thou sayest it; I am a King. This is why I was born, and why I have come into the world, to bear witness to the truth. Everyone who is of the truth hears my voice" (John 18.37). And history has confirmed his testimony, though Pilate shrugged his shoulders and in bitterness replied, "What is truth?" Truth was standing incarnate before him. The centuries have proved it. Like a sower, Jesus has walked the field of mankind, sowing his precious seed of eternal wisdom and power (cf. Esser, *Jesus Christus, der göttliche Lehrer der Menscheit,* p. 212).

Great teachers had already arisen before Jesus, claiming to announce the truth: Buddha, Zoroaster, Socrates, Plato, and all the philosophers, great and small, who believed they had something to say to mankind. In Jesus' time there were the wandering Cynics, who preached a popular version of the wisdom of the Stoa. And yet, of all these teachers of mankind great and small, what has remained? Zoroaster lives on only in the history of religion; Buddha's teaching has been so distorted that even the most laborious examination of the ancient texts can hardly ascertain what his original doctrine was. In its original form, it seems to have survived only on the little island of Ceylon. And all the other teachers of the ancient world, the Academics, the Stoics, the Neo-Platonists, and the rest—we would hardly know anything about them if their literary testimonies had not by fortunate accident been preserved. And it is not much different with the philosophers of the modern world. Their systems survive in their writings more than in the hearts of men. There is only one teacher who is still alive among us—Jesus. And we have no need of books and writings to learn what he taught. His knowledge has become our conscience. And today this teaching still pours out its infinite light upon the dark places of our existence.

How is this? The deepest and most secret reason is that he was an incarnate teacher, whose human thought was united to the Logos, who revealed not only one truth to us, but the absolute truth. All further questions cease before Jesus' message. There is no getting beyond it. Mankind can stray from Jesus' way of truth, and it can turn back to it. But we cannot make it straighter than it is, nor carry it further than Jesus has shown. The history of philosophy is the history of human inquiry and human error, not the history of truth. Truth has no history. It is an eternal present, the word of Jesus. The next reason for the enormously effective power of Jesus' message lies in the special way in which he offers it to us, but also in the mighty new thing that Jesus proclaims to us. Jesus is the divine teacher on account of his particular way of teaching, on the one hand, and on account of the richness of content in his doctrine, on the other; because of both the form and the substance of his message.

Jesus' unique way of teaching

From the point of view of form, the most striking thing about Jesus' message is its originality, springing directly out of the depths of his own consciousness. He grew up in the simple workshop of a carpenter, and was never exposed to the aids and expedients of human culture. There is no one who can boast of having been Jesus' teacher. When his fellow countrymen in Nazareth hear him preach, they are astonished, and ask, "How did this man come by this wisdom and these miracles? Is not this the carpenter's son? Is not his mother called Mary?" (Matt 13.53). The source of Jesus' teaching is not in what he has learned, but in his own soul. "I speak what I have seen with the Father" (John 8.38). "We speak of what we know, and we bear witness to what we have seen" (John 3.11). Certainly he is familiar with the books of the Old Testament, the written word of his Father, down to the last detail. He lives and moves and has his being in the language and ideas of the Old Testament. But he does not read it as a devout scholar or submissive disciple; he reads it as the Lord and Master who has come to fulfil it, down to the last iota. The written word of the Old Testament is not the ultimate to him. He bears the ultimate within his messianic consciousness. He reveals this even as a twelve-year-old in the temple. "And all who were listening to him were amazed at his understanding and his answers" (Luke 2.47). And when at the height of his powers he proclaimed his message to the Scribes and Pharisees, "the Jews marvelled, saying, 'How does this man come by learning, since he has not studied?' " (John 7.15). This was something the people sensed immediately, when they went from the Scribes to Jesus. "And they were astonished at his teaching; for he was teaching them as one having authority, and not as the Scribes" (Mark 1.22). Here a man of absolute greatness was at work, who did not search and question after truth, for he already possessed it, yea, he was truth incorporate. For this reason his message was so stirring and powerful, and yet on the other hand so simple and plain. If we may speak of Jesus' style, it lay in his marvellous art of saying the mightiest and most revolutionary things as simply and naturally as if they were self-evident. "Martha, Martha, thou art anxious and troubled about many things; and only one thing is needful." "Unless you turn and become like little children, you will not enter into the kingdom of heaven." "Render to Caesar the things that are Caesar's, and to God the things that are God's." "What does it profit a man if he gain the whole world, but suffer the loss of his own soul?" Vast stretches of humanity are illuminated by these Logia, and made a blazing path of sacrifice and surrender for many. And yet there is nothing bombastic, rhetorical, or forced about these words. The prophetic sermons break forth with incomparably greater violence, filled with rhetorical metaphor and holy wrath. Jesus' words are as quiet and calm, as simple and natural, as he himself was, or the child whom he blessed. Only in his sermons of judgement and battle (cf. Matt. 23) does he recall Jeremias and Osee. All his other sayings are like the flowers of the field. And yet they have become eternal words, as fresh today as when he first uttered them. They are "words of everlasting life," as Peter, the simple fisherman, described them (John 6.69). The simplicity of his greatness is the mark of his divinity. It is the work of man when narrow systems grind away, and the process of logic labours. But where truth shines pure and simple, bathed in its own radiance, there God is at work. Jesus confronts us as an intellectual miracle. And this miracle is revealed in its innermost powers because together with the moral miracle of his radiant sanctity it is comprehended into a *unity* of person. For Jesus did not merely teach as one having authority. He lived his teachings so intensely that the very life he led was the concrete expression of his teaching. Philosophers, as Voltaire once remarked, cannot even convert the people on the streets they live in, because their words are never entirely in accord with their deeds. But what Jesus taught was what he willed; and what he willed, he did. His life is marked by a miraculous unity of the outward and the inner man. There was no disharmony in it, nor any tension between word and deed, ideal and reality. If everything else in the Gospels were nothing but legend and fiction, this is the one thing the Evangelists could not have invented: the closed, firm unity of his life and experience. His doctrine has no better commentary than his own life. And when he went to meet his death, even from the pulpit of the cross, he taught mankind what dying is. Since then we know how we should die, in order to enter into eternal life.

The newness in Jesus' message

We have described the nature of Jesus' teaching from its formal side. Now we shall discuss what was so new in the content of his message. In general terms, we may say that Jesus' true achievement was to have proclaimed *God* to the world in the most consummate way, and this in two respects. Firstly, because he taught us to acknowledge the living God as the ultimate goal and true meaning of our existence. In pre-Christian times, among the Gentiles as well as the Jews, the concept of God had always been distorted in such a way that the Godhead was only the instrument of human needs. But it was Jesus' original achievement to uproot this anthropocentric concept of God and establish God in his absolute self-sufficiency and authority. God has no need of created beings. But created beings certainly have need of him. He alone is the meaning, goal, and content of their lives. Everything is to be given up for the sake of this one pearl, this treasure in the field. He begins the prayer he teaches to the disciples with the supplication, "Hallowed be thy name. Thy kingdom come, thy will be done on earth, as it is in heaven" (Matt. 6.9 ff., Luke 11.2 ff.). Thus Christ set man's devotion free from its bondage to earth, and lifted it up from earth to heaven. Religion was redeemed from the grasp of purely natural ends, and revealed in its true supernatural character.

The second corrective in the concept of God was Jesus' message that God is our Father. The veneration of the heavenly

Father was certainly not unknown even in pre-Christian times, among both Gentiles and Jews. But among the Gentiles it was far less important than the cult of gods and goddesses, while among the Jews the traditional faith in the All-Holy and All-Righteous One allowed no room for a warm and child-like relationship to God the Father. Among Jews and Gentiles, the fundamental emotion in their relation to God was fear. Not until Jesus proclaimed his message did the warm love of child for Father become the centre of religion. To him, the Old Testament commandment "Thou shalt love the Lord thy God with all thy heart" was not just one more commandment among all six hundred and thirteen drawn up by the rabbis; it was the absolute commandment, unique and all-embracing. Christ roused a new passion in mankind by calling up the child's love for the Father. Love, and no longer fear, becomes the basis of all religious devotion.

As Christ discovered God to man, he also revealed to us the mystery of *man*. Since Jesus' teaching we know what man is in himself, and what men are to one another. Before Christ, man was the servant of a tyrant or of the reigning caste; Christ led him to be aware of his own value, and created the ideal of personality that animates the Western soul. The ancient caste system was uprooted, and the human soul established as the highest value by his proclamation of its incomparable worth, of how it was intended for the kingdom of heaven and the Father's love; and again by his message that it was the poor and disinherited who would be called to the wedding feast; and finally, by the miracle of his incarnate sacrifice "for many." This was also the solution to the other question of what men should be to one another. If every man is of an unique and irreplaceable value, then charity, love of one's neighbour, is an incontrovertible command. We are all chil-dren of the selfsame Father, followers of the selfsame Sav-iour, companions of God. This Christian love is different from the abstract ideology of Stoicism, which certainly re-quires charity, but with its precepts of indifference and self-sufficiency deprives it of the warmth of human emotion and passion. Christian love is different from the Buddhist doc-trine of Metta, which understood "good will" to mean only the negative "release of the spirit." Christianity preached love as active, magnanimous, and joyful deeds, even towards one's enemy. It transformed the merely negative formulation, the so-called golden rule of antiquity, into a positive value: Do unto others as you would have them do unto you. By stressing the love of man as much as the love of God, Jesus elevated love of man into a religious demand and gave it the power and absoluteness that is the mark of the divine commandments.

So Jesus' message meant for mankind that the mystery of God and the mystery of man were both unravelled. And in doing this he also revealed the ultimate and most grievous mystery, which had confronted man like the riddle of the Sphinx—the riddle of suffering and death. If God is the meaning of our life, and if God is our Father, suffering and death cannot be the secret work of evil demons, as the heathen feared, nor the cruel issue of an iron law of nature, as the Stoics held, not the result of personal guilt, as the Jews believed. Rather, suffering is presented in its general validity and necessity as the expression of the divine will, the Father's will. But where the Father's will is, there also must be his blessing, his succour, and his salvation. And so suffering and death need no longer be absolute evil, or cruel fate. Because they are in the last analysis supported by the Father's will, they are a means of blessing, however they befall us. And so Christ proclaims the love of the cross. Ever since the day at Cæsarea Philippi when Peter avowed for the first time that Jesus was the Christ, to bear one's cross becomes an essential element in his following. "If anyone wishes to come after me, let him deny himself and take up his cross and follow me." To take up one's cross is an inseparable part of the true Christian way. It is the mystery of the future. It is the power of life. And so suffering, and with it the gloom of the entire ancient world, is changed. The true Christian can suffer and lament, but he can never despair. For it is the Father who sends our suffering.

The redemption of human will

Christ redeemed our erring thoughts through the truths he brought us. But he also redeemed our erring will through the Grace and love which radiate from his incarnate appearance, and which still shine upon us.

However, this is not to say that Christ in no way shared the pessimistic evaluation of the human natural will, or that the essence of his message was a blithe optimism; the marvellous fascination of his being was not that the morbid sense

of sin in the crowd should vanish before him like mist in the
sun, nor that men should come to him to be cured by his
soundness, kindliness, and sanctity, and return to certainty
and forgiveness, though there is a certain amount of truth in
this conception, which we shall discuss later. But it is quite
wrong to suggest that Jesus had no eyes or attention for the
twisted depravities of human nature. Rather does he judge
human nature pessimistically in that he sees it as distinctly
inclined to malice. It is true he describes his disciples in elevated terms. They are the "wedding guests," "sons of light,"
"the salt of the earth," "the light of the world." But he is
thinking of their supernatural calling, and their future ministry as the redeemed and the elect. There is a time, however, when he calls Peter "Satan," and he has his own disciples in mind when he laments, "O unbelieving generation
. . . how long shall I put up with you?" (Mark 9.18). He
himself is too pure, and too deeply understanding, not to be
moved at every turn by man's moral depravity. He says outright to those around him, "You, evil as you are" (Matt.
7.11); "you are evil" (12.34); "an evil and adulterous generation" (12.39). It is significant that the very first word he
addresses to mankind is "repent" (4.17). But certain as this
is, it is equally certain that Jesus has the very highest expectations of this depraved mankind. "You therefore are to be
perfect, even as your heavenly Father is perfect" (5.48). He
forbids all evil thoughts and intentions towards one's neighbour, and love of one's enemy is not a mere recommendation
but a categorical duty.

But how can Jesus make such demands, and proclaim that
the reward for their fulfilment is eternal bliss, if men are an
evil and adulterous generation? No doubt there is a contradiction here. We can solve it only if we try to understand it
from the viewpoint of Jesus himself, and of his awareness of
his messianic calling. When he spoke of the sins of men, he
had in mind the realities of the world around him. But when
he spoke of the obligation to be perfect as our heavenly
Father is perfect, he was drawing upon the world of his own
inner life, and requiring of his disciples what was life and
truth within himself. His strict moral imperatives are already
uttered out of his messianic awareness that he will communicate even his own being to those who believe in him. They
already bear the note of the Redeemer, and the Grace of redemption.

How is this Grace of redemption expressed in the Gospels?

It is constantly announced in Jesus' life, even where we least expect it, in his encounter with the men possessed of devils. These possessed men are wretched and divided in their souls, knowing themselves to be utterly abandoned to the daemonic powers of existence. Their sinful nature senses something strange, indeed hostile to their nature, the manifestation of sanctity. This manifestation of sanctity is so overwhelming that the wretched men are seized with sudden terror when they encounter Jesus. But the longer Jesus remains with them, the more his influence disarms them. Jesus' wakening, sanctifying power penetrates ever more deeply, ever more strongly, into their will. A new will arises in them. They are redeemed. "And as Jesus was getting into the boat, the man who had been afflicted by the devil began to entreat him that he might remain with him" (Mark 5.18). We may assume that Jesus did not undertake any healing of the sick that was not at the same time such a redemption of will, and an endowment with Grace. His thought and reflection were so completely full of the Father's glory and the kingdom of God that his entire ministry can be conceived only as a ministry of salvation. Jesus always regarded mind and body in man as one, he always saw the whole man in his outward and inward limitations. It was the whole man who was to be redeemed. When Jesus healed the paralytic at Capharnaum, Mark expressly points out that Christ saw body and soul as one (Mark 2.1 ff.). The sick man expected Jesus to heal his body, and yet the Master spoke of something that seemed completely remote from the sick man: "Son, thy sins are forgiven thee" (Mark 2.5). He saw not only the body broken by paralysis but also the soul tormented by guilt. "But that you may know that the Son of Man has power on earth to forgive sins, I say to thee, arise, take up thy pallet, and go to thy house" (2.10–11). Whoever came to Jesus with a thirsting soul plunged into a stream of power and purity of both body and soul, "rivers of living water," as Jesus himself put it (John 7.38). This was no potent material emanation, but something far more profound: intense love for God and man, founded upon the strongest vitality, which must have refreshed and restored the sick man as oxygen does our weary blood. All those who hungered and thirsted after righteousness, the souls of Zacheus and Nicodemus, Peter and John, the woman taken in adultery, Mary Magdalen—they must all have experienced the blessing that proceeded from Jesus as a rebirth, a new creation. In his conversation at night with Nicodemus, Jesus himself describes this great new experience as a rebirth from the Holy Spirit. "Unless a man be born again, he cannot see the kingdom of God" (John 3.3). The effect of this great new thing is given concrete expression in his inimitable metaphor of the true vine and the fruit. "I am the vine, you are the branches. He who abides in me and I in him, he bears much fruit; for without me you can do nothing" (John 15.5.) The Synoptic Gospels too describe this new thing as a living in Jesus, and drawing strength from his fullness. "Come to me, all you who labour and are burdened, and I will give you rest. Take my yoke upon you, and learn from me, for I am meek and humble of heart; and you will find rest for your souls" (Matt. 11.28–29). Here Christ's redemptive Grace reaches its culmination: it endows our poor will with a creative share in his own incarnate life. "Grace" is nothing more or less than the dawning of Christ's life within us.

Where does Jesus derive this redemptive power from? Its fountain head is revealed to us in the hypostatic union, the union of Jesus' humanity with the self of the Logos. So it will be our task to penetrate into the true redemptive content of the miracle of the incarnation, and find an answer to the question of how far the seeds of our redemption are planted in Christ's incarnation. In discussing the incarnation of our Lord, we shall make our way towards what is still deeper than his truth and his Grace—the mystery of his divine self.

XXI

THE INCARNATION AS THE BASIS OF OUR REDEMPTION

UP TILL now our discussion has centered on the incarnation in itself, its nature and constitution; but from now on we shall regard it under the aspect of its redemptive power. We are not asking what the incarnation is in itself, but what it signifies for us.

Original sin and redemption

Redemption presupposes the need for redemption, that is, the dogma of original sin. On the morning of creation, we all had the potentiality of living in Adam the life of original Grace—in that same Adam who held within his seed all the potentialities of humanity prescribed in the concept "man," all the possibilities of its concrete expression and individuation; he was the first man, and father of the entire human race, and as such was not man in the same way as we, his later descendants, are, single examples of the species; he was *man* absolutely, *totus homo*. In him we were all called to be the children of God, and to share in the divine life—indeed, more: potentially, in him we already did share in the divine life. This unity of life and Grace which our race enjoyed with the Father has its counterpart in our *common guilt,* when Adam of his own free will disobeyed the crucial commandment. In him, we also fell. In the will of the first man, the entire will of humanity rose up against God. Because Adam was in his person *totus homo*, all mankind fell through his act. Once and for all we fell from our original relationship of

335

life and love to God. We all died a death in respect of God. What was left to us was only our fallen nature, *natura lapsa*, a condition that essentially should not have been, because it was not at the beginning part of the divine ordination. There is no need here for us to discuss the question whether our nature became a fallen nature only because it fell through Adam's guilt from its supernatural fellowship of life and love with God, or whether, having lost its supernatural goal, it might not also have been weakened and wounded in its natural disposition for the divine and holy. We need establish here only that through Adam's fall our original bond of unity and love with God was once and for all objectively torn asunder. From now on human nature had no part in God; it belonged entirely to itself, and was nothing more than mere nature, just like a planet torn from the parent star, and whirling crazily on its own axis. So there weighs a guilt upon us: our original transcendent relationship to the Creator is destroyed. The roots of our being, from which our empirical being draws its existence and content, have been torn out of the original order of things and delivered up to a radical disorder and desolation. Could this mankind be redeemed? Because our guilt reached right to the roots, only God could free us from it. No human effort, no heroism of created being, was capable of bridging the monstrous abyss which had been cleft between the Creator and his creation by original sin. Humanity had been pushed back infinite distances from God, into the infinite remoteness of created being, and more, into the remoteness of sinful being, which bore the stain of being outside of God's order and decree.

And so only *God himself* could redeem us. But it was not a question of redeeming single human individuals, but the *totus homo*, the inclusive unity of all possible men. And so it was fitting to the wisdom of God that, just as the guilt had proceeded from the one first man, Adam, so the redemption should come from a new first man, a second Adam. The fact that potentially the entire human race lived in one single man, the father of mankind and was potentially tempted in him, and fell, had its counterpart in the new fact that the redemption too was fulfilled and realized finally and objectively in one single man, but in such a way that he redeemed us not as a single individual but as the representative of all mankind, as one in whom all possible examples of human nature are united. In God's eyes, it was part of the logic of the original idea of the creation—one father for mankind—that the *old*

Adam should have his counterpart in the new Adam, and that
the new Adam should be "man absolutely," "himself man,
Christ Jesus" (1 Tim. 2.5), "the first-born among many
brethren" (Rom. 8.29), one who opened the way to a completely new spiritual and supernatural line of development,
indeed, one who already potentially contained the new sequence of development within his own person, one in whom
the new following of the redeemed was already and finally
planted.

The redemptive function of Christ's theandric being

Two things are implied by the revealed fact that out of the
depths of his free, mysterious decree, it was God's will to
redeem fallen man in a manner similar to the way man fell
prey to sin. Firstly, the Redeemer would have to wear the
sacrificial garment of humanity, and yet himself be divine. As
man only, whose struggle and self-surrender are made out of
his own free decision, Christ stands upon the same plane as
fallen man, and only thus can he take our guilt upon himself
and atone for it. He became "like one of us." And because
this human atonement and expiation were at the same time
an atonement and expiation on the part of God, they possess
the power of forgiveness and abundant salvation. Only a *God-
man* could redeem us. Moreover, we may conclude that, as
the representative of redeemed mankind, he must stand in a
bond of unity with the entire totality of the redeemed. He is
in his person so related towards those in need of redemption
that his function as Redeemer is fulfilled only when this entirety becomes part of him. It is his consummation, his "fullness."

This allows us to probe still more deeply, and ask what is
the relationship between the divine Logos and the first-born
among many brethren, between the divinity and the humanity
in the ministry of redemption. Is the divinity the primary factor carrying out the actual work of redemption, or is it "the
man Christ Jesus" who fulfils it? In other words, is Christ our
Redeemer *in forma Dei* or *in forma servi*? Under either aspect
he is both God and man at the same time. For he can be the
"first-born among many brethren" only because in his metaphysical depths he is also God. He can embrace mankind in
its entirety, and set a new beginning and awaken a new

338 THE WORK OF CHRIST

generation of the redeemed through his divine nature, only because, as God, he is the creative principle of a new reality, mankind reborn. So more precisely our question is this: In what form do we behold the Redeemer? Do we encounter the triune God through Christ because he is divine, or because he is human? What is it precisely that redeems us in the figure of Christ—that his humanity is assumed into the Godhead, or that the Godhead became wholly and completely man? This question brings us to the ultimate depths of the mystery of the incarnation, and thus into the depths of the divine work of redemption.

The answer is given unambiguously in the revealed word of the Bible. We learn that the incomprehensible and overwhelming character of the figure of Christ is not that his humanity was assumed into the Godhead, but rather that the *Godhead became man,* and that we have among us a man who is God. The decisive thing is not the *ascendere,* the ascent of the human into the divine, but the *descendere,* the descent of the divine to mankind. The tremendous miracle is not to be found in the divinization of the flesh but in the incarnation of God. These are the glad tidings of Christianity: "And the Word was made flesh." The Epistle to the Philippians gives utterance to the same truth: "He emptied himself, taking the nature of a slave and being made like unto men. And appearing in the form of man . . ." (2.7). Christ's humanity is so much the instrument of divine redemption that in those passages where Paul wishes to express the Lord's mediatory function, he does so only in terms of Christ the man. "For there is one God, and one mediator between God and men, himself man, Christ Jesus, who gave himself a ransom for all" (1 Tim. 2.5). This text would imply that the triune God is the ultimate end and aim of our redemption, while the man Christ Jesus is its means and instrument. Therefore even the liturgies of the early Christian Church prayed to God the Father "through his servant Jesus" (*Didache*). Both Peter (I Peter 4.11) and Paul (Rom. 1.8; 16.27) pray to the Father through Jesus. In Paul (2 Cor. 1.20) the words already have liturgical overtones, though we must remember that in distinction to the name of "Christ" Paul uses the name of "Jesus" to mean God's human manifestation. There is another Apostolic formulation, which is to pray in the name of Jesus, "giving thanks for all things in the name of our Lord Jesus Christ to God the Father" (Eph. 5.20). "Do all in the name of the Lord Jesus, giving thanks to God the Father through him"

(Col. 3.17). Even today, Church liturgy is celebrated *"per Christum Dominum nostrum,"* which can be seen not only from the closing words of the collects but especially in the bidding-prayers and the canonical prayers. The great doxology of our canon runs thus: *"per ipsum et cum ipso et in ipso est tibi Deo Patri omnipotenti in unitate Spiritus Sancti omnis honor et gloria."*

Why does the decisive factor lie in the incarnation of God rather than in the divinization of a man? There is only one answer possible: Because the will of God to restore our up-rooted human nature to its old union of life with the living God has taken on substantial, existential form only in this in-carnation. From then on, it was no longer merely a glad promise and proclamation that we should be redeemed. Rather, our redemption has become objectively visible and concrete in the presence of this *homo* Jesus. Through the incarnation, humanity is already reunited, objectively and finally, with God. In this one new man, we are all existentially bound into a new unity with God. From now on, the chain of the generations, which was torn from God in its very first link, is once again united with God in this first-born among the brethren, and united in such a way that it can never again be broken. There will never again be a *natura humana* which is as such hostile to God, or the object of his wrath. In this new man Christ, all mankind is raised from a negation into a great affirmation, from the void into fullness, from worthlessness into worth.

We may say that none of the Church Fathers or the early Christian theologians emphasized this mediating significance of Christ's humanity as decisively as St. Augustine. It is the heart of his theology. And only this can give us a true under-standing of the importance he ascribes to the doctrine of Grace. As he frequently observes in his *Confessions,* even in the stormy years of his youth, the great Father of the Church never took complete pleasure in a book unless there were something in it about Christ. And when he became a theo-logian, a priest, and a bishop, this is what he wrote as his life's creed: *"Origo mea Christus est, radix meus Christus est, caput meum Christus est"* (*Contra Litteras Petiliani,* 1.7, 8). In his sermons he dwells with an especial love upon the pres-entation of the meaning and significance of Christ the media-tor. In his commentary on the Psalms (*Enarratio 2 in Psal-mum* 29.1), he asks, "What is it to be a mediator between God and men? Not between the Father and men, but be-tween God and men? What is God? Father, Son, and Holy

Spirit. What are men? Sinners, ungodly, mortals. Between that Trinity and the weakness and wickedness of men, Man was made mediator, not wicked, but yet weak; that inasmuch as he was not wicked, he might join thee to God, inasmuch as he was weak, he might draw near to thee: and so, that there might be a mediator between thee and God, the Word was made flesh, that is, the Word was made man." Similarly, Augustine emphasizes (*Enarratio in Ps.* 134.5), "But if he were man alone, by following what thou art, thou wouldest never reach him; if he were God alone, for lack of comprehending thou wouldest never reach him." "God with the Father, and Man with us men—*ecce Mediator.*" *Divinitas sine humanitate non est mediatrix, humanitas sine divinitate non est mediatrix, sed inter divinitatem solam et humanitatem solam mediatrix est humana divinitas et divina humanitas Christi* (*Sermo* 47.12, 21).

What position has the Godhead in Christ's office as mediator? This is the same question as the one we have just raised and answered. Augustine's answer to both is the same. Christ is the mediator not because he is God but because he is *God become man. Non enim per hoc mediator est, quod Deus est, sed per hoc mediator, quia factus est homo* (*Sermo* 293.7). Christ fulfils his office *in forma servi* (*Sermo* 279.8). He is the head of the Church *in forma servi* (*Enarratio in Ps.* 85.4). "He was the Word made flesh, that he might become the Head of the Church. For the Word himself is not part of the Church: but, that he might become the Head of the Church, he took upon him flesh" (*Enarratio in Ps.* 148.8). As man, he is the only one who may gaze upon God without sin (*Enarratio 2 in Ps.* 29.3) and without fear (*Quaestionum . . . in Matthaeum,* 13). And therefore he and he alone is the new Adam. "Just as all died in Adam, so now all live in Christ" (*Epistola* 140.8). *Venit ergo unus contra unum* (*Sermo in ed.* 31.1). "Just as no one can dwell in the realm of death except it be through Adam, so no one can dwell in the realm of life except it be through Christ" (*Epistola* 190.2, 8). *Nemo liberatus est, nemo liberatur, nemo liberabitur* (*De Civitate Dei,* 10.32, 2). *Via tua, veritas tua, vita tua Christus* (*Enarratio in Ps.* 85.15). We may depend upon Christ the way, because Christ is the truth. *Ambulare vis? Ego sum via. Falli non vis? Ego sum veritas* (*In Joannis Evangelium,* 22.8). "We are not the life, but partakers of the Life of Christ" (*In Jo. Ev.* 70.1). Thus Augustine makes use of every conceivable metaphor to impress upon his readers this central truth, that in Christ the man we have our all. Christ is the physic that cures us; he is the source of life for all creatures; the light that illumines us. Christ is our peace, our foundation, and the gates through which we enter into life. He is *hominis formator et reformator, creator et recreator, factor et refactor (In Jo. Ev.* 38.8).

It is the achievement of this great saint that he placed Christ's incarnation in the closest relationship to our redemption. It is not as though we were redeemed only by our imitation of Jesus' life in his meaning and spirit, and should follow his example. To Augustine that would be mere moralism, not Christianity. But also it is not as though we were redeemed only because in his incarnation Christ created the necessary basis and presupposition for our salvation, so that of our own accord we had to work out our own salvation upon this foundation. It is not as though Christ had merely built the bridge across the abyss separating us from God, and had now given us the opportunity of crossing this bridge of our own accord. In Augustine's eyes it is rather thus: Christ does not simply build this bridge; he is himself the bridge. He does not simply point the way to salvation; he is himself this way. He is not simply the necessary precondition for the new life; he is himself this new life. *Jam caro assumpta de nobis in domino non spe, sed re salva facta est (Enarratio in Ps.* 125.2). St. Thomas Aquinas gave the final clarification to this idea. He too is particularly inclined to demonstrate that all the tremendous work of salvation, this miraculous achievement of purest surrender to the *solus sanctus*, before whom the angels grow silent and the saints grow pale, has become in the light of Christ's incarnation our own achievement. Christ's life and suffering belong to us as truly as if we had fulfilled them in our own person. *Ex quo patet, quod omni baptizato communicatur passio Christi ad remedium, ac si ipse passus et mortuus esset (Summa Theologica,* III, qu. 69, a. 2). The substance of what we have to do to wipe out our sins has been achieved by Christ, yea, he is himself this achievement. All the good that germinates in our own life is only the unfolding of something that has received its form from Christ's life. We in our religious life are only the extension, the unfolding, of what occurred once in Nazareth, an historically unfolding incarnation of the God-man.

This already brings us close to the question of what relationship there is between the incarnation of the Son of God and his death for our salvation. What is the relationship between Nazareth and Bethlehem on the one hand and Golgotha on the other? By entering into human nature, the Son of Man from the start took upon him all the possibilities that come with the assumption of human nature—hunger and thirst, suffering and grief, struggle and death. And so the fact of the incarnation already implies the potentiality of Golgotha. By the free decision of his will, Christ transformed this potentiality into a reality, so that by taking human suffering upon himself he might free us all of it. Thus Bethlehem and Golgotha cannot be separated. The incarnation of the Son of God created the premises and foundation for that mighty, earth-shaking event when the Son of God died on Golgotha for our salvation. It is this death for our salvation that gives the incarnation its ultimate, terrible solemnity, and its special importance: the Son of God was born for us, that he might die for us.

XXII

CHRIST'S DEATH FOR THE
SALVATION OF MANKIND

*Biblical criticism and its denial of Christ's death for our
salvation*

NOWADAYS, destructive theological criticism regards it almost
as dogma that the Jesus of history had no intention of dying
for the salvation of mankind. All the historical Jesus intended,
they maintain, was to proclaim the imminent coming of the
Last Judgement. He simply carried on the message of John
the Baptist. Originally this Jesus lived in the happy optimism
and firm faith that Israel would even in his generation follow
his call to repentance and prepare themselves for the coming
kingdom of God. But when he transferred his mission from
the sunny valleys of Galilee and its simple, naïve, natural
people to the bitter party allegiances and pleasure-loving lux-
ury of Jerusalem, his spirit became increasingly aware of the
tremendous obstacles that stood in the way of his ministry.
It might have been, the critics say, that from time to time he
was seized with sorrowful premonitions, with the thought that
he himself would have to leap into the "gap," in order to
rouse the people with violence from their lethargy, and make
them ready for repentance over his own dead body. But at
that time his trust in his Father's aid was greater than these
cares. Even immediately before his arrest on the Mount of
Olives, he would not believe that the ultimate sacrifice was
about to become reality. "Father, take this cup from me."
So, on the whole, he regarded his arrest and execution as an
act of violence, forced upon him from outside against his own

343

true will. His death was not freely willed; it was not in the true sense a death for our salvation, but an admission of the divine will, which shook his own trust in the Father to its foundations. "My God, my God, why hast thou forsaken me?" Only after his death, when the belief that he had been resurrected spread abroad, and the scattered fellowship of the disciples came together again, was the need felt to relate his death to the belief in his resurrection, and ascribe significance to it within the divine Providence for our salvation. Biblical criticism would have it that Paul in particular followed the Judaic sacrificial speculation, and saw in Jesus' death a death of atonement; this led him to refashion the entire image of Christ after his own theology of the blood and the cross. What was for Jesus himself still unexpected and incomprehensible became in Paul's theorizing the true solution of the entire riddle of Jesus. And then the idea of redemption made its way from Paul into the Gospels. According to Luke, the pupil of Paul, the Transfigured One himself instructed the disciples at Emmaus on the necessity of his suffering. "Did not the Christ have to suffer these things before entering into his glory?" However, Wrede would maintain that these ideas of redemption have made their way into the Gospels only "a few times." They are scattered, and for that very reason can be proved to be secondary. The idea of Jesus' death for our salvation is the product of early Christian, and particularly Pauline, theology, and was only subsequently read into Jesus' message. The awareness of having to die for mankind was totally strange to Jesus himself.

In face of a theory such as this, which threatens the dearest memories of Christianity, we will find it necessary to pay the greatest attention to the origin and development of the idea of Jesus' suffering in the Gospels, and to see if it really does occur only incidentally, as an addition from outside, or whether it grows from the heart of his message, and forms an essential feature of his consciousness.

Christ's own statements about his death

We will ascertain that Jesus reckoned with the possibility and reality of a violent death *from the beginning,* and not just towards the end of his ministry. Ever since the day at Cæsarea Philippi, this possibility came to be a certainty to him. From then on, his messianic consciousness reached its culmination in the decision to give his life as a ransom "for many." This is already confirmed by certain general considerations. Jesus lives and moves and has his being in the Old Testament. Again and again he read there how stiff-necked Israel was in its opposition to its prophets, and how resolutely it tried to remove them and their burdensome exhortations. In his great tirades against the leaders of the nation he expressly refers this obstinacy of the Jewish nation throughout the entire length of the Bible, and the sorrowful fate of its prophets, to himself (Matt. 23.29 ff.; Luke 11.47 ff.; 13.34). To him the Jews are "the sons of those who killed the prophets," who "fill up the measure of their fathers." If there is anything to confirm Jesus' words, then it is the Old Testament, which he refers to himself: "A prophet is not without honour except in his own country" (Mark 6.4; Luke 4.24). Such an avowal from the start precludes an absolutely optimistic attitude. In addition, Jesus had the fate of John the Baptist before his eyes. John's execution must have drawn his attention afresh to the danger of his own situation. It was not only when he came to Jerusalem that he attracted the unrelenting hostility of the leading circles, but from the moment he entered upon his public ministry in Nazareth. Mark, who records the recollections of Peter, shows a special inclination to describe in detail how from the very beginning of his ministry in Capharnaum the Pharisees took offense at the free, self-confident way in which Jesus obeyed the Law; how the Scribes were angered at his claim to be Lord of the Sabbath, and to forgive sins; and how they joined with the followers of Herod in a conspiracy against him (cf. Mark 3.2, 6; Matt. 12.14; 5.11; Luke 4.28). Under these circumstances, how could Jesus, with his incomparable understanding of men, be for one moment uncertain about the fate that was awaiting him?

In the very beginning of his ministry, a slight premonition of his death breaks through. When the Pharisees reproach him because his disciples do not fast, his reply is significant: "Can the wedding guests mourn as long as the bridegroom is with them?" And he adds, solemnly, "But the days will come when the bridegroom shall be taken away from them, and then they will fast" (Matt. 9.15; Mark 2.19). It is so much labour lost to suspect these significant words of Jesus' as being a *vaticinium ex eventu*. Jesus' remark is in unforced harmony with his reply to John the Baptist's followers that they, John's disciples, do right to fast, since their master has

been taken away from them by Herod. It is true, he is not referring to an actual sacrificial death here, but certainly to a
violent end. For the bridegroom does not go away of his own
accord but is "taken away" from the disciples (ἀπαρθῇ), and
therefore they will fast.

Slight indications of the terrible fate that is awaiting him
are to be found in those parts of Jesus' message that form the
climax of his proclamation. "Blessed are you when men reproach you, and persecute you, and, speaking falsely, say all
manner of evil against you, for my sake. Rejoice and exult,
because your reward is great in heaven; for so did they persecute the prophets who were before you" (Matt. 5.11, 12).
At about the same time, Jesus takes the opportunity of proclaiming the Baptist to be the true Elias, who, according to
contemporary belief, was to precede the Messias. Referring
to his sorrowful end, he observes, "So also will the Son of
Man suffer in their hands" (Matt. 17.12). In the death of
John the Baptist, he sees the anticipation and confirmation of
his own death. Our Lord's reply to the request of the sons of
Zebedee points in the same direction. "Grant to us that we
may sit one at thy right hand, and one at thy left hand in the
glory," they ask. This request was certainly made at a time
when the threatening cloud was not yet visible, and the thought
of the glory was still in the forefront of the disciples' hopes.
Jesus made the significant reply, "Can you drink of the cup
of which I drink, or be baptized with the baptism with which
I am to be baptized?" (Mark 10.38). Here, too, Jesus does
not as yet refer to a sacrificial death in the narrower sense.
But he reveals clearly enough that he reckons with a violent
death as something inevitable. Luke repeats this same metaphor of the immanent baptism: "But I have a baptism to be
baptized with; and how distressed I am until it is accomplished" (12.50). The similarity of the metaphor would suggest that these words were uttered at about the same time.
There is no doubt that in all these sayings—which occur
comparatively early in his ministry—Jesus clearly announces
that he is reckoning with the possibility of a violent death.
However, there is still something tentative about all these
statements. They give no precise indication of what Jesus'
own interpretation of his violent death might be, whether he
regards it as a sacrificial death or as a destiny coming upon
him from without, against his will.

His words about the sign of Jonas the prophet take us
further. Matthew's version (12.40) is this: "For even as Jonas

was in the belly of the fish three days and three nights, so will the Son of Man be three days and three nights in the heart of the earth." If these words are original, then they already give some indication of Jesus' awareness of the close connexion between his death and his resurrection after three days; he already regarded his death as signifying triumph and salvation. The parallel passage in Luke 11.29 gives a simpler formulation to these words of our Lord: "No sign shall be given in [this generation] but the sign of Jonas. For even as Jonas was a sign to the Ninevites, so will also the Son of Man be to this generation." As we see, in this variant the point of comparison is not Christ's resurrection after three days in the grave, but Jonas' appearance and prophetic message as a whole. Which of these texts is original? Contemporary exegesis points out that in Biblical usage a "sign" ($\sigma\eta\mu\epsilon\bar{\iota}ov$) is never a purely human action, such as Jonas' call to repentance might have been. Rather, the expression "sign" always refers to God's direct intervention in history. The use of the future tense, too ($\delta o\vartheta\acute{\eta}\sigma\epsilon\tau\alpha\iota$)—"no sign shall be given it"—excludes the assumption that the reference might be to some sermon of repentance that the Lord had already preached, for the sign has yet to be made. So it can refer only to the miracle of Christ's resurrection after his three days' sojourn in the tomb. It would seem, then, that the original text is offered by Matthew. The sign of Jonas is to be repeated in Jesus' case, for he too will be reawakened to life after three days in the tomb.

The closer Jesus comes to Golgotha, the more frequent and detailed his references to his suffering become.

Jesus makes the first detailed prophecy of his suffering following Peter's avowal at Cæsarea Philippi (Matt. 16.21). Matthew expressly assures us that this was the first time that Jesus spoke in such detail of his suffering. Through Peter, the disciples had just acknowledged that he was the Messias. They were children of a nation whose dream was only of a Messias of glory, and they too understood Christ's calling to be a summons to glory and majesty. Jesus therefore realized that he had to oppose this misunderstanding in its inception, and enlighten them as to the *Christus crucifixus* This close connexion between his prophecy of suffering and Peter's previous affirmation that he was the Christ allows us to infer that our Lord himself gave a messianic interpretation to his suffering: because Jesus is the Christ, therefore he must suffer. This very passage is an indication of the divine decree through which his suffering becomes "the necessity of Providence."

"The Son of Man" must "go to Jerusalem." This is a decree of the divine will, not any mere accidental, historical fatality.

Jesus' second proclamation of his suffering was made during their time of wandering in Galilee. "Now while they were together in Galilee, Jesus said to them, 'The Son of Man is to be betrayed into the hands of men, and they will kill him; and on the third day he will rise again.' And they were exceedingly sorry" (Matt. 17.21, 22). Jesus must have been frequently compelled to speak of his suffering, and correct the constant surging of his disciples' false conception of a messianic kingdom of glory even in this aeon. The disciples' wakening from this pleasant dream, as it was to come on Good Friday, would have crushed them without some preliminary preparation for the possibility of his suffering. It is true, even now they could not measure the deep seriousness of his words. The idea of a suffering Messias was too remote for them. Contemporary Judaic theology had no conception of it. The Gospels expressly emphasize this incomprehension of the disciples' when Jesus makes the second prophecy of his suffering. "But they did not understand this saying, and it was hidden from them . . . and they were afraid to ask him about this saying" (Luke 9.45; Mark 9.32). They responded much more readily to the coming glory of the Messias, and to the thought of Jesus feasting with Abraham and Isaac and Jacob, as he had promised them. And so even Peter took the Lord "aside" when he first spoke of his imminent suffering. "He began to chide him, saying, 'Far be it from thee, O Lord; this will never happen to thee'" (Matt. 16.22). Because they were not strong enough to take serious account of the Lord's imminent suffering, they were not really able to understand his promise of the resurrection either. That was just as "hiden" from them as the Lord's cross. And so when the terrible thing happened, they had nothing firm and certain to build upon. When they beheld Jesus' death upon the cross, and his tomb, all their expectations of glory could not but collapse, and the little that they could understand of Jesus' resurrection was in no sense sufficient to help overcome the shock of our Lord's passion. It is not correct to infer—as theological criticism tries to do—that because of their hesitancy and timidity on the days of his suffering the disciples could have had no previous idea at all of the possibility of Christ's suffering and resurrection, and that therefore Christ's three prophecies of his suffering are to be regarded as a later insertion made by the devout community. The disciples could not possibly have ignored three clear prophecies of our Lord's suffering. They heard them clearly enough, but did not understand them with the same profundity and solemnity as Jesus had uttered them. In other cases, too, they frequently could not grasp what the Lord said, because, as the Gospel puts it, their hearts were "blinded." The selfish narrowness which concentrated all their thoughts and hopes upon the Christ of glory did not allow them to apprehend the gloom and sadness of his words, sadness unto death, nor to preserve it in their memory. They knew, certainly, that Jesus had spoken of death and resurrection, but their selfish expectations of the future had thrust this knowledge to the periphery of consciousness. They had retained only a little in their memory. But this little was sufficient to call his half-forgotten words back to mind the moment the Resurrected One did in fact appear. And so in the end Christ had not prophesied his suffering in vain.

The third prophecy of his suffering was made immediately before his final journey to Jerusalem, and his death (Matt. 20.17 ff.). "Behold, we are going up to Jerusalem, and the Son of Man will be betrayed to the chief priests and the Scribes; and they will condemn him to death, and will deliver him to the Gentiles to be mocked and scourged and crucified; and on the third day he will rise again." Jesus' passion loomed large on the horizon. The closer he knew he was to the terrible event, the more clearly his inward eye perceived the details of his suffering. This is why the third prophecy is the most circumstantial.

*   *   *   *

So now Jesus is in the stronghold of his enemies, Jerusalem. He is more oppressed than he has ever been by thoughts of his coming death. And in all frankness, he speaks them abroad. In the parable of the vine-dressers he says in the teeth of the Jewish elders that it has always been the Jewish way to kill the prophets sent them from the Master of the vineyard, and that in the end they would not even stay their hand from killing his only well-beloved Son (Matt. 21.33 f.). His opponents understood what he meant. "Though they sought to lay hands on him, they feared the people, because they regarded him as a prophet." Nor does Jesus hide from his disciples how much he is preoccupied by thoughts of the dark future. When they became indignant that Mary Magdalen should anoint his body with the precious ointment, which "might have been sold for much and given to the poor," he said pondering, "Why do you trouble the woman? She has done me a good turn. For the poor you have always with you, but you do not always have me. For in pouring this ointment on my body, she has done it for my burial" (Matt. 26.10 ff.).

And now Jesus celebrates the Passover with his disciples. As he breaks the bread and offers them the red wine, in his creative consciousness and of his creative will be becomes aware of his own suffering in the bread broken and the wine poured, his own body broken for many, and his own blood shed for many. The entire proceedings are dominated by the thought of suffering. This already brings us into the realm of "interpretations" of Jesus' death for our salvation. How did Jesus himself interpret the death he so clearly foresaw? Did he understand it, and will it as a death for the salvation of mankind?

Jesus' death for the salvation of mankind

The researches of religious history have shown that at the time of Jesus, the Jews did not cherish any belief in a Messias who was to suffer and to die. Only in post-Christian Jewry, in the Talmudic period, was there a tradition of a Messias Ben Joseph, or Ben Ephraim, who was defeated by his enemies. There is no purpose of atonement in the death of this Messias. In any case, there is no proof that the Jews had any idea of a suffering and dying Messias at the time the New Testament describes. This concept does not become alive until the second century after Christ. The first evidence of it is in the *Dialogus cum Tryphone* of St. Justin Martyr. According to Justin (89.90), Tryphon admits that the Bible prophesies a suffering Messias, and that this proclamation is particularly made in Isaias 53; but there is no reference here to death upon a cross, which, indeed, is cursed in the Law. The Talmudic texts also interpret Isaias 53 as referring to a suffering Messias. But they understand the value of this suffering for mankind's salvation in the usual sense, that the superabundant suffering of the righteous will also benefit the rest of mankind. They are not thinking of death for mankind's salvation in the narrow sense. This idea is quite specifically Christian. But it does have connexions with the Old Testament. The idea of the Messias' suffering for our redemption was not unfamiliar to the prophets, and was especially close to Isaias. But in Jesus' time, these prophetic ideas had already lost their force. National *amour-propre* would not endure the pitiful picture of a suffering Messias, and could reconcile itself only to the idea of a Christ of glory.

Unlike these nationalistic ambitions on the part of the Jews, there can be no doubt that Jesus understood his suffering, and took it upon himself, as a *suffering of atonement*. Immediately after Peter's acknowledgement that he is the Messias, he emphasizes for the first time the necessity of his suffering. "The Son of Man must suffer many things, and be rejected by the elders . . ." (Mark 8.31; Matt. 26.54). When the Lord here says "must," he does not mean that it is, for example, his fate that he should die like the prophets, a martyr to his faithfulness to his summons. Christ rather wishes to emphasize that he must suffer and die because he is the Messias. This is how we are to understand his words in Luke 12.50: "I have a baptism to be baptized with; and how distressed I am until it is accomplished!" This baptism is the part of the Messias. As his disciples are baptized with water, so he is with blood. This baptism in blood is the basis for the baptism with water. In the Gospel according to St. John, too, Jesus expresses this messianic necessity: "And as Moses lifted up the serpent in the desert, even so must the Son of Man be lifted up" (3.14). To all those who gazed upon it, the serpent was the sign of their redemption. And so Jesus' elevation, too, is something that will bring redemption. The expression "to be lifted up" has two meanings, for it indicates both Jesus' elevation upon the cross and his exaltation to the right hand of the Father.

All these passages in which Jesus' death is regarded as a necessary part of his calling as the Messias refer back to the Old Testament. Jesus repeatedly calls upon the words of the Scriptures to confirm the necessity of his suffering. In Matthew 26.24 he says, "The Son of Man indeed goes his way, as it is written of him" (cf. Mark 9.11). In Matthew 26.54, he asks, "How then are the Scriptures to be fulfilled, that thus it must take place?" Just as the murder of John the new Elias had been in accordance with the Scriptures, so it would also be in keeping with Old Testament prophecy that the Son of Man should have to go his way through suffering.

What passage is Jesus actually referring to, when he relates to the Scriptures the necessity of his suffering? The only certain passage in the Old Testament is Isaias 53, which portrays the suffering servant of God. In Luke (22.37) Jesus refers expressly to Isaias 53. "For I say to you that this which is written must yet be fulfilled in me, 'And he was reckoned among the wicked.' " This passage in Luke is by no means the only one. There are two other significant sayings of the Lord in which the reference to Isaias 53 strikes the eye at once. They are the final confirmation that Jesus understood his death as a death for mankind's salvation, according to Isaias 53.

The first important passage is to be found in Matthew 20.28 (= Mark 10.45). "The Son of Man has not come to be served, but to serve, and to give his life as a ransom for many" (δοῦναι τὴν ψυχὴν αὐτοῦ λύτρον ἀντὶ πολλῶν). In this passage, Jesus makes it perfectly clear that his task is "to serve," just as Isaias 53 speaks of the servant of God. Moreover, like Isaias, Jesus also speaks of sacrificing himself, and, borrowing Isaias' very phrase, he describes this sacrifice as a sacrifice "for many." The "ransom" (λύτρον) he gives for many is the ransom that is paid for someone in his stead. Thus his suffering is a suffering of atonement for many, that is, a suffering that is to liberate and redeem many from their servitude.

It would be strange indeed if liberal criticism had not done its utmost to dispute the authenticity of these important words of our Lord. For if they are genuine, there can no longer be any suggestion that Jesus encountered his death against his will, or that his sole intention had been to preach repentance like John the Baptist, or that the blood-stained mantle of mankind's Redeemer was first laid upon him by Paul.

Liberal criticism would have it that the saying about the ransom has a Pauline ring to it; they claim it was first coined by Paul's pupil, Mark, and made its way from Mark into the Gospel according to St. Matthew. The alleged basis for this assumption is that the saying about the ransom and the series of ideas it involves are not to be found elsewhere in the Lord's message. Moreover, it is remarkable that the variant in Luke 22.27 does not include this characteristic phrase. In this passage, Jesus declares quite simply, "I am in your midst as he who serves." It would seem that Luke's version is the original one, while the addition about giving his life as a ransom for many would simply be a commentary of Mark's upon the Lord's words, and, indirectly, a borrowing from Paul.

The first reply to this would be that in his Epistles, Paul himself never makes use of the expression "ransom." He certainly uses similar terms, and one in the first Epistle to Timothy is very closely related. Here (I Tim. 2.6) we may find the composite word ἀντίλυτρον, and the remainder of the passage, too, is strikingly reminiscent of the Lord's words, "who gave himself a 'ransom' for all" (ὁ δοὺς ἑαυτὸν ἀντίλυτρον). But this same liberal criticism holds that the first epistle to Timothy was written considerably later than the Gospel according to St. Mark. They assume that Mark was written before the beginning of the Jewish War in 66, and after the death of Peter, which would locate it between 64 and 66. On the other hand, they claim that the first Epistle to Timothy was written at a time when Pauline Christianity had taken its definitive form and was ready for literary evaluation. The time proposed is somewhere during the first ten years of the second century. If this is so, Mark cannot be dependent upon the first Epistle to Timothy, but, conversely, the Epistle to Timothy must be dependent upon Mark. In any case, so much is certain, that the saying about the ransom does not stem directly from Paul's vocabulary. For Paul himself does not use the word, and liberal criticism would have it that the apparently related expression ἀντίλυτρον is post-Pauline. Apart from the first Epistle to Timothy, the authentic Paul speaks quite simply only of "redemption" (ἀπολύτρωσις, 1 Cor. 1.30; Rom. 3.24; Col. 1.14; Eph. 1.7), or, using the metaphor of purchase, "redemption from the curse of the Law" (ἐξαγοράζειν, Gal. 3.13; 4.5), or of being "bought at a great price" (τιμή, 1 Cor. 6.20). Certainly these expressions echo the ransom of Matthew and Mark, but they are not absolute equivalents. There is a further doubt raised, for when Paul wishes to speak expressly of Jesus' sacrifice for many, at the Last Supper, he does *not* use Mark's (10.45) and Matthew's (28.28) phrase "for many," but "for you." There is no question he has the communion in mind, and not Jesus himself, as Matthew and Mark imply. So the expression "for many" is fundamentally as un-Pauline as the use of the word "ransom" (cf. Schweitzer, *The Mystery of the Kingdom of God,* Eng. tr., New York, 1950, p. 36). In fact, the ransom is not a borrowing from Paul at all, but from the Old Testament, and one which Jesus made himself.

But why does not Luke also speak of the ransom, in the same passage as Matthew and Mark speak of the Lord's having come "to serve"? It is certain that Luke did not omit this phrase because he did not regard the Lord's death as a death for mankind's salvation. After all, he was a pupil of Paul's and shared his clear doctrine that the Lord died for man's deliverance. In his account of the Last Supper, like Paul he reports those significant words of Jesus' in which he gives his flesh and blood to those present, which is testimony to his messianic sacrifice, even to death. It is equally certain that Luke, and Luke alone, reports a literal quotation of Jesus' from Isaias 53.12 (Luke 22.37). He is our sole testi-

mony that Jesus had already referred Isaias 53 to himself.
But it is precisely in Isaias 53 that the "servant of God" is
described as the one who will give his life for many. So even
though Luke does not report the saying about the ransom, he
nevertheless bears express witness that our Lord was familiar
with the prophecy from Isaias at the basis of the saying, and
indeed had applied it to himself. The deeper reason why
Luke omitted Jesus' words about the ransom is probably to
be found in the fact that, unlike Matthew and Mark, Luke
does not locate the disciples' contention about which of them
was reputed the greatest, and the Lord's subsequent words
about serving, in the Lord's time of wandering, more precisely, immediately before the Lord's entry into Jerusalem;
instead, he reports it in direct connexion with the Last Supper. But in his account of the Last Supper he had already just
pointed out the sense of atonement that characterized Jesus'
suffering when he wrote: "And having taken bread, he gave
thanks and broke, and gave it to them, saying, 'This is my
body, which is being given for you; do this in remembrance
of me.' In like manner he took also the cup after the supper,
saying, 'This cup is the new covenant in my blood, which shall
be shed for you.' " A few verses later, he reports Jesus' words
about his having come to serve. It was obviously against his
sense of style to link so closely a similar utterance of Jesus'
about his suffering and atonement.

The saying about the ransom has its most brilliant commentary in the accounts of the Last Supper, which we shall
not discuss in detail here. For our purposes, the question is
essentially one of the authenticity of the phrases about the
cup and the blood. Matthew and Mark read thus: "This is my
blood of the new covenant, which is being shed for many."
The Pauline tradition, however, reads thus: "This cup is the
new covenant in my blood" (1 Cor. 11.25). Luke adds to the
Pauline text, "This cup is the new covenant in my blood,
which shall be shed for you." All the accounts are agreed in
describing the contents of the cup as the blood of the covenant. In his account of the Last Supper, Paul expressly informs us that he "received it from the Lord" (ἀπὸ τοῦ
Κυρίου, 1 Cor. 11.23). He makes use of such an assurance
in only one other context—1 Corinthians 15.3, where he is
discussing another highly important part of the early Christian
tradition, the resurrection. Paul wants to give the assurance
that on this particular point he is not reporting in his own
words, but is drawing upon a source that goes back to the

Lord himself. It is probable that this source was Peter, for Paul tells us in Galatians 1.18 that he visited the disciple three years after his conversion. If he had heard these words from the Resurrected One himself, he would probably not have said "ἀπὸ τοῦ Κυρίου," but would have used a different preposition, such as παρὰ τοῦ Κυρίου. In any case, he regarded the words spoken at the Last Supper as well-established early Christian tradition, and thus as historical utterances of the Lord's. What is their meaning? Jesus is obviously performing a symbolical action, one that has reference to his death. The term "covenant" (*berith*) is rendered in the Septuagint by the translation "testament" (διαθήκη), and in New Testament usage this means the will, or testament, made by a testator in case of his death, which thus becomes effective in law only when he dies. So somehow it is Jesus' death that is at issue here. This is also indicated by the symbolism of the visible signs. The bread broken in pieces symbolizes his body destroyed in death. And the red wine poured from the cup symbolizes his blood shed in death. So this is a twin symbolism, in keeping with Jesus' custom of presenting the selfsame idea in twin parables (for example, the twin parables of the grain of wheat and the mustard seed, the lost sheep and the lost coin, the good and bad fish and the sheep and the goats). In offering the bread and the cup, and solemnly proclaiming "this is my flesh," "this is my blood of the covenant," he was not simply stressing in general terms that it was in his death, in the separation of his flesh and blood, that the new covenant was rooted, but also, and primarily, that this death and the covenant founded in it are already anticipated in this visible sign, that it is affirmed and apprehended in the bread broken and the cup poured. In other words, at this moment, here and now, Jesus' sacrificial death, founding the new covenant, takes on sacramental form. The sacrifice on Golgotha is here anticipated *in signo*. When Jesus adds, "Eat, this is my flesh. Drink, this is my blood," he is demonstrating that this his sacrificial death is for the salvation of his children, a good they should make their own, for their own salvation. And as they eat and drink of it, they are taken up into a communion of death with Jesus, and share the blessing of this communion.

We may affirm that Jesus could not have given clearer utterance to his awareness that his death was for the salvation of mankind than through this mysterious symbolism. To this extent, the Last Supper is a commentary on the true meaning of his death on the cross. What will take place tomorrow on

Good Friday for the whole world is fulfilled for the disciples today. They share in his flesh and blood.

The phrase "blood of the covenant" is taken from the ritual of the offering at Mount Sinai. When Moses came down from the mountain, he had young calves slaughtered "as pacific victims," and he sprinkled their blood upon the people and said, "This is the blood of the covenant which the Lord hath made with you" (Exod. 24.8). The expression is thus part of Old Testament sacrificial usage. When he chose it, Jesus had the sacrifice at Mount Sinai in mind. The children of Israel were taken into God's covenant through the blood of young calves, while his disciples were taken into the new covenant through his own blood.

Christ's proclamation of salvation apart from his death

There is one important question that arises from our discussion, and we may not close it until we have attempted an answer. If the Jesus of history already understood his death to be one of atonement, and established it as the true source of Grace and indispensable means of reaching God, and if this Jesus of history taught that we can achieve bliss only through his own death for our salvation, how can we explain that elsewhere—remarkably in the Sermon on the Mount— Jesus appears to ignore this mediating function of his death completely? Was it not Jesus who proclaimed the glad tidings of God's free, forgiving, fatherly love? Did he not clearly say that as long as man repents there is no sin that can separate him from the love of God, just as a little child cannot be separated from his father's love? Did not his parable of the prodigal son (Luke 15.11 f.) give concrete form to his promise that God's justice is not impaired, when he forgives? Does this not show a total absence of the idea that the Father can receive the prodigal son only because his own Son has sacrificed himself, even to death? And did Christ not himself teach us quite simply to pray for the forgiveness of our sins? Even before his death he forgave the adultress, the paralytic, and the thief at his right hand without any indication that his death was to atone for them.

This objection is certainly right in pointing out that Jesus' proclamation opened the way to the children of the new kingdom. All that is needed is repentance, and the Father's for-

giving love is there. This is an essential element in his proclamation of the Father. But it is equally certain that Jesus
alone appeared as *the bringer of the new kingdom*. Only where
he is are also the kingdom and the forgiveness of sins. All the
parables and sayings with which he proclaims the coming of
the kingdom of God take on the character of glad tidings only
because it is he, the Messias, who proclaims them. They become effective only through their inner dependency upon
Jesus. His promises and commandments draw their meaning
and strength only from his message that in him the new kingdom is come. It is come in him, and in him alone, because he
alone is the incarnate love of God. This love includes all that
is possible in sacrifice for God and man, even the sacrifice of
his life upon the cross. In surrendering to this all-embracing
love of Jesus', the disciples also gave their affirmation, at least
indirectly, to his cross. However much their will to live, and
their traditional Judaic image of the Messias, might resist
Jesus' prophecies of his suffering, their ideas were still overshadowed by the dark possibility that the Messias would suffer
and die, and that as his faithful disciples they themselves
would have to be prepared, like the sons of Zebedee, to drink
the cup of suffering with him. They gave their allegiance to
Jesus under the shadow of the cross. If our Lord's parables of
the prodigal son and of the lost sheep and other sayings are
silent about this mediating function of his death upon the
cross, it is only because they are concerned with the essence
of his message, which is to announce the unbounded fatherly
love of God; and this, unlike the Judaic law of *talion*, does
not make the forgiveness of sins dependent upon human merit
and achievement, but on inward conversion, which is, in its
ultimate depths, pure, unmerited Grace. The glad tidings of
pure Grace are not cancelled out by the Messias' subsequent
sacrifice upon the cross; on the contrary, his death bears fresh
witness to them, and gives them concrete and heart-rending
form.

We shall now go on to point out that the Apostles also
understood the Lord's death upon the cross only as the proof
of unbounded love and Grace. Our question is: How did the
Apostles judge Jesus' death upon the cross?

XXIII

THE APOSTLES' TEACHING CONCERNING CHRIST'S DEATH FOR THE SALVATION OF MANKIND

St. Paul's theology of the cross

IT was St. Paul who seized upon Jesus' message of redemption with all his heart and soul, and developed it in the theological terms of his age. He knows of nothing more sacred than Christ crucified: "For I determined not to know anything among you, except Jesus Christ and him crucified" (1 Cor. 2.2). It is the true theme of his theology of redemption, to trace *the objective value of atonement* in Jesus' death.

Three great questions engage the Apostle's contemplation: What is the nature of the distress from which mankind is delivered by Christ's act of redemption? In what way and by what means does the first-born among the brethren bring about this redemption? What is the issue, the fruit, of the redemption? We shall answer these questions in the light of St. Paul's Epistles, and in doing so we shall enter into the very workshop of the Apostle, and into the very heart of his religious thought.

What is the misery that redemption frees us from? According to Paul, it does not simply consist in sin, nor yet in the consequences of sin, but, in the most general sense, in man's entire situation at present, in the emptiness and inadequacy of concrete human existence. The entire world of the present is dominated by dark and evil forces. This is a supernatural, yea, a cosmic, evil, and not merely a personal grief. The

Apostle describes these forces as "the flesh," "sin," "the Law," and "death." These concepts, which may well seem abstract to our minds, are to him active forces. Sin appears in his work acting and moving almost like a living identity (Rom. 7.8 ff.). Death is ranged on the same plane with the supernatural spirits, and meets its destruction at Christ's hand like some individual being (1 Cor. 15.26).

These four powers are closely related to one another. Whoever is the victim of but one is the prey of the others as well. The most dangerous among them are sin and the flesh. To Paul, the word "flesh" (σάρξ) signifies primarily man's bodily nature. It is man as brute. Paul's view of man is marked by the dualism of the Hellenistic mind. The body is not the manifestation of the soul, but a burden cleaving to the soul. It is like a prison to the soul, and is therefore the ultimate cause of all the evil with which the human soul is weighed down. And sin cleaves to the flesh. Hence Paul's favourite expressions, "the body of sin," "sinful flesh," etc. (Rom. 6.6; 8.3; 7.13 ff.). Historically, it is true, our sin derives from the original sin of the first man (Rom. 5.12). But the first man himself sank into sin on account of the flesh. And his sin, moreover, was handed on to all other men, his descendants, again on account of the flesh. So sensual man is subject to the power of sin. The Law is in the service of "sinful flesh." It is the Law that transforms sin from an unthinking transgression of the Law into conscious sin and punishable trespass. And because the Law itself draws attention to all possibilities of its transgression, it even intensifies the sin. It is a power that convicts man of sin, not one redeeming him from it; it is one that wakens his sense of guilt. But where there is guilt, there is also punishment, and death. So the third power of the adversary enters the arena. For the wages of sin is death, and a death after which there is no more life. And so sinful man can only cry out in despair, "Unhappy man that I am! Who will deliver me from the body of this death?" (Rom. 7.24).

But in Paul's eyes, there are still higher supernatural forces labouring for man's destruction—the demons. He is convinced that fallen man wastes away beneath the influence of supernatural "angelic powers," of "thrones," "dominations," "principalities," and "powers" (1 Cor. 15.24; Col. 1.16). It is these angelic beings who really hold sway over this unredeemed world. And so they are called quite simply the "rulers of this world" (1 Cor. 2.6, 8). Mankind is in the hands of the malice and might of this realm of the spirits. It is only the redeemed who can be separated from the love of God by "neither . . . angels, nor principalities, nor powers" (Rom. 8.38). Human misery is thus played out both in the world of the senses and in the world beyond them. It is true, the domination of the demons cannot in fact be separated from the domination of the flesh, sin, death, and the Law. Indeed, it is the demons who seduce us to sin (1 Col. 10.20), above all to the sin of idolatry. They bring about the death of the flesh, and they propound the Law. For they delivered it to Moses (Gal. 3.19; cf. Heb. 2.2; Acts 7.38). There can be nothing more desolate than man's fallen state: sin within, and the devil above. The Apostle's fundamental conception is dominated by a dark pessimism markedly gloomier than that in Jesus himself. The influence of Judaeo-Hellenistic post-canonical writings, and their moral pessimism, can be traced here. An additional cause might well be the Apostle's personal disposition, his profoundly passionate nature, and his own personal experiences. But even if the Apostle's pen labours more mightily than the Lord himself, his fundamental view of man's unsaved state, and his desolation in sin and death, still correspond to the leading ideas in Jesus' message.

Is there any redemption from this abandonment to sin and death? In the Apostle's eyes, this is conceivable in only one way, that man should be raised up out of his fleshly, earthly existence, out of his fetters of flesh, sin, death, the Law, and the angelic powers, into a supernatural, heavenly kingdom, where righteousness rules instead of sin, and freedom instead of the Law, life instead of death, and instead of the reign of the evil spirits the reign of God. To Paul, this is not merely a spiritual, ethical redemption. Inextricably involved in the things of the spirit are the things of the body, and indeed the things of the cosmos. And so redemption embraces not merely the soul but the *whole man*. We are seized and transformed by the Grace of redemption even in our corporeality, so that our own body is filled with the divine Pneuma.

How is this redemption of the whole man brought about? According to Paul, it was because Christ, the Son of God, and a divine power high above all earthly things, entered into the distress of this flesh for my sake, and took upon himself the sin that permeates all earthly being; because he submitted himself to the Law, and out of his own depths conquered all —flesh, Law, sin, death, and the devil.

To be more circumstantial, because Christ entered into the same family with us men, he took upon himself wholly and completely the distresses of human corporeality. He became as one of us. The flesh that he took upon him was "sinful flesh," like ours (Rom. 8.3). "For our sakes he made him to be sin who knew nothing of sin" (2 Cor. 5.21). Paul does not mean by this that Christ himself had sinned in any way. Such a thought would destroy the coherence of his entire theology. Rather, he is thinking of an objective sinfulness in human nature, its abandonment to evil. This is already present before there is any question of a subjective guilt. In taking upon himself the likeness of sinful flesh, the Incarnate One also put himself in the power of the Law. Like all men, he too was threatened by its curse (Gal. 4.4). And finally, he also entered the realm of the demons' domination. In reality it was they who nailed him to the cross (1 Cor. 2.6 f.). And therefore, the Incarnate One cannot escape death either. He must die. Here is the tremendous solemnity of the incarnation, that it should thrust the Son of God into the ultimate human potentiality, even into death.

But his death was the great turning point. At this point, the Apostle's meditation shows a completely different aspect. For he who dies is no ordinary mortal, but the Son of God. A supernatural, divine being, high above all earthly being, is originally latent within him. His death only sets this latent divine power free. Death has become his liberator. "Death shall no longer have dominion over him" (Rom. 6.9). Through his resurrection, the Lord enters into a new being, one ordered high above all earthly powers. And so the resurrection is no accident. It is the triumph of the divine powers, hidden from the start within his human nature. At this point it is quite clear that the dominant factors in Paul's doctrine of the redemption are these: Jesus as *the metaphysical Son of God,* his *incarnation,* and finally the Lord's *resurrection* through the power of the incarnation. Through the incarnation Jesus enters into human misery, and through his resurrection he triumphs over it. The fundamental presupposition for both is his being the metaphysical Son of God.

How do we benefit from Jesus' liberation of himself? Pauline theology uses a different approach here. Christ is the *new Adam,* the first-born among many brethren. So what happened to Christ on that account happened in principle to all men who are related to this first-born. From the moment of Jesus' death and resurrection, all men are in principle redeemed from the adversaries, and translated into everlasting life. There is a characteristic phrase of Paul's, "since one died for all, therefore all died" (2 Cor. 5.14); Christ redeemed us from the curse of the Law, by becoming flesh himself, for our sake (2 Cor. 5.15; Rom. 8.3; Gal. 3.13). In this way, Paul was able to elevate the Lord's death, which had been to the Jews a stumbling block and to the Gentiles foolishness, into a decisive act of redemption. "O death, where is thy victory? O death, where is thy sting?" (1 Cor. 15.55). As he measures the redemption, so Paul also measures its fruit. Objectively, the redemption is already fulfilled in the death and resurrection of the Lord, so in the last analysis the faithful already assume *a priori* that they are redeemed. In principle, we are all of us already redeemed. Paul never fails to insist that "we have died with Christ"; "the body . . . is dead by reason of sin" (Rom. 6.4 f.; 8.10; Col. 3.1; 3.3; Gal. 2.19; 6.14, *et al.*). It would be mistaken, however, to regard those passages in Paul that express the objective side of our redemption as implying a redemption within our subjectivity. Antinomians ancient and modern have entangled themselves in this false interpretation. What Paul means is simply that, in being man, I have already in Christ, objectively and in principle, crossed the abyss that separated me from God. But of course, since I am this individual sinful man, I still have to bring my human self into subjective accord with that objective work of redemption. This is brought about by baptism. The objective achievement of the redemption still needs to be made inward and personal. In other words, our redemption is an *objective* fact, but not yet a subjective one. Only the future will bring its subjective realization. This is the element of tension. Our personal redemption is not finally fulfilled until the future when we ourselves come to die. And so for Paul, the *moment of our death* becomes especially important. For our death is our life. Paul often looks forward to his own hour of death, and the greater his yearning for resolution, the closer he believes his hour to have come. And so his hope is rooted in the imminent end of the world. The entire creation sighs towards its end. It is true, we are all of us objectively the sons of God. But Paul knows that "whosoever are led by the spirit of God, they are the sons of God" (Rom. 8.14 f.). But even though our subjective redemption is fulfilled only with our death, we already possess its germ in the "spirit of God" that dwells within us. This spirit is the "spirit of life" (Rom. 8.2). Through it, the powers of the world beyond work their way into my life here and now. They are characterized by the very things that work against his world in "peace, joy, faith, and love." The possession of this spirit is the "pledge" and "first fruit" (*arrha*) of eternal salvation. The true harvest is yet to come (2 Cor. 1.22; 5.5; Rom. 8.23).

A survey of the Apostle's doctrine of redemption will show that it coincides with the Lord's tidings of redemption in two main points: that fallen man is in distress, and that his redemption is objectively fulfilled by Jesus' death upon the cross. Christ proclaimed his message loosely and unsystematically, in single sayings, hints, and actions, like a rich man making gifts out of his own abundance. Paul, the theologian, takes them and develops them into a closed system, using the conceptual material he had retained from his rabbinical training. He penetrates deep into the ultimate moving causes of human life, and shows that the redemption is not merely external but brings movement and tension to our entire human existence, yea, even to the world of the spirits.

The Epistle to the Hebrews views Jesus' death for our salvation not so much in the perspective of rabbinical concepts as dependent upon the Jewish sacrificial cult. Christ, the high priest, is the true theme of the Epistle (4.14–10.29). He has been called by God higher than Melchisedech, higher than the priests of the Old Testament, whom he replaces. His priestly office will persist into eternity. The sublimity of this priestly office is in keeping with the sublimity of his sacrifice: "Nor again by virtue of blood of goats and calves, but by virtue of his own blood [he entered] into the Holies." "Through the Holy Spirit, [Christ] offered himself unblemished to God." And so his blood does not purify as the blood of animals does, externally, ritually, legalistically. It cleanses our "conscience from dead works to serve the living God." He has become our redemption through his life, and consummately through his death. It was a work full of sacrifice and surrender. Although he was the Son of God, he learned obedience from the things that he suffered, and when perfected, he became to all who obey him the cause of eternal salvation (Heb. 5.8 f.). In the will of Jesus, the Incarnate One, who said, "Behold, I come to do thy will, O God," we have been finally saved by the sacrifice of the body of Jesus Christ (Heb. 10.8).

The soteriology of the other Apostles

We still have to discuss the doctrine of redemption of the other Apostles, in order to show that St. Paul's soteriology is by no means the fruit of his own theorizings and his own brooding spirit, nor yet that he imposed it upon the Church; indeed, the doctrine of redemption bore the same essential characteristics in the non-Pauline communities as well, and especially in the teachings of the first Apostles. The other Apostles, however, were not especially concerned to clarify the concept of Christ's death for mankind's salvation. They were primarily missionaries, not theologians. It was enough for them to insist upon the fact of redemption through Jesus and his cross. Like Paul, Peter also describes Christ's sacrificial death as a sacrifice of atonement, "who himself bore our sins in his body upon the tree, that we, having died in sin, might live to justice" (I Peter 2.24). Jesus' objective death upon the cross for our salvation was to have the death of sin in us its consequence. Like Paul, Peter is concerned with the subjective result of Christ's sacrifice. "Christ also died once for sins, the Just for the unjust, that he might bring us to God" (1 Peter 3.18). Peter also uses a kind of liturgical formulation to express "the sprinkling of his blood" for the Christian community (1 Peter 1.2). Like Paul in the Epistle to the Hebrews, Peter also regards this blood sacrifice of the Lord as something utterly sublime: "You know that you were redeemed from the vain manner of life handed down from your fathers, not with perishable things, with silver or gold, but with the precious blood of Christ, as of a lamb without blemish and without spot" (1 Peter 18.19). In this passage Peter draws very close to Jesus' words about the "ransom for many." Jesus' blood is the price for which the Christians of Jewry will be redeemed from servitude to the Law and their tradition. Peter's soteriology is thus very close to Paul's. On the other hand, his words about "the Lamb without blemish and without spot" carry over into the sphere of Johannine ideas. According to John the Evangelist's account, John the Baptist had already described Jesus as the "Lamb of God, who takes away the sins of the world" (John 1.29, 36). In the Apocalypse of St. John, the redeemed in heaven sing their song of thanksgiving to this Lamb upon

the throne (5.9). They have been washed free of their sins
in his blood (1.5). Blessed are they who wash their robes in
the blood of the Lamb (22.14). In his first Epistle, John develops the significance for our salvation of Christ's work of
redemption. "To this end the Son of God appeared, that he
might destroy the works of the devil" (1 John 3.8). And to
this end he appeared, that he might "take away our sins" (1
John 3.5). And so John mentions deliverance from the devil
and from sin in one breath. At bottom they are one and the
same thing to him. It is typical of the Evangelist of love that
he should stress the love of God and the life it endows as the
dominant motive of the entire work of redemption. In the
last analysis, Jesus did not die to propitiate the wrath of divine
justice, or to give the devil his due; rather, "God has sent his
only-begotten Son into the world that we may live through
him. In this is the love, not that we have loved God, but that
he has first loved us, and sent his son a propitiation for our
sins" (1 John 4.9, 10).

In the Apostles' eyes, Christ's office as priest and mediator derives from the propitiatory nature of his death (1 Tim.
2.5). Like Paul (cf. 1 Tim. 2.5), John puts it thus: "If anyone sins, we have an advocate with the Father, Jesus Christ
the just" (1 John 2.1). And Peter too has similar words to
say, "that in all things, God may be honoured through Jesus
Christ" (1 Pet. 4.11; cf. Heb. 13.13 f.). And thus the formulation "through Jesus Christ" becomes the liturgical formula
to express Christ's mediation. The Apostolic liturgy was not
focused upon Christ's divinity, the Logos, but upon the God-
man, the Incarnate One, who put all his divinity behind him
that he might deliver us. And so, as we have already emphasized, the early Christian liturgy does not address its prayers
to Christ, but to the Father through Christ. A supplication of
this kind can be seen, for example, in Peter's prayer when he
healed the man born lame (Acts 4.24 ff.). Among the prayers
of St. Paul, we know only two addressed directly to Christ. On
the other hand, there are forty-five addressed to God the
Father. But at the same time, as we have indicated, the early
Christian Church is permeated with the idea that adoration is
due to Christ himself.

We may say that the concepts of "ransom" and "atonement for the many" are the dominant ideas of the Apostles'
soteriology. They are both present in the message of the *Lord
himself*. It was probably the unforgettable occasion of the
Last Supper which planted Jesus' words about the sacrifice of

his flesh and blood so deep in the disciples' hearts that they
never tire of repeating it. These Apostolic ideas of redemption
are summed up in St. Paul's short credo (1 Cor. 15.3), "For
I delivered to you first of all, what I also received, that Christ
died for our sins according to the Scriptures."

In the following chapter, we shall develop and extend the
soteriology of the Apostolic Fathers and theologians in all its
speculative breadth. In order to distinguish between what is
only theological opinion and what is revealed doctrine, we
shall first give an outline of the Church's dogma concerning
Christ's death for our salavation.

XXIV

THE CHURCH'S DOCTRINE OF REDEMPTION

Dogmatic decisions of the Extraordinary Office

It was the error of Pelagianism that first prompted the Holy Office to pronounce upon Christ's act of salvation. Pelagianism did not regard sin in its connexion with Adam's original sin, but as the free personal act of the individual, quite separate from the original sin of our nature. It did not regard original sin as an integral part of all mankind. It held that the individual can fall into sin through his own personal guilt. But he can also raise himself from the fall through his own personal effort. He needs Christ's example only in the sense of a *gratia externa*. Christ has become our pattern and example, but nothing more. For he took his death upon him for the sake of his own vindication. Thus Pelagianism denied the absolute necessity of the Grace that awakens and succours. It acknowledged a Grace of redemption only for the remission of sins. And in its early stages, it seems to have denied even this. It was compelled to admit the necessity of Christ's redemptive Grace at least for the remission of sins only when Augustine argued emphatically for the necessity and general validity of the baptism of infants. The Council of Ephesus made its decision against the Pelagians in canon 10: *Si quis ergo dicit, quod pro se obtulisset semetipsum oblationem et non potius pro nobis solis.* . . . Thus the Council defined the dogma that Christ did not die for his own sake, but for ours alone.

In the sixteenth century, Socinianism disputed the redemptive power of Christ's cross even more radically than Pelagianism. In keen opposition to the orthodox early Protestants, Laelius Socinus (d. 1562) and his nephew Faustus Socinus (d. 1604) not only denied the dogma of the Trinity and Jesus' divinity, but also with logical consistency went on to deny the necessity for any supernatural Grace or representative atonement on Christ's part. Later, a kind of intermediate position midway between the soteriology of the Church and that of Socinianism was put forward by Georg Hermes (d. 1831) and Anton Günther (d. 1863).

The superficial rationalistic doctrines of the Socinians had already been condemned by the Council of Trent, which established the following propositions (sess. 5, canon 3): 1. A deliverance from Adam's sin is necessary. 2. It is brought about only through Christ's merit (*meritum*). So there is a mediator, Jesus Christ. 3. Christ's act of redemption was accomplished *in sanguine, in ligno crucis, sua sanctissima passione*. 4. It is essentially a *satisfacere*, a *justificationem mereri*. 5. Its results are described by the expressions *regeneratio, justificatio, redemptio, justitia*. 6. This justification is by no means merely external; it does not merely cover up our sin, but makes it good within us. Through Christ the new justice becomes our own justice: *factus nobis justitia, sanctificatio, redemptio*.

As we may see from the foregoing points, Church dogma about redemption through Christ is fairly scant. This is because there have been only very few heresies within Christianity that have disputed the Christian doctrine of redemption. Apart from Pelagianism and Socinianism, it was actually the part of liberal historical theology and its successors to dismiss the Christian idea of redemption as mere untenable mysticism. On the Catholic side, the so-called modernists inclined towards the views of liberal theology, with its historical Jesus, that "the dogma of Christ's death for the salvation of mankind was not of the essence of Christianity, but was later imposed upon it by Paul." So the Holy Office was compelled to pronounce more profoundly upon Christ's act of redemption. In the new Syllabus (*Lamentabili, propositio* 38), it repudiated the proposition that the doctrine of Christ's death for mankind's salvation did not derive from Christ but from Paul. This was the last of the Church's doctrinal promulgations upon Christ's act of salvation.

Soteriology in the tradition of the Church

Starting from this ecclesiastical basis, we shall go on to evaluate the traditional theology of Christ's act of salvation subsequent to the Apostolic period. However various the interpretations of his death, they all start from the fundamental fact that Christ died for us, and that in his death we have our life. There are few Christian dogmas that from the beginning were confessed with such strength as this of the *Christus crucifixus pro nobis*.

The Apostolic Fathers

It is not strange that the Apostolic Fathers should not have entered upon theorizing of their own about Christ's act of redemption, but should simply have repeated the words of our Lord and the Apostles as they had been handed down. Ignatius of Antioch mainly defended Christ's capability of suffering against the Judaeo-Christian Gnostics. This led him to discuss Christ's act of redemption. The dominant idea in his teaching is that we were redeemed by the suffering of our God. Shortly before his martyrdom, he wrote in his *Epistle to the Romans* (6): "I seek him who died for us. I long for him who was resurrected for us." His devotion is the true mysticism of the cross. To St. Justin Martyr, redemption primarily consists in our deliverance from the sway of the demons. Otherwise, however, when the Apologists are not discussing Christ's office as high priest in disputing with the Gnostics, they especially emphasize the redemption of our knowledge through Christ. In their eyes, Christ is above all the perfect teacher of truth, the bringer of a new Law and a new ethics.

The doctrine of recapitulation

Independent speculation about Christ's act of redemption does not emerge until the third century. One of the oldest theories is known as the doctrine of recapitulation of St. Irenaeus. In this view, Christ's act of redemption lies not so much in his entire ministry, his life and death, as in his incarnation. Through his incarnation, Christ has become the new head of mankind. Mankind as a whole is summed up in him. He is the *compendium totius generis humani*. And so humanity, once separated from God by sin, is now reunited to God in him. In him, the God-man, the redemption is already objectively consummated, for it has abolished the infinite abyss between the Creator and his creatures, and re-established the old unity between God and man. The original head of mankind, Adam, signified the hostile separation between God and mankind. Christ, the new head, signifies their union. And so the essentials of the redemption were achieved in the moment of incarnation. Because at that moment divine life entered into flesh, the humanity was divinized and thus a reconciliation with God was objectively brought about. In the later disputes with the Arians, this doctrine of recapitulation was a welcome foundation for St. Athanasius and St. Gregory of Nyssa on which they could base their proof of the consubstantiality of Christ's divinity and the Father's. It is true, however, that in regarding the incarnation as the only essential factor in our redemption, Irenaeus and his successors reduced the content of Paul's soteriology. They discussed only the basis of our redemption, not its consummation; or rather, they did not regard the incarnation in all its effects as the entry of the Logos into the totality of human misery, even unto death; their dogmatic interest held solely to the mystical process of the incarnation.

The doctrine of restoration

As well as the doctrine of recapitulation, another theory showing the influence of St. Paul also emerged early: the doctrine of restoration. As a logical inference from his doctrine of original sin, the Apostle to the Gentiles taught that fallen man was under the dominion of the devil. Origen developed this conception so far as to regard fallen man as in the devil's possession. Sin delivers human souls into the devil's hands so completely that he does not simply hold sway over them, but owns them as his property. This theory is based upon the false dualistic assumption that the devil can exercise a certain independence and autonomy at least with regard to sinners. And consequently, we can be redeemed only by giving the devil a ransom, or due payment, for his possessions. Obviously, Origen forced the Lord's Logion of the ransom into a one-sided and legalistic theory of redemption. Salvation becomes something like a business transaction between Christ and the devil. The devil agrees to it because he has no inkling that the life of Christ delivered into his hands is the life of the Logos, and therefore divine and immortal. The adversary was deceived by the Lord's human nature, which hid his divine substance, and by the mystery of the virgin birth, which the devil knew nothing of. And so he was compelled to deliver up the soul of fallen mankind the moment Jesus died upon the cross. There are similar ideas already to be found in Ignatius of Antioch, who held that the devil was deceived by the mystery of Mary's virginity, and was wholly ignorant that Jesus had God alone for his father, and no mere earthly man. The moment Jesus died, the Lord's divine mystery was revealed. Jesus' divine power, which up till then had been hidden in his humanity, was liberated by his death. Jesus arose to a new life, and the devil was overcome. There is an unmistakable echo here of St. Paul's doctrine of Kenosis. And as well as Paul's ideas, there are also certain dualistic and Gnostic elements present. The dualism can be seen in the exaggeration of the devil's dominion into a formal right of possession over the human soul. The Gnostic influence is present in the sharp antithetical terms in which the divine and human natures in Jesus are conceived. The human nature has no value of its own. It serves only as an outward disguise, a means of deceiving the devil. The continued influence of this strange doctrine of restoration can be explained on the one hand by the great respect in which Origen was held, and on the other by the widespread popular belief in demons in the dying years of the ancient world. Those theologians who came under Origen's influence, such as the two brothers Basil the Great and Gregory of Nyssa, are especially inclined to regard Christ's humanity as the bait set to trap the devil. Only Gregory of Nazianzus repudiated the doctrine of the devil's right of possession over human souls, and called it blasphemous. There were certain of the Latin Fathers who came under the influence of the Cappadocian theologians, as far as they were in contact with the school of Alexandria—Ambrose, for example, and Augustine and Fulgentius as well. The strange theory came down by way of Augustine to some theologians of the Carolingian period, especially Alcuin and Rabanus Maurus. But today it is only of historical interest.

The doctrine of debt and satisfaction

The doctrine of debt and satisfaction appears to have the firmest Biblical foundation. It is based upon Jesus' saying about the ransom. It was primarily Tertullian, with his legal training, who defined Jesus' death as a *satisfactio* towards divine justice. His pupil Cyprian develops the fundamental features of this doctrine of Jesus' death to satisfy the debt of sin. Following Ambrose, a series of later Western theologians —Augustine, Jerome, Leo I, Fulgentius, and Gregory the Great—gave their own variations upon this idea of Christ's *satisfacere*. The sins of mankind were regarded as a debt which the just God requires us to pay. The passive state of debt and guilt is made good by the active deed of the Incarnate One's voluntary self-sacrifice. The theologians were then confronted with the question of why God should demand such a harsh penalty in the blood of his own Son. Anselm of Canterbury and Thomas Aquinas tried to solve this problem with the principle that the infinity of the guilt required infinite amends. They were trying to understand the inner necessity of Christ's redemption of mankind. The Son of God had to die because he alone was capable of making infinite amends, and thus of destroying the infinity of our guilt and debt. Later, when certain objections to this were raised, the Thomist school turned for support to the principle *honor est in honorante, injuria in injuriato,* which is to say that the extent of the "injustice" is proportionate to the dignity of him against whom it is committed. And because the injustice of sin was committed against the infinite God, an infinite atonement is necessary. On the other hand, however, because the extent of the "honor," the atonement, is proportionate to the dignity of him who makes it, it is insufficient if made by mere man. Because man is a finite being, the amends he could make have only a limited value, even though the injustice of his sin is infinite. Only God himself, God incarnate, is capable of an infinite atonement.

The doctrine of acceptation

Duns Scotus did not admit the doctrine of debt and satisfaction as it was put forward by Anselm and Thomas; in its stead he formulated what is known as the doctrine of acceptation, which held that it is the Father's gracious acceptation alone that gives the final value to Christ's work of atonement. By itself, Jesus' suffering and death would not have been adequate effectively to reconcile God to man. It would have been only a *satisfactio de congruo*. However, on account of the union of Jesus' humanity with the eternal Word, there was for God a *ratio extrinseca* to endow the atonement of Jesus' humanity with an infinite value. Thus Scotus also held fast to the central idea that Jesus' death upon the cross did in fact achieve a wholly sufficient, indeed superabundant, *satisfactio vicaria*. But the ultimate reason why these amends should be valid and more than valid is not the power of atonement immanent in Jesus' propitiatory suffering, but *God's will and God's Grace* alone. So in Duns Scotus' doctrine, the redemption appears far more strongly as the work of God's Grace than it does in the teaching of Thomas. The meritoriousness of the redemption, too, is supported solely by God's will and God's Grace. Even though the sacrificial death of the God-man may in itself be called an infinite act of atonement, this is still not a decisive reason why it should be regarded as a wholly valid act of atonement for *us*. God's gracious acceptance is the only explanation of the mystery of why Jesus' propitiatory death should benefit us even also. This theory of Duns Scotus' not only shook the foundations of Anselm's doctrine that Jesus' death for our salvation was absolutely necessary but superseded it. Theology today preserves only the notion of the appropriateness of Jesus' propitiatory death. God's righteousness would not have compelled him to demand any *satisfactio* at all. Still less would his righteousness have required him to insist upon the sanguinary form of *satisfactio* that took place upon Golgotha. Without contradicting his justice, God could have redeemed us out of his free, pure Grace.

Jesus' death as a mysterium tremendum et fascinosum

But as God did choose this sanguinary form, Christian thought has only been able to find expedient reasons, indicative of the *Christian concept of God.* Upon Golgotha more than anywhere else, the living God is revealed to us as the *mysterium tremendum et fascinosum.* Here at Golgotha our religious sense is vividly and compellingly confronted by the unfathomable aspects of God—the terror of his justice and the poignancy of his mercy. There is no other happening in history with such a shattering impact on man, nor one so conducive to repentance, as the events at the cross of our Lord. God is holy, holy, holy. In Christianity, the distance between Creator and created being has not been diminished —it has been made absolute. The first supplication we make in the Lord's Prayer is "Hallowed be thy name." The entire majesty and sovereignty of God, devouring all created being, as it were, is revealed in his claim to absoluteness. But this *tremendum mysterium* is at the same time a *fascinosum mysterium,* the eternal will of Grace, which to fallen man is all the more marvellous and overwhelming against the background of God's absolute sovereignty. The Christian doctrine of redemption is to be placed in the context of this tremendous breadth and depth of the divine mystery. God is the absolute mystery; what is related to God is bound to be overshadowed by mystery. And the more mysterious it is, the more "altogether different" it appears, the greater is the probability that here we are dealing with God. And because the nucleus, the innermost "heart" of the divinity, as it were, is revealed in Christ's act of redemption, this above all must be something altogether different from what our human thought could imagine God to be. When Paul writes of God's ways of redemption, praise and wonder come pouring from his lips: "Oh, the depth of the riches of the wisdom and of the knowledge of the Lord! How incomprehensible are his judgements and how unsearchable his ways!" (Rom. 11.33). And so any theory of redemption that speaks of a necessity in Christ's redemption is to be rejected from the start. It cannot be reconciled with the mysteriousness of God and his ways.

God is not only the *mysterium;* he is the *mysterium tremendum.* It is the fundamental function of the religious experience to bend in awe before God. And so the redemption upon Golgotha inevitably calls forth the same awe within us. How utterly different would the way of man have been towards redemption! Everything would have been completely rational and transparent to our petty human thought; it would be accessible to our understanding and our experience, there would be no tensions and enigmas. Isaias' pointing to the servant of God as one who takes upon himself the sins of his people is very hesitant. And he has hardly uttered what God has put into his mouth before he shrinks back at the thought of what he has said. And where the spirit of God was no longer present so vividly, mankind fled from the grievous picture of the servant of God, and, like post-canonical Jewry, took refuge in an image of the Messias of glory that was in keeping with normal human feelings and desires. And modern "liberal" theology, with its historical Jesus, also shrinks from a redemption through blood and wounds and the cross. If there is to be a Messias, let him be a radiant, happy figure, surrounded by flowers and children, the teacher of mankind before whom all error gives way and the mists of sin dissipate. But the thoughts of man are not the thoughts of God. The angels knew the eternal will, not, as we do, in reflections and symbols, but in its substance and truth, without restrictions or outward temptations; but when they rebelled against God, the answer of the *tremendum* was to cast them down. For, unlike ours, their sin was their own entire substance, not a part of it. And so they became devils. The first man was unable to sin as they did, and therefore he was unable to fall as they did, and therefore there is Grace for him. But the form in which this Grace was offered bore the awful mark of the Thrice-Holy. The wages of sin is death. The years before Christ came dwelt in this fear before the All-Holy, the altogether different. Hence there offerings of bloody propitiation. Hence Christ's act of atonement for sin bore within it the terror of death, in which the awfulness of divine justice is mirrored. But it does not stop at this terror. "God so loved the world," John cries, "that he gave his only-begotten Son." Even upon Golgotha, the *mysterium fascinosum* which is God shines out in two great acts of God's love. It is the Son of God who dies. God did not spare his own Son. He loved us first. We have shown that the incarnation of Christ is pure Grace, and laid the foundations for the deed upon Golgotha. And what was achieved by the events upon Golgotha was in turn also pure Grace and love, that God should give us the benefit of Christ's act of salvation, that in his Grace he should accept the heroic action and suffering of the first-born among the brethren as an action and suffering for us all. The Crucified One is God's love made visible, the *mysterium fascinosum,* both in what he is and in what he accomplishes for us. The Grace and the awe cannot be separated. They are both one in God, just as his justice and his mercy are one, the one God. The uniqueness and sublimity of the Christian concept of God shines forth here in this mysterious union of God's justice and God's mercy.

The redemption and moral responsibility

The foregoing clearly demonstrates the superficiality of the moderns' objection to the Christian doctrine of redemption. Their objection to a redemption from outside by something other than man, by Christ's death in our stead, is that it contradicts the first ethical requirement that all moral action should be answerable for itself. They object that the Christian dogma of redemption through the God-man destroys the high value of moral responsibility. It commits the new life to something other than the individual, an outside mediation, and this conflicts with the modern understanding of individual morality, and its autonomy. The truly ethical man can consider only self-redemption. This objection overlooks the fact that sin is not a question of purely ethical evil, accomplished in the will of man, but rather one of existential evil, affecting man's entire being and destroying his physical and metaphysical organization. Indeed, if sin were really only an event in our soul, a *passus praeter viam* within us, we could make amends for it at any time, and put it right by returning of our own accord to the one true way. We would be aided in this by a purely ethical education. And so any monistic ethics, or one founded on no religion at all, would be adequate, at least to avoid the more brutal excesses. But the man who submits to law is still a long way from the man of true goodness and purity. There are moral supermen whose morality fills us with a certain antipathy. We need think only of the Stoic, proud of his own virtue, the self-satisfied Pharisee, or the complacent Philistine of the Age of Prose and Reason. When this "moral" man, this acrobat of duty, is satisfied with himself and says, like the Pharisee in the temple, "O God, I thank thee that I am not like the rest of men . . . or even like this publican," it only means that he has not penetrated sufficiently into the hidden depths of his own being, that he lacks the refined sensibility which is the essence of all morality, the feeling that in comparison with the *solus sanctus,* the essential sanctity, goodness, and purity of God, all his own ethical perfection is hollow. Did not the last world war demonstrate to us what demons dwell within men, what monsters may be unleashed in us, how the beast can rise—no, not the beast, for the beast acts out of blind instinct, and innate unconscious impulse. An animal is innocent in comparison with the brutes who, in this war, consciously, deliberately, freely heaped outrage upon outrage. *Ecce homo*—behold the man, with all his most hidden possibilities come to light. The true Christian knows as the most elementary truth that all so-called morality is a superficial veneer of civilization. The history of religion and morality furnishes the conclusive proof that in all countries and at all times the human psyche has dwelt in the overwhelming sense of its impurity: I am impure, and was conceived in sin. The taboo rituals of primitive peoples, the propitiatory ceremonies of the higher religions, proceeded from the delicate sensibility of the *anima naturaliter christiana.* "Depart from me, for I am a sinful man, O Lord," cried Peter, out of his awareness of the evil of his nature (Luke 5.9). In his autobiography (*Briefe eines Obscuranten*) Professor Jocham tells of how his good mother lay upon her death-bed, praying fervently, and begging him to pray with her for her soul. Jocham was at that passionate and rebellious stage of youth which has a great belief in the self and its autonomy. It is an attitude neither ethical nor religious, but one of blithe optimism in its view of self and the world. And so his dying mother's supplication seemed strange to the young man. "Mother, you have always been so good. In all my memories of you, I cannot think of any wrong you have ever done. All your life you have taken care of us, with never a thought for yourself, and you have done so much for the poor. You really do not need to fear that God will not have mercy on you." Then his mother looked at him with a strange expression in her eyes, and with her ebbing strength she pointed to the picture of the Crucified One in the corner of the room. "Child," she said, "if it were not for him!" With the sure instinct of a simple child of nature, and with the alert conscience of the dying, this simple peasant woman knew how little our morality can boast of. Before the *solus sanctus,* our entire nature is impure and unhallowed. Only the Redeemer has the power. Only in his sacred being and in his union with God will we be well.

So our answer to the moralists' demand for self-redemption is this: We need succour from God outside ourselves; we need redemption through the Incarnate One, because in the very roots of our being we are sick, and therefore even our seemingly best actions are inadequate. Only when this our natural being is hallowed and united with God may a happy and blissful morality, a truly holy and divine life, develop out of this union with God. Only then is the Christian's striving after virtue freed of the oppressive awareness that we are planting a garden in bad soil, cultivating a morality that is false in its depths. Our morality has need of religion in order to be morality. And this brings another reason why those who disdain the tidings of redemption should pause and reflect. Redemption does not mean a mere external, mechanical reckoning of its results; it means over and above this that we surrender our entire existence to Christ the Redeemer, that we transpose ourselves existentially into his thought and will and action, that we become members of him, and continually draw impulse and movement from him, as the grape does from the vine. Redemption is not merely a gift but a task, a deed founded upon Christ's objective guaranty of our existence, the consciousness that through our baptism we are forever secure in Christ. This gives rise to yet a third objection to the advocates of self-redemption. Ernst Troeltsch takes his own theology of consciousness as his starting point, and repudiates any redemption from outside. "The doctrine of an unique act of redemption, achieved in Jesus' suffering, which is appropriated to the individual by faith, is quite untenable, for it goes against the metaphysical sensibility of our day, and cannot be reconciled with historical thinking. Moreover— and this is the most important religious objection—it presupposes a legalistic concept of God, the monstrous anthropomorphism of which contains the inner contradiction that fundamentally it should be God himself who in the institution of this redemptive death makes amends to himself" (*Glaubenslehre*, ed. Martha Troeltsch, 1911). What does Troeltsch mean by this "metaphysical sensibility"? In metaphysics, it is knowing, not feeling, that should be decisive. Sensibility is something purely subjective, and fades away before the immutable word of timeless revelation. And what he means by "historical thinking" is equally puzzling. It is probably his laws of "correlation and analogy" which we discussed earlier, and which precisely in Christology we reject because they are a hidden and disguised denial of the very problem that is the object of Christological scrutiny, the problem of Christ's divine claim and being. So we can understand only his third, religious objection that *God himself* in the institution of death upon the cross should *make amends to himself*. If we take the proposition literally, then of course it is a self-evident truth, and we can only wonder where Troeltsch has found his inner contradiction and his anthropomorphism. Rather, the proposition is the direct inference from the concept of God, and is *a priori* the very opposite of any anthropomorphism, because it ruthlessly carries through the *Deus solus Deo soli gloria*. Precisely because God is God, and because all the good we as created beings have, we have through God alone, a movement towards God can be only through God alone. There is no man, no created being, who can really give God something. God himself must, rather, give us the power to give. And similarly, if through sin man should fall from this movement towards God, it can be only God who will redeem him in his fall and thus make amends to himself. A finite being can never make amends to the *solus sanctus*. Only God himself, he alone can achieve a work of true atonement. The idea that a finite being could make amends to God would presuppose two completely separate spheres of being, realms of being, a metaphysical dualism. Within the one realm of God, every initiative, every decision, and every act of atonement can proceed only from God himself.

But probably Troeltsch does not mean that a man can make amends to God. What he objects to is that God killed his own consubstantial Son that he might make amends to Him. God rages against himself. He kills himself in his own Son that he might be able to live as one to whom atonement is paid. So what Troeltsch objects to is not that God makes amends to himself, but that he ensures the atonement in the way he does, by sacrificing himself, by this senseless, irrational, antirational act. What a bloodthirsty God he must be, to rage in his wrath against himself. What can we say to this? We can say that the whole difficulty of a bloodthirsty God fades away when we ask ourselves, in the light of dogma, what is the position in Christ's office as Redeemer of the *forma servi*, and what is the position of the *forma Dei*? What is the function of Christ's humanity in the work of redemption, and what is the function of his divinity? If Christ's humanity were extinguished in the Lord's office as Redeemer, if it were a question of a god who suffered and died, after the theory of Monophysitism or the pagan mythologies, then God would indeed be making amends to himself. But in reality the one who makes the amends is man, wholly and completely, who has received none of the divine properties from the divinity, apart from his autonomy. And this whole, complete man makes amends with the profoundest personal freedom. "I lay my life down of myself. I have the power to lay it down and I have the power to take it up again" (John 10.18). And what he sacrifices in this freedom is *not* the divinity, but his *natura humana*. This alone truly bears the guilt. It sinned in the first man and it sins in us, his descendants, continually. It bore the guilt and suffered and atoned upon Golgotha in the first-born among the brethren. Because it does not belong to itself, but to the Logos, its atonement is comprehensive and effective for all mankind. In the light of dogma, there can be no question of God's killing himself and his own divine substance. Troeltsch's objection is based upon the Monophysites' image of Christ, not the Church's.

Christ's redemption was not a one-time act, belonging to history. It is a continual reality. It is power and life, eternal rebirth and *reconciliatio*. The Church formulates this truth in its doctrine of Christ the King and his eternal sovereignty.

XXV

THE REIGN OF THE REDEEMER

Christ's kingdom in his Church

THE Old Testament already prophesies the eternal reign of the Messias. "But I have established my king upon Sion, my holy mountain" (Ps. 2.6; cf. Isa. 11.1 ff.; Mic. 4.7; Zach. 9.9). In the New Testament, the angel announces to Mary, "He shall be king over the house of Jacob forever" (Luke 1.32). In the Apostolic Creed, the glory of Jesus the Redeemer is affirmed in the simple words *"sedet ad dexteram Dei Patris omnipotentis."* And to sit thus signifies the power of king, ruler, and judge. Starting from Origen's presuppositions, Marcellus of Ancyra put forward the theory that at the end of time Christ would lay aside his human nature and give back his authority as head and king of mankind to the Father. But this was opposed by the Nicano-Constantinopolitan Creed, which made this addition to the Nicene Symbol: *cujus regni non erit finis.* It is John the Evangelist, especially, who raises the hymn of Jesus' kingship in his Apocalypse (1916). He sees in his vision how Christ in heaven bears the royal mantle, on which is written "King of kings and Lord of lords." For the early Christian world, Christ's kingly power was already ensured in the expression *Kyrios.* "No other name adhered to Christ so firmly as that of 'ὁ Κύριος' " (A. Harnack, *A History of Dogma,* Eng. tr, London, 1897–99, v. I, p. 183). In the patristic period, Origen and Augustine in particular attempted to view the entire course of history under the aspect of the reign of Christ. The history of the world is nothing more and nothing less than a progressive differentiation between the good and the wicked and a progressive conquest of the *civitas diaboli* by the victorious *civitas Dei.* In the high age of Scholasticism many theologians even adopted the view that Christ's kingly power held sway in earthly affairs also, and was realized in the supreme authority of his representative upon earth *in rebus spiritualibus et temporalibus*. However, the greatest spokesmen of high Scholasticism, above all St. Thomas Aquinas (*In Hebraios*, 1.1, 4), maintained that the power of Christ exercised by the popes upon earth applied directly to the values of soul and spirit, and only indirectly *ratione peccati* to earthly interests: *Non eripit mortalia, qui regna dat coelestia*. Whatever is holy and divine performed upon earth or in heaven, any good work and any stone contributed to the erection of the kingdom of God, is brought about by the sovereignty of Christ. Hence the Church's praise, *tu rex gloriae, Christe!* It is the living Church in which Christ's sovereign kingship is perpetuated throughout the ages. He continues his life, perpetuated in the Church's supernatural authority, and especially in her sacraments. Thus Christianity is not a perishable, or a dead, thing. It is not of yesterday, but of today. Whenever the Gospel is proclaimed, Christ preaches to us. Wherever a sacrament is administered, he heals body and soul, and delivers us from all our natural and supernatural fetters. As Christ eternal, he makes his way through time. Though all earthly thrones fail, the throne of this "King of kings" will never be destroyed, as long as the world lasts. The gates of hell will never conquer him.

In detail, there are three stages that lead up to the Redeemer's kingly throne. They are Christ's descent into hell, his resurrection, and his ascension.

Christ's descent into hell

It is Church dogma that after our Lord's death, Jesus' human soul descended to limbo, to the entrance of hell. It is true this article of faith did not find its way into the Credo until the fourth century. When Apollinaris of Laodicea denied Jesus' human soul, or rather its *pars intellectiva*, and maintained that its place had been taken by the Logos, the Church Fathers looked primarily to Jesus' descent into hell to prove the existence of his human soul. Since Jesus' body lay in the grave, it could only have been his soul that descended into hell. And so just at this time the attention of theologians was directed towards the *descensio ad inferos*. Since the eighth century the phrase *"descendit ad inferos"* is to be found in all versions of the Apostolic Creed. Finally in 1215, the Fourth Lateran Council defined the old belief in the new form, *descendit in anima et resurexit in carne ascenditque pariter in utroque*. The place to which Jesus descended is named *infernus*. This expression could actually designate hell itself, though it could also be a name for Purgatory, and for the entrance to hell, limbo, or the *limbus patrum et puerorum*. The name "limbo" derives from the Scholastics, who located the dwelling place of the Old Testament just men before the entrance of hell. However, the Protestant reformers retained the old concept of *infernus*, and taught that in order to demonstrate the Lord Jesus' victory over the devil, he descended to hell, himself destroyed it, and thus constrained the devil. Luther himself was a firm advocate of this opinion (cf. Loofs, *Dogmengeschichte*, p. 781). The dogma of the Church holds that after its separation from the body, Christ's human soul in its union with the Logos descended to the souls of the good men of pre-Christian times, bearing them the glad tidings of redemption. It is true, taken literally, the dogma says only *"descendit ad inferos,"* and admits only of the thought that Christ was really dead. But by the term *"descendere"* the Jews of the time meant only the process of dying (cf. Gschwind, *Die Niederfahrt Christi*, 1911), the soul's descent into Sheol, or Hades, to the fathers gathered there. In this case, our formula was simply an attempt to render the truth that at his death Christ was not carried off immediately from earth to heaven but, being truly dead, rested in the body for three days in his tomb. However, a glance at the Biblical and ecclesiastical tradition will show us that there is a deeper meaning to the *descendit;* it is an expression of Christ's kingly power over the dead. In his Epistle to the Ephesians (4.9), Paul writes, "Now this, 'he ascended,' what does it mean but that he also first descended into the lower parts of the earth?" Following the rabbinical method of proof, the Apostle infers a *descendere* from the *ascendere*. Most theologians regard this simply as a reference to the descent of the Son of God to earth. Paul gives no indication whatever that he is thinking of a descent of Christ into limbo. So as a proof for our dogma, Ephesians 4.9 is out of the question. However, the Lord himself seems to give a hidden hint of his *descensio*. Matthew (12.40) reports his Logion, "Even as Jonas was in the belly of the fish three days and three nights, so will the Son of Man be three days and three nights in the heart of the earth." If the Lord's comparison is to correspond, the Son of Man in "the heart of the earth" could not have been Jesus' dead body, but the living Jesus himself, or at least his living soul for Jonas was alive, not dead, when he was in the belly of the fish. Many theologians look for support to Jesus' words to the robber at his right hand, "This day thou shalt be with me in paradise" (Luke 23.43). But they have still to prove that by paradise Jesus really meant only limbo. Other theologians find a similar indication in Matthew (27.52): "[At Jesus' death] many bodies of the saints who had fallen asleep arose." They believe that the best way of connecting the awakening of the saints who had fallen asleep with Jesus' death is to regard it as an act of deliverance wrought by Christ's appearance in limbo. 1 Peter 3.18 ff. would seem to be closer to our dogma than these texts, "because Christ also died once for sins, the Just for the unjust, that he might bring us to God. Put to death indeed in the flesh, he was brought to life in the spirit, in which also he went and preached to those spirits that were in prison. These in times past had been disobedient when the patience of God waited in the days of Noe while the ark was building. In that ark a few, that is, eight souls were saved, through water." The passage is certainly difficult. Certain mythological elements have been found in it. Spitta, for example (*Christi Predigt an die Geister*, 1890), understands the spirits to whom Jesus preached to be those angelic beings who, according to Genesis 6, "went into the daughters of men." According to the Jewish legend, found in the Ethiopian Book of Henoch and also in the Book of Jubilees, and also certainly well known in early Christendom, as we may see from Jude 6 and 2 Peter 2.4, these spirits were bound in eternal fetters in the darkness of Tartary until the Day of Judgement, when they should be cast into the fiery abyss. Within the terms of this legend, there can be no question of a redemption of those spirits that were in prison. On the contrary, they are condemned to eternal torment. And so the preaching of Christ that Peter speaks of cannot be addressed to them. At most we would have to assume that Christ's "preaching" was the promise of future punishment. Moreover, Peter expressly observes that Christ preached to the spirits of those men who would not be converted in the days of Noe. It is wrong to contradict this clear indication, and apply it to the evil angels, and not to those who drowned in the Flood. The inclination to go hunting after mythological traces in the New Testament has obviously favoured this explanation. But according to the text, all that could be meant by the spirits in prison would be those who were drowned in the Flood. We may assume that in the days of Noe there were many who refused to listen to the call to repentance, but were converted to penitence shortly before their destruction, by the terrors of the Flood, and thus were accepted into Sheol as contrite penitents. And to them Christ proclaimed the redemption. But there were more in Sheol than these converted penitents of the Flood; there were the many souls since Adam who had turned to God, and so Jesus' message of salvation was no doubt intended for all men before Christ who had departed in penitence. At least, the Christian tradition is unanimous in assuming this. It interprets the text from Peter to mean that Christ brought the tidings of redemption not only to the penitents of the Flood but also to all good men who lived before Christ came to earth. By extending the interpretation of Peter's account to include all penitents before Christ came, the Lord is removed from a narrow historical perspective and set in the framework of a universal proclamation of salvation. The idea of a universal redemption, embracing the pre-Christian world too, was so near at hand that it would have been strange if the Christian tradition had not seized upon it. Assuming God's will to universal salvation and the general validity of the redemption, theology was bound to come to the thought that Christ redeemed more than those who came after him, eager for salvation; he was the Redeemer of mankind *in its entirety*.

But if we take 1 Peter 3.18 simply by itself, and not in the context of ecclesiastical tradition, the text is certainly not clear whether Christ's message was really intended for all the dead, or whether it was addressed only to the damned. If the latter, his sermon could only be the promise of punishment, the final proclamation of his victory over hell. There are some Fathers who regard this as the precise purpose of his *descensus*. What Christ intended by it was his final victory over death and hell. Luther, too, subscribed to this opinion. We learn from Church *tradition* only that Christ preached more than punishment to the dead, that he also brought tidings of salvation to the departed penitents. There are not a few Church Fathers who testify to this. And their testimony can be traced, as even Bousset admits (*Kyrios Christos,* p. 34), right back almost to the time of the first Christians. We already find Ignatius of Antioch drawing attention to this message of salvation to the departed (*Epistola ad Magnesios,* 9.2): "The prophets too, his disciples in spirit awaited him, and therefore he is . . . come, and has roused them from the dead" Tertullian (*De Anima*, 55) calls the prophets and patriarchs "appendages" (*appendices*) to our Lord's resurrection. Clement of Alexandria, Origen, and Methodius of Olympus had similar views. And there is similar testimony from certain apocryphal writings such as the "Ascension of Isaias," the Acts of St. Thomas, and others, that the conviction of Christ's descent to the underworld was deeply rooted in the early Christian faith.

Moreover, it is *of the essence of Christ and his mission* that Jesus should announce the tidings of salvation in limbo. After all, he came not as a judge but as a Saviour. Indeed, certain Western Fathers of the Church went so far as to extend this message of salvation of Christ's even to the damned. Origen's doctrine of Apokatastasis in the sense of ultimate pardon bestowed upon all men, even upon the damned, is apparent here. Under the leadership of Augustine, on the other hand, Western theology limited the redemptive achievement of Christ's descent to those who died in penitence under the old and the new covenants. St. Thomas Aquinas combines the view that Christ descended to the damned in the real depths of hell with the doctrine that he redeemed the patient just men of the old covenant. He had as yet no concept of limbo. The just as well as the unjust among the dead dwell in hell. But what they have in common is the separation from the living God. To give reasons for his doctrine, he put forward the view that Christ took upon himself all the punishments of hell caused by sin. In his *Summa*, however, St. Thomas rejects the idea that Christ endured punishment. In this later view, Christ descended to the underworld only "according to the place," only to deliver others from punishment, but not to endure punishment himself there.

And so it is the tradition of the Church that Christ's death for mankind's salvation also benefited the penitent and the just before his time. He redeemed them through his *descensio ad inferos*. But this is not to imply any idea of space in the realm of the spirit. This idea of space and place belongs to the outward form of the dogma, one of the means of the age of understanding and explaining the Christian doctrine. Nowadays we know that heaven is not up above, nor hell down below. Our affirmation of Christ's *descensio* is not tied to these spatial concepts. Our dogma simply means that Christ also died for the penitent world before his time. In the Latin text of Ecclesiasticus 24.45, the following words are spoken by

Wisdom: "And I will enter all the regions deep under the earth, and I will visit all those who sleep, and bring light to all those who hope in the Lord."

Historians of religion are fond of pointing out parallels to this dogma in the history of religion. They recall the journeys of the Greek heroes Odysseus, Heracles, Theseus, and Orpheus into Hades. However, apart from the fact that none of these journeys were made for the redemption of the inhabitants of Hades, and none of them were journeys of salvation, they all took place during the hero's lifetime, not after his death. The journeys of the Babylonian astral gods, particularly Marduk and Ishtar, as well as the descent into hell of the Nasoraean god Hibil-Ziva, are journeys of adventure, with battles and bloodshed, not true journeys of salvation. And in any case, what effect could these stories have had upon Christianity? At most, some influence would have been conceivable upon the Judaic world. But it is precisely among the Jews that no trace of any descent into hell is to be found in their picture of the Messias. (See Monnier, *Der erste Brief des Apostels Petrus,* 1900, p. 296). Such ideas do not make their appearance in Jewry until the post-Christian period. In Persian legend there is the tradition that the bird Karsipta preached Zoroaster's teaching in the underworld. But here too there is no question of a derivation of ideas, only of their similarity. Similar attitudes and similar needs also give rise to like-minded ideas. In this case the need to show that Zoroaster's office of redemption, too, was universal seems to have predominated. This same psychological need is also the explanation of Buddha's visit to hell, which is referred to in the *Lalita Vistara.* This visit, again, did not take place after Buddha's death, but during his lifetime. Nor did it serve to bring tidings of salvation. In any case, we may agree with Holtzmann ("Höllenfahrt im Neuen Testament," *Archiv für Religionswissenschaft,* 1908, pp. 285 f.) that these and similar ideas are to be explained as proceeding from psychological needs, above all from the expectation that the awaited Redeemer had come for all times and all peoples. For their part, these parallels from religious history are testimony that the human spirit is unable to imagine itself completely isolated from the supernatural world. It is bound by a thousand threads to the departed. And whenever a new saviour, Zoroaster or Buddha, comes upon the scene, man is ready to accept the belief that the world of the departed too will be affected by the new salvation. This need in the human spirit also lies at the foundation of the Christian faith in the *descensio ad inferos*. It is true, this need is not the exclusive source of the Christian dogma. The psychological need can be only the presupposition for the dogma, not its causal principle. For where need alone is at work, there will be nothing but hazy mythological figures and simple-minded belief in legends. But the Christian dogma has removed all the fantasies of mythology. Its basis lies in thoughts clear and profound. And these clear thoughts proceed from the Christian certainty that Christ, and he alone, is Lord over the living and the dead.

Christ's resurrection

Through his descent into hell, Christ showed that he was Lord and Redeemer of the penitents in limbo who had died before he brought his message to the world. Through his resurrection and ascension he reveals his glory to all beings upon earth and over the earth. They are the justification and confirmation of his life and death, his claim and his utterance, the solemn Amen to his incarnate office of Redeemer. But being such, they are at the same time also the creative beginning and the source of our new life. Ever since the events of Easter, we know that it is man's fate not to die but to live. Death is only the transition to life. Christ's resurrection testifies that Christianity is the religion of life. To be a Christian is to live.

This had already been perceived and stressed in St. Paul's work. "If Christ has not risen, vain then is our preaching, vain too is your faith. Yes, and we are found false witnesses [ψευδομάρτυρες]. . . . If with this life only in view we have had hope in Christ, we are of all men the most to be pitied [ἐλεεινότεροι πάντων]" (1 Cor. 15.14 ff.).

Denials of the resurrection

What we have said so far about Christ's death for the salvation of mankind receives its final triumphant testimony in the establishment of our belief in the resurrection. So there have been few dogmas that have been quite so passionately attacked by negative Biblical criticism as that of the resurrection. The critics start from the *a priori* assumption that Christ cannot have risen again, because there is no such thing as waking from the dead. And so when they probe the message of Easter, they do not ask, for example, whether Christ really arose from the dead, or what the historical sources can tell us of it. Their problem is how to explain the disciples' strange belief in the resurrection. It is a question worth noting. It means that from the start, even before the witnesses have been heard, the critics are already quite certain that nothing supernatural can have taken place. So what has to be proved is already an established dogma of unbelief. And now obviously critical theology is concerned only with how the belief in the resurrection entered into the history of the early Christians.

Reimarus, the author of the Wolfenbüttel fragments, derived the entire Pentecostal movement from a clever *deception*, played by the disciples. According to his theory, the disciples removed Christ's dead body, and announced that he had risen, and was no longer in his tomb. In Matthew's version, the Jewish Sanhedrin did maintain that the corpse had been stolen, and this is the interpretation held by the Talmud to this day. But nowadays, this particular hypothesis of a deception has been abandoned all along the line. The deceiver who cannot expect to derive the least temporal advantage from his deception, but only sacrifice, persecution, and death, simply does not exist. And so a different formulation of the hypothesis that some deception was practised has been adopted. The deception was practised not by the Apostles but by the members of the Jewish Sanhedrin, who deliberately removed Jesus' corpse in order to prevent the cult which Jesus' disciples had made of his living person from being kindled anew over his dead body (Réville). Because the Apostles found the Lord's tomb empty when they returned from Galilee, they believed that Jesus had really risen from the dead.

The mountain of objections that has been heaped up against this particular hypothesis has persuaded the most recent deniers of the belief in Christ's resurrection to eliminate altogether the idea of the Lord's tomb and to seek the deception not in the *empty* tomb but in the tomb itself. They declare that Jesus' tomb never really existed at all, but rather that as a blasphemer he was cast into a common criminal's grave immediately after the descent from the cross—a kind of mass burial, so that afterwards it was impossible to find his body. This was the starting point of the disciples' faith in his resurrection. It was encouraged by the visions of Peter and the women. Their loving imagination was all too eager to explain the disappearance of the corpse by its resurrection. "He is no longer here, so he must be risen again." And then later the story was invented of how Jesus had a tomb in the rocks covered with a stone, which had been opened by the angels. But at the back of this story there were only fiction-mongers, deceivers or else themselves deceived, and perhaps in the last analysis only purposeless fantasy and legend.

And so even today, the theory of a deception has its defenders. But since this can be dealt with only in close connexion with the criticism of Jesus' appearances, we shall have to come to it and evaluate it later.

The hypothesis that Jesus' death was only apparent, put forward by the Protestant theologian Gottlob Paulus, met a quicker and an easier end. It was later taken up again by Herder and Hase. According to this theory, when Jesus was buried he was in a state of motionless trance. The pungent aromatics with which he had been anointed, the coolness of the tomb, the lance-thrust which had brought him relief, all this roused him to life and consciousness once again. And his awakening brought about a reawakening of the disciples' waning faith in the Messias. David Friedrich Strauss made great sport of this theory. "It is impossible that a being who had stolen half-dead out of the sepulchre, who crept about weak and ill, wanting medical treatment, who required bandaging, strengthening and care, and who still at last yielded to his sufferings could have given to the disciples the impression that he was a conqueror over death and the grave, the Prince of life, an impression which lay at the bottom of their future ministry. Such a resuscitation could only have weakened the impression which he had made upon them in life and in death, at the most could only have given it an elegiac voice, but could by no possibility have changed their sorrow into enthusiasm, have elevated their reverence into worship" (*A New Life of Jesus,* authorized translation, 2nd ed., London, 1879, v. I, p. 412).

The pretensions of the *vision theory* are put forward all the more strongly, even today. Up till now it has been presented in two forms. The one school of thought—which counts among its members such important Protestant theologians as Keim, Schenkel, and Holtzmann, and the philosopher Lotze—maintains that the resurrection was an objective vision, aroused by the Transfigured One. The other school—Strauss, Renan, Hausrath—have decided it was a subjective visionary experience. As long as the vision theory was put forward on the basis of philosophical assumptions and psychological possibilities, it could be easily countered with factual historical source-material. But the situation was completely changed when its spokesmen set about supporting their conception upon the basis of historical textual criticism. And so today the problem of the resurrection has become not so much a dispute of philosophical attitudes as one of Biblical exegesis. Of course, the theory is ultimately founded upon a philosophical assumption. But nevertheless, the modern objections to Jesus' resurrection are not primarily philosophical, but exegetical, in nature. The Bible itself seems to be disputing with the Bible.

Historical evidence for the resurrection

Our first inquiry will be to find out what historical information has been handed down to us concerning the resurrection of our Lord. Not including the accounts of the resurrection in the Apocryphal Gospels, we have in all six Biblical accounts of Jesus' resurrection, the narratives of Matthew, Mark, Luke, and John, in addition to a few brief but significant indications in the Acts of the Apostles (1.3–9; 10.40 f.), and finally *Paul's* account of the resurrection in his first Epistle to the Corinthians (15.3 ff.). There is no doubt that from an historical point of view, this last account is the most valuable. Firstly, because from the point of view of writing, it is the oldest. It was written between 53 and 55, more than ten years before the Synoptic accounts, and more than twenty years before John's narrative. It is, moreover, handed down expressly as part of the Christian *tradition,* as one of the main parts of the Apostles' testament. For Paul emphasizes (15.3) that what he delivered "first of all" to the Corinthians about Jesus' resurrection he had himself "received" (ὃ καὶ παρέλαβον). This is the same phrase with which the rabbis in their time were wont to describe the traditional nature of their teaching. So we are not confronted with the special property of the Apostle, but with the broad stream of tradition of the early Christian community. This is also indicated by the peculiarly stylized terminology of the entire account. But Paul's narrative tells us still more. In assuring us that he received his tidings of the resurrection from the tradition, he also tells us the particular source upon which he drew. For we know from the Epistle to the Galatians (1.17) that immediately after his

experience on the road to Damascus, Paul did not go to Jerusalem, but to Arabia—probably to escape the pursuit of the
Jews, and in strict solitude to bring order to his overwhelming new experience. However, after three years, Paul went to
Jerusalem "to see Peter" (Gal. 1.18). He remained with him
fifteen days. In Jerusalem, he saw none of the other Apostles,
besides Peter, "except James, the brother of the Lord" (Gal.
1.19). This is none other than the Apostle James the Younger.
So we may conclude that Paul received his account of the
resurrection, as far as it did not concern his own conversion,
primarily from Peter the Apostle himself, and also from
James, the brother of the Lord. There is no doubt that, together with John, these two Apostles were regarded as the
most important witnesses, who had both heard and seen
Jesus. In the same Epistle, Paul described them as "the pillars"
(2.9) and "the men of authority" (2.6) in the Christian community. Moreover, the extent to which his account of the
resurrection is dependent upon Peter and James can be seen
from the fact that he first points out those manifestations
which were bestowed upon these very two disciples, Peter and
James. Only Luke (24.34) mentions briefly Peter's encounter
with the Resurrected One. It is clear that Paul learned of both
appearances directly from Peter and James in Jerusalem. So
we have to do with the personal account of the immediate
witnesses of Christ's resurrection.

How does Paul's account run? "For I delivered to you first
of all, what I also received, that Christ died for our sins according to the Scriptures, and that he appeared to Cephas, and
after that to the Eleven. Then he was seen by more than five
hundred brethren at one time, many of whom are with us still,
but some have fallen asleep. After that he was seen by James,
then by all the Apostles. And last of all, as by one born out of
due time, he was seen also by me. For I am the least of the
Apostles, and am not worthy to be called an Apostle, because
I persecuted the Church of God."

The first Apostles do not recount the single incidents in the
story of the resurrection, as Paul does; rather, they stress the
one great fact of the Lord's resurrection itself. They are well
aware of Joel's prophecy that the coming of the Holy Spirit
would pour out upon the new congregation of God an excess
of inward and mystical experiences. But they never call upon
these experiences for support of their faith in the resurrection.
Rather, they base their new faith exclusively upon what can
be exactly established on the historical level, and is vivid and

concrete to all. "Men of Israel, hear these words. Jesus of Nazareth was a man approved by God among you by miracles and wonders and signs, which God did through him in the midst of you, as you yourselves know. . . . But God has raised him up, having loosed the sorrows of hell . . ." (Acts 2.22 ff.). Like this first Pentecostal sermon of Peter's the preaching of all the Apostles reaches its culmination in the brief and solemn sentence, "This Jesus God has raised up, and we are all witnesses of it" (2.32; cf. 3.15; 10.41).

Because their preaching of the Pentecost deals with the historical and demonstrable events of the resurrection, when an Apostle has to be elected to complete their company, Peter makes a condition of the choice: "Of these men who have been in our company all the time that the Lord Jesus moved among us, from John's baptism until the day that he was taken up from us, of these one must become a witness with us of his resurrection" (Acts 1.21 f.). And so the first Apostles were exclusively concerned to bear testimony to the historical, demonstrable, objective events that took place on the day of the resurrection.

This is not the place to answer all the objections with which modern criticism had tried to break down the historical authenticity of the Apostles' testimony. In general these objections assume that it was solely the appearances of the Lord that to Paul and the other witnesses of the resurrection were the foundation of their faith. But in reality, it was not these appearances alone, but the fact of the empty tomb, an external, visible, demonstrable phenomenon, which supported the Apostles' belief in the reality of the appearances. With their Judaic frame of mind, the Apostles were by no means inclined to believe in the corporeality of these manifestations of the Lord, and would have regarded them as a mere ghostly apparition if they had not known of the empty tomb. The Evangelists are unanimous in their accounts of the empty tomb. And Paul, too, postulates the empty tomb, when he speaks of Jesus' burial. In the synagogue at Antioch he expressly declares that the Jews "took him down from the tree and laid him in a tomb" (εἰς μνημεῖον, Acts 13.29). And so he regards the resurrection simply as a "change," a "refashioning," or transformation (Phil. 3.21; 1 Cor. 15.52). And this change is not undergone by the transfigured spirit, but by the body that had been buried in the earth. "For this corruptible body must put on incorruption, and this mortal body must put on immortality" (15.53). So Paul's thought, too, is truly part of the Jewish tradition, for he does not preach a purely spiritual life after death but *the survival of the body, buried and now transfigured.* Consequently, it is not fitting that modern criticism should distinguish between two traditional accounts of the resurrection, one handed down in Galilee and the other in Jerusalem, or that it should maintain that the original, Galilean account, handed on by Paul, does not include the empty tomb, but only the manifestations of incorporeal spirit in Galilee, while the empty tomb was a legendary invention, and entered the Gospels of Luke and John only later, together with all the popular tales about touching Jesus' body, or how the Resurrected One ate and drank with the disciples. Now the existence of an hypothetical original Gospel according to St. Matthew, recording the Galilean account only, cannot be demonstrated without an arbitrary and violent elimination of Matthew 28.9, which recounts the appearance of the Resurrected One at the tomb (i.e., in Judea); nor is it admissible to identify the postulated original Gospel according to St. Mark with the account of the resurrection occurring in the Apochryphal Gospel of St. Peter, which was not written until later and was then derived from Luke and John. So this theory seems to break down against the fact that according to the original preaching of the Church, testified to by Paul (1 Cor. 15.4), Christ's resurrection took place on the third day after his death. Now since the Biblical accounts are unanimous that on the morning of the *third* day the disciples were still in Jerusalem, they could not possibly have been such a long way away in Galilee on the same day and entertained a vision of the Transfigured One there. And so from the beginning there must have been a Judaic tradition that told of the empty tomb and the corporeal appearance of the Resurrected One on the morning of Easter Sunday. The disciples could not ignore the corporeal quality of these manifestations of Christ, the less so since their idea of man was not dualistic, after the Hellenistic manner, but monistic. In their eyes, the living man can be only where there is a living body. In their eyes a spirit existing independently of the body would be an empty apparition, or ghost. According to the Semitic belief, the incorporeal spirits dwelling in Sheol are essentially inactive and withered. Incorporeal spirits cannot of themselves act or create. They can do so only through the instrument of the body. With such a view of man, the disciples could not have held to their belief in the resurrection if it were not supported by their knowledge of the empty tomb.

And so because the *empty tomb,* and not simply the impression of the appearances of the Lord, is the true basis of the disciples' Easter faith, any theory that attempts to understand their experience of the resurrection without taking account of the empty tomb is *a priori* untenable. For it does not take the Jewish pattern of thought as its starting point, but the critic's own dualistic view.

Soberly considered, the further attempt of the vision theory to find a place for the empty tomb in its explanation of the phenomenon of the resurrection, and to reason that the disciples' belief in the resurrection stemmed precisely from the fact that they found the tomb empty, is equally untenable. For in this case, the tomb would have had to be opened without the disciples' knowledge. Who could have done it? If it had been the members of the Sanhedrin who hid the body in order to prevent the disciples from setting up a cult of Jesus' dead body, why did they not produce the corpse when the disciples began to rouse all Jewry with their teaching: he is risen from the dead; he is no longer here? On the other hand, if Jesus' corpse had been thrown into a common criminals' grave, and for this reason could not be found by the disciples, why did not the members of the Sanhedrin draw attention to the criminals' grave when the disciples began to preach Jesus' resurrection? And how can we explain the unanimity of the Evangelists—and we have established that Paul is also to be reckoned among these witnesses of the tomb—in their account of Jesus' burial by Joseph of Arimathea? Are we to say they were all lying?

So now we are left only with the assumption that the disciples themselves removed Jesus' corpse, as the Talmud maintains to this day. But psychologically it is utterly incomprehensible that the disciples should have been so spellbound by their own deception that they left their families and their homes and led a life of sacrifice and self-surrender, and ultimately even died for the sake of their deception. And so the empty tomb remains perpetually an enigma.

But quite apart from the empty tomb, if we consider nothing but the appearances of the Transfigured One before the band of disciples, these are still so firmly founded in actual history that they cannot be regarded merely as psychogenetic experiences. The disciples do not hand down their testimony of the Transfigured One from hearsay, or from some occult proceedings; they have themselves consciously seen him, heard him, and touched him. They have learned of his resurrection by way of sober sense-perception, which is the only guarantee of genuine objective empirical knowledge. They are certainly familiar with purely psychogenetic experiences, within the soul. But they distinguish these clearly from their apprehension of objective realities outside the soul. When Peter was freed from the prison of Herod Agrippa by an angel, he wondered whether what had happened to him was a mere "vision" (ὄραμα) or whether it was "real" (ἀληθές, Acts 12.9). Paul too can tell of the "visions and revelations of the Lord" that had been made manifest to him (2 Cor. 12.1). But he never dreams of using these visions as the basis for his faith in the resurrection. Not even his experience on the road to Damascus is decisive and thoroughgoing enough to form the basis for the faith of the first Christian congregations. To Paul, this faith is rather founded solely upon what he himself "received" from the disciples, their word-of-mouth "Paradosis" (1 Cor. 15.3 ff.). So the foundation of the early Church's faith in the resurrection is in its decisive features the fact that the disciples, Cephas above all, were eyewitnesses. This is what gave the first Apostles the awareness of their calling and their sense of responsibility, that they should have been called by Christ himself to be "witness of his resurrection" (Acts 1.22), and "witnesses preordained by God" (10.41). There is no occasion whatsoever to doubt that the first Apostles were fully aware of the unusual, indeed, extraordinary nature of their tidings. But however miraculous their experiences, they shed all their strangeness in the light of the absolute certainty which their own eyewitness gave them. Of recent years, Rudolf Bultmann has demanded that for the sake of honest theological inquiry the Bible should be radically stripped of all mythological elements—above all, the accounts of the resurrection. But in doing so he misjudges the all-important fact that the first Apostles' proclamation of the resurrection is based upon the clear knowledge of their own beholding, which is one standard of truth to which every genuine scholarly method is committed. Eyewitness accounts are still to this day the surest means of true scholarly knowledge in all questions of historical reality. When Bultmann objects to the miraculous content of the accounts, he is unintentionally denying the main proposition of phenomenology, according to which every mode of knowing has to correspond to the object of knowing. In our case, it is a question of a religious phenomenon which by its very nature goes beyond the visible world of experience. It is not a question of any common history, but the history of our salvation, which necessarily involves the intervention of supernatural instances. And so in this case above all, mere eyewitness accounts are not sufficient for us to grasp the fullness of the Easter reality in its entirety. Because the Easter events were a question of real history, to that extent there was need of eyewitnesses to vouch for their authenticity. But because this history was at the same time the history of our salvation, to that extent for its complete comprehension there was need of the intervention of powers that are not of this world but of the Spirit on high. The disciples knew of these mysterious depths to their message; they knew that in being eyewitnesses they were at the same time vessels of the Pentecostal Spirit, which gave them the power to comprehend and testify to the events of Easter in their entirety.

The phenomenon of the resurrection and the faith of the disciples

This throws a great deal of light upon the peculiar nature of the disciples' faith in the resurrection. Because it was a matter of comprehending supernatural realities, there can on principle be no question of exact, scientific knowledge on the part of the disciples—which is what Bultmann at bottom demands. The faith of the disciples had to bear the stamp of the supernatural, *going beyond* mere natural knowing. The Biblical accounts tell us two things about the faith of the first Apostles in Christ's resurrection. Firstly, that the Lord did not appear in the public market place, before the eyes of the mob, nor yet before the seat of judgement of the Scribes. He appeared in all secrecy *only to the disciples,* only to those, that is, who already had some faith in him. In the seclusion of the garden at Gethsemane, the Transfigured One revealed himself to that same Mary from whom he had driven the seven devils (Mark 16.9; John 20.14), and to the mourning women (Matt. 28.9). On the lonely way to Emmaus, he appeared to two of the disciples (Luke 24.15). In the same seclusion, he revealed himself to Simon by himself (Luke 24.34), and to James by himself (1 Cor. 15.7). Behind closed doors (John 20.19, 20) and on the silent mountaintop (Matt. 28.17), he revealed himself to the assembled disciples. On lonely lake shores, he appeared to individual beloved Apostles (John 21.1 ff.). It is always to the disciples alone that the Resurrected One makes himself known. And it is always in seclusion, far from the crowd.

And the second feature that marks the Lord's appearances is very striking: the disciples are not immediately impressed or overcome by his presence. It is not as if the disciples were at once struck by the identity of this new figure and the old original one, long familiar to their sight. Rather, the disciples seem to need definite *personal* actions, characteristic of the Lord, before they become aware of this identity. In her confusion, Mary did not recognize that she was met not by the gardener but by the Master until the Resurrected One called her by name (John 20.15, 16). And similarly on the way to Emmaus, the disciples' "eyes were held, that they should not recognize him" (Luke 24.16), because he had appeared to them "in another form" (Mark 16.12). And only when "he took the bread and blessed and brake" in his own particular manner were "their eyes . . . opened" (Luke 24.31). And the disciples on the Lake of Galilee were equally unaware "that it was Jesus" (John 21.4). Only by the miracle of their great haul of fish did the disciple whom Jesus loved recognize him (21.7). And so it is understandable that the disciples should have "been startled" by his corporeality when he stood in their midst in Jerusalem (Luke 24.38), just as "some doubted" upon the mountain in Galilee (Matt. 28.17). For what appeared to the disciples was by no means a natural corporeality, demonstrable and three-dimensional. Just as Jesus' figure suddenly appears, so it vanishes with equal suddenness. And it appears behind closed doors. It is above and beyond the laws of space, and hence beyond all natural modes of experience. And so it could occur to the disciples that what they had seen was a ghost. The sovereignty of his corporeality over all the laws of space did not exclude the possibility that it could be seen and apprehended on the empirical level. The explanation given by St. Thomas Aquinas for this is that the presence of the Transfigured One had a specific effect upon the disciples' senses, above all their sense of sight, and that by a special miracle he made himself manifest to the eyes of the disciples. Christ's manifestation would necessarily change according to the situation in which he revealed himself, so that he encountered the disciples now as a gardener, now as a traveller, now in natural, now in supernatural form. "So it was within his power to present to the eyes of the beholders his form either glorified or not glorified, or partly glorified and partly not, or in any fashion whatsoever" (*Summa Theologica*, III, qu. 54, 1 ad 3). So what the disciples beheld and witnessed was not a purely natural perception, apprehended through the senses. It was also a supernatural experience, not unlike the experience of Christ known to many of the saints. Moreover, it was brought about because the person of the Resurrected One wrought upon the spirit and senses of the disciples. It was inspiration, it was Grace in the same sense as St. Paul's vision of Christ on the road to Damascus was Grace. It was not natural sight, but one *endowed by Grace*. And thus the foundation and the blissful content of their faith in the resurrection was not so much the resurrection as an historical event, as the presence of the *Resurrected One* himself. The actual resurrection itself had no immediate witnesses. And so it was Jesus' incarnate presence that drew the disciples into its supernatural realm of light and power, and bound them to him through his appearance to them even to the point where they were able to behold him, even to the point of entering the realm of time and space. They saw him in the body; they touched him; they ate with him.

This immediate impression made by the presence of the Lord transfigured explains the absolute *certainty* with which the first Apostles afterwards testify to the Lord's resurrection and ascension. As long as only the outward and visible manifestation of the Transfigured One wrought upon them, their faith was subject to all the uncertainty, doubts, and frailty natural to every perception made in time and by means of the senses. It was mere *fides humana*, that is, a certainty of belief based upon purely earthly understanding and peculiar to those *motivae credibilitas* which the historians and philologists are able to contribute with the means of their scholarship. And so some of the witnesses of the Easter events could "doubt" for a while. Doubt did not vanish until they were touched by the Lord's Grace, and then, penetrating through all the darkness and distortions of sense-perception, with supernatural sight they beheld the Lord himself. Their *fides humana* was transformed into *fides divina*, that certainty of faith which is absolute and infallible, because it is founded not upon human understanding alone but upon the immediate experience of the majesty of God, and the power of his truth and love.

Because the faith in the resurrection was wrought by God and brought about by Grace, it necessarily meant that it was not a faith for *anyone*, nor could it emerge from indifferent or hostile attitudes. It could take root and flourish only where hearts were prepared for the Lord, where men's minds kept watch in simplicity and humble awareness of their own inadequacy for the powers of redemption that issued forth from the figure of Christ. Only the pure in spirit, only those who hunger and thirst for justice, can gaze upon Christ and believe in the Resurrected One. And so in its depths, this faith is faith "in the Holy Spirit."

And therefore the Lord's resurrection is by no means a mere question of scholarship, a pure object of scholarly inquiry. Because it is in its deepest recesses an event supernaturally wrought, a void has been opened to human knowing that can be filled only by experiencing in faith. Therefore the Easter tidings are addressed not only to the brooding intellect but to the whole man, and above all to his conscience, that mysterious readiness of the soul to accept the world of the absolute and the holy, knowing that it must observe the standards of eternal goodness, truth, and beauty, and can attain to rest, wholeness, and inward peace only in their fulfilment. In other words, Christ's resurrection is a question of religion, not only of scholarship, summoning the relationship of our being and our action to the absolute, and claiming our entire existence. If there is an existential way of thinking anywhere, it must begin here, where the issue is the eternal being of Christ and Christianity.

From this we can distinguish between what is justified at the heart of the vision theory and what has been added by man. There is justification for the proposition that the appearances of the Resurrected One were primarily a subjective religious experience of the disciples, and not an occurrence for everyone. But what distinguishes the disciples' experience of the resurrection from mere visions is the fact that its content is the objective presence of the Transfigured One, coming from without their imaginations, just as to the disciples the empty tomb had the nature of an objective, ascertainable fact.

The religious significance of the resurrection

With this we have already made the transition to an appreciation in terms of dogma of the events of the resurrection. We will ask what *significance* Christ's resurrection had for the disciples and for the whole world. For the disciples the first and most important effect was that they now no longer beheld and experienced Christ *in forma servi*, but *in forma Dei*; they saw him as the *Christ of glory*; the divine mystery of the Lord, which previously they had been able to surmise only on a few sublime occasions, and even then obscurely, now confronted them more intensely than ever before, filling their entire being. Before the events of Easter, the disciples had beheld Jesus' humanity alone, only the reflection of his divinity as in a mirror obscurely, when it broke through Jesus' human garment in his miracles and words. But now it is his divinity that is at the centre of their faith, and their understanding of his humanity is only under the aspect of the divinity, *in lumine Dei*. To the disciples, the events of Easter meant a tremendous deepening and transfiguration of their image of Christ. Now they knew out of their own immediate experience that Christ, the son of Mary, was in his deepest reality the Son of God. And so from then on they never ceased to call upon him as the Kyrios. Thomas' avowal "My Lord and my God" when he touched the wounds of the Resurrected One (John 20.28) became from then on the chief message of their proclamation. In his very first sermon, Peter stressed this: "Therefore let all the house of Israel know most assuredly that God had made [him] both Lord and Christ . . ." (Acts 2.36).

Because the disciples first clearly understood Christ's divinity in the light of the resurrection, only in this light also were they able to understand and fully appreciate this act of redemption. Now for the first time they understood what had previously been unimaginable to them, and what Peter had called forth in Christ at Cæsarea Philippi, when Jesus carried his idea of suffering right through to its conclusion. "Did not the Christ have to suffer these things before entering into his glory?" (Luke 24.26). As the Resurrected One himself explained to the disciples at Emmaus, his suffering was the *necessary means of reaching the Father*. This was the culmination of his heroic surrender for the honour of his Father and the benefit of mankind. Now for the first time the Apostles understood Jesus' strange words of the "ransom for many" in all their depth and breadth, and now the unforgettable scene of the Last Supper, when Jesus offered them his own flesh and blood in the bread and wine, attained its final, overwhelming significance. Now for the first time they knew that at the Last Supper they had already been initiated into Jesus' death and partaken of the fruits of his sacrifice upon the cross.

From then on the blissful certainty of their *own resurrection* became the heart of their eschatological hopes. And it was not merely a matter of their souls' entering into bliss. It was rather the great new message of Christian hope that eternal life is essentially *resurrectio,* the resurrection and new creation of the whole man, body as well as soul. To the disciples, Jesus' resurrection was also a truly cosmic event, for it was their confirmation that all the dead would rise again. Paul was later to say, "For since by a man came death by a man also comes resurrection of the dead" (1 Cor. 15.21). Christ not only redeems us from sin and guilt, he also redeems the dead to life. "[God] raised us up together and seated us together in heaven in Christ Jesus" (Eph. 2.6). Now for the first time the disciples fully understand what Christ promised at the tomb of Lazarus: "I am the resurrection and the life; he who believes in me, even if he die, shall live" (John 11.25). That is Christianity: the tidings of the new life, the new heaven and the new earth. It is Paul once more who points to this new creation of the cosmos in his Epistle to the Romans. Thinking of the glory of Christ's resurrection, he affirms: "For I reckon that the sufferings of the present time are not worthy to be compared with the glory to come that will be revealed in us. For the eager longing of creation awaits the revelation of the sons of God. . . . For we know that all creation groans and travails in pain until now" (Rom. 8.18 ff.).

The ascension and the reign of Christ

Christ's resurrection is the crown and consummation of Jesus' ministry upon earth. From now on we have reached the immediate threshold of his heavenly power. The dogma of Jesus' *ascension* shows us Christ as the everlasting Kyrios, the *Christus triumphans,* sitting at the right hand of the Father, from whence he will come to judge both the quick and the dead.

It is *de fide* that of his own strength Christ rose in body and soul up to heaven. The heart of the dogma is that not only the transfigured spirit of the Lord was taken up into heaven, but also, through the power of his transfigured spirit, his *transfigured body* too. This assumption was wrought by the power of the Logos, who *mediante anima* also raised up the body of the Lord into heaven. And now a man, a new man, was "at the right hand of the Father," and all believing humanity who had a part in this new man also found its rightful home at the right hand of the Father.

Christ himself told the disciples at Emmaus of this his heavenly transfiguration. "Did not the Christ have to suffer these things before entering into his glory?" (Luke 24.26).

The classic text is to be found in the Acts of the Apostles. Luke's account here runs thus: "And when he had said this, he was lifted up before their eyes, and a cloud took him out of their sight" (1.9). In the same account, Luke informs us that between the Lord's resurrection and his ascension there passed forty days (1.3). The Apocalypse of St. John is in essence the Gospel of Christ transfigured, who is exalted to the right hand of the Father. The Apostles Peter and Paul also tell us of it. In his Epistle to the Ephesians, Paul observes: "He who descended, he it is who ascended also above all the heavens, that he might fill all things" (4.10). And similarly, the author of the Epistle to the Hebrews says: "Having therefore a great high priest who has passed into the heavens, Jesus the Son of God, let us hold fast to our confession" (4.14). Peter sums up the entire faith in the ascension in his first Epistle, with the words "the resurrection of Jesus Christ, who is at the right hand of God . . . for he went into heaven, Angels, Powers, and Virtues being made subject to him" (1 Peter 3.22). The Christian tradition is no less clear upon this question. All the versions of the Apostolic Creed include the sentence *"ascendit ad caelos, sedet ad dexteram Patris."* Just as the phrase *"descendit ad inferos"* does not express a place below, and excludes any idea of space or place, so the phrase *"ascendit ad caelos"* has a special sense, signifying a place above only for the disciples. And so they become witnesses of the assumption of Christ transfigured into the transcendent world. Only then did they grow certain that his ministry upon earth was fulfilled and his heavenly reign at the right hand of the Father had begun. The heart of the faith in Christ's ascension lies in the words *"sedet ad dexteram Patris."* The Church Fathers are agreed that this metaphorical expression signifies the participation of Christ transfigured in the Father's dominion over the world. From now on he is the king of heaven and earth, as the prophets envisaged him, "the Son of God in power," as St. Paul expressed it. This is so firmly engrained in the consciousness of the Apostles and disciples that they regard Christ's ascension as the true beginning of his office of Messias, whose ultimate foundation in their eyes is the resurrection and the ascension. In his very first sermon at the Feast of the Pentecost in Jerusalem, all the thoughts of the first Apostle are centred on Christ's ascension to the Father.

However, this heavenly reign of the Messias is not static, but dynamic, a perpetual ministry of salvation and redemption.

As the heavenly head of mankind the Transfigured One holds sway over *all members of his body*. As we have said, this continual ministry of Grace is designated by the theologians as the *gratia capitis*. The congregation at prayer is filled with the divine Pneuma of the Elevated One, and in the Eucharist they are fed with his transfigured flesh and blood. Thus Christ transfigured is the true object of our liturgy. The liturgies of the Greek Church in particular address their praise to the *majestas Domini*. From now on, Christ's promise has become reality: "And I, if I be lifted up from the earth, will draw all things to myself" (John 12.32). And from now on, in Paul's words, "at the name of Jesus every knee should bend of those in heaven, on earth, and under the earth" (Phil. 2.10). And from now on the joyful expectation of the Epistle to the Hebrews is fulfilled: "But he, because he continues forever, has an everlasting priesthood. Therefore he is able at all times to save those who come to God through him, since he lives always to make intercession for them" (7.24 f.). As the *everlasting high priest of the new covenant* he will always intercede for us until the hour comes which the Father has fixed by his own authority. And then the last act in the drama of the cosmos will be played. In the form of a servant, fettered before his judge, but gazing into the depths of time, he made his prophecy; and now it becomes a shattering reality. "I say to you, hereafter you shall see the Son of Man sitting at the right hand of the Power and coming upon the clouds of heaven" (Matt. 26.64). This sovereign power he attained through his sacrificial death. "Behold," says the Apocalypse of St. John (1.7), "he comes with the clouds, and every eye shall see him, and they also who pierced him." The Lord's office as judge of the world is the final act of his ministry as our Redeemer. When he has separated the sheep from the goats, the good fish from the bad, and the wheat from the tares, he will lead his own to the Father and deliver them into the Father's dominion. "And when all things are made subject to him, then the Son himself will also be made subject to him who subjected all things to him, that God may be all in all" (1 Cor. 15.28). The time of our Lord's ministry as our Redeemer is over. The time of the Messias is succeeded by the eternity of the Trinity.

INDEX OF PERSONS